A PROGRAM FOR LAND USE IN NORTHERN MINNESOTA

A TYPE STUDY IN LAND UTILIZATION

OSCAR B. JESNESS

CHIEF OF THE DIVISION OF AGRICULTURAL ECONOMICS
UNIVERSITY OF MINNESOTA

REYNOLDS I. NOWELL

AGRICULTURAL ECONOMIST
UNITED STATES DEPARTMENT OF AGRICULTURE

AND

ASSOCIATES

THE UNIVERSITY OF MINNESOTA PRESS

1935

PREFACE

Problems of land utilization are receiving greater attention at present than ever before. It is becoming more and more generally recognized that public interest calls for improvements in land policies and in programs of land use. The adoption of sound policies and the initiation of constructive programs of action are dependent upon facts regarding our land resources and the uses to which they are being devoted or for which they are best suited.

The object of the study on which this volume is based has been to assemble such facts and to develop their relationship to land use problems. Those who have participated in the work are not under the illusion that it speaks the final word on the subject. They look upon it rather as an introductory approach toward a better understanding of the problem and hope that it will be viewed as such. It should be followed by further study leading to greater refinement and accuracy and supplying additional details.

The initiation of the study was made possible by an assignment from the research funds of the Graduate School. In recognition of the importance of making the study as comprehensive as possible, the cooperation of the Division of Land Economics of the Bureau of Agricultural Economics, United States Department of Agriculture, was sought. That division had previously engaged extensively in land use studies both by itself and in cooperation with state institutions. The result was that the study became a joint undertaking of the University and the United States Department of Agriculture. The experiences of the federal department and the resources of staff and funds which it assigned to the project have made it possible to carry out a much more extensive study than would otherwise have been possible.

This is the second volume dealing with problems of land use to be published by the University of Minnesota Press. The first, *Land Utilization in Minnesota: A State Program for the Cut-Over Lands,* published in 1934, was the report of a committee appointed by the governor and is now out of print. To clear up any confusion that may arise over the publication of two separate reports dealing with the same general field, it may be well to point out their relationship and differences. The former report is that of a committee

iii

appointed to formulate specific recommendations. While the committee drew upon the results of previous research, it did not institute an independent survey. The present report presents the results of a specific research study in the field of land utilization. Necessarily, some of the same background material is included in both reports because it is essential to an understanding of the problem. However, such duplication as exists is incidental and unavoidable. There is no conflict between the two reports. The present report carries the analysis of some problems further than the earlier report and includes material not available at the time the former was written.

So many persons have assisted in the work that it is impossible to mention all of them. Dr. L. C. Gray and Mr. C. F. Clayton of the United States Department of Agriculture gave invaluable aid in formulating plans for the study. The burden of carrying out much of the work has rested upon Mr. R. I. Nowell, and particular mention should be made of the important service he has rendered. Professor Roy G. Blakey, under whose leadership a comprehensive study of taxation had previously been made, gave invaluable aid in directing the public finance and governmental aspects of the project. In addition to those listed elsewhere as participants in the study, acknowledgment is due Paul Kirk, state statistician, and Norman A. Borgen of the Minnesota Tax Payers Association, for supplying valuable data. County agents in the counties included were very helpful in making available their knowledge regarding local situations. Forest rangers cooperated generously in giving information about their districts. State, county, and township officials aided greatly by making data available and by giving the study the benefit of their suggestions. The services of Miss Florence Knox and Miss Frances Reiter have been especially helpful in connection with the preparation of the report.

O. B. JESNESS

University of Minnesota
    January 1, 1935

THE MINNESOTA LAND USE STUDY

DIRECTORS

OSCAR B. JESNESS, *Chief of the Division of Agricultural Economics, University of Minnesota*

LEWIS C. GRAY, *Principal Economist in Charge of the Division of Land Economics, Bureau of Agricultural Economics, United States Department of Agriculture*

ASSOCIATE DIRECTORS

EDWIN C. JOHNSON, *Associate Professor of Agricultural Economics, University of Minnesota*

CLAUDE F. CLAYTON, *Senior Agricultural Economist, United States Department of Agriculture*

RESEARCH ASSOCIATES, WRITERS, AND CONSULTANTS

JOHN H. ALLISON, *Professor of Forestry, University of Minnesota*

FREDERICK J. ALWAY, *Chief of the Division of Soils, University of Minnesota*

WILLIAM ANDERSON, *Professor of Political Science, University of Minnesota*

T. J. BERNING, *Director of Graded Elementary Schools, Minnesota State Department of Education*

ROY G. BLAKEY, *Professor of Economics, University of Minnesota*

G. G. BRADISON, *Examiner, Public Examiner's Division*

EDWARD G. CHEYNEY, *Professor of Forestry, University of Minnesota*

GROVER M. CONZET, *Director of the Division of Forestry, Minnesota State Department of Conservation*

CHLORUS W. CRICKMAN, *Agricultural Economist, United States Department of Agriculture*

RUSSELL N. CUNNINGHAM, *Forest Economist, United States Department of Agriculture*

T. C. ENGUM, *Director of Ungraded Elementary Schools, Minnesota State Department of Education*

LEWIS F. GAREY, *Assistant Professor of Agricultural Economics, University of Minnesota*

HAROLD F. HOLLANDS, *Instructor in Agricultural Economics, University of Minnesota*

v

NICHOLAS A. KESSLER, *Associate Land Clearing Specialist, United States Department of Agriculture*

PAUL H. KIRK, *Senior Agricultural Statistician, United States Department of Agriculture; in charge of Minnesota Crop Reporting Service carried on jointly by the United States Bureau of Agricultural Economics and the State Department of Agriculture*

THEODORE B. MANNY, *Senior Agricultural Economist, United States Department of Agriculture*

PAUL R. McMILLER, *Assistant Professor of Soils, University of Minnesota*

DALTON G. MILLER, *Senior Drainage Engineer, United States Department of Agriculture*

ROBERT W. MURCHIE, *Professor of Sociology, University of Minnesota*

REYNOLDS I. NOWELL, *Agricultural Economist, United States Department of Agriculture*

ARTHUR F. OPPEL, *Division of Forestry, State Department of Conservation*

GEORGE A. POND, *Associate Professor of Agricultural Economics, University of Minnesota*

MARK REGAN, *Research Assistant in Agricultural Economics, University of Minnesota*

HENRY SCHMITZ, *Chief of the Division of Forestry, University of Minnesota*

LAWRENCE H. SCHOENLEBER, *Assistant in Land Clearing, University of Minnesota*

MARK J. THOMPSON, *Superintendent of the Northeast Experiment Station and Associate Professor of Agricultural Engineering, University of Minnesota*

E. V. WILLARD, *State Commissioner of Conservation*

ARCHIE D. WILSON, *Project Director, Submarginal Land Projects, United States Department of Agriculture*

FIELD WORKERS AND ASSISTANTS

EDWARD AITON
WALLACE T. FERRIER
ROY M. GILCREAST
EDWARD G. GREST
HANS P. HANSON
KENNETH B. HEGGENHAUGEN

GERHARD J. ISAAC, *United States Department of Agriculture*
ALBERT R. JOHNSON
HARRY W. SODERBURG
ARTHUR W. TRUE
SYLVAN T. WARRINGTON

HERMAN WELCH

TABLE OF CONTENTS

LIST OF TABLES

PAGE

LIST OF FIGURES

PART I
THE PRESENT SITUATION IN LAND USE

CHAPTER I

THE BACKGROUND *

Some knowledge of past land policies is essential to a proper understanding of the present problems of land use in Minnesota and the adjustments needed to effect improvements. It may therefore be appropriate to sketch here briefly the history of land development in the nation and in the state.

The early pioneers who came to the New World were attracted by the abundant supply of land, which was being transferred from public to private ownership as a reward for services and as an incentive to settlement and development. When the United States became a separate nation, a public domain was created by the cession to the federal government of lands owned by seven of the states. This area was subsequently enlarged by purchase, conquest, and cession to a total of nearly a billion and a half acres.

The problem confronting the new country was how to handle or dispose of this great public domain. Some looked upon it as a national resource that should be handled primarily with a view to providing public revenue. Others were desirous that it be settled rapidly to stimulate development of the country. Public sentiment favored the latter course, and hence the country embarked upon the program that has resulted in placing much of the land in private ownership.

At first the land was offered for sale, usually at nominal prices. Early in the life of the nation the policy was adopted of setting aside certain lands for the support of education, and later specific grants were made to the states for the development of institutions of higher education. Grants were also made, both to the states and to corporations, to assist in the extension of railroads, the purpose being to encourage the settlement and development of the land. In 1841 the pre-emption system was adopted, which gave preference of purchase to persons who had established their residence upon and begun improvement of a tract of land. This was followed by the adoption, in 1862, of the homestead policy, under which settlers

* This chapter has been prepared by O. B. Jesness.

3

were given title to land in return for establishing residence thereon
and undertaking its development.

As a result of these policies, over a billion acres of the original
public domain have been disposed of by the federal government.
Part of the remainder has been reserved for national forests, Indian
reservations, and other public purposes, and part is still vacant
land. The following figures [1] summarize the situation as of 1931:

Number of Acres
Disposals 1,036,557,194
Withdrawals and reservations........................... 255,356,769
Vacant lands subject to applicable land laws............... 177,101,551
Pending entries 24,241,042

Total public domain 1,493,256,556

The chief feature of the land policy, as these figures reveal, has
been the transfer of land from public to private hands. By and
large, the states have disposed of their land grants.

From the vantage point of hindsight frequent criticism has been
directed against past policies of land disposal. For the most part
these criticisms have been aimed not so much at the policies themselves as at the lack of proper discrimination in their application.
It is easy to see now that in some areas the results would have
been more satisfactory had the policy of land disposal been based
to a greater extent upon the characteristics and qualities of the
land and the probabilities of successful development. Unfortunately, however, information regarding the quality of the land was
limited. Moreover, there seemed to be little need for concern about
a permanent supply of timber for a long time to come, and the popular demand was for the opening up of the lands for settlement and
agriculture, hence for their transfer to private ownership. In many
areas, timber was looked upon only as an obstacle to be overcome
in making the land ready for the plow.

Thus one of the consequences of the American land policy has
been the failure to harvest the timber crop with an eye to maintaining some land in timber production permanently. After the
original stand of timber has been removed, efforts have been made
to sell the land and to open it up for settlement as quickly as possible. In some areas this has led to general settlement and development; in others settlement has been very scattered. Settlers have

[1] Herman Stabler, G. W. Holland, and J. F. Deeds, *Rise and Fall of the Public
Domain Exclusive of Alaska and Other Outlying Possessions* (mimeographed report
of the United States Geological Survey).

been permitted, and even encouraged, to go on land that is unsuited to farm use because of its poor soil, the unfavorable climate, or the high cost of bringing it under cultivation. Unsatisfactory returns and low standards of living have resulted from such settlement, and in some areas, consequently, land abandonment has been extensive. Abandoned farms with fields, once cleared, reverting to their native state bear mute evidence of hardships, losses, wasted years, and disappointed lives.

Public as well as private expenditures enter into the picture. The settlement of land for farm use creates a need for public services, such as schools, roads, and local government. In a developing country, plans for the future are often built upon the expectation that the need for these services will increase. They may be projected on a scale entirely out of proportion to existing ability to pay, in the belief that future growth will provide the means. If debts are incurred and the tax base fails to grow, the financial load may become difficult, if not impossible, to bear. The next phase in the trend of events is an extensive tax delinquency and the return of land to public ownership.

Not only may the tax base fail to increase but it may actually decrease. In a timber area, for instance, taxes may be paid only so long as there is a timber crop. When the timber has been removed, much of the current value of the land may be gone. The owner finds himself unable or unwilling to continue paying taxes at a rate that previously was bearable, and so he allows the land to become delinquent.

Frequently the enthusiasm for development has led to land reclamation through drainage or irrigation projects which were expected to be self-liquidating; that is, the increased productivity was expected to more than pay the cost. Where it has done so, the development has been fully justified. However, inadvisable improvements have sometimes been undertaken, and in some places these represent such a heavy financial drain upon local units of government that they find themselves unable to meet their obligations and are threatened with bankruptcy. The obligation then rests upon the state to come to their aid, and the matter becomes one of concern to the citizens generally.

This broad picture of some of the acute problems of land use applies not only to the cut-over area of northern Minnesota but to many other parts of the country. There is widespread recognition of the need for land policies and programs that will improve the situation. Various states have undertaken land utilization studies and economic inventories. In Minnesota, for example, interim committees of the legislature have been created to consider various aspects of the problem. Reports regarding state lands have been drawn up. A detailed economic inventory of a representative cut-over county has been made as a result of legislative authorization and appropriation. A conservation commission and department have been created and land use problems occupy an important place in their sphere of activity. A committee of citizens appointed by the Governor has studied the problem, has formulated a series of constructive recommendations, and has prepared an extensive report dealing with the problems of land use in northern Minnesota.[2] Attention has been given to tax problems, and an extensive survey has been made of tax delinquency in the cut-over counties.[3]

Some of the problems involved have been the subject of legislative action. The state has come to the assistance of various localities that have been unable to meet obligations arising out of ill-advised drainage projects. State forests have been authorized. A permanent Minnesota Land Use Committee has been created by law, and provisions have been made for the organization of county committees to cooperate with this state committee in matters of land classification. Some consideration has been given to the enactment of zoning legislation to make more effective the results of classification.

The problems of land use may be expected to receive even more attention as understanding of the situation becomes more general. We have come to realize that we must rectify past mistakes and avoid similar mistakes in the future. It is now seen more clearly than formerly that the need for expansion of the agricultural industry is limited. Existing farms are supplying present markets abundantly and, since population is no longer expanding at a rapid rate, those markets will not expand greatly. Export markets are no longer clamoring for the products of our farms. Even if the extreme nationalistic policies of the present period of acute depression give way to a saner appreciation of the advantages of world trade, this country will continue to be faced with keen competition from other agricultural regions in the world markets. In the future

[2] *Land Utilization in Minnesota: A State Program for the Cut-Over Lands* (The University of Minnesota Press, 1934). For a description of this report and its relation to the present study, see above, page iii.
[3] Roy G. Blakey and associates, *Taxation in Minnesota* (The University of Minnesota Press, 1932).

the extension of agriculture to new lands will, in the main, succeed in proportion to the ability of such lands to take markets away from lands already in use.

This brief picture of the situation indicates why the land utilization study here reported was undertaken, and why it assumes the form it does. Many of the previous land utilization studies have been intensive ones — compilations of detailed facts about limited areas. It is no criticism of studies of this type to say that, under the circumstances, they were not adapted to the needs of the situation in northern Minnesota. The state is confronted with many pressing problems in the field of land utilization to which immediate attention should be given. Many of them relate to extensive areas. To have covered the entire region by means of intensive studies would have required more time and resources than were available. Some of the acute problems cannot be disregarded for another decade or longer while intensive research is carried on to supply the guides to their solution. Moreover, while detailed information is highly desirable, considerable progress in the solution of the pressing problems can be made on the basis of more general data.

Because of these considerations this study was planned along broad lines to cover the entire cut-over area, where land problems are acute. Much information about the area had already been assembled which proved decidedly helpful. Use was made of the geological surveys of the region; detailed soil surveys available for some areas, more general information available for others, and the extensive acquaintance of soils workers with the region; information regarding forest cover assembled by foresters; census records, which furnish data on population, settlement, and farm development; information in the possession of state and local officials; farm management studies available for some parts of the area and the maps that have been made of broad types-of-farming districts; taxation studies, including an extensive survey of tax-delinquent lands; and educational surveys, which supplied helpful data regarding school development and school problems.

The plan of approach was to bring together existing information having a bearing on the situation and to project the study on the basis of this information. For example, maps were made showing the distribution of population, existing settlement, crop lands, and so on. These gave a picture of existing development, by localities, within the area. This information, together with information on soils, drainage, forest cover, and tax delinquency, supplied a basis for a tentative delimitation of regions in which the problems of land use were substantially similar. Work was then carried on in the field to obtain additional data and to check and refine the districting previously made.

Problems of land use involve many factors. Desirable uses of land are determined by both physical and economic considerations. The suitability of the land for certain uses depends upon soil, climate, topography, the presence of stone and peat, drainage, and existing cover. The advisability of developing it for specific uses depends upon its location, transportation facilities, market requirements, and the cost of development. Land use is influenced by, and in turn itself influences, public services, tax rates, tax delinquency, and governmental organization. As much of this information was assembled as possible. Mere assembling of information, however, while it is necessary and very useful, is not enough. It must be classified and analyzed, and the results must be interpreted, to the end that a policy and a program of action are formulated which will lead to a solution of existing problems. It is to this end that the present report has been directed.

As part of the field work on the study, information was obtained from forest rangers regarding the forest cover in their districts. These men are well acquainted with their immediate territory and in a position to supply much information of this kind. Such information was mapped in order to apply it specifically to the areas involved.

Records at county courthouses were the source of data on income and costs of local government. Additional information was secured from township officials and others. This information was then summarized and analyzed to arrive at a picture of the situation and to determine ways of dealing with it. One argument in favor of the concentration of settlement is that it reduces the cost of public services. Efforts were made to set up estimates of possible savings. The possibilities of reducing costs through changes in the organization or functioning of local units of government were also considered. Naturally changes of this kind must meet the situation in the particular area or locality where they are adopted. The object was not to set up a stereotyped program of action adaptable to all circumstances but to illustrate possibilities. Local conditions must determine the program in each case.

Records regarding the operation of and the results obtained on farms were obtained by the survey method. Farms in areas suitable for further agricultural development as well as farms in areas where a relocation of population appears desirable were included. The data obtained from this part of the survey are useful as showing the possibilities for expansion and the limitations upon agricultural use of the land.

There has been widespread interest during the present depression period in the possibilities of combining part-time farming with other occupations. This has been proposed as a definite program in some forest areas, work in the forest to supplement the sustenance and income obtained from part-time farming. Records were secured on a number of part-time farms to throw light on the returns obtained from such farms.

A tentative districting of the area by defining boundaries of conservation zones that are not well suited to agricultural development was prepared, and this was refined by field inspections and by information obtained from local persons acquainted with the situation in their communities. This represents an approach to a broad land classification that will be helpful in formal classification and in the development of a program of zoning.

The first part of this report is given over mainly to a consideration of the present situation in land use in the fourteen northeastern counties. It pictures briefly the natural characteristics of the region, the present uses of the land, and some of the effects of existing land uses. Policies of land use are reviewed.

The second part outlines specific programs for bringing about improvements. The application of land classification and zoning to the area is developed in considerable detail. The private and public utilization of land for forestry is reviewed. Specific suggestions for improved utilization of agricultural land are offered. The movement of settlers from lands or localities not well suited to agricultural development is considered. Estimates of the possibilities of lowering the tax burden through suggested changes in governmental organization and settler relocation are presented. A concluding chapter summarizes the findings and offers suggestions for carrying the proposals into effect.

CHAPTER II

DESCRIPTION OF THE REGION *

NATURAL CHARACTERISTICS [1]

TOPOGRAPHY AND SOILS

Long ago great bodies of ice moved southward over much of the north-central part of the United States. These ice flows, or glaciers, carried with them great quantities of rock fragments and ground-up soil-building materials. As the ice sheets melted, their burden of boulders, cobbles, pebbles, sand, and clay was deposited in a jumbled mixture which the geologists call drift. Some of these ice bodies, originating east and south of Hudson Bay, left in Minnesota a reddish boulder clay, known as red drift. Still others originated west of Hudson Bay, in what is now Manitoba, and left a gray boulder clay containing many limestone fragments, which is known as gray drift.

The topographic features of northeastern Minnesota are largely glacial handiwork, modified in many places by the subsequent action of lakes and streams. Both the original soil and the subsoil in the northern parts of Cook, Lake, and St. Louis counties were scoured, the hard underlying rock being left exposed. Here and there depressions were scooped out, which now form the beautiful border lakes. Enough fine material was left among the boulders and exposed rocks to form a soil that would support a fair forest cover. Elsewhere the drift was deposited in a system of hilly moraines and undulating intermorainic till plains, among which are level outwash plains. Innumerable small pockets or basins were formed among the morainic ridges, knolls, and till plains and even on the outwash, giving origin to thousands of lakes, many of which have since been drained by stream action. It has been estimated that there are 5,650 square miles of lake surface in Minnesota ex-

---

* R. I. Nowell is primarily responsible for the preparation of this chapter.
[1] The basic material for this and the following sections was obtained from published reports on the geology, soils, and weather of the region, which includes the following fourteen cut-over counties: Aitkin, Beltrami, Carlton, Cass, Clearwater, Cook, Crow Wing, Hubbard, Itasca, Koochiching, Lake, Lake of the Woods, Pine, and St. Louis.

10

FIGURE 1. — RELIEF MAP OF MINNESOTA

(From a map of the Department of Geography, University of Minnesota, based on data of the United States Geological Survey and other surveys and maps)

clusive of Lake Superior.[2] This amounts to nearly 7 per cent of the entire surface area of the state. The total number of lakes is variously estimated between eleven and twelve thousand. Red Lake (440 square miles) and Mille Lacs (197 square miles) are the largest; probably three hundred or more exceed a thousand acres in area.

The last great ice sheet in Minnesota dammed the outlet of the Red River drainage basin and when it melted formed a large lake known as glacial Lake Agassiz, which occupied what is known as the Red River Valley of Minnesota, North Dakota, and Manitoba. A shallow arm of the lake extended as far east as northwestern St. Louis County and covered the whole of Lake of the Woods County, the northern half of Beltrami County, and most of Koochiching County. Agassiz was a temporary lake having a comparatively short existence, but it left unmistakable traces in the form of gravel beaches and reassorted sands, gravels, and clays. Finally, as the ice on its northern border melted, the lake drained to the north by way of Nelson River into Hudson Bay, leaving its bed available for plant growth. Subsequently a great thickness of partially decayed vegetation accumulated in some places. This gave rise to the extensive areas of peat that occur in parts of northern Minnesota.

The greatest relief of the state occurs in the northeastern corner. (See Figure 1.) Bluffs from 500 to 900 feet high rise abruptly from the shore line of Lake Superior, which is 602 feet above sea level. Inland the elevation ranges for the most part from 1,000 to 1,500 feet above sea level. The highest elevations are in the Iron Range hills and the rock knobs of Cook, Lake, and St. Louis counties, commonly known as the "Arrowhead" region. At one place in western Cook County the elevation rises to 2,230 feet, the highest in the state.

The soils of the fourteen counties may be considered to form eight broad groups [3] with respect to productivity and cultural possibilities. (See Figure 2.) Within any one group there are a great variety of soil types, but certain features characterize each group as a whole. Thus in the first group, in which outcrop rock and large

[2] Frank Leverett and Frederick W. Sardeson, *Surface Formations and Agricultural Conditions of Northeastern Minnesota* (Minnesota Geological Survey Bulletin No. 13, Minneapolis, 1917), p. 11.

[3] The description of these groups is based upon Dr. F. J. Alway's discussion of the soils of the state in an unpublished manuscript, "A Report of a Special Committee on Land Utilization," June, 1932.

boulders are predominant, there are numerous small bogs and a few scattered tracts of good loam with few stones. Small areas of excellent farm land are interspersed with large tracts worthless for farming.

Group 1 lies along the Canadian border east of International Falls and embraces the area stripped by the great moving ice

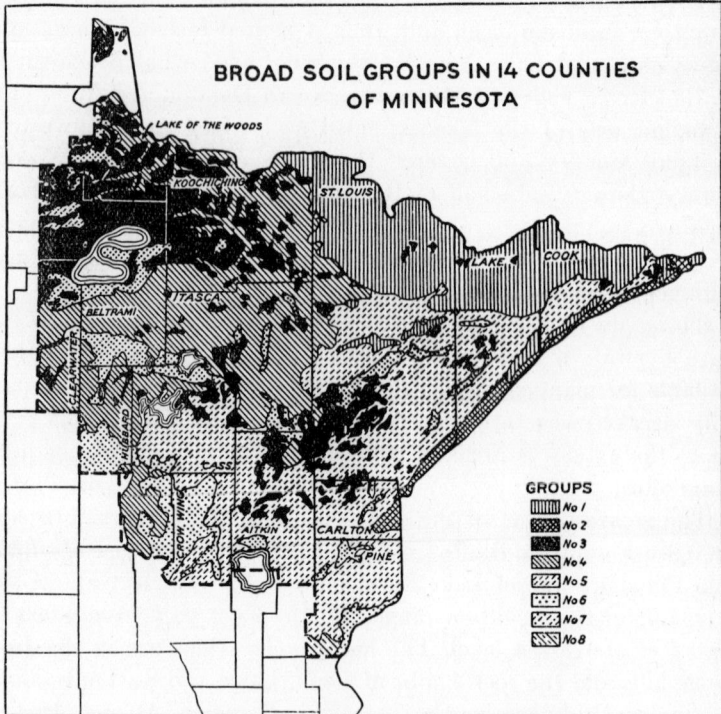

FIGURE 2. — SOIL GROUPS IN NORTHEASTERN MINNESOTA BASED ON PRODUCTIVITY AND CULTURAL POSSIBILITIES
(Drawn from a map prepared by the Division of Soils, University of Minnesota)

sheets, which left outcropping rock now covered by a thin mantle of drift. Large boulders were strewn over much of the surface. This region, except for a few small scattered tracts, is unfit for agriculture.

Group 2 is composed of lacustral soils along the shore of Lake Superior. Glacial Lake Duluth, about 550 feet higher than the present Lake Superior, formerly occupied the Lake Superior basin, and its shore line extended from one to five miles farther inland than the present shore line. The prevailing soil is a heavy reddish clay with a rather impervious subsoil, in which stone is absent or present only in small amounts. Deep gullies draining into Lake Superior occur at frequent intervals along the shore line. The tillable area is extremely limited. These soils are only moderately productive, and the heavy ones are difficult to work while wet or very dry.

Group 3 is comprised of large and continuous areas of peat bogs. In Figure 2 only about two-fifths of the entire peat acreage is shown. The remainder is in small or fair-sized bogs scattered throughout the various other groups. All the peat soils are naturally waterlogged and even after drainage are unproductive unless supplied with the proper plant nutrients, phosphate and potash. The necessity of supplying these in the form of commercial fertilizers makes the use of such soils expensive, especially those that must also receive an application of lime. All peat soils are subject to summer frosts and in dry seasons to fires. On part of the area included in this group the peat layer is less than three feet thick and in many places is being gradually burned off during dry seasons.

Group 4 comprises a complex of gray stony loams and peat bogs, small wet depressions of clay loam, sand plains, and sand ridges. The gray loams, which form the chief agricultural part, carry far less stone on the average than the soils of Group 5 to the south and east. Ordinarily they have an abundance of lime for alfalfa and sweet clover, for both of which they are well adapted. These soils are among the most productive in the cut-over region.

Group 5 represents a complex of gray stony loams with reddish subsoil, peat bogs, sand plains, and wet clay depressions. Between a fourth and a third of the area is occupied by swamps. There is considerable variation in the amount of stone on these soils. In some places stones are so numerous as to preclude the use of farm implements. Other fields have comparatively few. These soils are fairly productive after they are cleared and stoned, but the labor costs of stoning are usually excessive. The low-lying, stone-free clay depressions are productive when drained. Draining, however, frequently involves heavy outlays of both capital and labor.

The portion north of Lake Superior is decidedly inferior to that to the southwest because in general the stones are more numerous and the surface hilly or very rough. Much of it has a stony or gravelly subsoil which is very drouthy.

Group 6 includes all areas of considerable size that have a sandy or gravelly subsoil near enough the surface to make them distinctly drouthy. The surface soils range from loose, drifting sands to rather dark sandy loams. These are inferior agricultural lands but because of the ease with which they are cleared they have been extensively opened for farming.

Group 7 occupies a considerable acreage in the Red River Valley, but in the region under study is represented only by a narrow arm extending into the peat bog of northwestern Beltrami County. The soils are dark loams and dark sandy loams, very level, with an elevation only slightly higher than the surrounding swamp. Crops do well in years when moisture conditions are favorable.

Group 8 is represented only in southern Pine County, where the prevailing soils are productive gray loams with a heavy subsoil. Stones are present in small to moderate amounts. There are some inferior pieces with a gravelly subsoil and many peat bogs and deep potholes.

MINERALS

Geological ages before the glacial period an arm of the Labrador land mass extended down into the Great Lakes states. This formed a center or core of hard crystalline rocks, the oldest formation occurring in North America. Heaving and buckling of the earth's crust folded this material into a series of ancient mountain ranges running in a northeast-southwest direction. In the bases of these ranges pockets of concentrated iron ore occurred. While the mountains were young, volcanoes belched out great streams of molten copper-bearing lava from fissures in the iron ranges. This lava solidified, forming the copper ranges of Michigan, Wisconsin, and Minnesota. Ages of weathering, washing, and leaching disintegrated and wore the ranges away, leaving only the bases or stumps. Subsequent glacier action scoured the bases of the old ranges in some places and buried them under drift in others.

There are in Minnesota the remains of two copper ranges. One runs from Pine County into Wisconsin parallel to the south shore of Lake Superior; the other rises abruptly from and runs parallel to the north shore of Lake Superior. Although these ranges have not produced copper, they are of the same age and origin as the rich copper-bearing rocks of Keweenaw Point, Michigan.

Rich iron deposits occur in three ranges in northeastern Minnesota — the Vermilion in northern St. Louis and Lake counties, the Mesabi in St. Louis and Itasca counties, and the Cuyuna in Aitkin, Crow Wing, and Morrison counties. There are iron ranges in Wisconsin, Michigan, and Canada belonging to the same formation and extending in the same northeast-southwest direction; these produce some ore also, but they are much less important than the Minnesota ranges. The ore deposits on the Vermilion Range are located deep below the surface and are reached by shaft mines. On the Mesabi Range the ore is covered by a comparatively thin layer of glacial drift; when this is stripped off, the ore can be loaded from open-pit mines. On the Cuyuna Range both the open-pit and underground shaft methods are used.

CLIMATE

Northeastern Minnesota has long cold winters and rather short cool summers. The low summer temperatures and numerous lakes make it an ideal recreational area. There are wide variations in seasonal and daily temperatures, as is characteristic of inland climates. January is the coldest month, July the hottest. Annual temperatures average about seven degrees lower in the northeastern counties than in the southern part of the state. Lake Superior moderates the climate along its western and northern shores for a short distance inland. The prevailing winds, however, being from the northwest, tend to neutralize the influence of the lake. Over much of the area the growing season is too short for successful production of corn for grain, and in many parts even corn for ensilage is not a good crop. Oats, barley, alsike and red clover, alfalfa, timothy, potatoes, and vegetables are well adapted to the soil and climate.

Figure 3 shows the average length of the growing season in different parts of the state. This is perhaps the most important climatic factor in determining what crops shall be raised and what type of farming shall be carried on in an area. A small district along the banks of the Mississippi in southeastern Minnesota and another in the vicinity of the Twin Cities have the longest growing season — 160 days. In the extreme north the season is only 100 days, and much of the area has a season of 120 days or less. The moderating influence of Lake Superior is evident in the vicinity of Duluth, where the growing season is 130 days or longer.

Ordinarily all parts of Minnesota except where there is a drouthy subsoil receive enough precipitation to insure successful production of crops. Fortunately most of the precipitation (76 per cent) falls during the growing season, from April 1 to September 1. During the forty-seven-year period from 1886 to 1932 the average

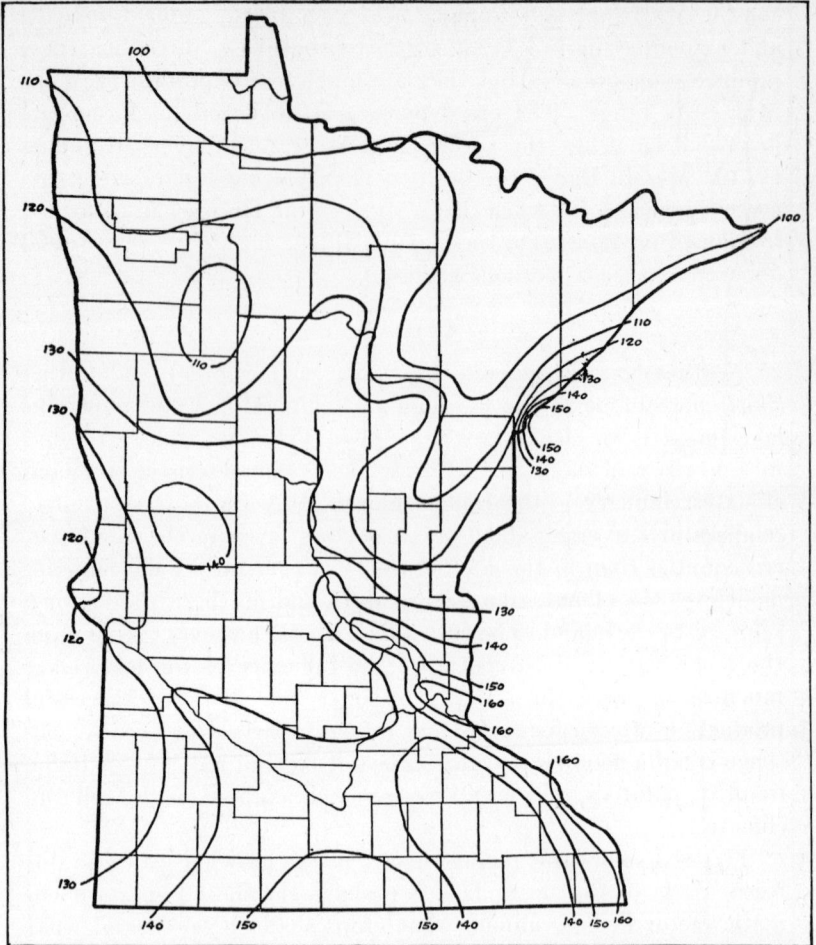

FIGURE 3. — AVERAGE LENGTH IN DAYS OF THE CROP-GROWING SEASON
IN MINNESOTA

annual precipitation for the state was 25.5 inches. As indicated in
Figure 4, the heaviest precipitation occurs in the eastern and
southeastern parts of the state, and the lowest in the extreme
northwest. Most of the storms move across the state from west to
east. These storms usually cause about two days precipitation and
are followed by fair-weather periods of about the same length.

VEGETATION

The original vegetative cover of the state comprised three
broad groups, the prairies on the west and south, the coniferous

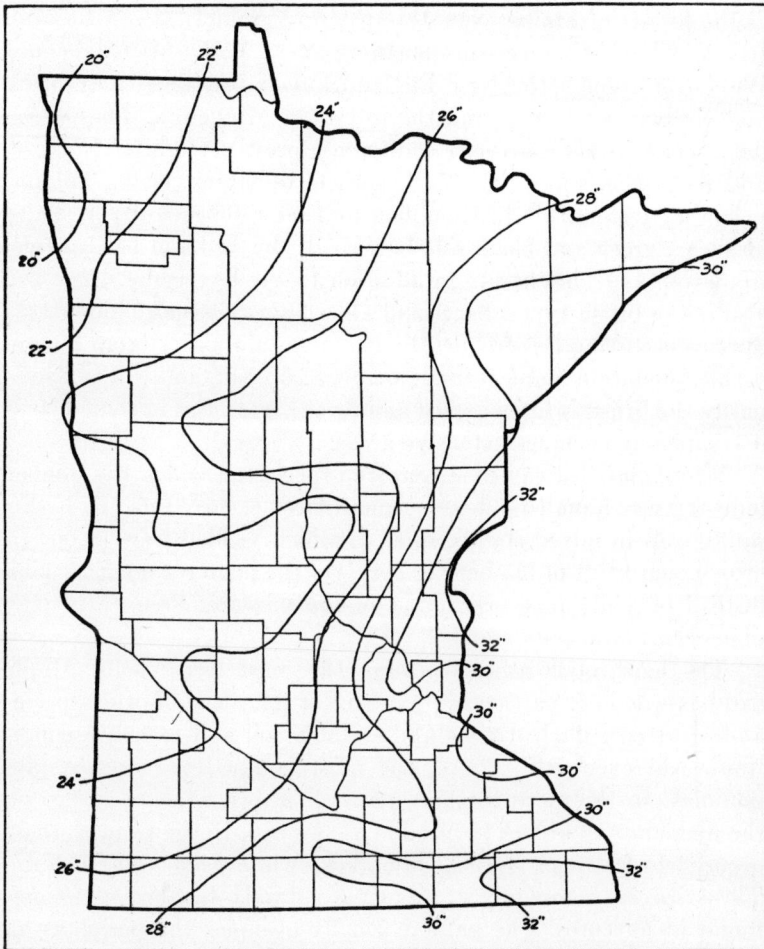

FIGURE 4. — AVERAGE ANNUAL PRECIPITATION IN MINNESOTA

forest in the northeast, and the hardwoods extending from the mouth of the Crow Wing River south and east to the boundaries of the state and west to the prairies. These groups were quite distinct. The prairies were treeless except along the banks of permanent streams. There were practically no conifers in the hardwood areas except within the transition zone, but within the coniferous forest several species of hardwoods were scattered. Climate has been the controlling influence in the differentiation of these vegetative areas.

In composition the coniferous forest was essentially the same as the forests of Maine, New Hampshire, Vermont, Massachusetts, Rhode Island, Connecticut, northern New York, Michigan, and Wisconsin, though the New England forests contained fewer jack and Norway pines than did the forests of Minnesota. The principal species in the northern coniferous forest are white, Norway, and jack pine, white and black spruce, tamarack, cedar, balsam, yellow and paper birch, trembling and large-toothed aspen, balm of gilead, green and black ash, basswood, elm, red and hard maple, ironwood, and pin cherry. In addition to the tree types, there are also many brush types, hazel and alder being the most important. Species occurring less frequently are mountain ash, swamp honeysuckle, mountain maple, service berry, scrub oak, and willow. Ordinarily the brush is interspersed among the trees, but in some places it completely occupies extensive areas.

White and Norway pine were the species on which the lumber industry was founded. These splendid trees occurred on the better sandy soils in mixed stands, some of which yielded from 20,000 to 60,000 board feet of lumber per acre. On the poorer sands jack pine instead of white pine was found in the mixture. Frequently jack pine occurred in pure stands.

The hardwoods usually occupy the most fertile soils. Maple and basswood are particularly tolerant of the shade of other species and, if given sufficient time and suitable soil and moisture conditions, will eventually crowd out most competitors. Spruce predominate in the more northern part of the state, white spruce on the highlands and black spruce in the swamps. In the swamps there occur, besides black spruce, tamarack, white cedar, and balsam. These species commonly grow in pure stands, but are sometimes found in mixtures. The balsam usually occupies the periphery of the swamps. Spruce and balsam are used extensively in the manufacture of paper.

Wet, poorly drained areas covered with trees are properly called swamps. Similar areas supporting grasses, sedges, and reeds but no trees are called marshes. When swamps or marshes grow up with deep accumulations of sphagnum or other peat mosses they are called muskegs. Large areas of open muskegs are interspersed throughout the northern forests. Tree growth is usually choked out or stunted by the sponge-like moss and the excessive moisture it holds.

The great hardwood belt of the central and southeastern part of the state was settled first. These were the most fertile lands and were cleared for the growing of crops. At the time of settlement there was no organized lumber market, so farmers used what lumber they needed for their farm buildings and destroyed the rest, except the small areas that were reserved for farm woodlots.

The exploitation of the northern coniferous forest, which was begun some years later, was quite different. A huge demand for building materials had developed with the settlement of the prairie lands. Cutting was done almost exclusively by highly commercialized lumber companies. On the assumption that all lands were to be cleared of stumps and developed into farms, the cutting was done ruthlessly, and young trees and seedlings were destroyed by slash fires, which were permitted to run wild. Recurrent fires since the logging operations have many times denuded vast stretches of land and have sometimes been attended by heavy loss of property and life.

Jack pine, white birch, aspen, and pin cherry are called fire types by foresters because of their habit of coming in on burned areas before other species. All these trees act as nurse crops for white and Norway pine and for many of the hardwood species. The forest of the present day is distinctly of fire-type complexion. Only a small remnant of timber of sawlog size remains. The bulk of merchantable timber is second growth of cordwood size. On vast areas the reproduction is of less than merchantable size. If given protection from fire and time enough, nature will restore the valuable species that were present when the white people took possession of the country.

WILD LIFE

Wild life constitutes one of the most important crops or products of the cut-over region, for upon it the tourist and recreational industry is dependent. Those who seek recreation are attracted by good fishing and hunting. The natural resources, climate, lakes and streams, woods, and wild life in a large part of the area are such that it can be best utilized for recreation. Since a thriving recreational industry is dependent upon an abundant and permanent supply of fish and game, it is imperative that wild life be cultivated and managed in such a way as to sustain the yield.

When Minnesota was first visited by white men, buffalo and antelope roamed over the western prairies and adjoining timber lands. These animals were ruthlessly slaughtered for their meat and skins, but more important in their extermination was the destruction of their range and native habitat. Similarly, the coniferous woods were originally full of American elk, moose, and caribou. With the draining of the swamps and the repeated burning of the forest lands, the number of large game has been greatly reduced. There remain in the state but a few hundred moose and only thirty or forty head of caribou.

The moose have retreated far to the north along the Canadian border, and the caribou to the vast impenetrable swamps north and east of Upper Red Lake. Even with continuous protection from hunters these animals are barely able to maintain their numbers. Both species are extremely intolerant of man. Even the occasional summer canoeist along the border waters seems to disturb the breeding and feeding habits of the moose. Perhaps if the great swamps were reflooded and fires kept out, the moose and caribou would again become more numerous. The active use of land for recreational purposes, however, is somewhat incompatible with the propagation of these two species of big game.

The common white-tailed deer is by far the most important of the remaining big game. Formerly this deer was restricted to the hardwood forests of the southern half of the state and was scarcely to be found in the coniferous forest of the northeast. But with the draining of the swamps, the cutting of the pine, and the repeated burning of the country a fire-type vegetation was established — aspen, birch, pin cherry, and various brushes — which created an ideal habitat for the white-tailed deer, and he moved in quickly. Today these animals are abundant. The deer population has been variously estimated at from 150,000 to 300,000 in the cut-over counties. The numbers are apparently being maintained despite the ten-day open hunting season in alternate years, when thousands are killed.

Black bear are fairly numerous, particularly in the Superior National Forest. Beaver have been so extensively trapped that they are almost extinct except in places where they have been rigidly protected. It has also become necessary to protect the muskrat, the supply of which for years seemed inexhaustible. The muskrat is extremely prolific, and the protective efforts of the state have been amply repaid.

The shallow lakes and marshes of northern Minnesota are important breeding and feeding grounds for migratory waterfowl. Some twenty-five species of ducks, four species of geese, and one species of swan are commonly found in Minnesota waters. Changes in water levels have destroyed many rice beds, however, which must be replaced if the supply of migratory birds is to be maintained.

In the cut-over counties there is an abundant supply of partridge, or ruffed grouse, and of sharp-tailed grouse. Prairie chickens are also present, though less numerous, along with a goodly supply of ring-necked pheasants in the more open farming sections.

Far more people engage in fishing than in the taking of any other kind of game. From the standpoint of the recreational industry, therefore, fish are the most important form of wild life. In the numerous small cold-water streams along the north shore of Lake Superior and elsewhere in the cut-over region, brook trout, rainbow trout, and brown trout are to be found. In the lakes are many different species of game fish, wall-eyed pike and bass being perhaps the most valuable and widely distributed. The pickerel or great northern pike (Essox estor) is found in most of the lakes in the region, and in the deep cold-water lakes along the border lake trout and Loch Leven trout are taken. The muskellunge is the largest of the native fish. Crappies, perch, sunfish, blue gills, lake carp, catfish, cisco, herring, and whitefish are among the many other valuable food fishes found in Minnesota waters. Despite the tremendous catches that are made every season the supply of fish is well maintained. The state hatcheries under the direction of the Game and Fish Division of the Department of Conservation are annually providing millions of fry and fingerlings for planting in the lakes and streams. During the fiscal year ended June 30, 1933, the following numbers by species were planted in the state:[4]

Small-mouth bass	2,135
Black bass	185,630
Crappies	101,857
Sunfish	192,948
Pickerel (northern pike)	2,250,225
Muskellunge	50,000
Cisco	400,000
Herring	5,050,000
Lake trout	2,941,253
Wall-eyed pike	617,286,272
Brook trout	1,745,787
Rainbow trout	1,145,504
Brown trout	855,096
Loch Leven trout	473,626
Albino trout	760
Whitefish	54,393,360
Total	687,074,453

[4] Dr. Thaddeus Surber, *The Minnesota Conservationist*, December, 1933, p. 13.

Much progress has been made in studying the feeding and breeding habits of the different species. Special efforts are being made to preserve such rare species as sturgeon and muskellunge. There remains the important job of applying knowledge of life history to the manipulation of environment. This process of "fish cropping" or management may be even more important than restocking in perpetuating food fishing in Minnesota waters.

SOCIAL AND ECONOMIC CHARACTERISTICS

POPULATION

In the fourteen northeastern counties there were on April 1, 1930, a total of 397,167 persons. These people, though they represented only 15 per cent of the total population of the state, occupied 36 per cent of its land area. The density per square mile of land area in the fourteen northeastern counties is about 14 persons, as compared with 32 persons per square mile in the state as a whole, 515 persons per square mile in Massachusetts, 41 persons per square mile in the United States as a whole, and 490 persons per square mile in the British Isles.

The geographical distribution of the population is shown in Figure 5. Centers of concentration occur around the wood-products and shipping industries of Cloquet and Duluth and the mines of the Mesabi Range. Other points of concentration occur at Ely on the Vermilion Range; at Aitkin, Crosby, and Ironton, on the Cuyuna Range; around the paper and lumber mills of International Falls; and at Bemidji, an old lumbering town. This map was so constructed as to present a maximum of detail in the sparsely settled regions. If a map were prepared on the same scale for the entire state, the dots in the south half would be so thick that they would blur together as they did on this map in the vicinity of Duluth and the Mesabi Iron Range.

Except around Cloquet and Duluth and the towns on the Mesabi Range, the population of the northeastern counties is comparatively sparse. By eliminating these two heavily populated areas from the calculation, the density for the outlying rural areas is reduced from about 14 persons to fewer than 8 persons per square mile.

In 1930, according to the census, 50.1 per cent of the population of the fourteen northeastern counties was living in cities of 2,500 or more. (See Table 1.) St. Louis County with 76.4 per cent, Lake with 62.6 per cent, and Crow Wing with 53.3 per cent were

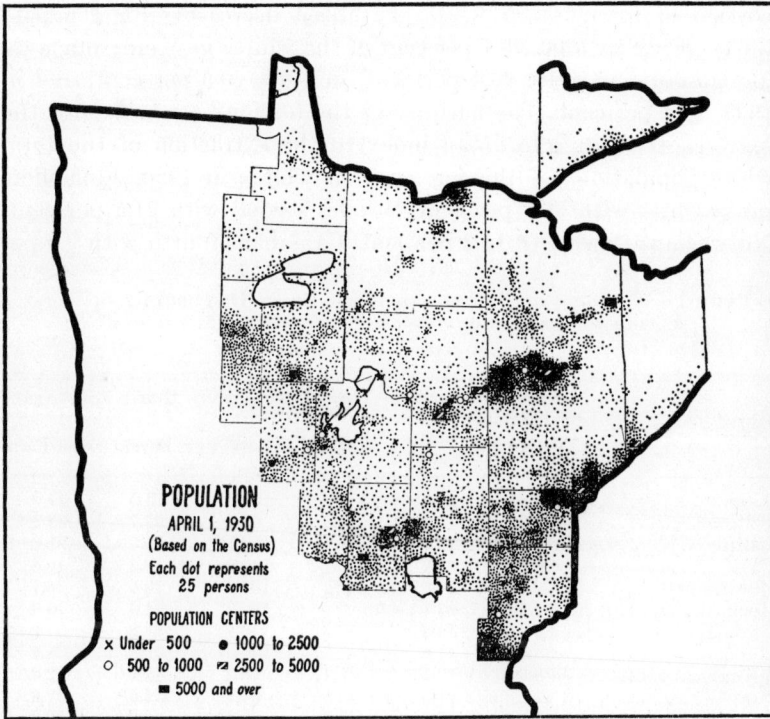

POPULATION
APRIL 1, 1930
(Based on the Census)
Each dot represents
25 persons

POPULATION CENTERS
x Under 500   • 1000 to 2500
o 500 to 1000 ⌐⌐ 2500 to 5000
■ 5000 and over

FIGURE 5. — POPULATION OF FOURTEEN NORTHEASTERN COUNTIES, 1930

the counties having the greatest proportion of urban dwellers. Seven of the counties — Aitkin, Cass, Clearwater, Cook, Hubbard, Lake of the Woods, and Pine — in which there were no cities as large as 2,500 population were classified by the census as 100 per cent rural.

The rural population was again subdivided by the census into two groups, rural-farm and rural–non-farm. Of the rural dwellers in the fourteen counties 58.9 per cent were classed as farm population, as compared with 68.0 per cent in the state as a whole and 56.0 per cent in the United States. Cook County with 76.0 per cent, Itasca with 52.8 per cent, and St. Louis with 52.5 per cent were the counties having the greatest proportions of rural–non-farm population.

The population of northeastern Minnesota is predominantly white (98.4 per cent). In 1930, 75.9 per cent of the whites were native-born and 22.5 per cent were foreign-born. In the state as a whole foreign-born whites comprised only 15.1 per cent. The proportion of foreign-born whites has been decreasing for the past thirty years. In 1900, 29.1 per cent of the whites in Minnesota were foreign-born, in 1910, 26.4 per cent, in 1920, 20.5 per cent, and in 1930, 15.1 per cent. The nativity of the foreign-born whites in the fourteen counties affords an index to the extraction of the total white population. Of the foreign-born whites in 1930, Finlanders ranked first with 22.5 per cent, Swedes second with 21.5 per cent, Norwegians third with 14.2 per cent, Canadians fourth with 9.0 per

TABLE 1.— NATIVITY OF WHITES AND RURAL-URBAN DISTRIBUTION OF TOTAL POPULATION IN 14 COUNTIES OF NORTHEASTERN MINNESOTA *
(in percentage of total)

COUNTY	NATIVITY OF WHITES		TOTAL POPULATION		RURAL POPULATION	
	Native	Foreign-Born	Urban	Rural †	Farm	Non-Farm
Aitkin	81.8	17.4	...	100.0	73.0	27.0
Beltrami	77.6	12.8	34.8	65.2	67.7	32.3
Carlton	74.6	23.1	31.9	68.1	68.8	31.2
Cass	82.3	9.2	...	100.0	59.2	40.8
Clearwater	78.4	16.8	...	100.0	73.9	26.1
Cook	64.5	27.1	...	100.0	24.0	76.0
Crow Wing	85.7	14.2	53.3	46.7	62.8	37.2
Hubbard	88.5	11.3	...	100.0	61.8	38.2
Itasca	78.5	19.7	21.2	78.8	47.2	52.8
Koochiching	77.2	21.5	35.8	64.2	52.4	47.6
Lake	67.9	32.0	62.6	37.4	49.2	50.8
Lake of the Woods..	79.0	20.8	...	100.0	61.1	38.9
Pine	79.3	19.7	...	100.0	72.1	27.9
St. Louis	72.5	26.9	76.4	23.6	47.5	52.5
Total 14 counties	75.9	22.5	50.1	49.9	58.9	41.1
State	83.9	15.1	49.0	41.0	68.0	32.0

* Source: Fifteenth Census of the United States, 1930, Population Bulletin, Second Series.
† Includes urban farm.

cent, and Germans fifth with 4.4 per cent. These same five nationalities occupied the first five positions in the state as a whole but in quite different order. Those of Swedish descent ranked first, Norwegian second, German third, Canadian fourth, and Finnish fifth. There is an interesting concentration of nationalities in the various counties. Finlanders comprise the highest percentage of foreign-born whites in Carlton, Itasca, and St. Louis counties, but in the western counties of Hubbard, Clearwater, Beltrami, and Lake of the Woods there are practically no Finlanders. Swedes predominate in Pine, Aitkin, Crow Wing, Lake of the Woods, Koochiching, and Lake counties, and Norwegians predominate in Beltrami, Cass,

Clearwater, Hubbard, and Cook counties. Canadians are most numerous in Beltrami and the border counties of Lake of the Woods and Koochiching.

TRADE CENTERS

Trade centers are by definition places where trading institutions are located. In agricultural areas the crossroads store is the nucleus of a trade center. Obviously trade centers may vary in size from

TABLE 2. — NUMBER OF CLASSIFIED TRADE CENTERS, BUSINESS UNITS, PROCESSORS
AND MANUFACTURERS, AND WHOLESALERS AND JOBBERS IN 14
COUNTIES OF NORTHEASTERN MINNESOTA, 1929 *

County	Trade Centers			Total Business Units	Gain or Loss 1915–29	Agricultural Processors or Other Manufacturing	Wholesalers and Jobbers
	Independent		Dependent				
	Major	Minor					
Aitkin	1	..	27	245	66	23	2
Beltrami	1	2	24	302	31	33	7
Carlton	1	3	15	314	59	47	1
Cass	..	3	23	236	45	27	1
Clearwater	..	3	8	109	27	17	..
Cook	..	..	7	60	38	5	..
Crow Wing	1	4	18	458	71	38	5
Hubbard	1	1	15	169	28	24	1
Itasca	1	3	30	396	69	38	4
Koochiching	1	3	32	249	33	10	3
Lake	1	..	9	119	41	5	..
Lake of the Woods	..	2	9	106	—16	10	..
Pine	..	5	22	314	63	47	1
St. Louis	5	6	71	1,512	37	118	17
Total	13	35	310	4,589	592	442	42

* Source: *Bradstreet's Book of Commercial Ratings*, July, 1929.

the one-store community to the large industrial cities. In 1930 there were in the fourteen northeastern counties 348 trade centers, of which 309 had 500 people or less; 40 had from 500 to 5,000 people; 6 had from 5,000 to 10,000; and four had populations in excess of 10,000: Duluth (101,463), Hibbing (15,666), Virginia (11,963), and Brainerd (10,221). (See Table 2.)

Rural sociology workers of the University of Minnesota have classified trade centers of northeastern Minnesota into three groups: major independent, minor independent, and dependent villages. Villages having a post office, a telegraph office, an express office, a publisher, and a bank were classed as independent and those lacking one or more of the five services were classed as dependent villages. Independent villages having 75 or fewer business units were classed as minor, and those with more than 75 as major. In the fourteen counties there were 13 major independent, 35 minor independent, and 310 dependent trade centers.[5] Included in the 300 dependent cities and villages were many very small places. Only 50 of the 300 were incorporated places that were enumerated separately by the census of 1930. There were in all trade centers a total of 4,589 business units, including 442 agricultural processors or other manufacturers and 42 wholesalers or jobbers.[6] During the period from 1915, when a similar classification was made, to 1929 the number of business units in the fourteen counties increased by 592 or 12.9 per cent. Increases occurred in all counties except Lake of the Woods.

INDUSTRIAL DEVELOPMENT

Mining.—The iron mines of northeastern Minnesota have a profound influence on social and economic conditions in the localities where they occur. While occupying only a negligible amount of land, they have a tremendous total value. In fact, the assessed value of unmined iron ore in 1932 was equal to 182.6 per cent of the value of all other real estate in the fourteen northeastern counties. The area directly influenced by the concentration of population and the mining activity embraces about a million acres. The three counties that enjoy the large mineral values as a tax base cover an area of about six million acres. By far the most important of the three ranges is the Mesabi, located in St. Louis and Itasca counties. Normally about 90 per cent of the total ore shipments from the state originate on this range. The Cuyuna Range in Crow Wing County ships about 5.4 per cent, and the Vermilion in northeastern St. Louis County the remaining 4.5 per cent. Minnesota is the most important iron-ore-producing state in the Union, being followed in order by Michigan, Alabama, and Wisconsin. During the years from 1927 to 1930 Minnesota produced 60 per cent of the total iron-ore output of the country and 21.5 per cent of the total world output.

In 1930 the United States Census reported that 8,593 men were employed in the iron mines of the state. The population in the areas adjacent to the mines aggregated about 80,000. These people were almost entirely dependent for their livelihood upon the mines and the business that the mines created. Because of the huge tax

[5] Exclusive of Duluth.   [6] Exclusive of Duluth.

base and the ease of collecting taxes from the mining companies, local expenditures for public purposes have been very liberal.

Forest products. — The lumber industry of Minnesota began in earnest about 1850, and from then until 1880 the annual cut increased gradually each year. During the next twenty years the annual cut increased very abruptly and reached an all-time peak about the year 1900. At the height of production the annual cut amounted to approximately two and three-tenths billion board feet and had an estimated value in excess of fifty million dollars. The decline from the peak of production was just as abrupt as the rise. The annual cut had declined to approximately a half billion board feet by 1920, and by 1930 to about a quarter billion board feet.

While the forests were being logged, many wood-using industries, such as planing mills, paper mills, and factories for the manufacture of sash, frames, doors, excelsior, etc., were attracted to Minnesota. At the peak of the logging operations there were in the state approximately 500 wood-using plants. When the timber supply became exhausted, many of the large sawmills were dismantled and moved to the forests of the South and West. Some of the wood-using industries followed the sawmills, others went out of business. Those that could use low-grade or small-sized material, such as the paper mills, excelsior mills, and more recently the insulation industry, have continued to do a fair volume of business. In 1929 a plant was established at Cloquet to use aspen and birch for the manufacture of toothpicks, match stems, and matchboxes. This has provided a market for a limited amount of second growth material that formerly was almost valueless. Today there are only a few sawmills left, mostly portable types that move from place to place clearing up the remnants of the old forest or sawing the best of the second growth material.

In 1929 the United States Census of Manufactures reported the value of lumber and a few miscellaneous wood products in Minnesota at $14,744,351; other wood-using industries had a total product valued at $62,718,943. Thus the total for lumber and wood products was $77,463,294. There were 221 establishments producing lumber and wood products. These employed approximately 10,930 men, or 10.6 per cent of the total employment in all industries, as compared with 62 per cent in 1857, 28.1 per cent in 1909, and 15.6 per cent in 1919. In the northeastern counties pulp and cordwood are now the most important forest products.

The Census of Agriculture in 1929 placed the farm value of

forest products sold, traded, or used by operator's family in the
fourteen counties at $1,402,833. In these counties income from for-
est products represented 4.9 per cent of the average farm income,
the range being from a maximum of 14.7 per cent in Koochiching
and Lake of the Woods counties to a minimum of 1.2 per cent in
Carlton and Pine counties, as compared with a mere 0.8 per cent
in the state as a whole.

Shipping and transportation. — The main railroads serving
northeastern Minnesota are those connecting Duluth with the
Twin Cities, International Falls, the iron mines, and northwestern
points in the state. In order to facilitate logging operations branch
lines were constructed extensively throughout the area. When the
timber supply became exhausted, the usefulness of many of the
branch roads ceased. Agricultural development was too slow and
the volume of freight and passenger traffic too small to justify continued maintenance of the lines. Consequently service has been reduced and some lines have been completely abandoned. In the
fourteen counties there were in 1931 approximately 2,144 miles of
trackage, 33.5 per cent of the total mileage in the state. The density of population per mile of road in the fourteen counties amounts
to 185 persons as compared with 401 persons per mile in the state
as a whole.

An important transportation industry has been developed for
the movement of ore from the mines to the lower Lake ports. Ore
is hauled by rail to docks at Duluth and Two Harbors, where it
is loaded on lake freighters, which transport most of it to Erie,
Pennsylvania. On the return trip the barges bring coal from Pennsylvania, automobiles from Detroit, and gasoline and various man-
ufactured commodities from the lower Lake ports. This lake-borne
freight is unloaded at Duluth and Superior and is then distributed
by rail and truck throughout the north-central and northwestern
states. Because of the great weight of coal and iron ore, the Duluth
port is second only to that of New York City in total tonnage
cleared.

In addition to the ore cargoes originating at Duluth and Two
Harbors, there is also an important traffic in wheat, butter, flour,
wool, flax, and other miscellaneous items. Iron ore accounted for
30.3 per cent of the total value of all shipments in 1933, wheat
24.8 per cent, butter 15.7 per cent, flour 10.9 per cent, and all other
commodities 18.3 per cent. The total value of all shipments in 1933
amounted to approximately $142,000,000 and the value of all re-

ceipts to $69,000,000. During the ten-year period 1924–33 the value
of lake shipments varied from a maximum of $412,000,000 (1924)
to a minimum of $74,000,000 (1932). Receipts during this period
ranged in value from $133,000,000 in 1929 to $59,000,000 in 1932.

The Great Lakes are unnavigable from about December 15 to
April 1 because of ice. During these months the transportation industry comes almost to a standstill. This seasonal nature of the
industry gives rise to rather extensive unemployment during the
winter months.

In recent years the highway system has been greatly expanded.
Every one of the fourteen cut-over counties now has hard-surfaced
or improved roads. Of the total road mileage in the fourteen counties state trunk highways comprise 1,643 miles (7.0 per cent), state
aid roads 2,238 miles (9.6 per cent), county roads 9,269 miles (39.7
per cent), and town[7] roads 10,217 miles (43.7 per cent). Generally
speaking, trunk highways and state aid roads are well constructed
and are kept in good repair. County roads are well maintained in
counties having iron ore and adequate tax money; elsewhere they
are inclined to be somewhat neglected. Town roads are much inferior to state and county roads. In some townships, however, town
roads are well constructed and kept repaired, while in others the
roads are impassable much of the year. Many town roads were constructed in anticipation of settlement that failed to materialize.
Towns have subsequently found it impracticable to keep such
roads repaired.

In the drainage districts miles of ditch banks were thrown out
when the ditches were dredged. These banks have been leveled and
sometimes graveled to provide a road system. Peat fires frequently
burn out the ditch banks, marooning the settlers who use them
for roads. The road system has in general been overbuilt in the
sparsely settled areas, and per capita costs of maintenance are excessive. In the better settled areas road facilities are adequate.
Farm produce in such areas can be trucked to railroad stations or
the entire distance to market in all seasons.

AGRICULTURAL DEVELOPMENT

The agriculture of northeastern Minnesota is built around
dairying as the major farm enterprise, butterfat for the manufac-

[7] The legal designation of an organized township in Minnesota is "town." In
popular usage (and at times in legislation as well), the terms "town" and "township" are used interchangeably. The term "town" is often used also in referring to
cities or villages. As used in this report, it refers to an organized township.

ture of butter being the principal product. Climatic conditions favor the growth of grasses and clovers. On extensive areas rocks are too numerous to permit plowing, so pasturing and hay meadows offer the best alternative use. On the tillable land oats and barley are the small grain crops most extensively grown. The growing season is too short for the successful production of corn for grain. Good ensilage corn, however, is produced on the southernmost edges of the area. Sunflower ensilage is used on many farms. Practically all the oats and barley are fed to dairy cattle, and in addition considerable quantities of grain are purchased. Clover seed along the Rainy River and potatoes elsewhere throughout the area are the principal cash crops. In the vicinity of Duluth and the towns of the iron ranges, truck crops such as cabbage, carrots, rutabagas, tomatoes, and peas are produced.,

Farm settlement, which was just beginning in 1880, increased only slightly during the next ten years. (See Table 3.) From 1890

TABLE 3. — AGRICULTURAL DEVELOPMENT IN 14 COUNTIES OF NORTHEASTERN MINNESOTA, 1880–1930

Census of	Acreage in Farms	Percent-age of Land in Farms	Number of Farms	Average Acreage of Farms	Acreage in Improved Land	Percent-age of Farm Land Improved
1880	51,580	.3	378	133.8	9,621	18.7
1890	258,249	1.4	1,829	141.2	48,274	18.7
1900	984,757	5.3	7,550	130.4	191,043	19.4
1910	1,893,874	10.2	14,275	132.7	413,009	21.8
1920	2,804,229	15.1	22,380	125.3	773,443	27.6
1925	3,192,119	17.2	29,446	108.4	854,049	26.8
1930	3,035,029	16.3	25,994	116.8	910,851	30.0

to 1925 the increase was rapid and at an almost constant rate. During that thirty-five-year period an average of 789 farms, including an average of 83,052 acres, were added annually. From 1925 to 1930 the number of farms and the total land area in farms decreased slightly. In those years farmers were abandoning some of the poorer pieces of land which had been brought under cultivation during the preceding development period. Since 1930 there has been an appreciable movement of population back to the country, and in 1933 many of the old abandoned shacks were being occupied by squatter families who did not intend to farm but were merely taking refuge from the insecure conditions of the cities.

In 1930 only 16.3 per cent of the total land area was in farms, as compared with 59.7 per cent in the state as a whole and 90 per cent in the southern half of the state. In certain southern counties nearly all the land was in farms in 1930 — in Yellow Medicine, for instance, 99 per cent, in Martin 97 per cent, and in Nobles 95 per cent. Within the fourteen counties agricultural development had been greatest in the western and southern border counties and least in the northern and eastern group of counties. The percentage of land in farms in the first group is as follows: Pine, 40 per cent; Clearwater, 36 per cent; Carlton, 34 per cent; Crow Wing, 33 per cent; Hubbard, 32 per cent; Aitkin, 24 per cent; and Cass, 22 per cent. Similar data for the less developed counties in the north and east of the region are: Beltrami, 17 per cent; Itasca, 13 per cent; Lake of the Woods, 13 per cent; St. Louis, 11 per cent; Koochiching, 8 per cent; Lake, 1.7 per cent; and Cook, 1.5 per cent. (See Figure 6.)

The size of farms decreased from 1890 to 1925; in 1930 the census revealed a slight increase. The acreage of improved land has increased throughout the entire period. Because of the rapid increase in the number of new undeveloped farms during the settlement period, the percentage of improved farm land remained almost constant until 1910. Since 1910 the percentage of improved land in farms has gradually increased.

Of the 910,851 acres of improved land in 1930 over half, or 58.9 per cent, was in hay, 14.1 per cent in oats, 5 per cent in corn, 4.3 per cent in barley, 4 per cent in potatoes, 3 per cent in wheat, and the remaining 10.7 per cent in other miscellaneous crops.

The 1930 Census of Agriculture listed certain items of farm income: sale of crops, livestock and livestock products, and forest products; receipts from boarders; and the value of produce used by the operator's family. These data reveal clearly the type of farming in the cut-over counties. The income from the items listed amounted to $1,107 per farm, which is about half the average income per farm in the state ($2,267) from the same items. (See Table 4 on page 34.) The farm produce used by the operator's family in the northeastern counties amounted to 23.3 per cent of the total income from the items listed, whereas the state average amounted to only 13.8 per cent. Crop sales in the fourteen counties amounted to 12.9 per cent of the total; for the state, 21.3 per cent. Receipts from livestock and livestock products represent 56.7 per cent of the total in the northern counties and 63.9 per cent of the total in the state.

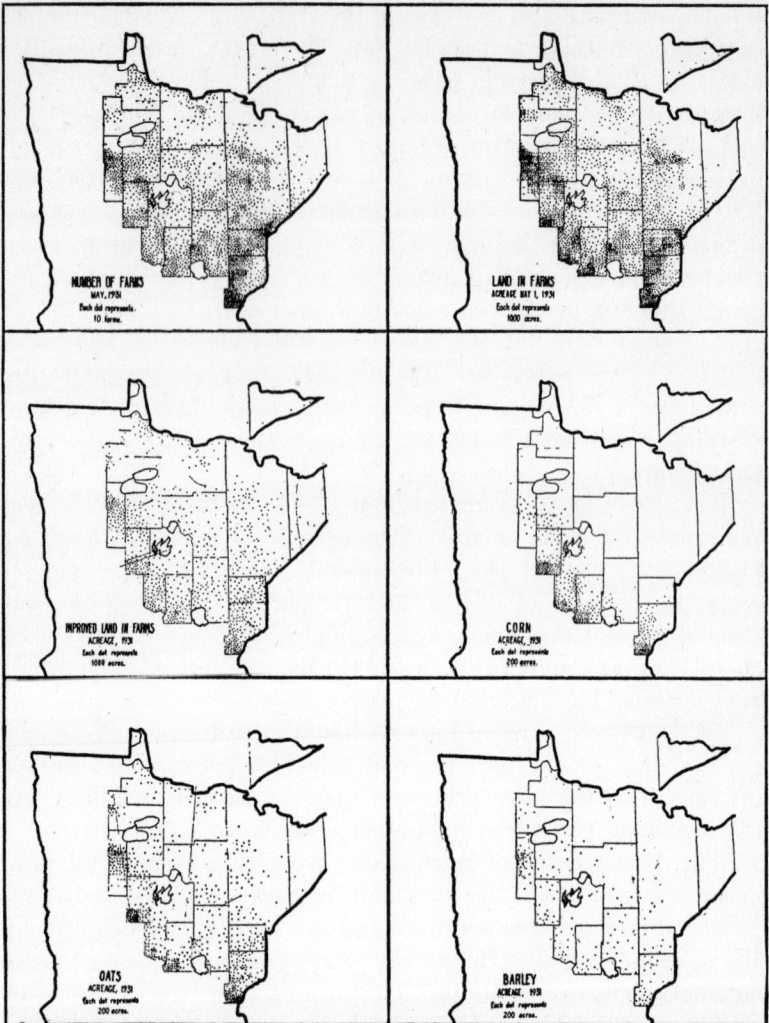

FIGURE 6. — FARM DEVELOPMENT AND ACREAGE IN CORN, OATS, AND BARLEY IN FOURTEEN NORTHEASTERN COUNTIES, 1931

1. Number of farms, each dot representing 10 farms. 2. Amount of land in farms, each dot representing 1,000 acres. 3. Amount of improved land in farms, each dot representing 1,000 acres. 4. Acreage in corn, each dot representing 200 acres. 5. Acreage in oats, each dot representing 200 acres. 6. Acreage in barley, each dot representing 200 acres.

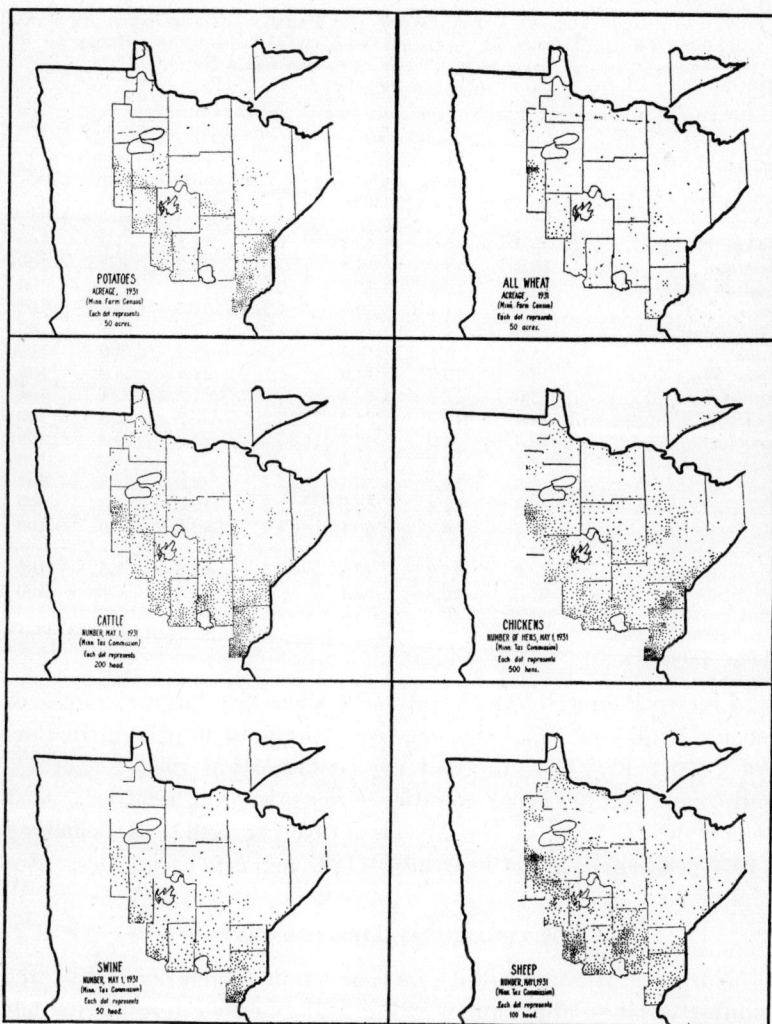

FIGURE 7. — ACREAGE IN POTATOES AND WHEAT AND NUMBER OF LIVESTOCK IN FOURTEEN NORTHEASTERN COUNTIES, 1931

1. Acreage in potatoes, each dot representing 50 acres. 2. Acreage in wheat, each dot representing 50 acres. 3. Number of cattle, each dot representing 200 head. 4. Number of chickens, each dot representing 500 hens. 5. Number of swine, each dot representing 50 head. 6. Number of sheep, each dot representing 100 head.

33

TABLE 4. — PERCENTAGE OF TOTAL INCOME OF FARMERS REPRESENTED BY FARM
PRODUCTS SOLD, TRADED, OR USED BY OPERATOR'S FAMILY, AND RECEIPTS
FROM BOARDERS, ETC., IN 14 CUT-OVER COUNTIES OF NORTHEASTERN
MINNESOTA, 1929 *

County	Crops	Live-stock	Live-stock Products	Forest Products	Products Used by Operator's Family	Receipts from Boarders	Total
Aitkin	8.2	17.8	45.7	4.3	22.1	1.9	100
Beltrami	15.9	13.2	38.3	9.2	21.9	1.5	100
Carlton	16.2	10.4	53.7	1.3	18.1	.3	100
Cass	9.0	21.2	39.8	4.0	22.5	3.5	100
Clearwater	18.6	17.4	42.1	4.2	17.4	.3	100
Cook	11.2	4.4	40.2	4.5	37.7	2.0	100
Crow Wing	9.8	16.7	42.9	2.7	22.9	5.0	100
Hubbard	13.0	18.7	42.4	3.7	21.8	.4	100
Itasca	12.7	13.2	34.2	10.2	26.9	2.8	100
Koochiching	19.3	11.0	28.7	14.7	24.9	1.4	100
Lake	5.4	9.3	46.0	6.5	31.5	1.3	100
Lake of the Woods...	19.3	12.5	30.4	14.7	22.3	.8	100
Pine	13.3	17.4	48.8	1.2	19.0	.3	100
St. Louis	9.5	9.7	50.1	5.0	24.8	.9	100
Total.............	12.9	14.2	42.5	5.6	23.3	1.5	100
State.............	21.3	29.8	34.1	.7	13.8	.3	100

* Source: Fifteenth Census of the United States, Statistics by Counties, Third
Series, Table III.

Livestock and livestock products were the largest source of
income in all counties, being relatively the most important in Pine
(66.2 per cent), Carlton (64.1 per cent), Aitkin (63.5 per cent),
and Cass (61.0 per cent) counties. Crop sales were relatively most
important in Lake of the Woods (19.3 per cent), Koochiching
(19.3 per cent), and Clearwater (18.6 per cent) counties. (See
Figure 7.)

RECREATIONAL DEVELOPMENT

Northern Minnesota, with its cool summer climate and its large
number of lakes, abundant wild life, and extensive forest areas has
a combination of conditions that makes it ideal for summer recreational purposes. Because of the dearth of lakes and the oppressive
summer temperatures in the prairie states to the west and south,
people from these areas come to Minnesota for a vacation of fishing, bathing, and boating. Many of these people own lake shore
property and maintain their own cottages; others rent cottages and
facilities or go to the resort hotels.

An important recreational industry has been developed around
this stream of tourist traffic. Outside capital is brought in for the
development of property, payment of taxes, and purchase of sup-

plies. In many parts of the northeast, vacationists provide the principal source of income. The farmers furnish milk, eggs, vegetables, and fuel to the tourists during the summer and watch the properties in the winter. Many farmers rent cottages and boats to vacationists and act as guides for fishing and hunting parties. In many places where the soil is extremely poor, farmers would find it impossible to make a living without the supplementary income they receive from recreation. The commercial life of many of the small towns is also dominated by and dependent upon the tourist industry.

According to estimates of the Ten Thousand Lakes Greater Minnesota Association, the total number of tourists vacationing in Minnesota exceeds two million annually. The annual number of tourists approximately doubled during the ten-year period 1920–30. But during the lean years of the economic depression recreation expenditures, which are of a luxury type, have been greatly curtailed. It is estimated that there are in the state about thirteen hundred tourist resorts and hotels in addition to some three or four hundred tourist camps. The tendency in recent years has been toward the development of better equipment and facilities at the resorts and away from the poorly equipped open campsites. The number of persons who vacation at privately owned summer homes and lake cottages greatly exceeds the number who stop at commercialized resorts.

There are two principal lake areas in the northeastern counties; one centers around Leech Lake and includes the lakes of Crow Wing, Cass, Hubbard, Beltrami, and Itasca counties; the other is the mass of lakes in northern St. Louis, Lake, and Cook counties. The first group is easily accessible and has been thoroughly developed. Practically all the desirable lake shore property is in private ownership, and good roads reach the most remote beach properties. Lake shore within the Chippewa National Forest is leased to private individuals for the construction of summer homes. Conditions are quite different with respect to the northern group of lakes. This is a wilderness area for the most part, accessible only by canoe. Cottages have been built only on the outer fringe of lakes. The charm of the region is enhanced by its remoteness, and there are many who oppose the building of roads to make the area accessible to motor cars. Future development, however, will probably tend to open up this area and make it available to a much larger number of people.

GOVERNMENTAL CHARACTERISTICS *

UNITS

Table 5 indicates the local governmental structure of the counties considered in this report. Every resident is directly concerned with three units of local government in addition to the state and the nation. For the man on the farm there is a county, a town, and a school district government. In urban places every resident is af-

TABLE 5. — NUMBER OF LOCAL UNITS IN 14 COUNTIES OF NORTHEASTERN MINNESOTA

County	County Government	Cities and Villages	Towns *	Common School Districts	Other School Districts	Total Units
Aitkin	1	6	51	103	5	166
Beltrami	1	10	51	71	4	137
Carlton	1	10	25	32	8	76
Cass	1	10	52	19	6	88
Clearwater	1	5	21	62	4	93
Cook	1	1	8	5	1	16
Crow Wing	1	10	35	92	5	143
Hubbard	1	4	27	60	4	96
Itasca	1	16	42	5	4	68
Koochiching	1	7	32	..	3	43
Lake	1	1	7	..	1	10
Lake of the Woods	1	3	29	11	3	47
Pine	1	11	36	100	10	158
St. Louis	1	29	74	16	18	138
Total	14	123	490	576	76	1,279

* The figures here given take no account of recent dissolutions, to be mentioned hereafter.

fected by a county, a city or village, and a school district. These are in all instances separate units of government, operating through their respective boards, councils, and other elective officers.

From the legal point of view, the framework of local government is the same in the northern as in the southern part of the state, but in fact there are some very notable differences. With the exception of the areas about Duluth and the Iron Range, population in the northern counties is sparse. In southern Minnesota the agricultural population generally accounts for over half of the total, in some cases for over two-thirds, but in the northern counties about half the population is in cities and villages. Related to these differences are the following differences in local government:

1. County areas in northern Minnesota are relatively very large, but

* This discussion is based on material prepared by Professor William Anderson.

2. County populations average much smaller than they do farther south.

3. Large areas in a number of northern counties have neither organized town governments nor ordinary school districts. In such areas the county authorities provide for local roads and schools in so far as these are needed.

4. The average town in northern Minnesota, while it has about the same area as one farther south, has a much smaller population.

5. School districts in the northern counties, including the so-called "unorganized districts," are fewer, and larger in area, than in the southern part of the state. The number of common (ungraded elementary) school districts is much larger in the southern counties.

6. Outside of St. Louis, Itasca, and Crow Wing counties, which have valuable mineral deposits, the taxable wealth per capita, per town, and per county for the support of local government services is much smaller in the northern than in the southern counties. At the same time, because certain services have seemed necessary, the northern communities have raised approximately as much revenue per capita for local purposes as have the southern.

ORGANIZATION

The governmental organization of local units is substantially the same in all parts of the state. The county, which is the principal general agent of the state for local purposes, has a county board of five members (seven in St. Louis County) elected by districts, and a series of officials (auditor, treasurer, attorney, sheriff, coroner, superintendent of schools, register of deeds, surveyor, judge of probate, court commissioner, and clerk of the district court) elected at large. The usual term of office is four years. Salaries are provided for some offices, which vary roughly in proportion to the wealth and population of the county. Some officers are permitted by law to collect and retain all or part of certain fees for services. This may be in lieu of or in addition to fixed salaries.

In its organization the county government is a house divided against itself. On one side stands the board of county commissioners, which represents the county as a corporation and has powers with respect to the construction and maintenance of certain county institutions and the courthouse, and the levying of the county tax. On the other side stands the series of county officers already named. They are all provided for by statutes, are elected directly by the voters, and are responsible only to the voters and the state. The board of county commissioners has very little control over them, and must provide them with such office space, supplies, equipment, salaries, and assistance as the law specifies. Thus a large part of the county budget is really beyond the control of the county board, and the county administration lacks a central responsible head.

The policy of direct popular election of officers has been carried to the extreme in the organization of the county. Even such unimportant officers as the coroner and the surveyor must be chosen through the process of popular nomination and election. Since every officer of importance is elective, no important provision has been made for the selection of deputies and other county employees on the basis of merit.

Finally, it is noteworthy that the law provides for practically the same number of elective officers and the same organization in all counties, large and small, rich and poor. Cook County with 2,435 inhabitants (1930 census) and Lake of the Woods with 4,194 have the same elective officers as Crow Wing with 25,000 and Itasca with 27,000, and practically the same number as St. Louis County with 204,000 inhabitants. If the organization is adequate for the larger counties, it would seem to be topheavy for the smaller ones.

The town is the organized rural township. For all towns there is provided a local organization consisting of a town board of three members, a town clerk, a town treasurer, an assessor, an overseer of highways, who is usually one of the board members, two constables, and two justices of the peace, all elected at the town meeting. In addition there may be other elective officers. The town board members, or town supervisors, serve for three years, justices and constables for two years, and the other officers generally for one year. Most salaries are merely nominal, but the overseer of highways may be paid a monthly wage, the assessor receives a per diem, and certain other officers receive designated fees.

In practice the construction and maintenance of town roads and the maintenance of certain county roads are the principal and most expensive of the town's functions. A few of the northern counties also have the "town system" of poor relief, which places some responsibility for the care of the poor upon the towns, cities, and villages. Local provisions for public health, for law enforcement, for the conduct of elections, and for licensing and regulating certain businesses, also fall upon the town, but receive relatively little attention.

In general school districts are of two types in Minnesota. First come the common or ungraded elementary districts. These are relatively much more numerous in the southern counties, but even in the fourteen northern counties under consideration there are more than seven times as many of these as of all other types. As a rule the voters in each of these districts at an annual school meeting elect the members of the board of three and determine the school tax and other matters of policy. The board in turn selects and employs the teacher and perhaps a janitor or caretaker of the school and manages the other affairs of the school. As implied in the name, there is usually only one school in the district, an ungraded elementary school, with but a single teacher. Enrollments are also small as a rule. In fact, the 576 common school districts in the fourteen counties had only 16,069 pupils enrolled in 1931, whereas the 76 other districts had 86,751, or more than five times as many. The average of nearly 28 pupils per common district was better, however, than the average for the state.

Contrasting with the common school districts are the various districts of larger size. In the laws these are usually called special and independent districts. These terms cover the various types of consolidated districts as well as the city and village districts. Lake County schools are all included in a single county district. In a number of other northern counties there are so-called "unorganized" county districts, or areas in which the county provides the schools through a special board consisting of the chairman of the county board, the county superintendent of schools, and the treasurer.

Special and independent districts are usually governed by boards of five or more members elected from the districts at a regular election. There is usually no annual school meeting, and hence the full responsibility for managing the schools devolves upon the elective board. The terms of the members are usually three years, overlapping, and salaries are a rare exception.

The board in such districts elects a superintendent, who reports directly to it and to the State Department of Education. Thus the county superintendent, who superintends the ungraded schools in common school districts, is not needed in special and independent districts and usually has little or no jurisdiction over them. The local superintendent, in turn, nominates the teachers and other employees, and has general control of the schools under the authority and supervision of the elective board, to which he is responsible.

FUNCTIONS

Education, both elementary and secondary, constitutes practically the sole function of the school districts. In performing this function the districts are supervised and aided by the state, and are also assisted by the other local units. Towns, cities, and villages provide the assessors, who assess property for all purposes, many of the roads which serve the schools, and in many cases the facilities for conducting school elections. Counties collect taxes for all units, including schools, raise a separate tax levy for school purposes, and handle and distribute other funds for the school districts.

Urban places excepted, the remaining functions of local government are divided between the counties and the towns, a constantly increasing share going to the counties.

Many roads originally built and maintained by the towns have been taken over by the counties and the state. Today the state maintains some eleven thousand miles of trunk highways, and collects and distributes to the counties a one-mill property tax and one-third of the gasoline tax, which the counties expend upon the state aid and county aid roads. The counties construct and in part maintain practically all the traffic-bearing roads of second-rate and third-rate importance. What is left to the towns is a considerable mileage of town roads, and some work of maintenance on certain county roads.

Before the extension of the trunk highways in 1933 there were in the state nearly 7,000 miles of trunk highways (state), nearly 17,000 of state aid roads (county), nearly 9,000 of county roads (constructed by counties but maintained in part by towns) and over 78,000 miles of town roads. The state then took over 4,000 miles of important roads from the counties to add to the trunk highway system, but did not reduce the amount of state aid given to counties for road purposes. The result was that the counties were able to take over more miles of the most traveled town roads as "county aid" roads under the gas tax diversion law. This left the towns with a still less important task of road building and maintenance.

Law enforcement in rural districts is divided between a number

of agencies, including the state highway patrol, the State Bureau
of Criminal Apprehension, and other state agencies; the sheriff and
his deputies, as well as the coroner, for the county; and the constables elected by the towns. As new state agencies have been put
in at the top in recent years and the sheriffs have obtained more
deputies, the constables in the towns have become increasingly less
important. They are, as a rule, practically unpaid, although they
get some fees. They have almost no equipment, no headquarters,
and no local jails. They carry on their daily work as farmers or in
some other capacity, and are in most cases seldom called upon to
make an arrest. The sheriffs of the counties are also elective officers
and without police training, although many of them have had long
experience. Upon them and their deputies falls the main work of
law enforcement in rural areas, and they also cooperate with the
police in cities and villages. Many counties provide only an inadequate staff of deputy sheriffs, so that regular patrolling of rural
districts is the exception found only in a few of the most populous
counties. A number of counties do not even maintain adequate
jails, and must take their prisoners to adjoining counties. As with
roads, so with law enforcement, the trend is away from the town
as a unit and toward the county, the state, and the nation.

The towns have justices of the peace for minor civil cases, mis-
demeanors, and "binding over" proceedings in connection with major crimes. A constable usually attends the justice in his court, but
there is no town officer to correspond to the county attorney for
prosecuting offenders. Indeed the justice himself is in practically
all cases without any legal training.

In the counties the prosecutor of all criminal offenders is the
county attorney. The district court is the court of general jurisdiction in Minnesota, for criminal as well as for civil matters. A district judge holds court at every county seat at stated times, usually
at least twice a year. Each county, besides paying a part of the
judge's salary, provides a local resident clerk of the district court,
a court room, chambers for the judge, and a small law library. Outside of the larger cities, where municipal courts have acquired
substantial jurisdiction, the district courts handle practically all
important cases in the first instance, and also hear some appeals
from justice courts and probate courts. Each county maintains
also a probate court for probating wills and administering the
estates of deceased persons. The judge need not be learned in the
law.

In the field of public relief and welfare work, Minnesota gives its several counties the option of deciding by popular vote whether the "town" or the "county" system of poor relief shall prevail. Originally these two systems were more clearly distinguishable from each other than they are today. Under the town system, each town, village, and city in the county levied its own tax and expended its own funds for all relief purposes. Under the county system, poor relief was a duty of the county alone. By recent legislation the county has been required to assume certain burdens, such as mothers' pensions and old age pensions, and has also been authorized to provide a poor farm or home, whichever system of relief prevails. Furthermore, if the expense of relief in any town under the town system exceeds the yield of a one-mill tax, the county is compelled to provide 75 per cent of the revenue needed above such one-mill levy. The result is that the county may foot a large part of the relief bill even under the town system, though it has no real control of the expenditure of the funds.

Because of the option they have, counties are constantly shifting from one system to the other. In 1932 eleven of the fourteen counties discussed herein had the county system. Carlton, Clearwater, and Crow Wing had the town system, and Beltrami has now adopted this plan.

Property assessment for tax purposes continues to be the function of town, village, and city assessors. Town assessors are elected at the annual town meetings. They work for a short time each year on personal property assessment, and a longer time each even-numbered year on real estate assessment. Their compensation is a per diem for the time employed.

Tax collection, on the other hand, is a county function. The county auditor calculates the rates of both real and personal property taxes for all local units of government each year and extends the charges upon his books. The county treasurer receives the taxes for all units, and the auditor and treasurer together distribute the proceeds to the units and officers entitled to receive them.

Public health is, in most rural districts, a rather neglected function. Each town board is ex officio a board of health for the town, but as such it is relatively inactive. When epidemics break out, the state health authorities have to step into the situation. Except in St. Louis County and a few others which provide for county nurses, there is practically no county health work being performed in the fourteen counties.

CHAPTER III

PRESENT USES OF LAND : NATURAL AREAS *

Statistical data descriptive of land use are compiled and published according to political subdivisions. Township data are usually combined to form county totals and averages. Where natural conditions, such as soil, topography, climate, etc., are essentially uniform throughout a county, there is no objection to this procedure. Unfortunately, however, county boundaries do not ordinarily conform to natural boundaries. Within most counties greatly differing natural conditions are to be found, and hence county statistical averages are almost meaningless.

In part the difficulty may be overcome by summarizing township data in groups classified on the basis of natural conditions. In Figure 8 the fourteen counties have been divided into twelve broad groups, principally on the basis of topography and soil productivity.[1] Each group constitutes an essentially "natural area." The line of demarcation between areas is not, of course, clear-cut, and there are many variations in topography and soil within a single area. Therefore such a districting must necessarily be an approximation.

The boundaries of the natural areas shown in Figure 8 are superimposed upon a relief map. Within each area the topographic

* This chapter has been prepared by R. I. Nowell. C. F. Clayton was responsible for much of the plan of approach and supervised the assembling and tabulation of the data on soils ratings and timber surveys.

[1] Only about 19 per cent of the land area of the fourteen counties has been covered by soil surveys. However, on the basis of the surveys and various other supplementary data, such as the geological surface formation map of the Minnesota Geological Survey, cover maps, timber cruisers' reports, original government survey plats, etc., interviews with township assessors, county agricultural agents, and others, indexes of soil productivity have been prepared for every township. The index represents a weighted average for the entire township. Numerical values ranging from 1.0 to 10.0 were assigned according to agricultural productivity. The best soils in Minnesota were given a rating of 1.0 and the poorest a rating of 10.0. The ratings were determined on the basis of the amount of cleared land used in the production of crops normally grown in the locality. The average rating for the fourteen counties is 7.5; the state average is 4.5. If the fourteen counties are excluded, the average for the state is about 3.0. The best lands in the fourteen counties have a rating of 3.0. The acreage of this grade of land is very small, amounting to only about 2.3 per cent of the area. In some instances the indexes are based upon scant information. These indexes were used as the principal basis for differentiating the natural areas of Figure 8.

characteristics display a certain degree of homogeneity. Area I embraces well-drained lands adjacent to the Rainy River and its tributaries. Area II is a flat, featureless, poorly drained area the greater part of which is covered with peat. Area III is largely rock outcrop or is rough and broken, strewn with boulders and pitted with lakes. Area IV, in which numerous small streams have their origin, is fairly well drained, and includes much of the best agricultural land in the fourteen counties. Area V is so very rough that it is unadapted to agriculture. Area VI is spotted with lakes and has a variety of soils. Area VII embraces the Mesabi Iron Range. Area VIII is a prairie region, comparatively flat. Area IX is sandy and spotted with lakes. It represents a transition zone between the well-developed agricultural land to the south and the comparatively undeveloped land to the north. Area X is flat and predominantly swampy, though some good agricultural lands occur along the stream courses. Area XI has more relief than Area X, which lies to the west. It is very stony but moderately productive when stoned. Area XII is stony, sandy, and inferior to Area XI for agricultural purposes.

While this division of the fourteen counties is based primarily upon physical factors, the areas differ distinctly in economic and social development. This must logically follow, since economic and social development is so intimately dependent upon natural factors, such as soil, timber, and minerals. A striking illustration is afforded by comparing the economic development of Area VII, the Mesabi Iron Range, with Area II, the big peat area. Figure 8 represents a generalized land classification on the basis of natural factors. In Chapter VI is presented a more detailed tentative land use classification based on social and economic factors in addition to natural factors.

In this chapter the present use of land in each of the broad natural areas is described. All lands have been grouped into five classes according to use: agriculture, urban, forest, open meadow, and muskeg. The agricultural class includes all land in farms; the urban all land within the boundaries of incorporated cities or villages; the forest all timbered or cut-over land not in farms, farm woodlots being excluded from this figure. The three classes designated forest, open meadow, and muskeg are descriptive of natural cover rather than of economic use. The natural cover, however, has economic significance in that it defines to a certain degree the potential economic uses. Mineral lands were not classified separately

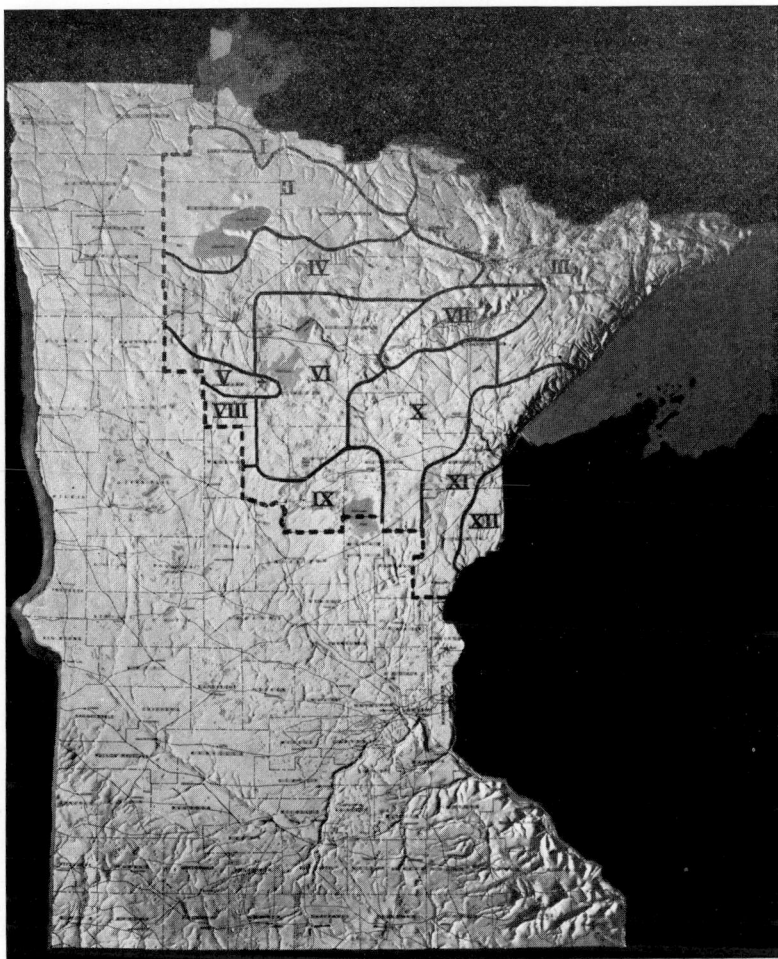

FIGURE 8. — BROAD NATURAL AREAS IN FOURTEEN NORTHEASTERN COUNTIES

because of the difficulties of classification. Large acreages of low-grade mineral lands are held for speculative purposes. Either a great increase in the price of iron or new discoveries in the arts of refinement, or both, would be necessary to permit the working of these deposits. Other lands without known mineral deposits are held in anticipation of future mineral discoveries. Pending such uncertain future use the lands are now in agricultural use, forest, or some other cover. The acreage of mineral lands that have actually been worked or are workable under present conditions constitutes a negligible percentage of the total land area. Mineral lands were, therefore, thrown into the class represented by the prevailing present use. Similarly, flowage rights are held on a few lands by power companies. At some future date these lands may be used for power purposes, but in the meantime agriculture and forestry are the prevailing uses.

Nor has recreation, while it is very important in northern Minnesota, been recognized as a separate land use in this study. Some lands are used exclusively for recreation, but more frequently recreation is supplementary to agriculture or forestry. It was found most difficult to reduce the recreational use of land to an acreage basis. As an alternative the rodage of developed lake shore line was compiled as an index of recreational use. Because the areas are of varying sizes, developed lake shore rodage in the various districts could not be compared directly. To make comparisons possible, developed shore line rodage of each area has been expressed as a ratio to total land area and the ratio in turn expressed as an index. The average for the fourteen counties is represented by 100.

Table 6, which presents a few of the principal characteristics of the twelve natural areas in summary form, is presented for the readers who may wish to make comparisons of the various areas described in the following pages. Figure 9, showing land use and selected forest items for the fourteen northeastern counties is also presented for comparison with similar charts for each of the twelve natural areas.

Area I

The topography of this area is flat, interrupted only by stream courses which drain from the big swamp on the south into the Rainy River. Much of the area is covered with peat. Below the peat are mineral soils, some of which are very productive. Between the streams the swamp extends well down to the banks of the

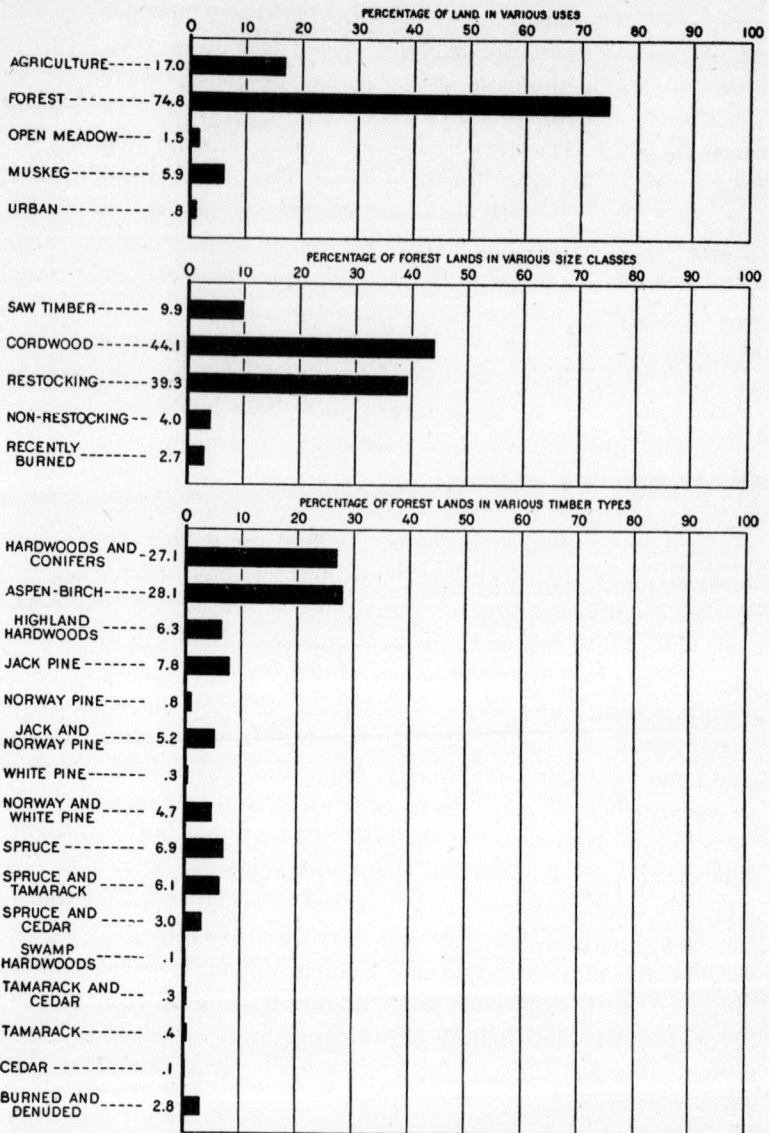

PERCENTAGE OF LAND IN VARIOUS USES

| | 0 | 10 | 20 | 30 | 40 | 50 | 60 | 70 | 80 | 90 | 100 |

AGRICULTURE----- 17.0
FOREST --------- 74.8
OPEN MEADOW---- 1.5
MUSKEG--------- 5.9
URBAN---------- .8

PERCENTAGE OF FOREST LANDS IN VARIOUS SIZE CLASSES

SAW TIMBER------ 9.9
CORDWOOD------44.1
RESTOCKING------39.3
NON-RESTOCKING-- 4.0
RECENTLY BURNED -------- 2.7

PERCENTAGE OF FOREST LANDS IN VARIOUS TIMBER TYPES

HARDWOODS AND CONIFERS -27.1
ASPEN-BIRCH-----28.1
HIGHLAND HARDWOODS ----- 6.3
JACK PINE ------- 7.8
NORWAY PINE----- .8
JACK AND NORWAY PINE----- 5.2
WHITE PINE------- .3
NORWAY AND WHITE PINE ----- 4.7
SPRUCE --------- 6.9
SPRUCE AND TAMARACK ----- 6.1
SPRUCE AND CEDAR ----- 3.0
SWAMP HARDWOODS ------ .1
TAMARACK AND CEDAR --- .3
TAMARACK------- .4
CEDAR ---------- .1
BURNED AND DENUDED ----- 2.8

FIGURE 9. — DISTRIBUTION OF LAND USES AND OF TIMBER OF VARIOUS TYPES AND SIZES IN FOURTEEN NORTHEASTERN COUNTIES

46

TABLE 6. — PRINCIPAL CHARACTERISTICS OF NATURAL AREAS IN
NORTHEASTERN MINNESOTA

Natural Area	Total Acreage	Percentage in Several Classes of Ownership			Percentage Tax Delinquent ‡	Percentage in Several Uses			Soil Productivity Rating **	Index of Recreational Use ††
		Federal	State	Private		Agriculture	Forest	Other §		
I	878,371 *	3.1	17.6	79.3	58.9	19.9	56.8	23.3	5.9	3.0
II	2,033,584 †	6.7	25.5	67.8	74.2	5.8	61.5	32.7	9.1	...
III	4,102,445	24.1	13.9	62.0	47.1	2.0	97.6	.4	9.2	100.0
IV	2,407,898	.6	12.5	86.9	43.5	27.1	70.7	2.2	5.8	40.7
V	413,373	2.2	8.1	89.7	86.8	13.3	84.8	1.9	7.8	192.6
VI	2,177,333	11.2	7.8	81.0	52.7	16.5	76.4	7.1	7.0	251.8
VII	930,940	...	6.6	93.4	24.5	15.0	81.6	3.4	7.8	92.6
VIII	257,253	...	.7	99.3	32.2	48.7	43.4	7.9	6.7	188.9
IX	761,785	...	1.5	98.5	27.7	45.8	45.0	9.2	6.6	218.5
X	2,039,309	.1	7.9	92.0	46.7	17.7	74.2	8.1	7.7	85.2
XI	1,413,625	.1	.6	99.3	29.3	39.5	55.6	4.9	6.4	122.2
XII	412,786	.1	.6	99.3	61.7	14.5	84.0	1.5	7.5	...
14 counties	17,828,702	8.0	11.2	80.8	47.6	17.0	74.8	8.2	7.6	100.0

* Exclusive of Angle Township, Lake of the Woods County, 79,421 acres.
† Exclusive of Red Lake Indian Reservation, 407,928 acres.
‡ Percentage of total taxable area delinquent for general property taxes in 1931 and prior years.
§ Includes open meadow, muskeg, and urban.
** See page 43, footnote 1.
†† Based on developed lake shore rodage in relation to total land area, the average for the fourteen counties being represented by 100.

Rainy River. The area has an agricultural productivity rating of 5.9 if the best lands in the state are rated 1 and the poorest 10.

A total of 878,371 acres [2] of land is included in Area I, of which 19.9 per cent is in farms, 56.8 per cent in forest, 22.6 per cent in open muskeg, .3 per cent in open meadow, and .4 per cent in urban sites.[3] In Figure 10 are presented graphically the percentages of land in various uses and certain pertinent data relating to the forests. The state owns 17.6 per cent of the land in the area, the federal government 3.1 per cent, and 79.3 per cent is in private or corporate ownership. In 1931, 408,320 acres, or 46.5 per cent of the total and 58.9 per cent of the taxable land area, was delinquent for

[2] Exclusive of Angle Township, Lake of the Woods County, 79,421 acres.
[3] Data on the acreage of land in different uses were obtained from three sources: land in farms, from the United States Census of Agriculture, 1930; urban land, from maps showing boundaries of incorporated places; and lands in forest, open meadow, and muskeg, from fire-plan books of Minnesota forest rangers.

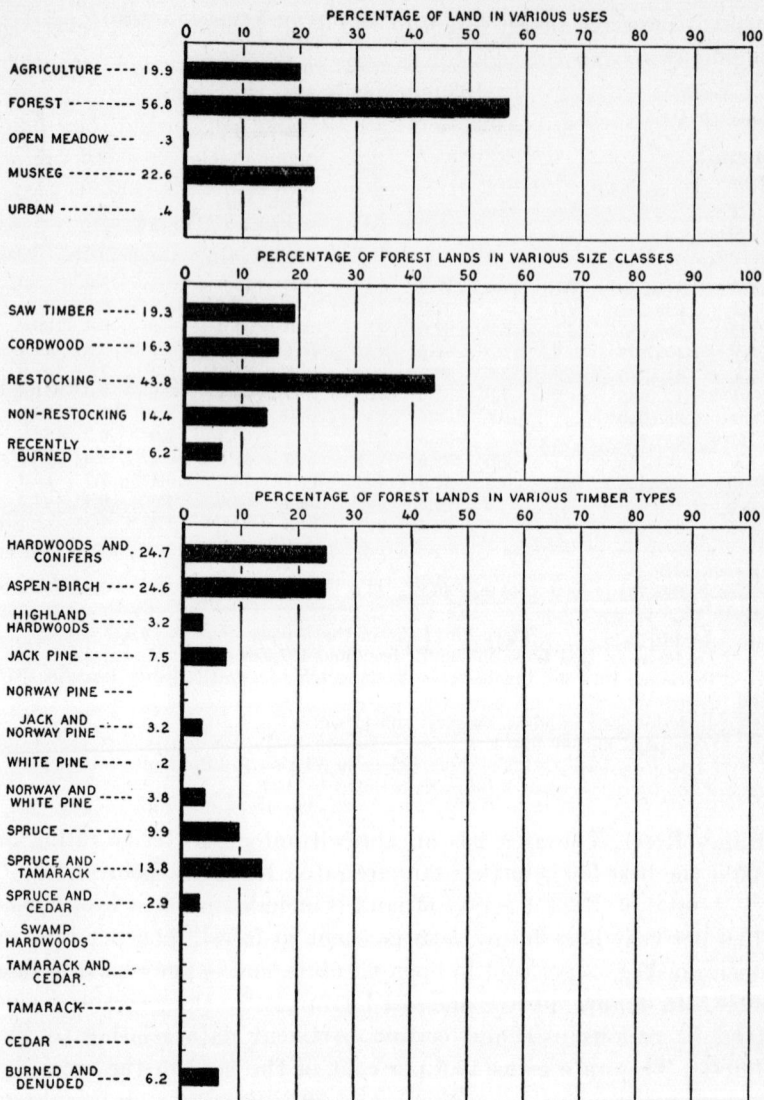

PERCENTAGE OF LAND IN VARIOUS USES

AGRICULTURE ---- 19.9
FOREST --------- 56.8
OPEN MEADOW --- .3
MUSKEG --------- 22.6
URBAN ----------- .4

PERCENTAGE OF FOREST LANDS IN VARIOUS SIZE CLASSES

SAW TIMBER ----- 19.3
CORDWOOD ------ 16.3
RESTOCKING ----- 43.8
NON-RESTOCKING 14.4
RECENTLY BURNED ------- 6.2

PERCENTAGE OF FOREST LANDS IN VARIOUS TIMBER TYPES

HARDWOODS AND CONIFERS 24.7
ASPEN-BIRCH ---- 24.6
HIGHLAND HARDWOODS ------ 3.2
JACK PINE ------- 7.5
NORWAY PINE ----
JACK AND NORWAY PINE ----- 3.2
WHITE PINE ----- .2
NORWAY AND WHITE PINE ----- 3.8
SPRUCE --------- 9.9
SPRUCE AND TAMARACK ------- 13.8
SPRUCE AND CEDAR ------- .2.9
SWAMP HARDWOODS ------
TAMARACK AND CEDAR ----
TAMARACK ------
CEDAR ---------
BURNED AND DENUDED ---- 6.2

FIGURE 10. — DISTRIBUTION OF LAND USES AND OF TIMBER OF VARIOUS TYPES AND SIZES IN AREA I

48

general property taxes. Much of this land probably will revert to public ownership through the process of tax delinquency.

Land in farms. — In 1930, according to the United States Census of Agriculture, 175,002 acres, or 19.9 per cent of the total land area, was in farms. There were 1,258 farms in the area, averaging 139.1 acres each, of which 31.2 acres were in crops, 2.2 acres in plowable pasture, 6.6 acres in other pasture land, 78.9 acres in woodlots, and 20.2 acres in all other land. Crop land represented 22.4 per cent of the total acreage in farms and only 4.5 per cent of the total land of the area. In 1931 the important crops and the respective acreages per farm were as follows: hay, 19.7 acres; oats, 6.7 acres; barley, 2.6 acres; clover seed, 2.3 acres; wheat, .8 acres; and potatoes, .8 acres.[4]

Dairy cattle and sheep are the most important livestock enterprises. In 1931 there were 6.6 cattle per farm, 4.5 sheep, .6 hogs, 19 hens, and 1.5 horses.[5] Because of the great distance to outside markets production for sale is limited mainly to concentrated products such as butter, wool, and clover seed. The city of International Falls and the village of Baudette afford markets for very limited quantities of other farm produce. Practically all the hay and grains produced are fed on the farms, and the farm family consumes a goodly portion of the other farm produce. Long winter feeding periods are necessary for livestock because of the low winter temperatures and deep snow cover.

Physical conditions in the area are excellent for the production of alfalfa and alsike clover seed. The average yield of cleaned alsike seed is about 200 pounds per acre. In recent years this has sold for from 8 to 15 cents a pound at the farm. Approximately 45 cars of seed are shipped out of the area every year.

The lands classed by the census as farm woodlots are for the most part unreclaimed portions of the farms. Some of them are too wet to be reclaimed and some probably are too stony, although lands in this area are comparatively free of stone. Very few, if any, are being managed as woodlots on a sustained yield basis. Cattle are pastured on the woodlot portion of the farms as well as on the wild adjoining lands. In past years the timber on the farms has been a source of considerable farm income, but it has been cut and recut so many times that very little merchantable material remains. Descriptive data on farm woodlots are not available, but it

[4] Minnesota State Census of Agriculture, 1931.
[5] From assessment records of the Minnesota Tax Commission.

is assumed that they have a cover similar to adjoining lands primarily in forest use.

Land in forest use.[6] — As indicated previously, 56.8 per cent, or 499,024 acres of the area, is classed as forest lands. (See Figure 10.) This includes all timbered or cut-over lands not in farms. A considerable portion of the forest is potential farm land of fair quality. There are no federal or state forests in Area I. For much of the area agriculture appears to be the most appropriate use. Approximately 67 per cent of the forest land is covered with highland types of timber, and 27 per cent with swamp types. Peat accumulations up to two feet in depth are sometimes found on lands supporting highland timber types.

Mixed hardwoods and conifers, occupying 25 per cent of the forest land, and aspen-birch, occupying 25 per cent, are the most extensive forest types in the area. Jack pine occupies 7 per cent, and all other highland types 10 per cent. The predominant types in the swamps are black spruce, in pure stands or combined either with tamarack or cedar. Even before the summer of 1933 burns so

---

[6] Timber cover and size classes were taken from fire-plan books of Minnesota forest rangers in so far as they were available. For areas not covered by fire plans, forest rangers or subdistrict patrolmen mapped cover and size classes within their districts as best they could from memory. No cruising was done specially for this study. Accurate maps were available for the national forests and for some state forests. Acreages were estimated from the cover maps by planimeter. Attempts were made in mapping to recognize all types of 640 acres or larger. These data are admittedly inaccurate in detail for small areas, but it is believed that when the data are totaled and averaged by natural areas, a fairly accurate picture of timber cover is obtained. Preliminary results of a detailed timber survey being made by the Lake States Forest Experiment Station indicate that these data from forest rangers tend to exaggerate the amounts of available sawtimber and merchantable cordwood and to minimize the amounts of poor or unsatisfactory reproduction.

The following timber types were recognized: mixed hardwoods and conifers, aspen-birch, highland hardwoods, jack pine, Norway pine, mixed jack and Norway pine, white pine, mixed Norway and white pine, spruce (including balsam), mixed spruce (including balsam) and tamarack, mixed spruce (including balsam) and cedar, swamp hardwoods (yellow birch, balm of gilead, and black ash), tamarack, cedar, and mixed tamarack and cedar. To be included within a given class, 80 per cent or more of the trees had to be of the designated type. In mixtures, the two types combined, but neither singly, had to equal 80 per cent or more of the total.

Forest lands were divided in size classes as follows: *sawtimber areas,* including stands where a large proportion of the timber is large enough for manufacture into lumber in accordance with the prevailing logging and milling practice of the region; *cordwood areas,* stands where the bulk of the timber is less than sawtimber size but six inches diameter breast height or larger; *restocking areas,* lands that once supported a stand of timber now being renewed, on which the bulk of the growth is less than cordwood size; *burned and denuded areas,* lands burned so recently that reproduction has not become sufficiently established to justify classification under an established forest type but which in time if protected will restock to merchantable timber; restocking areas were subclassified as: *good,* lands 70 per cent or more restocked with commercial species; *fair,* lands 40 to 69 per cent restocked; and *poor,* lands 10 to 39 per cent restocked.

recent that reproduction had not yet started covered 6 per cent of the area, and the fires that occurred in 1933 materially increased the percentage of burned area.

About 84 per cent of the original forest has been cut or burned over, leaving 16 per cent of old growth of sawtimber size. About 4 per cent of the second growth material has attained sawlog size, making a total of 20 per cent. While this is a comparatively small figure, the area ranks second to Area II, which borders on the south and has a total of 23 per cent of sawlog size. Roughly three-fourths of the old growth timber is black spruce in pure stands or mixed with tamarack or cedar. The second growth that has attained sawlog size is about nine-tenths jack pine and one-tenth aspen-birch.

Approximately 16 per cent of the area is second growth material of merchantable cordwood size. Mixed spruce and tamarack, mixed hardwoods and conifers, and jack pine are the principal timber types in the cordwood size class. About 44 per cent of the area is of restocking sizes less than six inches diameter breast height. Of the restocking sizes 10 per cent is classed as having a good stand, 23 per cent as fair, and 11 per cent as poor. On the highlands reproduction is predominantly aspen-birch, mixed hardwoods and conifers, and jack pine; in the swamps it is black spruce. About 14 per cent has been burned or grazed so recently that it has not as yet had a chance to restock.

In addition to the forest lands there are almost 200,000 acres, or 23 per cent of the area, which are covered with muskeg. The peat accumulations in the muskegs are so deep and the drainage so poor that tree growth is practically choked out. Stands of tamarack in the muskeg about three inches in diameter are estimated to be about 150 years old. Muskegs have no economic value except perhaps for grazing big game such as moose and elk.

A very small amount of land is classed as wild open meadows, and a negligible amount is in urban sites. Power dams in the Rainy River have raised the water level and largely destroyed its natural beauty. Except along the shore of Lake of the Woods, therefore, practically no recreational development occurs. Lake of the Woods has a rocky shore line in places and does offer recreational possibilities. But very little development has thus far taken place.

Partridge and grouse are abundant on the highlands, and deer abound throughout the entire area. While hunting is very good, practically no land has been exclusively dedicated to recreational use. The newly created Red Lake Game Preserve embraces about the western half of the area. This preserve was created primarily to afford the state legal authority to assume a part of the bonded indebtedness on drainage ditches. Wild life conservation was decidedly a secondary consideration.

AREA II

A shallow arm of glacial Lake Agassiz at one time covered Area II completely. The flat topography is largely a result of wave action. Perhaps its most distinctive characteristic is the great peat bog which covers approximately 68 per cent of the area. Two of the largest bodies of water in the state are located in this region, Upper and Lower Red Lake. Both are very shallow. Scattered irregularly throughout the peat are ridges or islands which emerge just a few feet above the surrounding bog. These ridges range in agricultural productivity from very poor to good. Until drained the peat has absolutely no agricultural value, and even after draining applications of phosphorous and potassium fertilizers are necessary. Thousands of miles of open drainage ditches have been constructed in Area II in attempts to reclaim the peat lands. Special assessments against lands presumably benefited by the ditches have been so great that practically every project has been forced into delinquency and abandonment.[7] The drainage ditches have not only failed to convert the area into a farming community but have also been a positive evil in causing fire hazards. In recent years beaver have dammed many of the ditches, and the rest should be dammed to remove the fire hazard and to restore the original conditions of the forest. Except for a very restricted section in northwestern Beltrami County east of Grygla, Natural Area II is to be considered distinctly non-agricultural. The agricultural productivity rating of the area is 9.1.

Parts of the bog, notably in western Koochiching County, are almost impenetrable in the summertime. Logging operations are conducted during the winter months, when the surface is covered with snow and ice. The peat averages from eight to ten feet in depth and makes road construction extremely difficult. If the peat is not removed, the weight of gravel or surfacing material causes it to squash out the sides, making it difficult to maintain a firm, smooth surface. When dry the peat is combustible and great holes are frequently burned in roadbeds.

[7] See Chapter IV for a more complete discussion of drainage problems.

This area embraces a total of 2,441,512 acres of land surface. The Red Lake Indian Reservation occupies 407,928 acres in the southwestern portion. Since the acreage within the reservation has been permanently dedicated to an appropriate use, it has been omitted from all consideration in this study of land use problems. Exclusive of the reservation there are 2,033,584 acres. In 1930, 67.8 per cent of the area was in private ownership, 25.5 per cent in state ownership, and 6.7 per cent in federal ownership. The state-owned lands are mostly valueless open muskegs obtained from the federal government under the swamp grant. In 1931 some 1,023,280 acres, or 50.3 per cent of the entire area and 74.2 per cent of the taxable area, were delinquent for general property taxes. This is mostly logged-off swamp land, a substantial portion of which will probably revert to the state. Federal lands include small remnants of the original public domain and a few lands held in trust for the Indians.

Land in farms. — In 1930 only 5.8 per cent, or 118,532 acres, was in farms. (See Figure 11.) Natural Area III, of which 2 per cent was in farms, was the only area having a sparser agricultural settlement. According to the United States Census of Agriculture there were 715 farms in the area in 1930. Most of these farms were located along the Black and Sturgeon rivers in Koochiching County, on the jack pine sands of southwestern Lake of the Woods County, along the eastern shore of Upper Red Lake, and on the higher land which emerges from the swamp in northwestern Beltrami County. Natural Area II was once settled much more densely than at present, but it is so poorly adapted to farming that abandonment has been extensive. The farms along the rivers in Koochiching and Lake of the Woods counties are on comparatively good soil, but are severely handicapped by lack of adequate market outlets. The farms on sand in southwestern Lake of the Woods County are isolated and unproductive. Those in northwestern Beltrami County are comparatively large, are much more productive than those in Lake of the Woods County, and have better market outlets.

The average size of all farms in the area in 1930 was 165.8 acres. Only in Area VIII, which is an open prairie section, did farms average larger. In Area II, 72 acres per farm were cleared and about 52 acres per farm were in crops. Area VIII, again, is the only area having more crop acres per farm than Area II. Hay, pasture, oats, and barley are the important crops, and dairying and sheep the important livestock enterprises.

PERCENTAGE OF LAND IN VARIOUS USES

	0	10	20	30	40	50	60	70	80	90	100

AGRICULTURE ---- 5.8

FOREST --------- 61.5

OPEN MEADOW --- 1.9

MUSKEG --------- 30.8

URBAN -----------

PERCENTAGE OF FOREST LANDS IN VARIOUS SIZE CLASSES

	0	10	20	30	40	50	60	70	80	90	100

SAW TIMBER ----- 23.0

CORDWOOD ------ 32.6

RESTOCKING ----- 22.4

NON-RESTOCKING 3.7

RECENTLY BURNED ------ 18.3

PERCENTAGE OF FOREST LANDS IN VARIOUS TIMBER TYPES

	0	10	20	30	40	50	60	70	80	90	100

HARDWOODS AND CONIFERS 9.0

ASPEN-BIRCH ---- 9.5

HIGHLAND HARDWOODS ------ 4.5

JACK PINE ------- 6.4

NORWAY PINE ---- 1.4

JACK AND NORWAY PINE ----- 2.4

WHITE PINE ----- .4

NORWAY AND WHITE PINE -----

SPRUCE --------- 4.9

SPRUCE AND TAMARACK ------ 24.3

SPRUCE AND CEDAR ------ 14.2

SWAMP HARDWOODS ------

TAMARACK AND CEDAR ---- 1.5

TAMARACK ------ 3.0

CEDAR --------- .2

BURNED AND DENUDED ---- 18.3

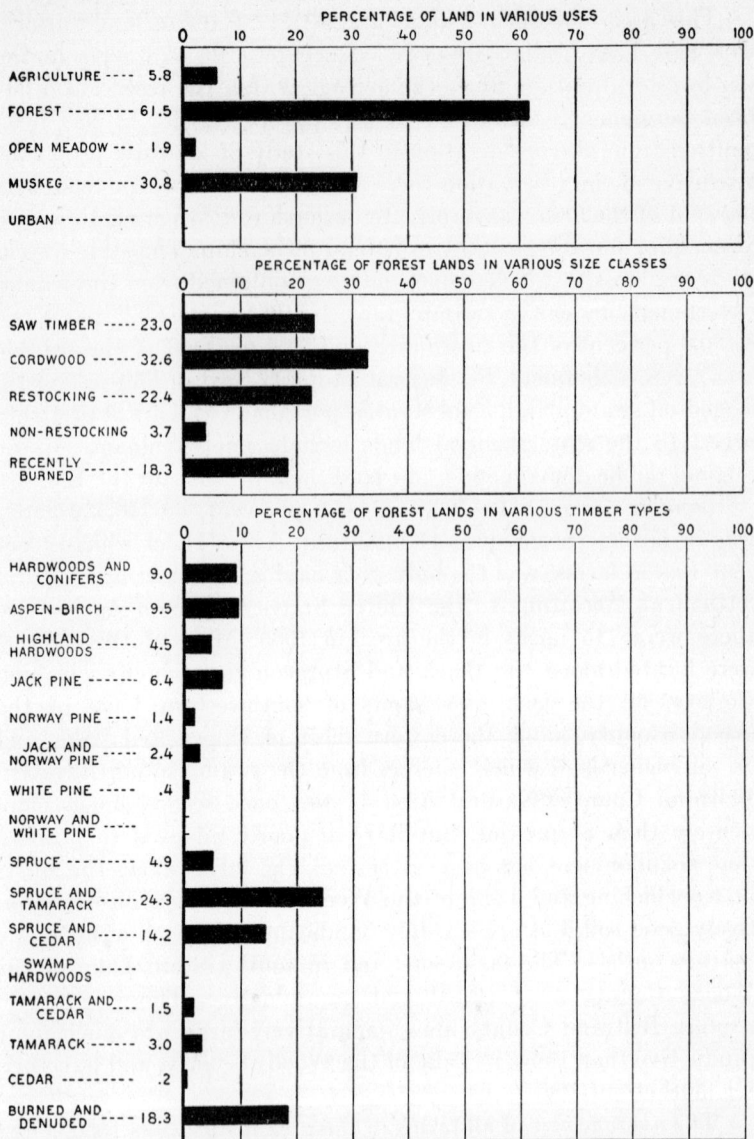

FIGURE 11. — DISTRIBUTION OF LAND USES AND OF TIMBER OF VARIOUS TYPES AND SIZES IN AREA II

Farms in Area II have a larger acreage classed by the census as woodlot than farms in any of the other areas.

Land in forest use. — Forest land, representing 61.5 per cent of the total area, is by far the most important use class. Forestry and game conservation are the uses to which most of Area II is best adapted. Within this area is located part of the Beltrami Island State Forest and all of the Pine Island State Forest. Together these forests embrace 1,014,817 acres, or approximately half of the area, exclusive of the Indian Reservation. The rest of Area II, with the exception of three townships in Koochiching County, is included in the Red Lake Game Preserve.

Approximately 34 per cent of the forest land supports highland timber types and 48 per cent lowland types. The remaining 18 per cent has been recently burned and denuded. The original timber types on the burned lands have not been recorded. Spruce and tamarack, and spruce and cedar are the most important timber types in the swamp. On the highlands aspen-birch, mixed hardwoods and conifers, jack pine, and highland hardwoods are the important types, in the order named.

Fires in this area have caused great damage in recent years. Before the summer of 1933, 18 per cent of the total area had been so recently burned that reproduction had not yet started. This is three times the acreage burned in Area I and more than that in all other areas combined. Peat fires once started are extremely difficult to control. For months they will smolder deep below the surface with comparatively little damage; then suddenly a wind will whip them into a raging surface conflagration. Drainage ditches have dried out much of the peat and made large acreages combustible. Farmers ignite the peat in burning meadows and clearing timber lands. The fire-fighting expenditures of the State Division of Forestry in Areas I and II are greater than in all the rest of the state. Reflooding of the swamps and relocation of the isolated settlers would go far toward controlling fires.

Timber of sawlog size covers 23 per cent of the forest lands of Area II. This is the largest percentage, as well as the largest absolute acreage, of sawlog timber in any of the twelve natural areas. The sawlog material consists mostly of spruce and tamarack, mixed hardwoods and conifers, and aspen-birch. Cordwood timber, predominantly spruce and cedar, and spruce and tamarack mixtures, occupies about 33 per cent of the forest lands. Restocking sizes occupy 22 per cent of the forest area. About three-fourths of the restocking lands have a fair to good stand of timber, and on one-fourth the stand is poor. The highlands are restocking largely to aspen-birch, jack pine, and mixed hardwoods and conifers; the swamps to spruce and tamarack, and spruce and cedar. Almost a third (31 per cent) of Area II is classed as open muskeg.

Since there are few lakes in Area II, recreational activities are limited to the hunting of upland game birds and deer. The area provides an ideal habitat for other big game, such as moose and elk. If properly managed it is possible that these species may at some future date become sufficiently numerous to permit the public to take limited numbers.

Area III

Area III is predominantly in forest use. (See Figure 12.) The topography is rough and broken, and the area has many beautiful lakes. In the northern part underlying native rock crops out at the surface or is covered with a very thin mantle of soil. Huge boulders are strewn promiscuously over the landscape. In the southern part the soil is a rough stony loam, interspersed with many small peat bogs. The growing season is short, averaging about 98 days. All other uses of land, including agriculture, open meadow, muskeg, and urban, appear negligible in comparison with the land in forest use. Of a total of 4,102,445 acres, 97.6 per cent is in forest, 2.0 per cent in agriculture, 0.2 per cent in open meadow, 0.1 per cent in muskeg, and 0.1 per cent in urban use. The federal government owns 24.1 per cent, the state 13.9 per cent, and private individuals or corporations 61.9 per cent. In 1931, 29.2 per cent of the total area and 47.1 per cent of the taxable area, or 1,196,360 acres, was delinquent for general property taxes.

Land in forest use. — Within Area III are included the Superior National Forest and five state forests — Kabetogama, Burntside, Grand Portage, Finland, and Cloquet Valley. Together these forests cover 3,323,902 acres, or 81 per cent of the entire area. The region is well suited to the production of forest products. Forest lands of the state and federal government could well be extended and consolidated for more efficient management.

About 90 per cent of the lands in forest use support highland timber types and 9 per cent swamp types. In recent years fires have been so well controlled that only 0.5 per cent of the forest land has been recently burned. Approximately 60 per cent of the forest lands support timber of merchantable cordwood size; 29 per

PERCENTAGE OF LAND IN VARIOUS USES

	0	10	20	30	40	50	60	70	80	90	100

AGRICULTURE ---- 2.0
FOREST --------- 97.6
OPEN MEADOW --- .2
MUSKEG --------- .1
URBAN ----------- .1

PERCENTAGE OF FOREST LANDS IN VARIOUS SIZE CLASSES

	0	10	20	30	40	50	60	70	80	90	100

SAW TIMBER ----- 8.2
CORDWOOD ------ 59.8
RESTOCKING ----- 29.3
NON-RESTOCKING 2.2
RECENTLY BURNED ------- .5

PERCENTAGE OF FOREST LANDS IN VARIOUS TIMBER TYPES

	0	10	20	30	40	50	60	70	80	90	100

HARDWOODS AND CONIFERS 33.4
ASPEN-BIRCH ---- 22.8
HIGHLAND HARDWOODS ------ 1.1
JACK PINE ------- 9.3
NORWAY PINE ---- 1.1
JACK AND NORWAY PINE ----- 6.4
WHITE PINE ----- .3
NORWAY AND WHITE PINE ----- 16.0
SPRUCE --------- 7.1
SPRUCE AND TAMARACK ------ .9
SPRUCE AND CEDAR ------ 1.1
SWAMP HARDWOODS ------
TAMARACK AND CEDAR ----
TAMARACK ------
CEDAR ---------
BURNED AND DENUDED ---- .5

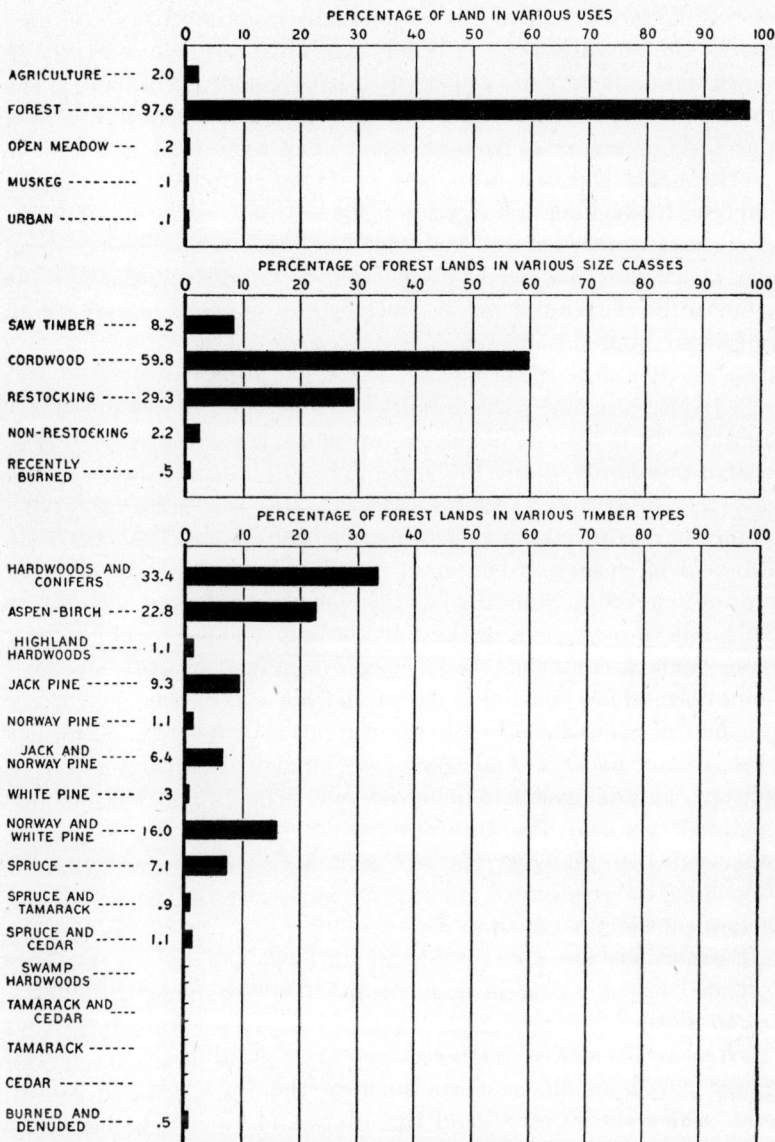

FIGURE 12. — DISTRIBUTION OF LAND USES AND OF TIMBER OF VARIOUS TYPES AND SIZES IN AREA III

cent is of restocking sizes; and 8 per cent is old growth of sawtimber size. The cordwood material runs about 41 per cent mixed hardwoods and conifers, 18 per cent mixed Norway and white pine, 15 per cent jack pine, 14 per cent aspen-birch, 9 per cent spruce, and the balance miscellaneous types. The sawtimber is predominantly mixed Norway and white pine, and mixed hardwoods and conifers. Restocking areas run heavily to aspen-birch, mixed hardwoods and conifers, mixed jack and Norway pine, and mixed Norway and white pine. About 85 per cent of the restocking areas has a fair to good stand of young trees and 15 per cent a poor stand. Pulpwood from this area supplies the paper mill at Cloquet with a large portion of its requirements. The wood-using industries of Duluth and eastern lake ports also draw heavily on this area for timber supplies.

Land in farms. — In 1930 there were 679 farms in the area, embracing a total of 77,947 acres. Many of these farms were scattered along the north shore of Lake Superior in Cook and Lake counties. Commercial fishing is the main source of income, farming being only a side issue. Similarly, in the vicinity of Tower and Ely in St. Louis County, men working in the iron mines part of the year have small places where they keep a cow, a few chickens, and raise some vegetables. Around some of the lakes part-time farming is pursued in combination with the recreational industry. Elsewhere throughout the area lumberjacks acquired land when the timber supply became exhausted, hewed out logs for cabins, and attempted to farm. The Brimson community in St. Louis County was settled in this way. The soil around Brimson is so stony that from four to six hundred loads of stone per acre must be removed before plowing is possible. Throughout the entire extent of Area III conditions are unfavorable to farming, and unless there are outside sources of cash income it is practically impossible for farmers to make a living.

Recreation. — Area III possesses great possibilities for recreational development. In it are many of the finest lakes in Minnesota. Along the International Boundary and among the numerous inland lakes, hundreds of miles of canoe routes penetrate a wilderness area of exceptional beauty.

Comparatively few of the shore lines have been developed with summer homes and cottages. Since there are few roads in the area, most of the lakes are inaccessible by car. Kabetogama, Pelican, Vermilion, and Burntside lakes have the greatest development. Despite its inaccessibility almost a fourth of the developed lake shore line of the fourteen counties is located in Area III. The ratio of developed shore line to land area is exactly the same as the average for the fourteen counties. Opportunities for future recreational development are much greater in Area III than in any other natural area of the state.

Area IV

A rather wide range of soil types is included in this area. A productive clay loam interspersed with swamp is found at the eastern extremity of the area around the village of Cook, and a gray loam comparatively free of stone, interspersed with swamp, occurs at Effie, Northome, and Blackduck. For some distance west of Bemidji the land is sandy with wet peat depressions. Stone is most abundant in the eastern parts of Area IV, but constitutes a serious problem elsewhere. With an index of 5.8 the productivity rating is the best of the twelve natural areas.

Area IV embraces a total of 2,407,898 acres, 27.1 per cent of which is in farms, 70.7 per cent in forest, 1.2 per cent in open meadow, 0.4 per cent in muskeg, and 0.6 per cent in urban use. (See Figure 13.) Most of the land (86.9 per cent) is privately or corporately owned; 12.5 per cent is in state ownership; the amount in federal ownership is very small (0.6 per cent). In 1931 tax delinquency amounted to 43.5 per cent of the taxable area and 37.5 per cent of the total area.

Land in farms. — In 1930 there were 651,967 acres of land in farms and 4,808 farms, averaging 135.6 acres, in the area. Farm settlement is densest in the west, in Clearwater and Beltrami counties. Another well-settled region occurs in the eastern part of the area, in St. Louis County. All of Area IV in Itasca County except two or three townships is sparsely settled. In 1930 about 44.7 per cent of the land in farms was cleared, and 28.5 per cent was in crops. Woodlots averaged 87.3 acres per farm. Pasture, hay, and small grains are the principal crops, and dairying and sheep the important livestock enterprises.

Most of the mineral soil of the area is well adapted to the production of alfalfa and other leguminous forage crops. In some parts alfalfa and clover seed are produced very successfully. The average length of the growing season is about 111 days. This is too short a season for the production of corn for grain, but about 1.4 acres per farm are put into ensilage. Potatoes are raised as a cash crop.

PERCENTAGE OF LAND IN VARIOUS USES

	0	10	20	30	40	50	60	70	80	90	100
AGRICULTURE ---- 27.1											
FOREST --------- 70.7											
OPEN MEADOW --- 1.2											
MUSKEG --------- .4											
URBAN ----------- .6											

PERCENTAGE OF FOREST LANDS IN VARIOUS SIZE CLASSES

	0	10	20	30	40	50	60	70	80	90	100
SAW TIMBER ----- 11.6											
CORDWOOD ------ 45.0											
RESTOCKING ----- 37.2											
NON-RESTOCKING 2.2											
RECENTLY BURNED ------- 4.0											

PERCENTAGE OF FOREST LANDS IN VARIOUS TIMBER TYPES

	0	10	20	30	40	50	60	70	80	90	100
HARDWOODS AND CONIFERS 28.2											
ASPEN-BIRCH ---- 26.7											
HIGHLAND HARDWOODS ------ 9.3											
JACK PINE ------- 8.4											
NORWAY PINE ---- 1.6											
JACK AND NORWAY PINE ----- 3.9											
WHITE PINE ----- 1.1											
NORWAY AND WHITE PINE ----- .3											
SPRUCE --------- 8.8											
SPRUCE AND TAMARACK ------ 3.5											
SPRUCE AND CEDAR ------ 2.9											
SWAMP HARDWOODS ------- .5											
TAMARACK AND CEDAR ---- .4											
TAMARACK------- .3											
CEDAR --------- .1											
BURNED AND DENUDED ---- 4.0											

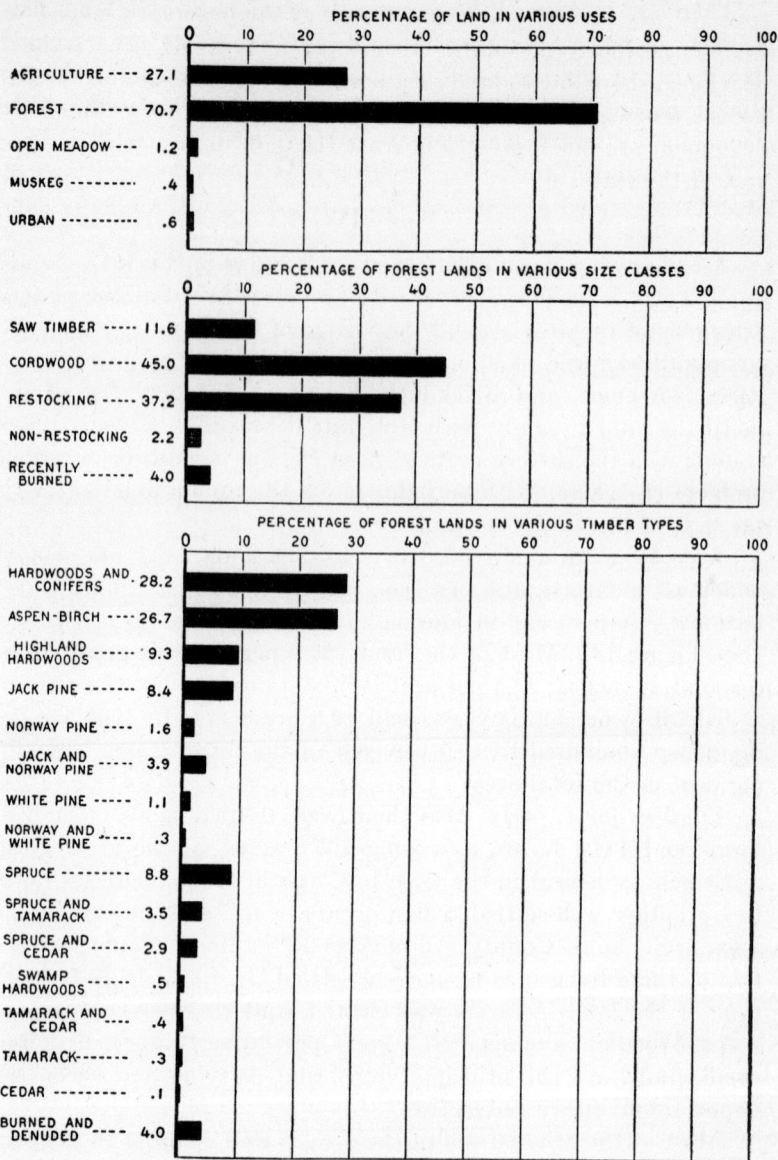

FIGURE 13. — DISTRIBUTION OF LAND USES AND OF TIMBER OF VARIOUS TYPES AND SIZES IN AREA IV

There are in Area IV large acreages of wild cut-over land, particularly in Koochiching and Itasca counties, which have a good clay loam soil and are suitable for agricultural settlement. At the same time considerable acreages of poor lands which offer little chance for successful operation are being farmed.

Land in forest use. — As indicated previously, 70.7 per cent of Area IV is classed as forest lands. The heavy soils originally supported a magnificent stand of white and Norway pine. A few blocks of virgin white and Norway pine still stand in northern Itasca County. Old growth sawtimber amounts to about 11 per cent of the total land in forest use. Mixed hardwoods and conifers, and white and Norway pine are the principal species of sawlog size. About 45 per cent of the forest supports trees of merchantable cordwood size, and 37 per cent trees of restocking size. The cordwood material is mostly mixed hardwoods and conifers, and aspen-birch. Restocking areas are about a third aspen-birch and two-thirds all other types common to the north woods, except white and Norway pines, which for some reason are not restocking properly. Fires in recent years have burned and denuded about 4 per cent of the forest area.

Recreational use of land. — There are a few fine lakes north of Bemidji in Beltrami County and in northern Itasca County. Scenic State Park is located in the northern part of Itasca County. Nine and one-half townships of Area IV are included in the George Washington Memorial State Forest. Deer, upland game birds, and waterfowl are abundant in the area. Despite these recreational opportunities the area does not have the charm or possibilities of either Area III or Area VI. The index of shore line development for the area is only 40.7 per cent of the average for the fourteen counties.

AREA V

Area V consists of a stony and extremely rough chain of hills. The western part extends into the White Earth Indian Reservation and the White Earth State Forest. It also includes Itasca State Park. The western boundary of the area was not determined in this study, but conditions throughout much of the White Earth Indian Reservation are essentially the same as the mapped portion of the area. A narrow chain of hills about four miles wide and twenty-five miles long angles south from the area, just inside the Cass County boundary line. This chain constitutes the Foothills

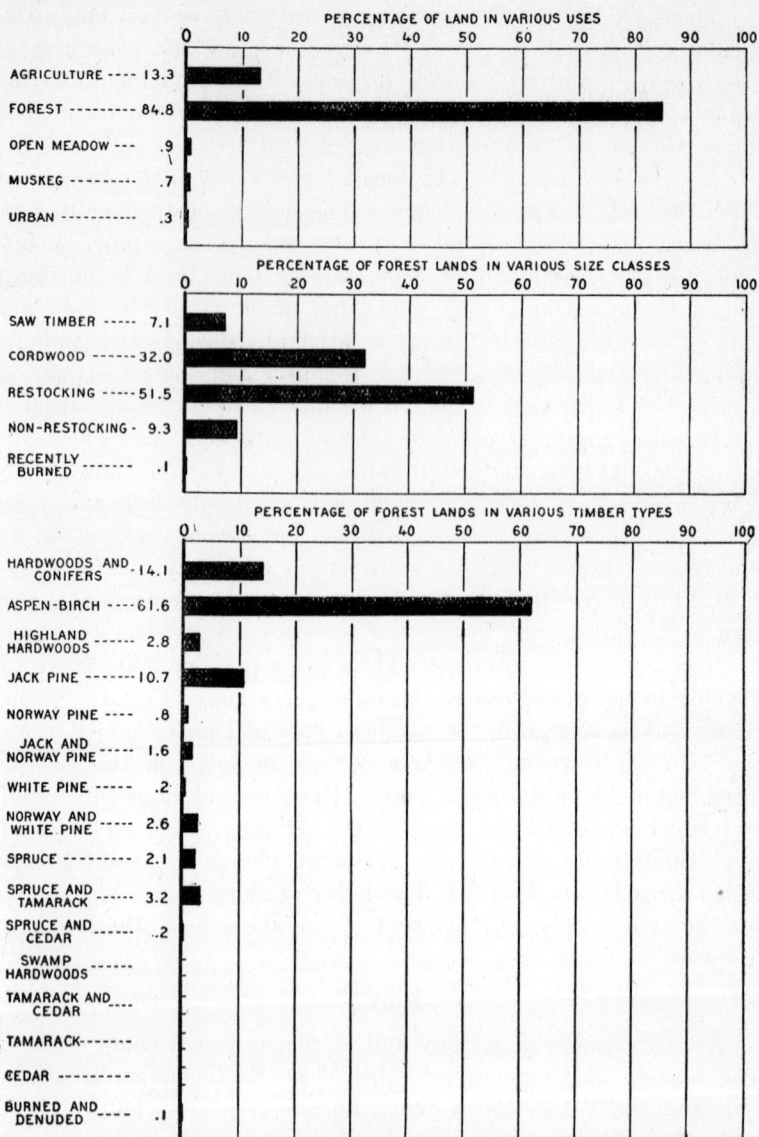

PERCENTAGE OF LAND IN VARIOUS USES

| | 0 | 10 | 20 | 30 | 40 | 50 | 60 | 70 | 80 | 90 | 100 |

AGRICULTURE ---- 13.3
FOREST --------- 84.8
OPEN MEADOW --- .9
MUSKEG --------- .7
URBAN ----------- .3

PERCENTAGE OF FOREST LANDS IN VARIOUS SIZE CLASSES

| | 0 | 10 | 20 | 30 | 40 | 50 | 60 | 70 | 80 | 90 | 100 |

SAW TIMBER ----- 7.1
CORDWOOD ------ 32.0
RESTOCKING ----- 51.5
NON-RESTOCKING - 9.3
RECENTLY BURNED ------- .1

PERCENTAGE OF FOREST LANDS IN VARIOUS TIMBER TYPES

| | 0 | 10 | 20 | 30 | 40 | 50 | 60 | 70 | 80 | 90 | 100 |

HARDWOODS AND CONIFERS -14.1
ASPEN-BIRCH ----61.6
HIGHLAND HARDWOODS ------ 2.8
JACK PINE -------10.7
NORWAY PINE ---- .8
JACK AND NORWAY PINE ----- 1.6
WHITE PINE ----- .2
NORWAY AND WHITE PINE ----- 2.6
SPRUCE --------- 2.1
SPRUCE AND TAMARACK ------ 3.2
SPRUCE AND CEDAR ------- .2
SWAMP HARDWOODS ------
TAMARACK AND CEDAR ----
TAMARACK------
CEDAR ---------
BURNED AND DENUDED ---- .1

FIGURE 14. — DISTRIBUTION OF LAND USES AND OF TIMBER OF VARIOUS TYPES AND SIZES IN AREA V

62

State Forest. Area V is distinctly non-agricultural and should be
devoted entirely to forest use, recreation, and Indian reservations.
The productivity rating of the soil is 7.8, which is the same as that
of Area VII, the Mesabi Iron Range.

Land in farms.—Agricultural development in the area is widely
scattered. One entire township has only two farms. In the total
area there were 440 farms in 1930. These farms occupied 54,973
acres, or 13.3 per cent of the land. (See Figure 14.) Their average
size was 125 acres, 34 acres of which were in crops, 57.7 acres were
cleared, and 67.2 acres were in woodlots. A growing season of about
119 days prevails, which permits the production of ensilage corn.
About 4.2 acres of corn per farm was raised in 1931, 6.3 acres of
oats, 2.3 acres of potatoes, and 15.6 acres of hay. Sheep and dairying are the most important farm enterprises. In 1930 there were an
average of 9.9 sheep and 8.8 cattle per farm. The area ranked first
in number of sheep per farm. If it were possible to produce enough
hay for winter feeding, sheep grazing would provide a profitable
use for much rough land in the area. Moderate grazing by sheep
aids reforestation by clearing out the grass, ferns, and underbrush,
and thus reducing the fire hazard.

Land in forest use.—Roughly 85 per cent of the area is classed
as forest land. Of the land in forest use about 7 per cent is of sawlog size. Much of this timber is in Itasca State Park, where one of
the few stands of virgin white and Norway pine remaining in the
state is found. Cordwood timber amounts to 32 per cent of the
total and consists mainly of mixed hardwoods and conifers, aspen-
birch, and jack pine. Approximately 52 per cent of the forest lands
is of restocking sizes. Aspen-birch makes up 88 per cent of the restocking class, spruce and tamarack 6 per cent, and all other types
6 per cent. About 9 per cent of the forest lands has been burned
or grazed so heavily that it is not restocking to timber types. Timber burns in this area have been negligible in recent years, however.

The White Earth State Forest covers about 80,811 acres of the
area, and Itasca State Park an additional 25,209 acres, the two
covering 26 per cent of the total area. The state owns 33,641 acres,
or 8 per cent of the land, the federal government about 2 per cent,
and private or corporate interests 90 per cent. Tax delinquency
runs higher in Area V than in any other part of the state. In 1931,
77 per cent of the total area was delinquent. Lands in this area are
poorly adapted to private ownership. When the state gets title

through reversion this land should be retained and managed for conservation purposes. If protected against fire, the lands will produce a good crop of forest products.

The area has some excellent lakes that are well developed. The index of recreational use is 192.6.

Area VI

The soils in Area VI vary greatly. Sands prevail over much of the southern third of the area and in the vicinity of Cass Lake. In some places there is a sandy loam underlain with porous gravel which causes the soil to be droughty. Lands south of Leech Lake and those embraced by the Foothills State Forest are extremely rough and stony. In the vicinity of Grand Rapids there are some good agricultural lands. Peat bogs are smaller and less numerous in Area VI than in Areas II and X. The index of agricultural productivity of the soil is 7.0, and the average length of the growing season about 119 days.

Many beautiful lakes are located in Area VI. Leech, Winnibigoshish, and Cass lakes are the largest, and there are hundreds of small ones. Many of the lakes have clean sandy beaches ideal for bathing. The recreational industry is highly developed, about 31.2 per cent of the developed shore line of the fourteen counties being located in this area. The index of recreational development is 251.8, the highest of all twelve areas.

There are some 2,177,333 acres of land in the area, of which 16.5 per cent are in agriculture, 76.4 per cent in forest use, 3.6 per cent in open meadow, 3.1 per cent in muskeg, and 0.4 per cent in urban uses. (See Figure 15.)

The federal government owns 11.2 per cent of the area, the state 7.8 per cent, and private or corporate interests 81 per cent. Most of the area in federal ownership consists of forest and Indian lands in the Chippewa National Forest. The present forests include 310,511 acres, or 14.3 per cent of the entire area. Established federal purchase areas encompass an additional 279,739 acres. One small state forest, Land O'Lakes, lies entirely in Area VI, and three others, Foothills, Third River, and George Washington Memorial, are partially included. The state forests occupy 9.3 per cent of the area, state and federal forests, 23.5 per cent. Tax delinquency runs comparatively high, and the state will probably acquire title to a large acreage through reversion. In 1931, 925,280 acres, or 42.5 per cent of the total area and 52.7 per cent of the taxable area, were

PERCENTAGE OF LAND IN VARIOUS USES

```
                 0   10  20  30  40  50  60  70  80  90  100
AGRICULTURE ---- 16.5
FOREST --------- 76.4
OPEN MEADOW --- 3.6
MUSKEG --------- 3.1
URBAN ----------- .4
```

PERCENTAGE OF FOREST LANDS IN VARIOUS SIZE CLASSES

```
                 0   10  20  30  40  50  60  70  80  90  100
SAW TIMBER ----- 12.0
CORDWOOD ------ 66.2
RESTOCKING ----- 19.2
NON-RESTOCKING - 2.6
RECENTLY
BURNED
```

PERCENTAGE OF FOREST LANDS IN VARIOUS TIMBER TYPES

```
                         0   10  20  30  40  50  60  70  80  90  100
HARDWOODS AND .43.7
  CONIFERS
ASPEN-BIRCH ---- 24.0
HIGHLAND ------ 6.8
HARDWOODS
JACK PINE ------- 3.4
NORWAY PINE ---- 1.0
JACK AND ----- 14.4
NORWAY PINE
WHITE PINE ------
NORWAY AND ----- .3
WHITE PINE
SPRUCE --------- 1.0
SPRUCE AND ------ 4.2
TAMARACK
SPRUCE AND ------ .9
  CEDAR
SWAMP ------
HARDWOODS
TAMARACK AND ---- .3
  CEDAR
TAMARACK ------
CEDAR ---------
BURNED AND ----
DENUDED
```

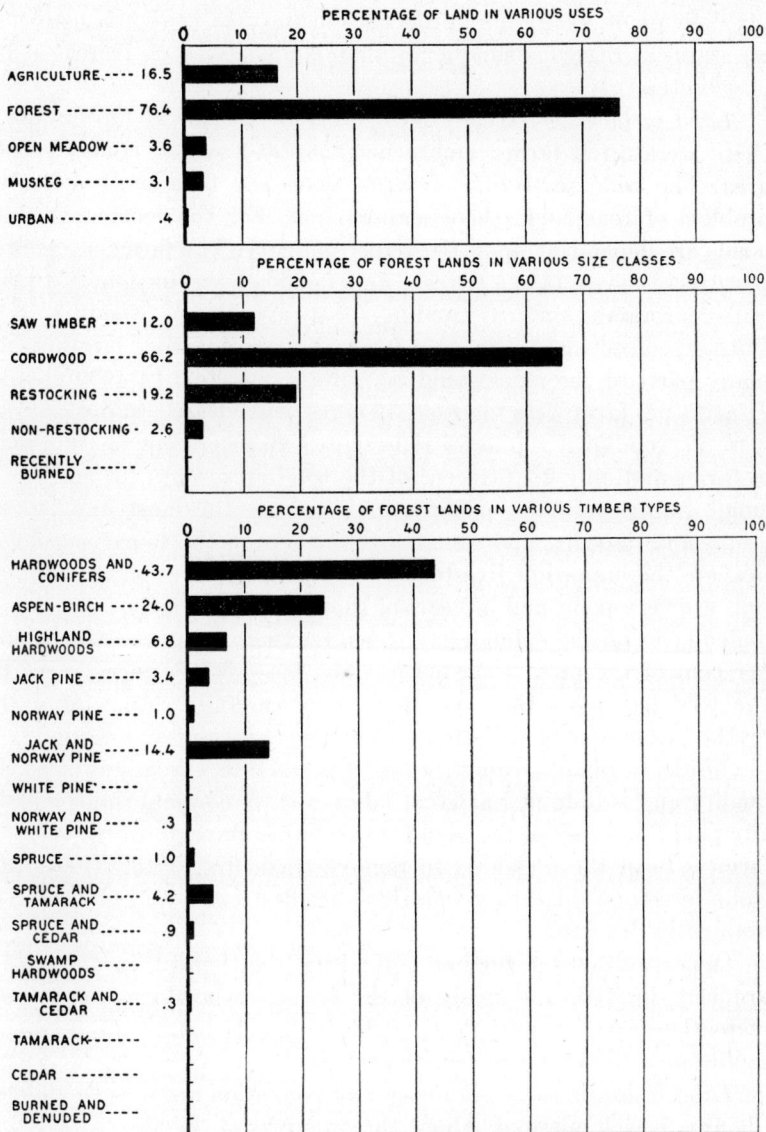

FIGURE 15. — DISTRIBUTION OF LAND USES AND OF TIMBER OF VARIOUS TYPES AND SIZES IN AREA VI

tax delinquent. Lake shore properties in the area have a much better status as regards delinquency than lands having no recreational
possibilities.

Land in farms. — According to the 1930 Census of Agriculture,
there were 3,130 farms, embracing 358,490 acres of land, in the
area. The wide scattering of farms gives rise to a most difficult
problem of road and school maintenance. For the most part the
farms are dependent upon the resort industry. The farms are comparatively small (114.5 acres), and much of the income is from
outside sources, such as guiding, boat livery, and woods work.
Without supplemental income from the resort trade, farming in
many parts of the area would be quite impossible. In 1930 about
31 acres per farm were in crops, 49 acres were cleared, and 65 acres
were in woodlot. Crop acres represented 26.7 per cent of the land
in farms and only 2.7 per cent of the total area. Corn for ensilage,
small grains, potatoes, pasture, and hay are the most important
crops, and dairying and sheep, as elsewhere in the fourteen counties, are the important livestock enterprises. Pastures on the sandy
soils are very poor, and in years of short rainfall farmers experience
difficulty in raising enough hay to winter their livestock. About 3.6
per cent of the area is classed as open meadow. Farmers harvest
the wild hay from these meadows very carefully. Much of it is
scythed from among the stumps and snags by hand and carried on
pitchforks to small openings, where it is stacked. The hay is of poor
quality and is obtained at great labor cost. A nominal sum is usually paid the owner of the land for this hay stumpage. In the spring
farmers burn the meadows to remove trash. In burning, nests of
game birds and migratory waterfowl are destroyed, and forest fires
frequently develop.

Opportunities for further agricultural settlement in the area
are very limited, and many of the farmers who do not enjoy a
recreation-farm combination would be much better off if they
could move to more promising locations.

Land in forest use. — Forestry and recreation are uses to which
the area is well adapted. About three-fourths of the area is classed
as forest lands. Second growth timber of cordwood size covers 66
per cent of the forest. Restocking sizes cover 19 per cent, and sawtimber 12 per cent. The area ranks first in percentage of cordwood
sizes, last in percentage of restocking sizes, and fourth in percentage of sawtimber. About 94 per cent of the timber is of upland
types and only 6 per cent of lowland types. Mixed hardwoods and

conifers account for about 60 per cent of the cordwood material, and the rest consists mainly of jack and Norway pine, and aspen-birch. The sawtimber also runs largely to mixed hardwoods and conifers, aspen-birch, and jack and Norway pine. Aspen-birch represents 66 per cent of all restocking lands, and jack and Norway pine most of the balance. Fifty-nine per cent of the restocking lands has a good to fair stand of young trees, and 41 per cent a poor stand.

AREA VII

Area VII encompasses the Mesabi Iron Range. The land area occupied by the mines is very small, but the area used for dumps, concentration plants, machine shops, railroad yards, and other industrial-urban development is considerable. Many of the mines are within city or village limits. Hibbing, Virginia, and Chisholm are the largest centers, and there are fifteen or twenty smaller villages in the area. Cities and villages occupy 3.3 per cent of the area. Only in Area XI is the proportion of urban land greater. There is a huge concentration of wealth in the iron deposits, which serve as a tax base for the local governments. When the mines were operating at maximum capacity, a generous labor supply was attracted. Labor-saving devices and decreased activity have since greatly reduced employment and caused a serious surplus of labor in the area. Units of local government, having what seemed an inexhaustible source of revenue, have attempted to alleviate unemployment by placing large numbers on the public payroll. Partly to supply the excellent market that exists for fresh farm produce and partly to supplement the income from part-time employment, settlers have attempted to farm the most obstinate of land. The area is poorly adapted to agriculture, except in a few townships along the southern slope of the range and in the northern tier of townships in the vicinities of Embarrass and Pike. The productivity rating of the soil for the area is 7.8, and the average length of the growing season about 95 days.

Lands in Area VII are for the most part privately or corporately owned (93.4 per cent). The state owns the balance. Tax delinquency prior to 1932, when it amounted to 22.1 per cent of the total area and 24.5 per cent of the taxable area, was the lowest of all the areas. A large proportion of the wild land in the area is held speculatively for possible mineral deposits.

Land in farms. — In 1930 there were 1,689 farms in the area,

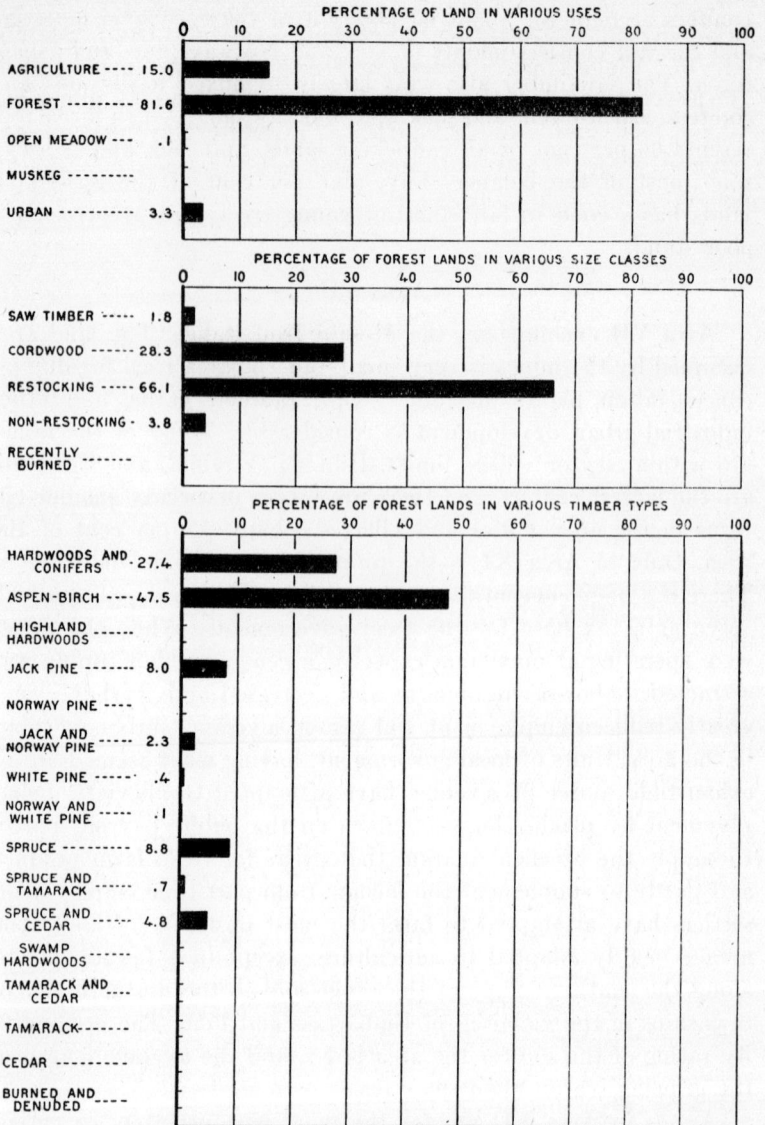

PERCENTAGE OF LAND IN VARIOUS USES

| | 0 | 10 | 20 | 30 | 40 | 50 | 60 | 70 | 80 | 90 | 100 |

AGRICULTURE ---- 15.0
FOREST --------- 81.6
OPEN MEADOW --- .1
MUSKEG ---------
URBAN ----------- 3.3

PERCENTAGE OF FOREST LANDS IN VARIOUS SIZE CLASSES

SAW TIMBER ----- 1.8
CORDWOOD ------ 28.3
RESTOCKING ----- 66.1
NON-RESTOCKING - 3.8
RECENTLY BURNED -------

PERCENTAGE OF FOREST LANDS IN VARIOUS TIMBER TYPES

HARDWOODS AND CONIFERS - 27.4
ASPEN-BIRCH ---- 47.5
HIGHLAND HARDWOODS ------
JACK PINE ------- 8.0
NORWAY PINE ----
JACK AND NORWAY PINE ----- 2.3
WHITE PINE ------ .4
NORWAY AND WHITE PINE ----- .1
SPRUCE --------- 8.8
SPRUCE AND TAMARACK ------ .7
SPRUCE AND CEDAR ------ 4.8
SWAMP HARDWOODS ------
TAMARACK AND CEDAR ----
TAMARACK-------
CEDAR ---------
BURNED AND DENUDED ----

Figure 16. — Distribution of Land Uses and of Timber of Various Types and Sizes in Area VII

68

occupying 139,805 acres, or 15 per cent of the total land. (See Figure 16.) These farms averaged only 82.8 acres, the smallest of all the areas. About half the land in farms was in woodlots, about half was cleared, and about a fourth was in crops. Hay, pasture, and oats are the principal feed crops, and rutabagas and potatoes are the important cash crops.

Practically all the farmers in the area depend upon the mines or upon the local government for some work during the year. Aside from a few large dairy farms, most of the places are small; and the productivity of most of the soil is very low. Farming sections of the area give the impression of being badly overpopulated. In many places men have crowded out on lands that offer little except exercise and fresh air. Physical limitations on further agricultural expansion are great.

Land in forest use.— Approximately 82 per cent of the area is classed as forest lands. These lands once supported a heavy growth of white and Norway pine. Today scarcely a seed tree remains. An occasional rotting stump gives mute evidence of the exploited forest. Less than 2 per cent of the area supports timber of sawlog size, and most of this is cull hardwood trees. About 28 per cent of the forest is of cordwood size. The cordwood material is mostly mixed hardwoods and conifers, and jack pine. Most of the cordwood timber is located in the Mesabi National Forest purchase area north of the Range proper. About two-thirds of the forest is of restocking sizes, predominantly of the aspen-birch type. (See Figure 16.) People from the range towns go out in cars equipped with trailers to gather firewood from large areas of surrounding territory. They have picked up practically all the dead timber on vacant lands and are now cutting green aspen saplings for fuel.

Recreation.— There are comparatively few good lakes, but the lakes of both Areas III and VI are so close at hand that the residents of this area do not want for recreational opportunities. Merchants in the range towns obtain a considerable volume of business from tourists going to and from lake resorts in other areas. Within Area VII the index of recreational development is 92.6.

Area VIII

Area VIII has the largest percentage of land in farms and the smallest percentage of land in forest use of all the twelve areas. There is a fairly even balance between land in farms and land in forest use. (See Figure 17.) The topography is flat to gently un-

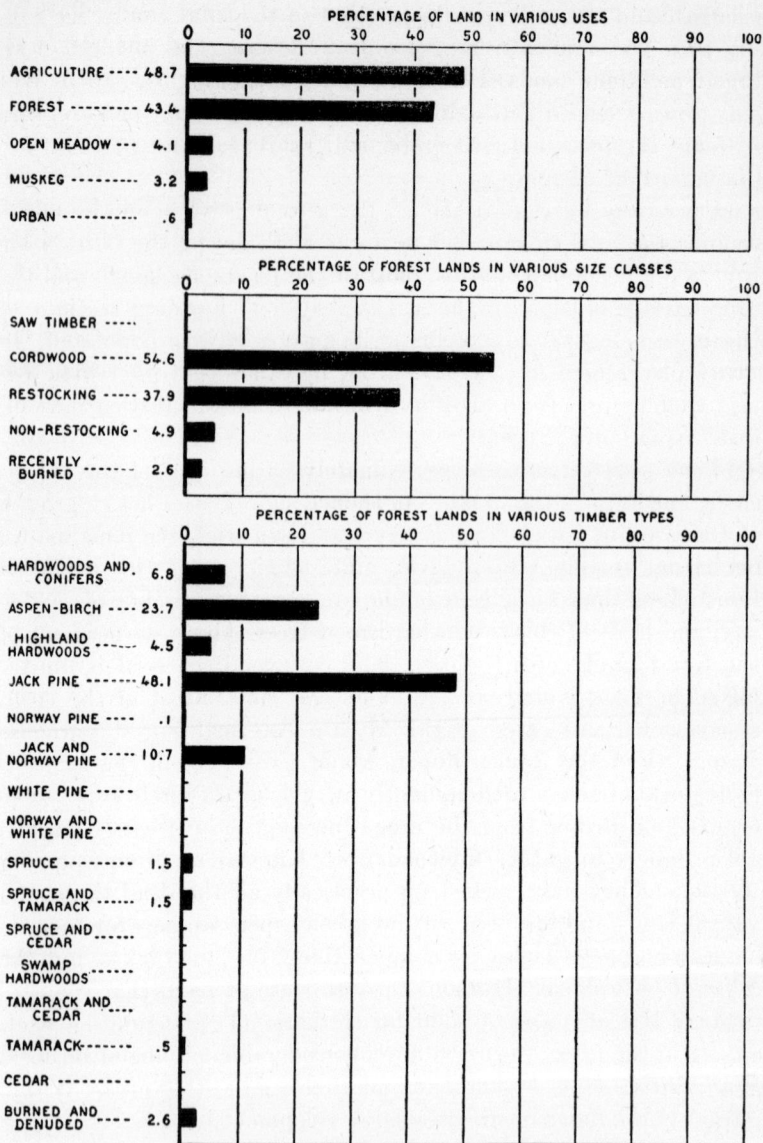

FIGURE 17. — DISTRIBUTION OF LAND USES AND OF TIMBER OF VARIOUS TYPES AND SIZES IN AREA VIII

dulating, and the soils are sandy loams and loamy sands. Part of this area was originally an open grass prairie, and the rest was largely jack pine sands. The productivity rating for the area is 6.7. The growing season averages about 124 days.

Land in farms.—In 1930 the 720 farms of this area occupied an average of 174 acres each, or a total of 125,333 acres. About 79 acres per farm were in crops, 118 acres were cleared, and 56 acres were in woodlots. In 1931, according to the state census of agriculture, the important crops and their respective acreages were as follows: oats, 22.1; hay, 20.5; corn, 14.7; barley, 3.6; potatoes, 3.0; and wheat, 1.8. According to township assessors' reports there were in 1931 an average of 3.1 horses per farm, 10.9 cattle, 6.3 sheep, 2.4 hogs, and 31.6 chickens. The area ranked first in acreage per farm of all the important crops except hay, first in the number of horses and hogs, second in the number of poultry, third in the number of cattle, and fifth in the number of sheep.

Despite the large acreages of crops, yields in the area are low, and farm incomes comparatively small. In recent years the area has suffered from insufficient rainfall, and forage supplies have been short. Some 4 per cent of the area is classed as wild open meadow. Farmers near by harvest the hay on these meadows most diligently. The problems of the area seem to be more those of farm management than those of land use maladjustments.

Land in forest use.—The forest lands in this area are predominantly covered with second growth jack pine in pure stands or mixed with Norway pine. There is nothing of sawtimber size left in the area. About 55 per cent is of merchantable cordwood size, 38 per cent of restocking sizes, and 7 per cent non-restocking or recently burned timber. The cordwood sizes run about 85 per cent jack pine, and jack and Norway pine mixed; the restocking sizes about 24 per cent jack pine and 57 per cent aspen-birch.

Area VIII is well supplied with lakes. The beaches are of smooth clean sand and well developed for recreational use. The area is within easy driving distance of the Twin Cities (about 160 miles). The index of recreational development is 188.9.

Area IX

Area IX includes the best parts of three cut-over counties: Aitkin, Crow Wing, and Cass. In much of the Aitkin County portion a stony loam pitted with wet peat or clay depressions with an occasional gravelly ridge prevails. Eastern Crow Wing County is

very similar to southwestern Aitkin County. In western Crow
Wing and southern Cass counties a sand with a jack pine cover
prevails. For agricultural purposes the soils of the area are comparatively good, having a productivity rating of 6.6. With favorable price relationships farming in much of the area would be
moderately successful. In central Crow Wing County is located
the Cuyuna Iron Range, on which have developed several important mining towns, the largest of which are Crosby, Ironton, and
Deerwood. The largest city of the area is Brainerd, the county seat
of Crow Wing County.

Several very lovely lakes besides Mille Lacs are situated in the
area, and an important recreational industry has been developed.
The index of recreational use, which is 218.5, is surpassed only by
Area VI to the north. Farmers enjoy a good summer market for
fresh fruits, vegetables, and dairy and poultry products. Many
farmers have small lakes on their farms with a few cabins and a
boat or two which they rent to vacationists. Additional income is
obtained from bait, guiding, pulpwood, fuel, etc.

Tax delinquency is less in Area IX than in any other of the
twelve areas except one, amounting in 1931 to 27.7 per cent of all
taxable land. Most of the delinquent lands are in Cass and Aitkin
counties, where tax rates and assessments are high. Crow Wing
County, having mineral deposits as a source of revenue, has kept
rates and assessments on farm property comparatively low. Practically all land in Area IX (97.8 per cent) is privately owned.

Almost equal percentages of land are in farms and in forest use
(45.8 and 45.0 per cent, respectively). (See Figure 18.) The area
ranks first in land in open meadow, 7.4 per cent being in this classification.

Land in farms. — In 1930 there were 2,562 farms in the area
and 348,757 acres of land in farms. The average farm contained
136.1 acres, had 48.5 acres in crops, 78.1 acres cleared, and 58 acres
in woodlot. Dairying was the most important farm enterprise. The
area ranked first in number of cattle per farm, with an average of
13.7 head. The cropping system was built largely around the dairy
enterprise. Hay was produced on 13.5 acres, oats on 9.4 acres, corn
on 6.4 acres, and barley on 2.7 acres. An average of 7.6 sheep per
farm were raised and only enough hogs and poultry for family use
were kept.

Land in forest use. — Of the forest lands in this area 95 per cent
are covered by highland timber types, 4 per cent by lowland types,

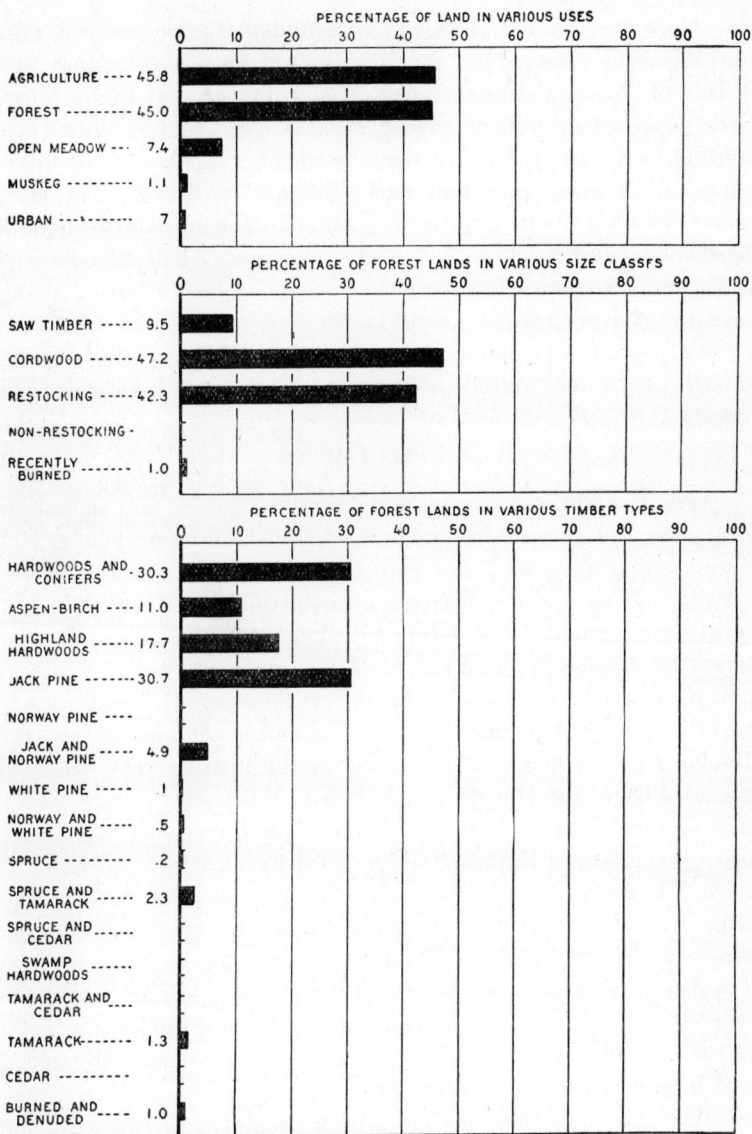

PERCENTAGE OF LAND IN VARIOUS USES

| | 0 | 10 | 20 | 30 | 40 | 50 | 60 | 70 | 80 | 90 | 100 |

AGRICULTURE ---- 45.8
FOREST --------- 45.0
OPEN MEADOW --- 7.4
MUSKEG --------- 1.1
URBAN ---------- 7

PERCENTAGE OF FOREST LANDS IN VARIOUS SIZE CLASSES

SAW TIMBER ----- 9.5
CORDWOOD ------ 47.2
RESTOCKING ----- 42.3
NON-RESTOCKING -
RECENTLY BURNED ------- 1.0

PERCENTAGE OF FOREST LANDS IN VARIOUS TIMBER TYPES

HARDWOODS AND CONIFERS - 30.3
ASPEN-BIRCH ---- 11.0
HIGHLAND HARDWOODS ------ 17.7
JACK PINE ------- 30.7
NORWAY PINE ----
JACK AND NORWAY PINE ----- 4.9
WHITE PINE ----- .1
NORWAY AND WHITE PINE ----- .5
SPRUCE --------- .2
SPRUCE AND TAMARACK ------ 2.3
SPRUCE AND CEDAR
SWAMP HARDWOODS ------
TAMARACK AND CEDAR ----
TAMARACK ------- 1.3
CEDAR ---------
BURNED AND DENUDED ---- 1.0

FIGURE 18. — DISTRIBUTION OF LAND USES AND OF TIMBER OF VARIOUS TYPES AND SIZES IN AREA IX

73

and 1 per cent has been burned and denuded. Two types, jack pine, and mixed hardwoods and conifers combined, make up almost two-thirds of the total timber cover. About 10 per cent of the forest area supports growth of sawlog size, 47 per cent cordwood size, and 42 per cent restocking sizes. Sawtimber is about half mixed jack and Norway pine and half highland hardwoods. The cordwood sizes are about two-thirds jack pine and one-third highland hardwoods, and hardwoods and conifers mixed. The restocking of forest lands is proceeding very unsatisfactorily in this area, chiefly because of over-grazing. About 72 per cent of the restocking lands have a poor stand of young trees. The restocking types are mainly mixed hardwoods and conifers, aspen-birch, and highland hardwoods.

Area X

Area X contains a considerable number of large and small peat bogs. The soil between the bogs is a complex of stony loams, sand plains and ridges, and wet clay depressions. The area is poorly adapted to agriculture because of inadequate drainage. Agricultural development is most favored along stream courses, particularly the Mississippi and the St. Louis and its tributaries, where natural drainage is afforded. Jacobson, Floodwood, Meadowlands, and Swan River are communities representing the best of the area. Boulders are so abundant on many of the upland tracts that the use of tillage implements is precluded. When the stones are removed the better soils are moderately productive, as is exemplified by the Grand Rapids Experimental Farm, which is located in Area VI. Some areas of stone-free land occur. One rather large stone-free area is worthy of special mention. Located about nine miles north and west of Floodwood, centering in Cedar Valley Township, is an area having roughly a seven-mile radius that has scarcely a stone. The soil is a productive mellow gray loam. Parts of the upland soils are rough and hilly and have a gravelly subsoil which renders them very drouthy.

Many drainage projects have been promoted in this area, but most of them are now delinquent and abandoned. The peat lands when drained are similar to those of Area II, deficient in phosphorous or potassium, or both, and sometimes in lime, and subject to frosts and fires. In the vicinity of Sax and Fens in St. Louis County head lettuce and celery are being produced on peat land with a fair degree of success. Pasture and meadow are probably the best uses to which peat land can be put after it is drained and cleared, but these uses are unable to support the burden of general property taxes and special ditch assessments usually imposed upon such lands. The large proportion of the area is undrained swamp and has a comparatively low productivity rating of 7.7.

Area X is far more heavily settled than Area II (6.6 as compared with 1.1 persons per square mile), but the settlement is more generally distributed, and the problem of maintaining roads and schools for the more scattered population is consequently greater. St. Louis and Itasca counties have been very generous in providing services for isolated families, but Aitkin County has been financially unable to do so.

About three-quarters of Area X is in forest use, almost a fifth in agriculture, and the balance in muskeg, open meadow, and urban sites. (See Figure 19.) Ownership is 92 per cent private or corporate, 7.9 per cent state, and 0.1 per cent federal. Tax delinquency in 1931 amounted to 43 per cent of the total area and 47 per cent of the taxable area.

Land in farms. — In 1930 there were 361,099 acres of land distributed among 3,554 farms in the area, an average of 101.6 acres per farm. Only 27.8 acres per farm were in crops in 1930, and 48.8 acres per farm were cleared. In 1931 the farms averaged about 0.5 acres of corn, 3.5 acres of oats, 1.25 acres of barley, 1.5 acres of potatoes, and 11.5 acres of hay. In addition to these field crops most farms in the area have a garden and raise an abundant supply of rutabagas, which are an important item in the family's diet.

In 1931 the livestock consisted of 1.6 horses per farm, 9.3 cattle, 3.3 sheep, 0.6 hogs, and 19.4 chickens. Though livestock numbers are comparatively small, farmers have difficulty securing adequate forage for winter feeding. Wild hay from the meadows is carefully harvested, much of it by hand with scythe and pitchfork. Frequently the hay is mixed with golden rod and thistle and is of extremely poor quality.

Land in forest use. — Of the land in forest use about 60 and 40 per cent, respectively, are of highland and lowland types. The highland types are principally mixed hardwoods and conifers, aspenbirch, and highland hardwoods; the lowland types are mainly spruce in pure stands and in mixtures with tamarack and cedar. About 10 per cent of the forest land bears timber of sawlog size, 30 per cent of cordwood size, and 53 per cent of restocking sizes. Burned and non-restocking lands amount to 7 per cent of the total.

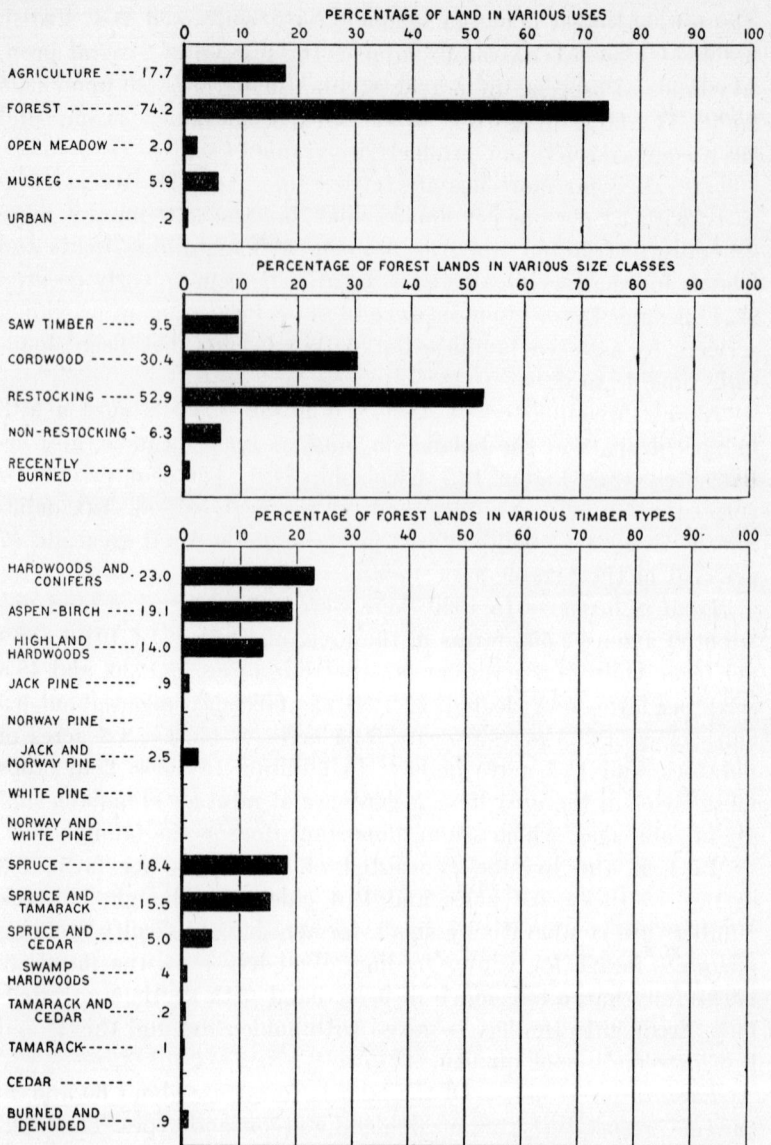

PERCENTAGE OF LAND IN VARIOUS USES

AGRICULTURE ---- 17.7	
FOREST --------- 74.2	
OPEN MEADOW --- 2.0	
MUSKEG --------- 5.9	
URBAN ----------- .2	

PERCENTAGE OF FOREST LANDS IN VARIOUS SIZE CLASSES

SAW TIMBER ----- 9.5	
CORDWOOD ------ 30.4	
RESTOCKING ----- 52.9	
NON-RESTOCKING - 6.3	
RECENTLY BURNED ------- .9	

PERCENTAGE OF FOREST LANDS IN VARIOUS TIMBER TYPES

HARDWOODS AND CONIFERS . 23.0	
ASPEN-BIRCH ---- 19.1	
HIGHLAND HARDWOODS ------ 14.0	
JACK PINE ------- .9	
NORWAY PINE ----	
JACK AND NORWAY PINE ----- 2.5	
WHITE PINE -----	
NORWAY AND WHITE PINE -----	
SPRUCE --------- 18.4	
SPRUCE AND TAMARACK ------ 15.5	
SPRUCE AND CEDAR ------ 5.0	
SWAMP HARDWOODS ------- 4	
TAMARACK AND CEDAR ---- .2	
TAMARACK------- .1	
CEDAR ---------	
BURNED AND DENUDED ---- .9	

FIGURE 19. — DISTRIBUTION OF LAND USES AND OF TIMBER OF VARIOUS TYPES AND SIZES IN AREA X

76

The sawlog timber is mostly highland hardwoods, and mixed hardwoods and conifers. The cordwood material is largely mixed hardwoods and conifers, and aspen-birch. The reproduction sizes are about 28 per cent spruce, 23 per cent aspen-birch, 18 per cent spruce and tamarack, 13 per cent mixed hardwoods and conifers, and the balance miscellaneous types.

There are two state forests in Area X, the Savanna and Fond du Lac. The Savanna occupies 203,548 acres, and the Fond du Lac 90,932 acres. Most of the state forests have only recently been created, and very little improvement work has been done.

The Savanna State Forest includes some very beautiful lakes and offers an excellent opportunity to develop recreation and the conservation of timber and game in one large project. The swamp lands within and adjoining the forests provide good cover for moose and other big game. Aside from the lakes of the Savanna State Forest, Area X has little to offer in the line of recreation. The index of recreational development is 85.2.

Area XI

Widely divergent topographic conditions are included in Area XI. Relief in the northern part, particularly along the shore of Lake Superior, is much more pronounced than in the southern half of the area. The soils are predominantly red drift which carry a heavy burden of stone. Along the lake shore in the vicinity of Duluth and Two Harbors the drift has been reassorted by water action, and a red clay practically free of stone prevails. Small swamps are found in the area, but with much less frequency than in Area IX to the west. When cleared of stumps and stone the soils are moderately productive, the rating being 6.4. The area is about 120 miles in length from north to south, and the growing season varies from less than 100 days to over 140 days. In the southern part of the area the soil is more productive and stones are fewer; in this section, around Pine City, corn for grain is produced successfully.

The area is traversed by the main highway and rail lines between the Twin Cities and Duluth. Partly as a result of the excellent transportation facilities in the area, considerable urban and rural development has taken place. With 69.7 persons per square mile, the area has more than five times the average population density of the fourteen counties. Excluding the city of Duluth, the density is 23.8 persons per square mile. In 1930 there were 5,839 farms in the area, an average of 3.5 farms per square mile as compared with 0.9 farms per square mile in the fourteen counties as a whole. Of the total land in the area 4.2 per cent is used as urban sites, which is a much greater percentage than in other areas. Two Harbors, Duluth, Cloquet, Carlton, Moose Lake, Sandstone, and Pine City are among the population centers.

Although the area is fairly well settled, there are still large acreages of unoccupied land. Approximately 55.6 per cent of the total is classed as forest lands and only 39.5 per cent is in farms. Most of the wild land remains unsettled by reason of physical limitations, such as inadequate drainage or excessive stone.

Practically all the land is in private ownership (99.3 per cent). That in state ownership, which amounts to only 0.6 per cent, consists of a few scattered pieces of school land. Tax delinquency in 1931 amounted to 29.3 per cent of the taxable area. At that time delinquency was limited almost exclusively to wild lands.

Land in farms. — Farms occupy a little over a half million acres of land. Crop land amounts to 34.5 per cent of the land in farms and 7 per cent of the total area. The farms are small, averaging only 95.6 acres. An average of 33 acres per farm are in crops, 52.9 acres are cleared, and 42.7 acres are in woodlot. Near each of the cities a considerable acreage is devoted to the production of truck crops, such as rutabagas, cabbage, cauliflower, tomatoes, carrots, and peas. Rutabagas are produced on a rather extensive commercial scale, and the area is one of the most important carlot shipping areas in the United States. On the lighter soils potatoes are an important cash crop. Poultry production is highly commercialized in certain sections, particularly around Barnum in Carlton County. The poultry products of the area are noted for superior quality. Dairying is, as elsewhere throughout the northern counties, by far the most important source of farm income. With 11.3 cattle per farm, the area ranks second in number of cattle. In 1931 there were in the area 21 cities and villages in which there were creameries receiving butterfat. The aggregate volume of these receiving points is approximately five million pounds annually. Sheep play a very minor rôle in the organization of farms.

In the vicinity of Duluth, Two Harbors, and Cloquet, part-time farming assumes considerable importance. Employment in all industries dependent upon lake traffic is highly seasonal, since the lakes are navigable for only about eight months of the year. To supplement incomes from part-time jobs many of the laboring

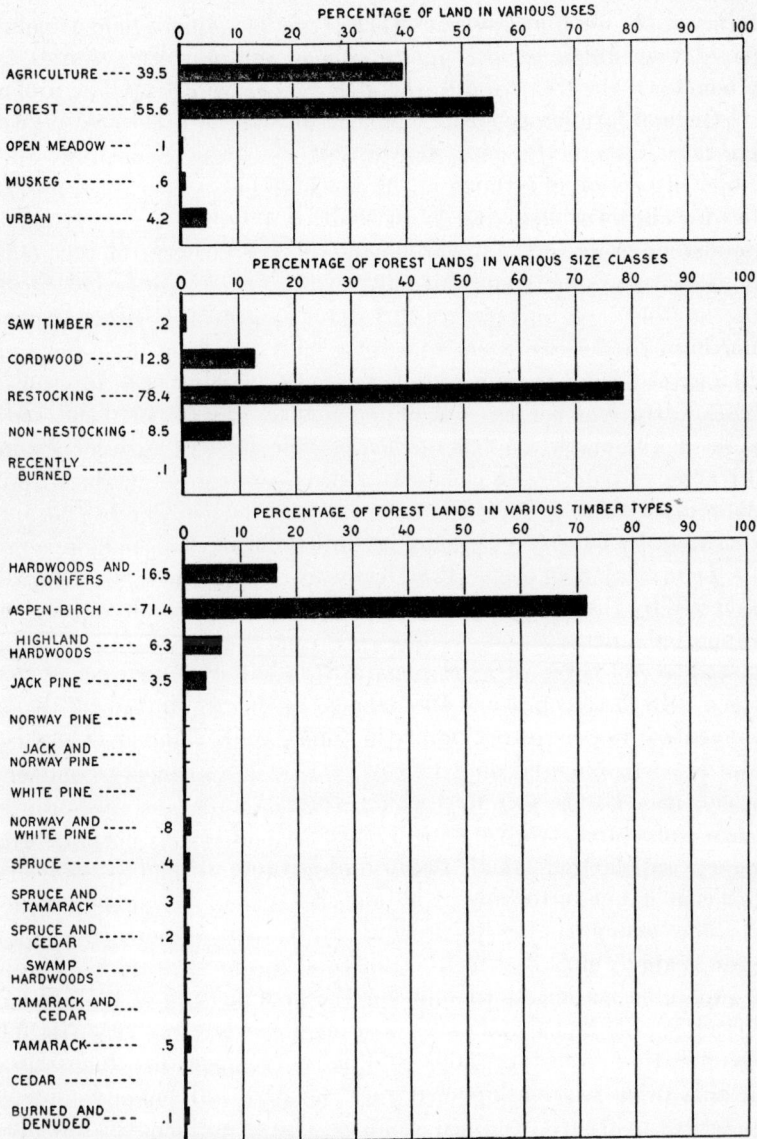

FIGURE 20. — DISTRIBUTION OF LAND USES AND OF TIMBER OF VARIOUS TYPES AND SIZES IN AREA XI

classes have obtained small acreages on which they produce small fruits, vegetables, poultry products, and occasionally some dairy products.

General farming conditions in the southern part of Pine County are noticeably better than in the rest of the area. To permit a closer inspection of farming in the southern part of the area, statistics for all townships lying south of the first township line north of Sandstone were summarized separately from those for the rest of the area. Some significant differences are revealed. Farms in the southern part averaged 20.3 acres larger than those in the northern part. There were 24.3 acres more per farm in crops, and 16.5 acres more per farm were cleared. In 1931 farms in the south of the area had 6.0 acres of corn per farm as compared with 4.0 acres in the north, 2.5 acres of barley as compared with 0.7 acres, 3.1 acres of potatoes as compared with 2.0 acres, 15.7 acres of hay as compared with 10.4 acres, 14.6 cattle as compared with 9.9 cattle, and 2.7 hogs as compared with 0.8 hogs.

Land in forest use.— Practically all of Area XI was burned severely by the fires in 1894 and 1918. Prior to these fires the area supported a dense stand of white and Norway pine. Today scarcely a seed tree of these varieties remains standing. Frequent grass fires since 1918 have completed the damage to the old timber and have prevented proper restocking of the forest lands. Timber of sawlog size is negligible, and only 12.8 per cent is large enough for cordwood. (See Figure 20.) Restocking sizes cover 78.4 per cent of the area. Unfortunately a very small percentage of the restocking lands have a satisfactory stand. Because of burning or over-grazing, 8.5 per cent is not restocking at all and 27.1 per cent very poorly.

The young timber is predominantly aspen-birch. This type grows rapidly if protected from fire, and in recent years has found a profitable market at Cloquet for the manufacture of toothpicks, match stems, and matchboxes. During the winter of 1933–34, for the first time in history, mills paid more for aspen than for spruce. If this price relationship continues, farmers will probably adopt practices to secure sustained yields of aspen. Problems of fire control in the area will be greatly reduced when farmers come to regard aspen stands as potential sources of farm income.

Area XII

The topography of Area XII is rather flat and featureless. Approximately 10 per cent of the area is wet, poorly drained swamp

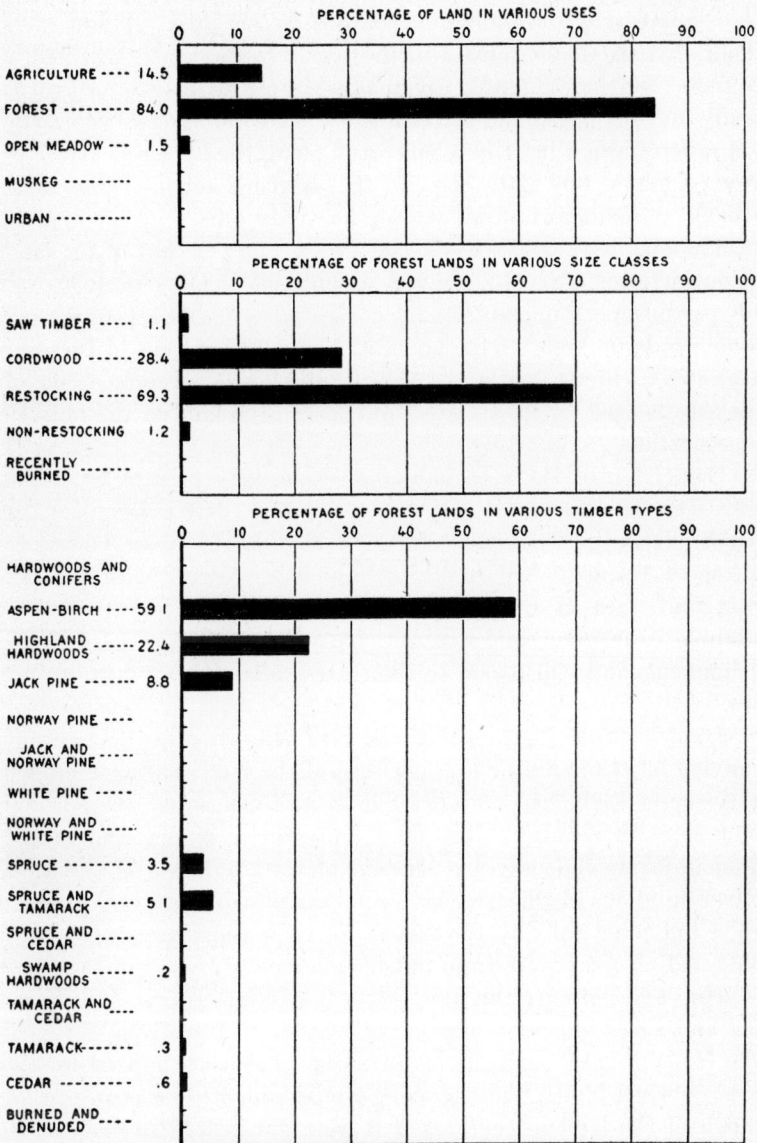

PERCENTAGE OF LAND IN VARIOUS USES

AGRICULTURE ---- 14.5
FOREST --------- 84.0
OPEN MEADOW --- 1.5
MUSKEG ---------
URBAN -----------

PERCENTAGE OF FOREST LANDS IN VARIOUS SIZE CLASSES

SAW TIMBER ----- 1.1
CORDWOOD ------ 28.4
RESTOCKING ----- 69.3
NON-RESTOCKING 1.2
RECENTLY BURNED -------

PERCENTAGE OF FOREST LANDS IN VARIOUS TIMBER TYPES

HARDWOODS AND CONIFERS
ASPEN-BIRCH ---- 59 1
HIGHLAND HARDWOODS ------ 22.4
JACK PINE ------- 8.8
NORWAY PINE ----
JACK AND NORWAY PINE -----
WHITE PINE -----
NORWAY AND WHITE PINE -----
SPRUCE --------- 3.5
SPRUCE AND TAMARACK ------ 5 1
SPRUCE AND CEDAR ------
SWAMP HARDWOODS ------ .2
TAMARACK AND CEDAR ----
TAMARACK------- .3
CEDAR --------- .6
BURNED AND DENUDED ----

FIGURE 21. — DISTRIBUTION OF LAND USES AND OF TIMBER OF VARIOUS TYPES AND SIZES IN AREA XII

81

land. Some relief is afforded, however, by the beds of numerous small streams that originate in the area. On the south the area is bounded by the St. Croix River, the Minnesota bank of which is sandy and steep in some places and low and rolling elsewhere. The soil ranges from a light jack pine sand along the St. Croix River to a very heavy obstinate clay at the extreme north of the area. Stones are abundant on all except the sandy soils.

The area is very sparsely settled, only 14.5 per cent of the land being in farms. (See Figure 21.) Population density in 1930 was 4.9 persons per square mile as compared with 69.7 persons per square mile in Area XI to the west. About 84 per cent of the area is classed as forest land and 1.5 per cent as open meadow. None of the area is used for urban sites, and there is no land in the muskeg classification.

Ownership of the area is almost exclusively private or corporate. Tax delinquency is very heavy. In 1931, 61.7 per cent of the taxable land was delinquent for general property taxes. Only two of the twelve areas had greater delinquency: Area V with 86.8 per cent and Area II with 74.2 per cent. Area XII is very poorly adapted to farming, and it is anticipated that a major part of the delinquent land will revert to the state under the tax delinquency law.

Land in farms. — In 1930 there were 513 farms in the area, occupying 59,718 acres, or 14.5 per cent of the land. Farms averaged 116.4 acres each, had 33.7 acres in crops, 78.3 acres cleared, and 38.1 acres in woodlot. Crop land represented 29 per cent of the land in farms and only 4.2 per cent of the total land of the area. Farm buildings in the area have a rather pleasing external appearance, but practically all the money for their construction has been obtained on mortgages from outside sources.

Hay and oats are the most important crops grown, and dairying and sheep the most important livestock enterprises. Many of the farmers have small bands of sheep, which are grazed on the wild cut-over lands. Sheep grazing would constitute a good use for much of the land in the area if it were not grazed so close as to interfere with reforestation.

Land in forest use. — In this area the original stand of timber has been quite depleted. Only 1 per cent supports growth of sawlog size, and this consists for the most part of old deformed hardwoods having no commercial value. About 28 per cent of the forest cover is of cordwood size and 69 per cent of restocking sizes. The cordwood sizes are about a quarter jack pine and three-quarters highland hardwoods. The restocking areas are predominantly (89 per cent) aspen-birch and are growing very nicely where protected from fire.

Farmers in the area have been unsympathetic toward efforts to promote reforestation. Theirs has been a logical reaction, since they are attempting to extract a living from soils of low yield. From their point of view it was highly imperative that the lands be cleared as rapidly as possible and placed in crops.

There are no lakes in the area, but there are several very excellent trout streams. Game, both large and small, is abundant in the St. Croix Wild Life Sanctuary. The St. Croix River possesses unusual scenic beauty and might well be developed for recreational purposes.

CHAPTER IV

THE ECONOMIC AND SOCIAL CONSEQUENCES OF PLANLESS LAND USE

The removal of merchantable timber from the lands of northern Minnesota has left the people living on these lands largely dependent upon agriculture. If farming yields an adequate return under conditions regarded as normal, there is no question of the advisability of such use of the land. If it does not, it is obviously a mistake to foster its development. The present chapter considers some aspects of this question.

INCOME AND STANDARD OF LIVING *

It is to the interest of society that its members enjoy the highest possible standard of living. Living standards are difficult to measure exactly, but because they are determined by income to a large extent, income figures are useful as indicators of possible standards of living. Data from the 1930 census are used in the comparisons that follow. As these clearly show, there are many areas in northeastern Minnesota where agriculture cannot be advantageously developed. An analysis is presented of the gross farm incomes in the fourteen northeastern counties and comparisons with the remaining counties and with data for the state as a whole.

Gross farm income figures in the federal census reports include the value of all farm products sold, traded, or used by the operator's family, and receipts from boarders. Because of differences in the size of the counties and in the number of farms in each, the figures must be reduced to a per farm basis to make them comparable for different counties or other areas.

Table 7 gives the average income per farm obtained from the various sources in each of the fourteen counties, in the fourteen counties as a group, in the remaining counties of the state as a group, and in the state as a whole. To facilitate comparisons of different areas, a series of maps, based on the data in Table 7, has been prepared (Figure 22). For each source of income the counties are divided into three classes on the basis of the amount of in-

* This section has been prepared by H. F. Hollands.

TABLE 7. — INCOME PER FARM DERIVED FROM EACH OF SEVERAL SOURCES IN 14
COUNTIES OF NORTHEASTERN MINNESOTA, 1929 *

County	Crops	Livestock and Livestock Products	Forest Products	Products Used by Family	Receipts from Boarders	Gross Farm Income
Aitkin	$ 86	$666	$45	$232	$20	$1,049
Beltrami	152	493	88	210	14	957
Carlton	198	786	16	222	4	1,226
Cass	103	701	46	259	40	1,149
Clearwater	230	735	52	216	4	1,237
Cook	90	358	36	302	16	802
Crow Wing	107	649	29	251	54	1,090
Hubbard	129	603	37	216	4	989
Itasca	138	512	111	290	30	1,081
Koochiching	158	327	120	204	11	820
Lake	52	524	62	299	12	949
Lake of the Woods....	146	325	111	169	6	757
Pine	200	995	18	285	5	1,503
St. Louis	102	643	54	266	10	1,075
14 counties	$139	$653	$54	$245	$16	$1,107
All other counties....	540	1,579	11	323	4	2,457
State as a whole....	483	1,449	17	312	6	2,267

* Source: United States Census of Agriculture, 1930, Third Series, County Table III.

come per farm from the particular source. Accompanying each map
is a set of horizontal bar diagrams, which show the average income
from this source for the fourteen counties, for all other counties,
and for the state as a whole.

Map 1 in Figure 22 is a comparison by counties of the average
income per farm from the sale of crops. That income varied from
$52 in Lake County to $230 in Clearwater. In six counties the average income per farm from the sale of crops was less than $108.
These were the three extreme northeastern counties and Cass,
Crow Wing, and Aitkin, with their extensive sandy or swampy
areas. The five northwestern counties of the region, with their
somewhat heavier soils, came in the intermediate income group,
$120 to $190. Several of these counties produce quantities of alsike
and red clover, timothy, and alfalfa seed. Three counties in the
southern part of the region had average incomes per farm of more
than $190. Of the three, Carlton and Pine produce crops that can
be sold in Cloquet, Duluth, and the Twin Cities, the markets of
which are accessible by paved highways. Clearwater County, with
the largest crop income per farm of any of the fourteen northeastern counties, has some land which resembles that of the grain-
producing counties farther west. As indicated by the bar graph,

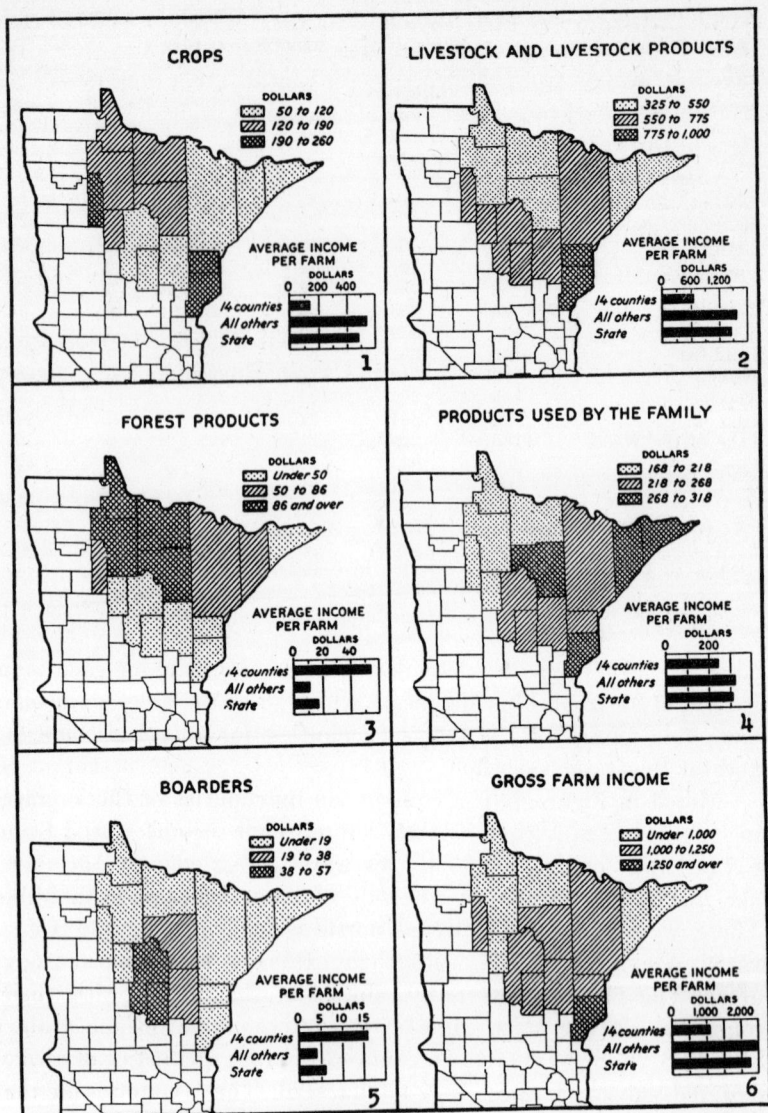

CROPS

DOLLARS
⬡ 50 to 120
▨ 120 to 190
▩ 190 to 260

AVERAGE INCOME
PER FARM
DOLLARS
0   200 400
14 counties
All others
State

1

LIVESTOCK AND LIVESTOCK PRODUCTS

DOLLARS
⬡ 325 to 550
▨ 550 to 775
▩ 775 to 1,000

AVERAGE INCOME
PER FARM
DOLLARS
0   600 1,200
14 counties
All others
State

2

FOREST PRODUCTS

DOLLARS
⬡ Under 50
▨ 50 to 86
▩ 86 and over

AVERAGE INCOME
PER FARM
DOLLARS
0   20   40
14 counties
All others
State

3

PRODUCTS USED BY THE FAMILY

DOLLARS
⬡ 168 to 218
▨ 218 to 268
▩ 268 to 318

AVERAGE INCOME
PER FARM
DOLLARS
0   200
14 counties
All others
State

4

BOARDERS

DOLLARS
⬡ Under 19
▨ 19 to 38
▩ 38 to 57

AVERAGE INCOME
PER FARM
DOLLARS
0   5 10 15
14 counties
All others
State

5

GROSS FARM INCOME

DOLLARS
⬡ Under 1,000
▨ 1,000 to 1,250
▩ 1,250 and over

AVERAGE INCOME
PER FARM
DOLLARS
0   1,000 2,000
14 counties
All others
State

6

FIGURE 22. — AVERAGE FARM INCOME FROM DESIGNATED SOURCES IN
FOURTEEN NORTHEASTERN COUNTIES, 1929

the average for the fourteen counties was $139, as compared with $540 for all other counties, and with $483 for the entire state. The average income from the sale of crops in all other counties of the state was almost four times that of the fourteen northeastern counties in the year considered.

Map 2 shows the average income per farm from the sale of livestock and livestock products. Income from this source was larger than that from any other single source, ranging from $325 to $995. In general, the northern counties of the group had the lowest income from this source, the western the next largest, and the two southeastern counties, Carlton and Pine, the largest. Proximity to relatively large centers of population helped to increase income from this source in some counties, especially Lake, St. Louis, Carlton, and Pine. Although this type of income was large as compared with incomes from other sources, the average was only $653 for the fourteen counties, whereas it was $1,579 for the group of all other counties. The $325 income from this source in Lake of the Woods County was less than half the average for the group of fourteen counties; even in Pine County, in which the income from sales of livestock and livestock products was noticeably higher than in any other northeastern county, it was $454 smaller than the state average — $995 as compared with $1,449.

In the northeastern counties the income per farm from forest products was larger than the average for the rest of the state. However, in 1929 the income from this source was relatively unimportant even in these counties. The southern counties of the area (see Map 3) had very low incomes per farm from forest products, being less than $50 in every case. Three counties came in the range of $50 to $85 per farm, while the largest incomes from this source were received in the northwestern counties of the group. In Koochiching the income per farm was $120. The fourteen counties as a group averaged $54 income from forest products. The average for all other counties was $11 and for the state $17 per farm.

Another item of farm income and one having special significance in an analysis of living standards is that of products consumed by the operator and his family. Lake of the Woods County stood at the bottom of the list with an income of $169 per farm in the form of produce consumed by the operator's family. Four other counties in the northwestern part of the area were also low, each of them having less than $218 income per farm. The south-central counties of the area, Carlton, Aitkin, Crow Wing, and Cass, together with St. Louis, come in the next income class, $218 to $268. In only four counties did the income from this source range between $268 and $318. The average for the entire fourteen counties was $245, as compared with $323 for all other counties. Cook County, with an income of $302, had the largest income from this source, but even this was less than the state average of $312.

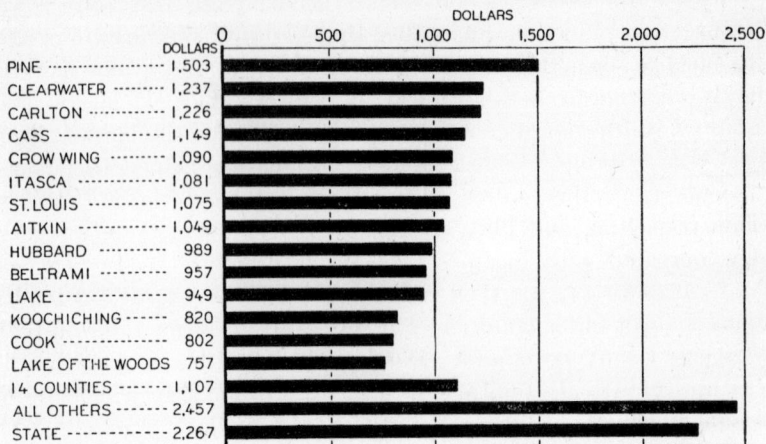

FIGURE 23. — AVERAGE GROSS FARM INCOME IN EACH OF FOURTEEN NORTHEASTERN COUNTIES, IN THE REST OF THE STATE, AND IN THE STATE AS A WHOLE, 1929

Receipts from boarders is the other type of farm income which in this region exceeds that received by the farmers of the state as a whole. But this source is even less important than receipts from forest products, varying from $4 per farm in Carlton, Clearwater, and Hubbard counties to a maximum of $54 in Crow Wing County. The average for the fourteen counties was $16; for all other counties $4; and for the entire state $6. The somewhat higher average income per farm derived from boarders in the northeastern counties is a reflection of the greater recreational advantages existing in this part of the state.

Figure 23 has been prepared from the data in the last column of Table 7, in order to give a better picture of the farm income and of the standard of living in the fourteen northeastern counties. In this chart the average gross farm income per farm in each county, in the group of fourteen counties, in all other counties, and in the state as a whole are shown by horizontal bar diagrams.

Pine County, with an income of $1,503 per farm, had the largest farm income of any of the fourteen counties in 1929, being $266 greater than that of Clearwater County, which had the next highest. This favorable position of Pine County is due to the fact that the southern portion of the county is relatively well developed agriculturally. The northern portion of this county, on the other hand, being similar in general characteristics to the other counties in the cut-over region, has the same types of land use problems.

Clearwater County had a total farm income of $1,237 per farm. Natural conditions in the central part of this county are suitable for farming and the average farm income for the county is relatively high, despite the fact that it includes two regions not well adapted to farming, one in the northern and one in the southern part of the county.

Carlton County ranked third with an income of $1,226 per farm. This relatively high income is in part the result of agricultural development due to favorable market outlets for farm products.

Cass County, with an average farm income of $1,149, had the smallest income of the four counties in which the average income was larger than the $1,107 average for the entire group of northeastern counties. In each of the ten other counties of the group the average income per farm was less than the average in the fourteen as a group.

In Lake of the Woods, Cook, Koochiching, Lake, Beltrami, and Hubbard counties the gross farm income was less than $1,000 per farm. St. Louis County would have an even lower income were it not that in the extreme southern part of the county the income per farm is materially increased by the Duluth markets. These data indicate that the counties along the Canadian border, together with Beltrami and Hubbard, had the lowest farm incomes during 1929.

The three bars at the bottom of Figure 23 aid in comparing the gross farm income of this group of fourteen counties with that of other groups in the state. The gross farm income in these northeastern counties was relatively low, being $1,107 in 1929. This was approximately 45 per cent as large as the $2,457 average gross farm income in all other counties, and 49 per cent as large as the $2,267 gross farm income in the state as a whole.

FARM RECORD DATA, 1932 *

Several areas in each of six counties in northern Minnesota were selected for a special study of the financial success of settlers and the possibilities of further development. Two types of areas were

* This section has been prepared by G. A. Pond and C. W. Crickman.

chosen: tracts representing the best developed and most successful agricultural lands, which will be referred to as "development
areas," and tracts where conditions are relatively less favorable to
agricultural development and where settlers have made little financial progress. In some cases this latter type includes contiguous settlements and in others scattered settlements. These are designated
"relocation areas."

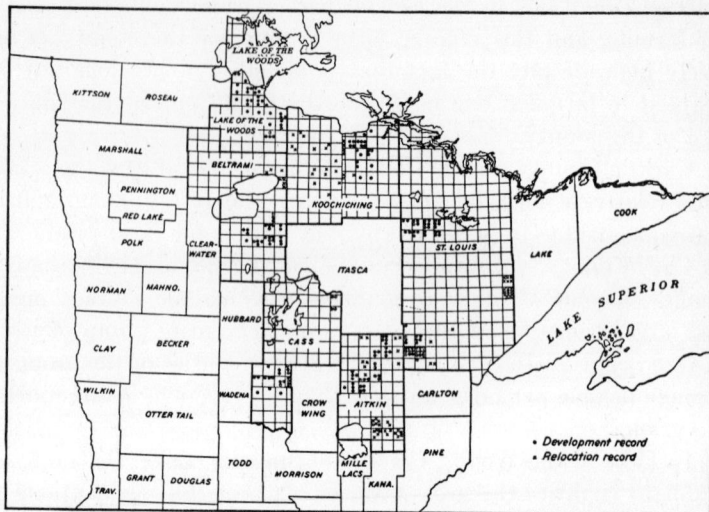

FIGURE 24. — LOCATION OF FARMS STUDIED IN DEVELOPMENT AND
RELOCATION AREAS

SOURCE OF DATA

From the development areas 188 records were obtained, distributed by counties as follows: Aitkin, 30; Beltrami, 25; Cass, 21;
Koochiching, 26; Lake of the Woods, 32; and St. Louis, 54. The 83
relocation records were distributed as follows: Aitkin, 31; Beltrami, 7; Cass, 2; Koochiching, 18; Lake of the Woods, 4; and St.
Louis, 21. Because the number of relocation records from Cass and
Lake of the Woods counties was too small to represent any considerable area, they were omitted from the tabulations. The location of the farms covered by these records is shown above.

The records from these farms were obtained by the survey
method. They include: a complete physical inventory and description of the farm and all assets and liabilities of the operator at the
time of settlement and in 1933; an estimate of crop acreages and
yields in 1932 and of normal yields; data covering cash receipts and

TABLE 8. — COMPARISON OF AVERAGE INCOME PER FARM IN DEVELOPMENT AND RELOCATION AREAS

SOURCE OF INCOME	DEVELOPMENT AREAS (188 farms, averaging 175 acres)		RELOCATION AREAS (77 farms, averaging 122 acres)	
	Per Farm	Per Acre	Per Farm	Per Acre
Dairy products	$334	$1.90	$95	$.78
Cattle	72	.41	30	.24
Poultry and eggs.....................	77	.44	32	.26
Sheep and wool......................	33	.19	7	.06
Hogs	15	.09	1	.01
Crops	148	.85	22	.18
Wood products	10	.06	29	.24
Miscellaneous	3	.02	..	..
Total cash farm receipts............	$692	$3.96	$216	$1.77
Farm produce used by family..........	245	1.40	167	1.37
Rental value of dwelling..............	99	.57	36	.29
Total farm income.................	$1,036	$5.93	$419	$3.43
Cash income from labor off farm.......	89	.34	149	1.22

expenditures for the year ending June 30, 1933; the products of the farm consumed by the farm family for the year; and estimates of the cost of land development. In addition, a history of settlement, a record of outside sources of income since settlement, and personal data regarding the farm operator and his family were obtained. All this information was secured by an enumerator who visited the farm during the summer of 1933.

COMPARISON OF FARM INCOMES IN DEVELOPMENT AND RELOCATION AREAS

The average cash and non-cash farm income of the farms in the development and relocation areas are shown in Table 8. In development areas the cash income per farm was more than three times as great as in the relocation areas. About the same proportion was received from the sale of livestock and livestock products in each, but the farmers in the development areas received relatively more income from crop sales and less from the sale of forest products. In addition to the cash income the farm family has the use of the farmhouse and consumes a portion of the products of the farm. These have been credited as income. The rental value of the farmhouse was estimated at 10 per cent of the present replacement value. Since the farms in the development areas are considerably larger than those in the relocation areas, the income has also been computed on an acre as well as on a farm basis.

Besides the income from the farm these operators secured some cash income from work off the farm. This outside work included a wide variety of jobs, but chiefly work on public roads. This has not been included in the farm income because in many cases, especially in the relocation areas, it represents a form of public relief. The settlers are frequently given this work so that it may not be necessary to carry them on regular county relief rolls. Since it was impossible to determine how much of the outside work was of the relief type, all income from this source has been listed separately.

The average cash expense per farm and per acre in the development and in the relocation areas is shown in Table 9. Expenditures for all items except feed are less in the relocation areas. The interest charge includes only actual interest incurred on indebtedness. In some cases, interest, taxes, and other items of expense incurred have been entered even though they were still unpaid at the end of the year. The table shows the expense incurred rather than the actual monetary expenditure.

TABLE 9. — COMPARISON OF AVERAGE CASH EXPENSE PER FARM IN DEVELOPMENT AND RELOCATION AREAS

ITEM OF EXPENSE	DEVELOPMENT AREAS		RELOCATION AREAS	
	Per Farm	Per Acre	Per Farm	Per Acre
Power and machinery	$122	$ .70	$ 42	$ .34
Buildings and improvements	10	.06	3	.03
Labor	40	.23	16	.13
Feed	39	.22	39	.32
Livestock purchases	25	.14	13	.11
Other livestock expense	7	.04	4	.03
Crop expense	18	.10	5	.04
Taxes and insurance	126	.72	61	.50
Interest on indebtedness	58	.33	24	.20
Total cash expense	$445	$2.54	$207	$1.70

The net cash farm income, the net farm income, and the family labor earnings in the development and in the relocation areas are shown in Table 10. The net cash farm income together with any income he derives from labor off the farm is what the farmer has to spend for personal and living purposes and for principal payments and savings. If he fails to pay any bills incurred during the year, his cash available for spending is increased by that amount. It is apparent from these data that the farm operators in the relocation areas must depend very largely upon outside work for funds with which to support their families. The cash income from the farm is obviously little more than enough to cover the necessary current cash expenditures.

The net farm income is the sum of the net cash farm income and the non-cash income. It represents the return the farmer receives

TABLE 10. — COMPARISON OF NET CASH FARM INCOME, NET FARM INCOME, AND FAMILY LABOR EARNINGS PER FARM IN DEVELOPMENT AND RELOCATION AREAS

ITEM OF COMPARISON	DEVELOPMENT AREAS		RELOCATION AREAS	
	Per Farm	Per Acre	Per Farm	Per Acre
Cash receipts	$692	$3.96	$216	$1.77
Cash expenses	445	2.54	207	1.70
Net cash farm income.................	$247	$1.42	$ 9	$ .07
Non-cash income	344	1.97	203	1.66
Net farm income.....................	$591	$3.39	$212	$1.73
Interest on farmer's equity at 5 per cent	276	1.58	71	.58
Family labor earnings.................	$315	$1.81	$141	$1.15

for the use of his own capital, for management, and for the labor of himself and members of his family. Since the amount of capital associated with the family labor is much greater in the development areas than in the relocation areas, the family labor earnings are also shown in Table 10. This is computed by deducting from the net farm income interest at 5 per cent on the farmer's equity in his business. It is the return for the labor of the farmer and his family after all expenses have been paid and a remuneration for capital allowed.

In the comparisons shown in Tables 8, 9, and 10 all farms in development areas have been combined and likewise all farms in relocation areas. In Table 11 comparisons between the development and the relocation areas within the same county are shown. The same general results appear in the individual counties as were shown for the combined figures. In Koochiching and St. Louis counties the cash farm expenditures exceeded the cash farm income in the relocation areas. The income from labor off the farm was comparatively large in these areas and provided funds for family living.

TABLE 11. — COMPARISON OF NET CASH FARM INCOME, NET FARM INCOME, AND
FAMILY LABOR EARNINGS IN DEVELOPMENT AND RELOCATION AREAS
OF 4 COUNTIES

ITEM OF COMPARISON	AITKIN COUNTY		BELTRAMI COUNTY		KOOCHICHING COUNTY		ST. LOUIS COUNTY	
	Development	Relocation	Development	Relocation	Development	Relocation	Development	Relocation
Number of farms.....	30	31	25	7	26	18	54	21
Acres per farm.......	156	100	157	88	198	163	164	129
Cash farm receipts...	$855	$234	$602	$176	$863	$252	$522	$175
Cash farm expenses...	561	190	385	123	495	302	299	181
Net cash farm income	$294	$ 44	$217	$ 53	$368	$—50	$223	$—6
Non-cash farm income	387	182	324	188	325	184	362	257
Net farm income.....	$681	$226	$541	$241	$693	$134	$585	$251
Interest on farmer's equity at 5 per cent	315	73	197	53	292	81	257	69
Family labor earnings	$366	$153	$344	$188	$401	$ 53	$328	$182
Cash income from labor off farm.......	53	56	25	25	126	231	101	256

PHYSICAL DIFFERENCES BETWEEN FARMS IN DEVELOPMENT AND RELOCATION AREAS

The smaller earnings of farmers in the relocation areas as compared with those in the development areas are due, to a considerable extent, to physical differences in the farms in these areas.
In the first place, these farms are 30 per cent smaller than those in
the development areas. Furthermore, only 23 per cent of the farm
area is crop land, as compared with 56 per cent in the development
areas. Of the crop land 62 per cent is tillable, as compared with 94
per cent in the development areas. Considering the farms as a
whole, 34 per cent is tillable land in the development areas and only
12 per cent in the relocation areas. The relatively large amount of
stone in the relocation areas has made it difficult to bring the land
under cultivation. Nineteen per cent of farm lands in these sections
were so stony that the operators considered the cost of stone removal prohibitive. The corresponding proportion in the development areas was 4 per cent. The remainder of the land in the relocation areas was more stony and the stones were larger. Farmers in
the relocation areas estimated that it required 76 man hours, 65
horse hours, and 48 pounds of explosive to remove the stone from
a single acre. Estimates for the development areas were 18 man

hours, 19 horse hours, and 2 pounds of explosive. This difference alone accounts for much of the difference in the proportion of land under cultivation.

The relative proportion of different soil types in the two types of areas is shown in Table 12. In the development areas there was a larger proportion of the heavier soil types and less peat. That the soil in the development areas was more productive is indicated by

TABLE 12. — PERCENTAGE DISTRIBUTION OF FARM LAND OF VARIOUS SOIL TYPES IN DEVELOPMENT AND RELOCATION AREAS

Areas	Sandy	Sandy Loam	Clay Loam	Clay	Peat
Development areas	4	28	48	11	9
Relocation areas	4	34	31	8	23

the crop yields. With the exception of clover and timothy hay and wild hay, the yield of every crop grown in both types of areas was greater in the development areas. The average difference in yield of the principal crops was 7 per cent in favor of the development areas.

The farms in the relocation areas were 1.6 miles farther from town and 5.2 miles farther from a railway shipping point than those in the development areas. The roads to town were also of poorer quality in the relocation areas. Twelve per cent were unimproved dirt roads, 13 per cent improved dirt roads, and 75 per cent graveled roads. In the development areas 18 per cent of the roads were improved dirt, 80 per cent gravel, and 2 per cent hard surface.

DIFFERENCES IN ORGANIZATION OF FARMS IN DEVELOPMENT AND RELOCATION AREAS

A larger proportion of the farm acreage in the development areas was in crops and pasture than in the relocation areas and less in woods and waste land. The distribution of crops, however, was very similar in both types of areas. In the development areas relatively more small grain was raised and less hay. More of the hay, however, was raised on tillable land. The proportion of land in cultivated crops was about the same in both areas. There were more than twice as many head of livestock on the farms in the development areas as on the farms in the relocation areas, but the proportion of the different kinds of livestock was about the same. The larger area of crop and pasture land per farm and the higher yields in the development areas made it possible to support this larger amount of livestock. The livestock in the development areas was more productive than that in the relocation areas. The average value of dairy products per cow in the development areas was $49, as compared with $33 in the relocation areas. The value of poultry and egg production per hen was $2.89, and of sheep and wool per ewe $3.75, in the development areas; in the relocation areas, $2.32 and $2.67, respectively. The larger return in the development areas was in part due to better market outlets and in part to a better quality of livestock and a more adequate supply of suitable feed.

DIFFERENCES IN FINANCIAL PROGRESS AND STATUS OF SETTLERS IN DEVELOPMENT AND RELOCATION AREAS

The settlers in the development areas had a net worth at time of settlement one-third greater than that of settlers in the relocation areas. On July 1, 1933, they had a net worth more than three and one-third times as large. The gain in the net worth of settlers in both types of areas is shown in Table 13. The settlers in the devel-

TABLE 13. — CHANGES IN NET WORTH PER FARM SINCE SETTLEMENT, IN DEVELOPMENT AND RELOCATION AREAS

Items of Comparison	Development Areas		Relocation Areas	
Resources per farm, July 1, 1933	$6,519		$2,134	
Liabilities per farm, July 1, 1933	1,188		553	
Net worth per farm, July 1, 1933		$5,331		$1,581
Resources per farm at settlement	$2,809		$1,912	
Liabilities per farm at settlement	737		411	
Net worth per farm at settlement		$2,072		$1,501
Gain in net worth since settlement		$3,259		$ 80
Years since settlement		21.0		15.5
Gain in net worth per year		$ 155		$ 5

opment areas have made slow but substantial financial progress since settlement, whereas those in the relocation areas have a gain in net worth of only $80 in more than fifteen years. This difference in financial progress is apparently due to differences in the returns from the farms rather than to unequal opportunities for income from outside the farm. In fact, the average annual outside income per farm was $159 in the relocation areas and only $124 in the development areas.

The estimated present value of real estate in the development areas is about two and one-half times as great as in the relocation areas. The original purchase price was only 50 per cent higher. These figures are shown in Table 14. The cash cost of development, including cash expenditures for land clearing, building construction, fences, and all other real estate improvements, was much higher in the development areas. At the present time the estimated value of the real estate in the development areas is within less than 5 per cent of its cash cost. In the relocation areas the present value is 28 per cent less than the cash cost of purchase and development.

TABLE 14. — COST OF REAL ESTATE AND PRESENT VALUE PER ACRE IN DEVELOPMENT AND RELOCATION AREAS

Items of Comparison	Development Areas	Relocation Areas
Purchase price	$12.19	$8.18
Cash cost of development	15.17	6.37
Total cost	$27.36	$14.55
Estimated market value	26.10	10.43
Percentage ratio of present value to cost	95.4	71.7

The extent to which farmers are delinquent in the payment of taxes and interest is an indication of their financial status. In the development areas 56 per cent of the settlers studied were delinquent in the payment of taxes, and in the relocation areas 73 per cent. The amount of delinquent taxes was also relatively greater in the relocation areas, amounting to 170 per cent of the tax levy due in 1933 as compared with 81 per cent in the development areas. Only 20 per cent of the settlers studied in the development areas were delinquent in interest payments, and the total amount of the delinquency was 59 per cent of the interest due in 1933. In the relocation areas the corresponding figures were 40 and 79 per cent, respectively.

COMPARISON OF FARM EARNINGS IN AREAS STUDIED WITH FARM EARNINGS IN OTHER PARTS OF THE STATE

A comparison of income, expenses, and earnings of the farms studied in northeastern Minnesota and those of two other groups of farms in the state is shown in Table 15. The data covering the farms in northern and southeastern Minnesota were obtained through a supervised farm-accounting study. They do not cover exactly the same time period as the survey, but the years covered overlap sufficiently to permit use of the figures for rough comparisons. Some of the 44 farms covered in the accounting study were in the counties covered by the survey, and most of them were in the same general area. They were, however, larger, more fully developed farms and more intensively operated than the farms included in the survey. They are operated by some of the most successful farm operators in northern Minnesota. The farm receipts, net cash income, and net farm income were greater than those of the farms surveyed in the development area. The family labor earnings, however, were lower because of the high interest charge resulting from the higher capitalization of these farms.

TABLE 15. — COMPARISON OF FARM EARNINGS IN AREAS STUDIED WITH FARM EARNINGS IN OTHER PARTS OF MINNESOTA

	SURVEY		FARM ACCOUNTS	
ITEMS OF COMPARISON	Development Areas	Relocation Areas	Northern * Minnesota	Southeastern † Minnesota
Number of farms...........	188	77	44	143
Acres per farm.............	175	122	184	201
Crop acres per farm.........	58	23	78	138
Period covered by record	July 1, 1932–June 30, 1933		April 1, 1932–Mar. 31, 1933	Jan. 1–Dec. 31, 1932
Cash farm receipts..........	$692	$216	$1,135	$2,748
Cash farm expenditures ‡....	386+	184+	729	1,674
Net cash farm income.......	$306	$ 32	$ 406	$1,074
Non-cash farm income.......	344	203	340	383
Net farm income...........	$650	$235	$ 746	$1,457
Interest at 5 per cent on entire investment	326	107	470	926
Family labor earnings.......	$324	$128	$ 276	$ 531

* Includes farms in Beltrami, Carlton, Clearwater, Hubbard, Itasca, Polk, St. Louis, and Wadena counties.
† Includes farms in Dodge, Freeborn, Goodhue, Le Sueur, Mower, Rice, Steele, and Waseca counties.
‡ Does not include interest paid on indebtedness.

The farms in southeastern Minnesota were dairy farms. In general they were operated by farmers of more than average ability and financial success. They probably do not, however, represent as carefully selected a group as the farmers in northern Minnesota or perhaps even those in the development areas. According to every measure, income and earnings were much higher on these farms than on any of the groups in northern Minnesota. Since the farmers in southeastern Minnesota are on a more commercialized basis than those in the northern part of the state, it is likely that their earnings have declined more during the present depression than the more nearly self-sufficing farms of northern Minnesota. It is probable that over a period of years the difference in earnings in favor of the southeastern Minnesota farmers would be greater than is shown in Table 15. It must be remembered that, as the data in this table indicate, while farmers in northern Minnesota do not make as large earnings as those in the more fully developed sections of southern Minnesota, they have much less capital invested in their business. Furthermore, there is a wide variation, as regards earnings of farmers, between different areas in northern Minnesota.

SOCIAL SERVICE *

Social institutions such as schools, medical services, and religious organizations play an important part in community life. They are closely related to land utilization in that the use of land for agriculture entails the provision of these services for the settlers. They are also related to land use from the standpoint of financial support, because their development is dependent upon the availability of income. When settlement extends to areas unsuited to agricultural use, lower standards of social service are likely to be found.

Public School Education

The measurement of the educational status of the cut-over area, especially if it is to be compared with that of other areas in Minnesota, is made difficult by two conditions. One is the existence of a law, applicable throughout the entire state and in general rather uniformly enforced, that requires school attendance between certain ages or until satisfactory completion of the work in the eighth grade. The other is that attempts have been made by various grants and special aids to provide equal educational opportunities for all children of the state regardless of residence.

Apparently there is no marked variation among larger regions of the state in the extent to which educational facilities are available or in the number of years of school attendance. However, considerable variation is found among the counties.

The maintenance of satisfactory educational opportunities is particularly difficult in those counties where the farm income is low, and it would be impossible were it not for large contributions made by the state to the schools in these counties. Table 16 indicates for

* This section was prepared by H. F. Hollands on the basis of data compiled by R. W. Murchie, professor of sociology in the University of Minnesota.

TABLE 16. — NET STATE SCHOOL AID PER PUPIL FOR THE SCHOOL
YEAR 1929–30 BY COUNTIES

County	Total State School Aid	Contribution to State School Aid from General Property Tax	Excess Receipts over Contribution	Number of Pupils Enrolled	Excess per Pupil
Aitkin	$112,662	$ 11,919	$100,743	4,068	$24.76
Beltrami	165,416	9,373	156,043	4,598	33.94
Carlton	153,204	14,925	138,279	5,455	25.35
Cass	141,032	9,585	131,447	4,035	32.58
Clearwater	65,119	5,771	59,348	2,397	24.76
Cook	10,891	2,861	8,030	473	16.98
Crow Wing	162,426	19,192	143,234	6,646	21.55
Hubbard	81,008	7,738	73,270	2,635	27.81
Itasca	251,832	41,257	210,575	8,140	25.87
Koochiching	108,886	8,492	100,394	3,299	30.43
Lake	58,742	5,430	53,312	1,695	31.45
Lake of the Woods..	36,110	3,517	32,593	1,038	31.40
Pine	139,719	14,993	124,726	5,174	24.11
Average 13 counties	$114,388	$ 11,927	$102,461	3,819	$26.83
St. Louis	877,353	516,719	360,634	52,800	6.83
Average 14 counties	$168,886	$ 47,984	$120,902	7,318	$16.52
All other counties..	97,029	32,742	64,286	6,155	10.44
County average in state as a whole..	$108,592	$ 35,195	$ 73,397	6,342	$11.57

each of the fourteen counties, for these counties as a group, and for
the state as a whole the amount of school aid received from the
state in excess of the amount levied for payment to the state school
aid funds from the general property tax in the area. For the purpose
of comparing counties and regions this excess of receipts over contributions from the general property tax was reduced to a per-
pupil-enrolled basis. An average for thirteen northeastern counties,
exclusive of St. Louis, was computed. St. Louis County was omitted
because the public school situation there differs from that in the
northeastern counties as a group. The iron ore deposits in the
county give it a high assessed valuation and greater revenue than
is received by other counties. The situation in St. Louis County
is also affected by a law [1] applying to it under which a special tax
is levied in the county to create a fund for apportionment to school
districts in which a tax levy of 30 mills does not bring in a revenue
equal to $90 per pupil. The larger amount of local funds provided
in this county results in a smaller proportion of the total school
support coming from state aid. The situation in St. Louis County
is also affected by the larger school enrollment, the school systems

[1] Laws of 1921, chapter 357.

of Duluth and the Iron Range cities being in this county. Excluding St. Louis County, the excess of receipts over contributions per pupil for public school costs ranged from $16.98 in Cook to $33.94 in Beltrami County. Cook County differed from other counties of the group in having only a few large organized school districts with relatively small enrollments, so that the assessed value per pupil was almost sufficient to provide the $40 limit.[2] Under this law the supplemental school aid received by Cook County schools was small.

The data indicate that the average excess of receipts over contributions in the thirteen northeastern counties was $26.83 per pupil as compared with $10.44 in all other counties of the state. The average excess in the state as a whole was $11.57 per pupil, which was less than half as much as the excess received by eleven of the thirteen northeastern counties. If St. Louis County is combined with the other northeastern counties, the average excess of the group was $16.52 per pupil, which was 58 per cent higher than the average for all other counties of the state.

MEDICAL SERVICES

The services of doctors, nurses, and hospitals are considered essentials of any modern community. Table 17 gives the population and the number of square miles per general hospital bed, per nurse, and per doctor. These data, which provide only for quantitative analysis, are relative rather than absolute because their nature precludes absolute reliability; that is, the number of beds varies according to needs, the number of nurses on the staff varies from time to time, and there is the inevitable factor of mobility among doctors.

There was, on the average, one hospital bed to every 500 persons in the fourteen counties, as compared with an average of one bed to 226 persons in all other counties, and to 241 persons in the entire state. With respect to distribution, there was one hospital bed to every 49 square miles of land area in the cut-over counties, as compared with an average of one to every 5 square miles in all other counties, and one to every 8 square miles in the state as a whole.

[2] Section 3030 of the General Statutes of 1923 provides that the state pay supplemental school aid sufficient to make a total of $40 per pupil in those cases where a twenty-mill levy on real and personal property is not enough to raise the entire $40 locally. In recent years the full $40 has not been paid because of a deficiency of funds.

TABLE 17. — DISTRIBUTION OF MEDICAL SERVICES BY POPULATION AND LAND AREAS
IN 14 COUNTIES OF NORTHEASTERN MINNESOTA, 1931

County	POPULATION PER			SQUARE MILES PER		
	General Hospital Bed	Doctor	Nurse	General Hospital Bed	Doctor	Nurse
Aitkin	469	3,002	2,502	57	366	805
Beltrami	668	2,071	1,726	80	248	206
Carlton	386	1,930	1,633	16	79	67
Cass	623	1,417	3,118	84	191	421
Clearwater	734	2,386	2,386	78	255	255
Cook	...	1,217	....	..	749	...
Crow Wing	237	1,507	3,661	10	62	151
Hubbard	960	1,919	3,199	96	192	319
Itasca	534	1,512	3,403	54	152	341
Koochiching	370	1,564	1,760	83	349	393
Lake	272	2,356	1,010	81	700	300
Lake of the Woods......	4,194	1,398	4,194	1,346	449	1,346
Pine	...	1,689	....	..	118	...
St. Louis, excluding Duluth	511	1,517	2,515	32	96	159
14 counties	500	1,661	2,816	49	163	277
All other counties.....	226	818	903	5	19	21
State as a whole......	241	869	980	8	27	31

For each doctor there were 1,661 persons in the cut-over counties, 818 in all other counties, and 869 in the state as a whole. In
terms of land area, there was one doctor for every 163 square miles
in the northeastern counties, one for every 19 square miles in all
other counties, and one for every 27 square miles in the entire state.

For each nurse there were 2,816 people in the fourteen counties,
903 people in all other counties, and 980 people in the state as a
whole. The distribution by area also showed a relative scarcity of
nurses in the northeastern counties.

Possibly this relative scarcity of medical facilities would not be
serious if the existing facilities were readily accessible when needed.
It was found, however, that while in the southern part of Minnesota practically all the people lived within ten miles of one or more
doctors, in the northeastern counties more than 50,000 rural people,
representing approximately 24 per cent of the rural population,
were more than ten miles from a doctor, and nearly 11,000, or
about 5 per cent, lived more than twenty miles from a resident
physician. Moreover, of the medical services that did exist in these
northeastern counties, a large part were supported independently
of the farm income of the area, since the mining, lumber, and paper
companies provided a considerable part of the services.

Religious Institutions

The extent to which a region is supplied with adequate religious institutions is another indication of its ability to support needed social services. For purposes of analysis the counties of the state were divided into six groups and the percentage of the population not associated with any church was computed. Non-affiliation with any church varied from 30 per cent of the population in the southern parts of the state to 60 per cent in the northern parts. However, with relatively less church affiliation in the northern counties the variety of church organizations was just as great as in the southern.

Study of the location of priests and ministers led to the conclusion that in thickly settled regions there were many churches and religious leaders, but in the sparsely settled regions, especially in the northern section of the state, there were large areas without churches, priests, or preachers. Furthermore, available data indicated that a large number of rural churches were dependent on the city or larger village churches for support. In some instances the village churches themselves received from 10 to 50 per cent of their support from the home mission fund of their respective denominations. Despite considerable subsidization from outside sources, the religious institutions of the rural areas of the north were relatively inadequate.

Sparsity of population and isolated settlement evidently are factors limiting the availability of social services. This is another reason why it is advantageous to concentrate settlement in the areas best suited to agricultural development.

FARM ABANDONMENT *

Planless land use permits the settlement of land so unsuited to farm purposes that it is unable to supply the returns necessary for the subsistence of the operator and his family and the maintenance of the needed social organization in the community. One consequence of such ill-advised settlement is farm abandonment.

In passing through territory in which farms have been abandoned, one can see some of the results of abandonment: fields growing to weeds, brush, or second growth timber; fallen-down fences; caved-in wells; and decaying and collapsing buildings. These visible evidences of failure suggest the losses of capital, time, effort, and morale of the men, women, and children who, after years of

* This section has been prepared by H. F. Hollands.

effort, have been forced to leave "home" and search elsewhere for opportunities to make a living. Past abandonment is water over the dam, but it should lead to the realization that this sacrifice of time, energy, and savings could often have been prevented.

Data from the federal agricultural census have been used to give some indication of the extent of land abandonment in the fourteen counties. Table 18 shows the number of farms in each of the northeastern counties for each census year from 1900 to 1930. In every county the number of farms increased to the year 1925, when the number in St. Louis and Itasca counties was nine times

TABLE 18. — NUMBER OF FARMS IN 14 COUNTIES OF NORTHEASTERN MINNESOTA IN CENSUS YEARS, 1900–30

County	1900	1910	1920	1925	1930
Aitkin	768	1,348	1,945	2,569	2,467
Beltrami *†	1,243	1,577	3,065	2,534	2,083
Carlton	605	1,195	1,917	2,287	2,070
Cass	668	948	1,579	2,143	2,010
Clearwater †	...	1,055	1,253	1,539	1,500
Cook	36	146	141	192	127
Crow Wing	1,241	1,148	1,281	1,452	1,696
Hubbard	641	843	1,252	1,442	1,304
Itasca ‡	217	830	1,436	2,148	2,278
Koochiching ‡	...	444	944	1,474	1,278
Lake	19	210	208	444	298
Lake of the Woods §	...	...	...	945	723
Pine	1,416	2,066	3,088	3,326	3,288
St. Louis	696	2,465	4,271	6,951	4,872
Total	7,550	14,275	22,380	29,446	25,994
State as a whole	154,659	156,137	178,478	188,231	185,255

* Part of Beltrami County organized as Lake of the Woods County in 1922.
† Clearwater County organized in 1903 from Beltrami County.
‡ Koochiching County organized from a part of Itasca County in 1906.
§ Lake of the Woods County organized from part of Beltrami County in 1922.

that in 1900. After 1925, however, there was a significant change. In twelve of the fourteen counties the number decreased during the period 1925–30; and in only two, Crow Wing and Itasca, did it increase. There were 3,452 fewer farms in the entire fourteen counties in 1930 than in 1925, a decrease of 11.7 per cent. The largest actual decline in number of farms occurred in St. Louis County, where there was a decrease of 2,079 farms, or of 30 per cent, during the five-year period.

The decrease in the number of farms is not in itself indicative of farm abandonment, since it might have resulted from consolidation into larger units. Not only did the number of farms decrease, however, but also the number of acres in farms. As is shown in Table 19, the number of acres in farms reached a high point in 1925. In 1930 the acreage in all counties except Cass, Clearwater, Crow Wing, and Pine was less than in 1925. The largest relative decrease occurred in Cook County, where there was a decline of 36 per cent; the next largest was 28 per cent, in Lake County; and in both Lake of the Woods and St. Louis counties a decrease of more than 18 per cent took place. The total land in farms in the fourteen counties declined by 157,090 acres from 1925 to 1930, a decrease of 4.9 per cent.

TABLE 19. — ACREAGE IN FARMS IN THE 14 COUNTIES OF NORTHEASTERN MINNESOTA IN CENSUS YEARS, 1900–30

County	1900	1910	1920	1925	1930
Aitkin	112,712	175,796	231,221	300,564	286,650
Beltrami *†	186,716	223,764	459,487	297,806	265,842
Carlton	67,092	120,505	185,199	194,270	189,273
Cass	104,577	147,081	240,733	276,645	293,300
Clearwater †	......	174,616	203,168	223,439	233,352
Cook	5,523	23,769	18,334	23,371	14,856
Crow Wing	170,509	168,771	190,100	207,004	225,373
Hubbard	99,143	151,984	191,996	202,488	197,052
Itasca ‡	27,641	108,380	168,976	229,513	219,383
Koochiching ‡	......	73,245	152,507	184,512	167,813
Lake	2,435	22,279	26,739	32,394	23,108
Lake of the Woods §	......	......	......	139,146	113,078
Pine	148,459	230,689	333,418	335,805	361,838
St. Louis	59,950	272,995	402,351	545,162	444,111
Total	984,757	1,893,874	2,804,229	3,192,119	3,035,029
State as a whole	26,248,498	27,675,823	30,221,758	30,059,137	30,913,367

* Part of Beltrami County organized as Lake of the Woods County in 1922.
† Clearwater County organized in 1903 from Beltrami County.
‡ Koochiching County organized from a part of Itasca County in 1906.
§ Lake of the Woods County organized from part of Beltrami County in 1922.

FARM ABANDONMENT IN HUBBARD COUNTY *

In order to obtain more detailed information on farm abandonment and the conditions associated with it, a special study was made in Hubbard County in the summer of 1932. The abandoned farms in the county were visited, and information was obtained by inspection of the property. Supplementary information was obtained from neighboring farmers, from relatives of the farmers who had moved away, and from official county records. For purposes of comparison, the field workers also visited occupied farms in the

* The survey on which this section is based was carried on under the supervision of E. C. Johnson by W. T. Ferrier and H. W. Soderburg.

same locality and obtained detailed information regarding such farms, their occupants, and the farm business. County records furnished data on taxes and tax delinquency.

For the purposes of this study an abandoned farm was one on which land previously cleared, broken, and used for crops was lying unused during the summer of 1932. If the house was being occupied by some squatter who merely used a small area for garden crops, the farm was considered to be abandoned. A property with unoccupied buildings was not considered an abandoned farm unless it included, in addition to a garden plot, some land which had previously been in crops. This requirement eliminated pieces of property on which people had lived only until the timber was removed or while a living could be made off the farm in a lumber camp, sawmill, or village.

Data for the 301 abandoned farms of Hubbard County typify farm abandonment in many parts of the fourteen northeastern counties, and they serve, together with the data from the farms that were occupied, as a basis for the discussion that follows.

In Table 20 are presented some of the general characteristics associated with farm abandonment in Hubbard County. Part A gives data relating to the time of abandonment. Ninety-one, or 30 per cent, of the farms were abandoned before 1920; and the number abandoned during the three ensuing periods averaged about 67 farms per period, the range being from 62 to 79 farms.

The number of years that the farms were operated is given in Part B. Of the 194 farms for which this information was obtained, 90, or 46 per cent, had been farmed for fifteen years or longer. Fifty-two of the 194 farms, or 27 per cent, had been farmed from ten to fourteen years; and only 8 farms had been occupied for less than five years.

The type of tenure of the last farmer to occupy the land is given in Part C of the table. These data were obtained for 266 of the abandoned farms; of this number 208, or 78 per cent, were abandoned by the owner; and 23, or 9 per cent, were abandoned by tenants. The remaining 13 per cent were last farmed by squatters.

The present ownership of 252 of these abandoned farms is given in Part D of Table 20; 129 farms, or 51 per cent, were owned by individual nonresidents, some of whom had gone elsewhere to make a living; 51, or 20 per cent, were owned by banks and investment corporations; 43, or 17 per cent, by individuals living in the immediate vicinity; and 14, or 6 per cent, by timber or land companies.

TABLE 20. — CHARACTERISTICS OF AND REASONS FOR FARM ABANDONMENT
IN HUBBARD COUNTY

PART A: YEAR ABANDONED

	No.	Per Cent
Prior to 1920	91	30
1920–1923	62	21
1924–1927	79	26
1928–1932	69	23
Total	301	100

PART B: NUMBER OF YEARS FARMED

	No.	Per Cent
Less than 5	8	4
5–9	44	23
10–14	52	27
15 and more	90	46
Unknown	107	..
Total	301	100

PART C: TENURE WHEN ABANDONED

	No.	Per Cent
Owner	208	78
Tenant	23	9
Squatter	35	13
Unknown	35	..
Total	301	100

PART D: TYPE OF OWNERSHIP

	No.	Per Cent
Individual resident	43	17
Individual nonresident	129	51
Timber or land company	14	6
Banks-investment	51	20
Miscellaneous	15	6
Unknown	49	..
Total	301	100

PART E: CONDITION OF BUILDINGS

Usable houses
Number ... 166
Percentage ... 55
Average replacement cost ... $350
Usable barns
Number ... 126
Percentage ... 42
Average replacement cost ... $146

PART F: YEAR TAXES FIRST BECAME DELINQUENT

	No.	Per Cent
Before 1927	49	23
1927	41	19
1928	34	16
1929	20	10
1930	33	16
1931	36	16
Total	213	100

PART G: AVERAGE INCOME PER FARM *

295 occupied farms ... $ 719
All farms in Hubbard County .. 769
All farms in 14 counties ... 846
All farms in other counties ... 2,130
All farms in state ... 1,949

PART H: REASONS FOR ABANDONMENT

	No.	Per Cent
Inadequate income	69	31
Foreclosed	62	28
Owner died	34	15
Bought for investment	19	9
Poor soil	19	9
Miscellaneous	17	8
Unknown	81	..
Total	301	100

* Income from sale of crops, livestock, livestock products, and forest products. The average income of the 295 farms was $440 in 1931. Considering the difference in the price levels of 1929 and 1931, this figure is equivalent to an income of $719 in 1929, the year for which the other incomes are given.

The condition of the buildings on these abandoned farms in the summer of 1932 is indicated in Part E of Table 20. There was no usable house on 135 of the farms, and 166 of them, or 55 per cent, had usable houses of a sort that could then have been replaced at an average estimated cost of $350. There were only 126 usable barns on the 301 farms, and these could have been replaced at an average outlay of $146.

The extent of tax delinquency is of interest in connection with abandonment in this county. Part F of the table indicates that 213 of the farms were tax delinquent in 1932. The owners of the other 88 abandoned farms continued to pay taxes. Forty-nine farms became tax delinquent before 1927, and since then the number of farms becoming delinquent each year varied from 41 in 1927 to 20 in 1929.

Part G of the table gives the average gross income per farm derived from the three principal sources by the 295 occupied farms adjoining the ones abandoned, and by other farms in the state. The average income per farm for the 295 farms was $719, which was $50 less than the average for all farms in Hubbard County. The average income per farm in this county was in turn lower than that in the fourteen counties, and still lower than the average income per farm in the state as a whole.

Answers were obtained for 220 farms to the question, "Why was the farm abandoned?" A summary of the reasons is given in Part H of Table 20. The reply received most frequently (69 times) was that the occupant could not make a go of it and so packed his belongings and left. In 62 cases the property was foreclosed and the farmer moved voluntarily or was evicted; on 34 farms the owner died and left no heirs, or at least none who desired to occupy the farm. There were 19 farms which had been bought as an investment, in several cases without inspection of the property, and for which the owner could secure no tenant; another 19 were abandoned because of poor soil.

Assessors' valuations, the amounts of the real estate taxes, tax delinquency, and mortgage indebtedness of the abandoned and the occupied farms are compared in Table 21. The true and full value of the abandoned farms averaged $1,245, as compared with $3,763 for the occupied ones; the value per acre of the occupied farms was $23.69, which was more than twice as much as the $11.58 per acre value of the abandoned farms. The 1931 tax levy averaged 38 cents an acre on the abandoned farms and 55 cents on the occupied. Two hundred and thirteen of the abandoned farms, or 71 per cent, were tax delinquent, as compared with 138, or 47 per cent, of the occupied farms. The amount of accumulated delinquent taxes per acre of land in the farms averaged $1.77 an acre for the abandoned and 42 cents for the occupied farms.

TABLE 21.—ASSESSORS' VALUATION, TAXES, DELINQUENCY, AND MORTGAGE IN-DEBTEDNESS OF FARMS INCLUDED IN THE HUBBARD COUNTY SURVEY, 1932

	Total	Per Farm	Per Acre
True and full value			
Abandoned farms	$ 374,738	$1,245	$11.58
Occupied farms	1,110,059	3,763	23.69
Real estate taxes			
Abandoned farms	12,342	41	.38
Occupied farms	25,633	87	.55
Tax delinquency			
Abandoned farms	57,297	190	1.77
Occupied farms	19,508	66	.42
Mortgage debt			
Abandoned farms	224,752	1,270	11.81
Occupied farms	334,535	1,134	7.14

Information concerning the amount of mortgage indebtedness was obtained for 177 abandoned farms and for all the occupied farms, 60 per cent of which were mortgaged. The average mortgage per acre on the 177 abandoned farms for which data were available was $11.81, as compared with $7.14 per acre for the occupied farms.

In order to facilitate comparison between the physical characteristics of the abandoned and the occupied farms included in this study, Table 22 has been prepared from the data gathered by the survey. For example, the average acreage of the abandoned

TABLE 22.—PHYSICAL CHARACTERISTICS OF FARMS VISITED IN HUBBARD COUNTY, 1932

	Abandoned		Occupied	
Number of farms...................	301		295	
Acres in farms....................	32,366		46,871	
Acres per farm....................	107.5		158.8	
Area plowable per farm	Acres	Per Cent	Acres	Per Cent
Now plowable	18.5	17	67.4	42
Once plowable	21.5	20	67.4	42
Topography				
Level	22.1	20	65.3	41
Gently rolling	54.6	51	79.8	50
Rough to hilly	30.8	29	13.7	9
Total	107.5	100	158.8	100
Soil classification				
Group 1 (most desirable)..........	28.9	27	56.3	36
Group 2 (less desirable)...........	18.7	17	63.9	40
Group 3 (least desirable)..........	59.9	56	38.6	24
Total	107.5	100	158.8	100

farms was 107.5 and that of the occupied farms 158.8. Of special significance is the average number of acres plowable per farm, which at the time of most extensive use averaged 21.5 acres, or 20 per cent, on the abandoned farms as compared with 67.4 acres, or 42 per cent, on the occupied farms.

Some of the land in the county is too rough for crop use. Not all of the soil is well adapted to farming. A comparison of topography and soils indicates why the abandoned farms had relatively less crop land. Table 22 shows the amount of level, gently rolling, and hilly land on both the abandoned and the occupied farms. In contrast to the average of 22.1 acres of level land per abandoned farm there were 65.3 acres of level land per occupied farm. These acreages of level land agree very closely with the average number of plowable acres per abandoned and per occupied farm. Since the occupied farms are larger, percentage figures furnish a better basis of comparison of the topography of these two groups of farms. On the average, only 20 per cent of the area of the abandoned farms was level, as compared with 41 per cent of the occupied farms. In each group about 50 per cent of the farm acreage was gently rolling; but of the occupied farms only 9 per cent of the acreage was rough to hilly, as contrasted with 29 per cent of the abandoned farms.

The soils in this county are varied, but in general they may be classified into nine soil types. For the purposes of this discussion these nine types have been combined into three groups on the basis of general suitability for agricultural purposes. Group 1 includes the most desirable types in the county; Group 2 the less desirable but usable types; and Group 3 those which, if included in farms, are generally used only for permanent pasture or woodlot. On the abandoned farms 27 per cent of the acreage was composed of Group 1 soils, as compared with 36 per cent of the area of the occupied farms. Forty per cent of the acreage of the occupied farms, as contrasted with 17 per cent of that of the abandoned farms, was composed of Group 2 soils. These two groups include the soil types ordinarily usable for fields in Hubbard County, and together they represented 76 per cent of the acreage of the occupied farms and only 44 per cent of the acreage of the abandoned farms. Group 3 soils, however, constituted 56 per cent of the area of the average abandoned farm, but less than half as much, or only 24 per cent, of that of the occupied farms.

The data on topography and soils are important indicators of

TABLE 23. — OUTSTANDING INDEBTEDNESS OF 14 COUNTIES OF NORTHEASTERN MINNESOTA ON DECEMBER 31, 1932, WITH PERCENTAGE CHANGE FROM DECEMBER 31, 1929 *

Form of Indebtedness	Eleven Counties (Crow Wing, St. Louis, and Itasca omitted)	Percentage Increase or Decrease from December 31, 1929	Crow Wing, St. Louis, and Itasca	Percentage Increase or Decrease from December 31, 1929	Total Fourteen Counties	Percentage Increase or Decrease from December 31, 1929
County bonds	$5,925,674.38	—26	$1,248,800.00	—42	$7,174,474.38	—30
County warrants	1,048,777.08	—15	1,120,244.94	223	2,164,022.02	34
Total	6,969,451.46	—25	2,369,044.94	—7	9,338,496.40	—21
Town bonds	797,735.14	—5	157,064.67	—25	954,799.82	—9
Town warrants	230,575.27	—26	830,052.86	.3	1,060,628.13	—7
Total	1,028,310.42	—11	987,117.53	—5	2,015,427.95	—8
City and village bonds	925,903.20	—5	14,201,169.07	—12	15,127,072.27	—12
City and village warrants...	168,963.08	—23	1,764,602.03	15	1,933,565.11	10
Total	1,094,866.28	—8	15,965,771.10	—10	17,060,637.38	—10
School bonds	2,587,772.90	—19	6,837,562.79	—29	9,425,335.69	—26
School warrants	603,692.53	8	2,303,275.90	21	2,906,968.43	18
Total	3,191,465.43	—15	9,140,838.69	—21	12,332,304.12	—19
Total bonds	10,237,085.63	—21	22,444,596.53	—20	32,681,682.16	—21
Total warrants	2,052,020.02	—12	6,018,175.73	29	8,065,183.69	16
Grand total	$12,289,105.65	—20	$28,462,772.26	—13	$40,746,865.85	—16

* County figures from public examiner's reports. Trunk highway reimbursement bonds have been deducted. Town, city and village, and school figures from *Interest Bearing Debts of the State of Minnesota and Its Municipalities*, compiled by the Minnesota Tax Commission, June 1, 1933, and July 1, 1930.

the reasons for abandonment. They illustrate the importance of directing settlement to the land that is best adapted to successful farming, and warn against indiscriminate use of land for farm purposes without regard to its suitability.

Measures of living standards and data on farm incomes are not available for farms now abandoned. But the data presented in the above analysis, such as those related to tax delinquency, mortgage indebtedness, replacement cost of buildings, and natural conditions of topography and soil constitute strong evidence that the income received on these abandoned farms was far less than was necessary for the maintenance of a satisfactory standard of living.

PUBLIC FINANCE *

A detailed analysis of the financial status of the units of local government in each of the fourteen northeastern counties is given in Chapter XI. It is the purpose of this section to outline briefly those aspects of public finance that are the outgrowth of planless land use. Perhaps the major problem of public finance has resulted from indiscriminate settlement. Large capital outlays have been necessary to provide road and school facilities for scattered settlements. These, together with expenditures on drainage projects, account for the major part of the present indebtedness of the fourteen northeastern counties. Table 23 shows the total outstanding indebtedness on December 31, 1931, for local government units and the percentage changes that have taken place since December 31, 1929.

Fifty-four per cent of the bonds of these counties outstanding on December 31, 1932, were issued for the construction of ditches and 28 per cent for the building of roads; 16 per cent were refunding bonds and the remaining 2 per cent were for county buildings. Of the total indebtedness of all units, 54 per cent was for buildings, 15 per cent for roads and bridges, 21 per cent for ditches, and 10 per cent represented refunding bonds.

Although substantial reductions have been made in debts, they still remain a heavy burden. Some measures of this burden are given in Table 24.

The debt per capita of comparable units of government in the rest of the state, excluding Hennepin and Ramsey counties, is $49, slightly more than in Carlton, which has the lowest per capita of the fourteen counties. The remainder of the state (excluding

* This section has been prepared by Mark Regan.

TABLE 24. — MEASURES OF INDEBTEDNESS FOR 14 COUNTIES OF
NORTHEASTERN MINNESOTA, 1932

County	Net Indebtedness December 31, 1932	Debt per Capita	Indebtedness per $1,000 Assessed Valuation	Debt per Taxable Acre
Aitkin	$1,946,857.21	$130	$429	$1.70
Beltrami	1,678,654.83	81	341	1.38
Carlton	856,711.28	40	104	1.66
Cass	1,769,239.80	113	426	1.72
Clearwater	482,684.22	50	200	1.01
Cook	415,485.60	171	402	.82
Hubbard	447,053.93	46	128	.78
Koochiching	2,364,994.97	168	564	2.30
Lake	385,007.29	54	149	.48
Lake of the Woods......	874,942.54	204	512	1.25
Pine	1,067,473.98	53	166	1.20
Above 11 counties.....	$12,289,105.65	$ 88	$281	$1.38
Crow Wing	$ 1,198,764.08	$ 47	$109	$1.91
Itasca	1,541,171.63	57	61	1.11
St. Louis	25,722,836.55	126	86	7.90
Above 3 counties......	$28,462,722.26	$111	$ 85	$5.40
14 counties	$40,751,827.91	$103	$107	$2.88

Hennepin and Ramsey counties) had an indebtedness of $90 per $1,000 of assessed valuation and $2.12 per taxable acre. In all the northeastern counties, excluding Itasca and St. Louis, the ratio of debt to assessed value was greater than this state average. Because of the large areas included in the northern counties, the debt per taxable acre is lower, except in Koochiching and St. Louis, than in the rest of the state. Five counties in the northeastern group have an indebtedness exceeding 40 per cent of the assessed valuation and two have over 50 per cent.

The capital outlays for roads and bridges, schools, and ditch improvements have placed a heavy burden of debt upon many of the counties in the cut-over group. Costs of maintenance also have been high, especially in relation to taxpaying ability. Table 25 shows the per capita cost and the cost per $1,000 of assessed valuation of county and school operation. In six of the fourteen counties the expenditures for school and county purposes are in excess of $100 per $1,000 of assessed valuation. Were the counties obliged to bear the entire cost, a tax levied on the basis of 100 per cent tax collections would mount as high as 172 mills in Cook County for schools and roads alone, to say nothing of debt service and city and

TABLE 25. — SCHOOL AND COUNTY OPERATING COSTS PER CAPITA
AND PER $1,000 OF ASSESSED VALUATION IN 14 COUNTIES
OF NORTHEASTERN MINNESOTA *

County	Per Capita	Per $1,000 Assessed Valuation
Aitkin	$31	$102
Beltrami	30	126
Carlton	26	68
Cass	29	109
Clearwater	22	86
Cook	73	172
Hubbard	27	73
Koochiching	33	112
Lake	50	137
Lake of the Woods	34	84
Pine	24	76
Crow Wing	27	63
Itasca	63	68
St. Louis	59	40

* Township and city and village costs omitted.

village and township costs. Substantial state aid has been received
by the counties for roads and schools.[3] Assistance in meeting interest and principal payments on ditch obligations has been received
by some of them.

Table 26 shows the comparative assessed valuations, levies, and
mill rates in each of the fourteen counties for 1929 and 1931. The
decline in valuation was great in all the counties except Carlton,
Crow Wing, Itasca, and St. Louis. Except in these four and in Lake
County, mill rates were higher in 1932 than in 1929.

Though total tax levies have been reduced in all but Lake of
the Woods County during the four years, the reductions have been
more than offset in most counties by the increasing percentage of
uncollected taxes. Table 27 shows the percentage of uncollected
taxes for each of the four years in each county.

The percentage of tax delinquency had attained considerable
proportions in all but four of the northeastern counties by 1929.
In all but Cook there have been increases since that time. The
state has come to the aid of four of the counties that could not
meet their outstanding ditch bonds.

Table 28 shows the ditch mileage constructed, the capital invested, and the interest and principal payments from the state in
the counties of the northeastern group that are within the Red
Lake Game Preserve or the reforestation and flood control areas.

[3] State aid provides for a large share of the school costs in all these counties
except St. Louis.

TABLE 26.— ASSESSED VALUATIONS, TAXES LEVIED ON REAL AND PERSONAL PROPERTY, WITH PERCENTAGE CHANGE AND MILL RATES, 1929–32, IN 14 COUNTIES OF NORTHEASTERN MINNESOTA *

County	Assessed Valuation		Percentage Change	Taxes Levied †		Percentage Change	Mill Levy	
	1929	1932		1929	1932		1929	1932
Aitkin	$ 7,591,038	$ 4,542,244	—40	$ 749,155	$ 598,856	—20	99	132
Beltrami	5,969,217	4,921,258	—18	727,694	696,338	— 4	122	141
Carlton	9,505,427	8,230,797	—13	863,642	697,961	—19	91	85
Cass	6,104,137	4,157,561	—32	667,358	555,972	—17	109	134
Clearwater	3,675,283	2,412,708	—34	281,729	208,524	—26	77	86
Cook	1,824,247	1,034,083	—43	262,553	220,058	—16	144	213
Hubbard	4,928,146	3,486,875	—29	356,232	295,756	—17	72	85
Koochiching	5,407,941	4,191,265	—22	916,354	779,208	—15	169	186
Lake	3,457,914	2,587,552	—25	403,359	293,536	—27	117	113
Lake of the Woods	2,239,886	1,706,641	—24	228,108	243,437	6	102	143
Pine	9,548,424	6,416,627	—33	765,683	559,651	—27	80	87
Crow Wing	12,222,626	10,997,659	—10	1,220,191	1,012,658	—17	100	92
Itasca	26,275,053	25,171,480	— 4	2,560,614	2,276,265	— 7	97	90
St. Louis	329,078,576	299,880,620	— 9	23,414,700	21,230,404	— 9	71	71

* Compiled from biennial reports of the Minnesota Tax Commission.   † Except special assessments.

115

TABLE 27. — PERCENTAGES OF TAX DELINQUENCY IN 14 COUNTIES OF NORTHEASTERN MINNESOTA, 1929–32 *

County	1929	1930	1931	1932
Aitkin	48.83	55.61	64.40	69.98
Beltrami	51.22	53.05	61.13	66.37
Carlton	11.45	12.18	30.95	24.89
Cass	46.11	48.56	60.38	65.40
Clearwater	34.44	36.53	47.95	54.41
Cook	39.76	38.62	31.08	30.55
Hubbard	35.28	39.34	45.40	52.94
Koochiching	28.43	45.00	54.00	55.12
Lake	23.59	22.89	35.74	28.29
Lake of the Woods	66.14	68.46	78.81	78.46
Pine	28.52	30.76	36.49	45.51
Crow Wing	11.53	12.93	23.92	28.46
Itasca	8.77	10.00	12.58	12.20
St. Louis	3.22	4.54	7.67	18.26
State as a whole	7.74	9.52	15.79	20.18

* From compilations by the Minnesota Tax Commission.

Ditches were constructed in all the northeastern counties except Lake and Cook. Sixty-two per cent of the total ditch mileage and 68 per cent of the capital invested in the remaining twelve counties were in the four counties listed in Table 28. Of the ditch bonds outstanding on December 31, 1929, 75 per cent were obligations of these four counties.

Under the Red Lake Game Preserve [4] and the reforestation and flood control projects [5] the state assumed liability for deficits on interest and principal payments on ditch bonds chargeable to ditches within the Red Lake Game Preserve and the reforestation and flood control areas. Under these acts the state had made interest and principal payments of over $1,775,000 by December 31, 1932.[6] It is estimated that the state had assumed responsibility for interest and principal payments on $2,306,426.41, or 75 per cent of the ditch obligations outstanding in the four counties on that date.

It was these principal and interest payments by the state on ditch bonds that made possible large reduction in county bonds. The state contributions are equivalent to 84 per cent of the reduction that was made by the group of eleven counties over the period and 58 per cent of the total reduction by all units of local government in these counties.

[4] Session Laws of Minnesota, 1929, chapter 258.
[5] Session Laws of Minnesota, 1931, chapter 407.
[6] Of this amount about $1,645,000 represented payments to the three counties in the Red Lake Game Preserve. The current total (August 28, 1934) paid these counties was about $2,472,000.

TABLE 28. — DITCH MILEAGE, CAPITAL INVESTMENT, AND STATE AND COUNTY DRAINAGE OBLIGATIONS IN COUNTIES WITHIN RED LAKE GAME PRESERVE, REFORESTATION, AND FLOOD CONTROL PROJECTS

County	Miles of Ditches*	Original Capital Invested*	Total Ditch Obligation December 31, 1929 †	Interest and Principal Received from State to December 31, 1932	Ditch Obligation December 31, 1932 †	Estimated Obligations of State December 31, 1932 ‡
Aitkin	427.9	$1,223,274	$ 896,763	$ 132,213 †	$ 796,100	$ 372,500
Beltrami	890.2	1,896,123	2,036,530	823,865 ‡	1,172,400	801,304
Koochiching	568.6	1,520,886	957,000	338,285 ‡	553,000	474,300
Lake of the Woods	624.4	1,378,327	1,036,352	483,746 ‡	658,320	658,320
Total	2,511.1	$6,018,610	$4,926,645	$1,778,109	$3,054,300	$2,306,424

* United States Census, 1930, Drainage of Agricultural Lands. † Public examiner's records. ‡ Reports from county auditors.

117

CHAPTER V

PRESENT POLICIES AND PROGRAMS OF ADJUSTMENT*

While it is true that no comprehensive, well-coordinated public policy dealing with problems of land use has been formulated, a number of policies and programs of action that have been adopted have a more or less direct bearing upon these problems. For instance, as already pointed out,[1] the policies that guided the federal and state governments in the disposal of public lands have had an important bearing on land utilization. The purpose of this chapter is to review some of the present public policies and programs relating to land use.

FEDERAL POLICIES AND PROGRAMS

NATIONAL FORESTS

The timber culture act of 1873 was enacted to stimulate the planting of trees and, while its results were limited, it is suggestive of the developing interest in forests. There was also a legislative proposal in the seventies looking to the creation of forest reserves, but action along this line did not come until 1891, when an act of Congress authorized the president to set aside public lands as forest reserves. This marked the beginning of the actual establishment of national forests. The enactment of this legislation was soon followed by executive orders withdrawing various public lands for forest purposes.

It would be a mistake to assume that the creation of national forests was the result of a sudden awakening to the importance of permanent provision for the timber requirements of future generations. The adoption of the program came after years of discussion and in the face of considerable opposition. Nor did the opposition cease after the enactment of the legislation. It finally led, in 1907, to legislation requiring congressional approval for the creation or extension of national forests in some of the western states.

The mere withdrawal of lands did not, of course, suffice to establish satisfactory public forests, as was appreciated by those who

* This chapter has been prepared by O. B. Jesness.
[1] See Chapter I.

118

were instrumental in having land reserved for forest purposes. After several years' efforts, provisions were made for the development of an effective federal forest service.

While the greater part of the existing national forests has resulted from the setting aside of public lands for this purpose, provision has also been made for the acquisition of additional land by purchase or exchange. The adoption of a program of purchase was urged particularly in eastern areas, where public timber lands no longer existed in any quantity. After several years' effort, the Weeks law was enacted (1911), authorizing the purchase of forest lands needed in the protection of the flow of navigable streams and appropriating money for such purchases. Later legislation extended the scope of these purchases. Such national forests as have been established in the eastern states have resulted mainly from the purchase program.

The total area in national forests on June 30, 1933, was about 187,000,000 acres, of which approximately 162,000,000 acres were owned by the United States, the balance of about 25,000,000 acres being in state and private ownership.[2] In 1932 the area owned by the federal government in national forests in Minnesota amounted to 1,127,051 acres.

INDIAN LANDS

Some of the lands in the United States have remained under public control as a result of policies adopted in dealing with the Indians. For a considerable time the government followed the practice of entering into treaties with the Indians for the cession of lands to the government. Under such treaties certain lands were reserved for the use of the Indians. In 1871 an act of Congress ended the making of formal treaties with the Indians and made them subject to direct legislation. The policy of setting apart reservations of land for Indian use was continued, however.

In 1887 Congress passed the allotment law, which provided for individual land grants to Indians, the land to be held by the government in trust for a time and then to be turned over to the allottee in fee simple. Allotments of considerable areas have been made to individual Indians as part of this program.[3]

[2] Annual Report of the United States Forest Service, 1933.

[3] No detailed consideration of this policy or its effects can be given here. As pointed out by the commissioner of Indian affairs (in the Annual Report of the Secretary of the Interior, 1933, p. 108), "This law in its origin was intended to be a civilizing instrument for the Indians. . . . But, in fact, the allotment law turned out to be principally an instrument to deprive the Indians of their lands. The suc-

The Indian lands in the United States include an area of about 71,000,000 acres, of which 39,000,000 acres are allotted and 32,000,000 are unallotted lands.[4] The area in Minnesota totals 1,491,026 acres, of which 935,299 acres are allotted lands and 555,727 acres are unallotted.[5]

The significance of Indian lands for a program of land utilization is that such lands, at least until title has passed fully into private hands, are subject to governmental control. It therefore becomes important that this control be so exercised as to facilitate the carrying out of satisfactory land programs in the areas where they are located.

AGRICULTURAL ADJUSTMENT PROGRAM

The current federal program of agricultural adjustment being carried out under the law approved on May 12, 1933, and activities related thereto have an important bearing on immediate land policies and, to some extent, may affect the land use program of the future.

Because of certain features inherent in agriculture, the farmer does not follow the example of many other lines of industry in a period of depression. In industry reduced outlets commonly lead to reduction of output. Farming, on the other hand, tends to maintain its production and to take the necessary readjustment in the form of reduced prices for its products. The object of the Agricultural Adjustment Act is to restore price parity for farm products, that is, to re-establish the relationship that existed in an earlier period between the prices received by farmers for a unit of commodity and the prices paid for commodities bought by farmers.[6] The chief method employed to attain this result is the curtailment of output. Funds obtained through the collection of processing

cessive steps of loss are easy to trace: Each Indian on the allotted reservations was given an allotment of about 160 acres, which was held in trust by the government for a time and then turned over in fee simple to the allottee. In most cases, the allottees sold their land to white settlers in order to have 'easy money' for quick spending. If the allottee died before the end of the trust period, the land passed to his heirs. Often there were numerous heirs, and the practicable method of settling the estate was to sell it and divide the money among the claimants. A third step in the loss of Indian land came from the disposal of so-called 'surplus' lands which were left after allotments had been made to all Indians of the reservations. These surplus lands were then opened to entry and were homesteaded by white settlers." The unsatisfactory results of this policy have led to a demand for its revision and legislation to that end has been proposed.

[4] *A National Plan for American Forestry*, 1:611 (73d Congress, 1st Session, Senate Document No. 12).

[5] *Ibid.*

[6] 1909–14, except in the case of tobacco, for which the years 1919–29 are used.

taxes may be used for benefit or rental payments to farmers in order to effect the reduction program.

For the time being, the agricultural adjustment program modifies decidedly the use of land for agricultural purposes. This is likely to be a temporary situation, however, and not one that will materially alter long-time programs of land use. The present adjustment program is designed to help farmers curtail output in a period when supplies have accumulated and prices are extremely low because of reduced domestic outlets and the disruption of foreign trade. As industrial activity recovers, domestic outlets will tend to improve. Some of the restrictions on international trade will probably be lifted. To the extent that long-time curtailment may be needed, however, it is likely to be brought about by changes in farming methods and by removing entire farms or areas from agricultural production rather than by keeping parts of farms in idleness.

Perhaps the most significant aspect of the agricultural adjustment situation is the emphasis it places upon the limitations of agricultural use of land. These limitations must be recognized in planning programs of land use. Market requirements as well as potential agricultural possibilities must be considered in dedicating additional lands to agricultural uses.

Among the longer-time programs that are in process of development at the present time is the acquisition of land that is submarginal for agricultural purposes. An allotment of funds has been made to the Federal Emergency Relief Administration to initiate such a program, and a division has been set up in the Agricultural Adjustment Administration to cooperate in carrying it out. Other federal agencies are also cooperating in this program. While governmental acquisition of land submarginal for agricultural purposes has been recommended in some quarters as a means of reducing agricultural output, the possibilities in this direction are at best limited. Such lands are not an important factor in farm production. To have any material effect, so large an area would need to be purchased that very difficult problems of human adjustments would result. Little justification can be found for buying truly submarginal land for the purposes of production adjustment. But such a program may serve highly useful ends in other ways. The land-acquisition program may be employed as an aid in overcoming the undesirable effects of scattered settlement in some areas. Settlers in such regions may be helped to locate in more advantageous sur-

roundings, and local units of government may be relieved of some
of their burdens in the process. The program may also be desirable
in so far as it releases land that can be used to good advantage for
forestry or other purposes. It undoubtedly is an important step in
the direction of better land utilization.

SUBSISTENCE HOMESTEADS

In 1933 Congress appropriated $25,000,000 for the establishment
of so-called "subsistence homesteads." [7] This term is unfortunate
in that it suggests the possibility of moving persons onto the land
under circumstances where they will become wholly self-sufficient.
This, of course, is not practicable. Modern standards of living include requirements that can be satisfied only by purchase, and for
this a cash income, either from the sale of farm products or from
other sources, is necessary. Cash is also required for meeting interest, installments on the principal, and tax obligations. The program
contemplates rather the fostering of part-time farming by persons
who have or can obtain other employment from which they will
obtain a cash income. It is not, as some persons have assumed, a
program for moving urban unemployed generally onto land. To
attempt to solve unemployment by such a process would be to
ignore the fact that there is already more than enough land in agricultural use and that to extend it greatly would be unfair to existing agriculture.

The subsistence homestead program need not receive detailed
consideration in connection with a land use program for Minnesota, for the amount of land likely to be employed in such projects
in this state is decidedly limited. Two such projects, one at Duluth
and the other at Austin, have been approved, and others may develop in the vicinity of urban centers or where work in forests may
be combined with part-time farming. But at the most they will
involve only a negligible proportion of the land area.

STATE POLICIES AND PROGRAMS

The state, like the federal government, was for a long time
primarily concerned with getting public lands into private owner-

[7] Section 208 of the National Industrial Recovery Act, reading as follows: "To
provide for aiding the redistribution of the overbalance of population in industrial
centers $25,000,000 is hereby made available to the President, to be used by him
through such agencies as he may establish and under such regulations as he may
make, for making loans and otherwise aiding in the purchase of subsistence homesteads. The moneys collected as repayment of said loans shall constitute a revolv-
ing fund to be administered as directed by the President for the purposes of this
section."

ship to stimulate development. It welcomed the sale of public lands
and settlement thereon by homesteaders. It disposed of the lands
it received from the public domain as rapidly as buyers could be
found. Federal grants of land to Minnesota totaled nearly seventeen million acres. About half of this represents grants to railroads
for the promotion of transportation. Of the balance, only a little
over two million acres remain in state ownership, mostly swamp
lands unsuited to private ownership.

As we have said, forest resources during the early days of settlement appeared to be so plentiful that there need be little concern about future requirements. But interest in forestry and the
growth of trees has been manifest for some time. As early as 1889
the legislature appropriated two thousand dollars for the use of the
Minnesota State Forestry Association in preparing and distribut-
ing a manual of information on the planting and cultivation of
trees.[8] A few years later, in 1893, a grant of three thousand dollars
was made to promote the raising of forest trees on the prairies.[9] In
1895 the legislature passed an act [10] to provide for the prevention
and suppression of forest and prairie fires, and in 1899 it recognized
the desirability of creating forest reserves, to consist "of all such
tracts and parcels of land as shall be set apart from any state lands
by the legislature for forestry purposes; or which shall be deeded,
devised, or granted to the state for forestry purposes." [11] In 1903
the State Board of Forestry was authorized to purchase lands suitable for forestry at not to exceed $2.50 an acre, "preferably at the
sources of rivers . . . but not to exceed in any one congressional
township one-eighth part of the area of such township." [12]

While this act suggests that there was a growing recognition of
the value of state forests, it reveals that the importance of setting
aside solid blocks of land was not appreciated. A grant of twenty
thousand acres of land from the United States for forestry purposes
was accepted in 1905. A constitutional amendment was proposed
by the legislature in 1913 to authorize the legislature to set aside
"such of the school and other public lands of the state as are better
adapted for the production of timber than for agriculture . . . as
state school forests, or other forests as the legislature may provide." [13] The proposed amendment was adopted at the general election in 1914, and the legislature was thereby given a limited power
to create state forests.

[8] Laws of 1889, chapter 54.
[9] Laws of 1893, chapter 241.
[10] Laws of 1895, chapter 196.
[11] Laws of 1899, chapter 214.
[12] Laws of 1903, chapter 134.
[13] Laws of 1913, chapter 592.

With the passage of time the interest in conservation has increased and the policy has been firmly established of developing state forests and protecting timber resources from destruction by forest fires. The Department of Forestry and Fire Prevention and the Fish and Game Department were established in response to such interest. More recently the various state departments for the conservation and control of lands have been brought together into one administrative unit, the Department of Conservation.

A constitutional amendment, first proposed by the legislature in 1923, authorizing legislation for special tax treatment of forest lands in order to foster private forestry, was approved by the voters in 1926. A special forest tax law was passed in 1927 under the authority granted by this amendment.[14] The Red Lake Game Preserve was created by legislative act in 1929. This measure, however, was more in the nature of assistance to counties overburdened with bonded indebtedness arising out of ill-advised drainage projects than a conservation measure. In 1931 similar assistance was provided for other areas. The 1931 legislature also established the boundaries of a number of state forests and withdrew from sale public lands located in these areas. Further provision of this nature was made by the legislature in 1933. These measures are the result of a growing recognition of the need for changed land policies in the state.

TAX DELINQUENCY

As discussed elsewhere, tax delinquency is one of the chief problems in much of the area considered in this report. Tax delinquency may be temporary, the result of an acute economic depression which for the time being wipes out the income needed for meeting the tax. An improvement in the economic situation brings such property back into the tax-paying class. On the other hand, the delinquency may be of a permanent character, as is the case with much of the land in the cut-over area. Taxes were paid as long as valuable timber remained on the land. With the removal of the timber the owners were unable or unwilling to continue meeting the tax burden, since the land was not needed for other uses. It should be obvious that these two types of tax delinquency are essentially different and call for different treatment. Delinquency of the second type is frequently more a problem of land use than one of taxation.

[14] Laws of 1927, chapter 247.

The tendency has been to temporize with the problem of tax delinquency by permitting "bargain" settlements, the assumption having been that it was better to obtain some revenue than none at all and that it was important to return delinquent land to the tax rolls in order to obtain future revenue from it. Mounting delinquency, however, set limits to the continuance of such a policy. In 1927 the legislature [15] provided that title to land remaining delinquent for five years should revert to the state to "be held by it in trust for each and all the tax districts interested in the taxes and assessments, penalties, interest, and costs accrued therein." The act further provided that "all such parcels of land becoming the absolute property of the state, in trust as aforesaid, under the provisions of this act, shall be classified and appraised by the county under the supervision of the state auditor, as agricultural and nonagricultural, and shall be sold by the state, at not less than the appraised price." The time at which this act should become effective was later extended to 1935.

The trend has been toward a recognition of the need for a policy that would fit the facts of the case. While many inconsistencies still exist, indications are that definite progress has been made. For one thing, there is a growing realization that bargain settlement of taxes for the purpose of retaining property on the tax rolls fails to attain its object if recurring delinquency is the consequence, and that bargain settlement may in fact be a cause of recurring delinquency, because taxpayers may come to regard it as a means of scaling down their tax bills. There is, therefore, a growing sentiment that such settlements are unwise and that they should be discontinued.

The viewpoint also is gaining ground that land reverting through tax delinquency should be sold only if private ownership is desirable and is likely to become permanent. The undesirability of sale of tax-delinquent land that will result in an unnecessary scattering of settlement, and of land not suited to private development, should be self-evident.

In short, the policy of handling tax-delinquent lands is in a transition stage. The defects of past methods are becoming more evident, and it is being recognized that tax delinquency may be a phase of land use. In the future we may expect that the problem will more frequently be attacked from the point of view of land utilization.

[15] Laws of 1927, chapter 119. See also Laws of 1929, chapter 415.

LOCAL INDEBTEDNESS

Local units of government frequently resort to borrowing as a means of financing various activities and improvements. When such improvements are really self-liquidating, and the benefits derived from them justify the outlay and extend over a period of time, this method of financing is satisfactory if it is not overdone. These limitations are less likely to be recognized in a new and developing area than in one that is already well established. The former frequently has expectations of development and growth in population and an increasing tax base. The existing taxpaying ability may not be great enough to pay for the schools and roads which are needed at the moment and which it is believed will be needed to take care of expected growth. Drainage and other land reclamation projects may be undertaken at public expense as part of the development program. If it later develops that anticipation has exceeded realization, the local debt burden may not only become heavy but may even become unbearable, with the result that taxes on some of the property remain unpaid and the tax load on the rest is increased. Under such circumstances an acute situation may arise. This is what has happened in some parts of northern Minnesota.

Where such a situation develops, the question arises as to whether or not it is a matter of direct concern to the state as a whole. Should the state ignore the difficulties of local units in meeting their indebtedness or should it assume responsibility for these debts and participate in their retirement? Various considerations enter into the problem. Default by local units may affect the credit standing of other local units and perhaps even that of the state itself. To the extent that this occurs, the results are not without concern to the people generally. Moreover, while the state has no direct financial responsibility for debts incurred by local units as a result of their own policies, it is in some cases partly responsible for the situation because it has permitted, if not actually encouraged, the adoption of certain policies resulting in debt creation. A case in point is that of drainage ditches. An act of the legislature made these ditches possible. The theory was that the improvements would be self-liquidating through the collection of special assessments on the benefited properties and that the counties which issued their bonds to finance such projects were merely lending the use of their credit. But when the special assessments went unpaid, the burden of retiring the bonds fell back on the counties. Under such circumstances the state may be charged with some responsibility for the situation.

It was the recognition of this responsibility that caused the legislature of 1929 to provide for the creation of the Red Lake Game Preserve as a means of taking over certain lands and assuming the indebtedness outstanding against them as a result of drainage projects.[16] The following quotation from this legislative act is indicative of the reasoning on this point.

Whereas, pursuant to such laws [relating to drainage ditches] the counties of Beltrami, Lake of the Woods, and Koochiching have heretofore incurred obligations to finance and refinance such ditches upon lands which it now appears were and are not suitable for agriculture, and the assessments levied upon lands supposedly benefited thereby cannot be collected in a sum sufficient to pay such bonds and the payment of such bonds by the use of the taxing powers of such counties would result in confiscatory rates such that taxes so levied would not be paid, and

Whereas, default in the payment of such bonds by such counties is imminent, and the general credit of the State of Minnesota and all its political subdivisions and municipal corporations would thereby be damaged, resulting in greatly added interest charges on all public financing for many years to come, and

Whereas, certain lands in said counties hereinafter described will become available for state ownership by reason of delinquent tax liens thereon, and such lands are suitable for state ownership and administration for use as a wild life preserve and hunting ground and other state purposes, and will produce revenues to assist in relieving the tax burdens and preventing such bond default.

Under the provisions of this act the state assumed the obligations outstanding against certain lands for drainage developments and in return acquired full title to the lands involved. This policy was extended to other lands by an act of 1931.[17]

While no policy has been evolved with regard to the state's relationship to local debts generally, various aspects of the problem have received considerable attention. Some have urged that the state should make an annual payment to local units of government in lieu of taxes on land controlled by the state. Some would extend this policy to tax-delinquent land generally. But such an arrangement, it will be seen, would be purely arbitrary; payments would have no direct relationship to local needs or to the state's responsibility for the local situation. It would be unfortunate if the state should obligate itself to such annual payments. Where land is taken over by the state for a specific purpose, settlement with the local units on the basis of its reasonable value in such use may be justified. It would also seem reasonable to require that such pay-

[16] Laws of 1929, chapter 258.
[17] Laws of 1931, chapter 407.

ments be applied first to existing local debt rather than to current operating expenses.[18]

School Aid

Another state policy bearing directly upon the land use problem is that of providing state aid for the support of local educational facilities. State aid is a recognition of the fact that education is not purely a matter of local concern, that the state generally is interested in having educational opportunities available to all its children of school age. Education is a matter of general interest not only because all the people have economic, social, and governmental relationships but also because of the mobility of the population. The long-time trend of population movement has been from rural areas to urban centers. The latter have a direct concern in the education of its future population, and it is not unfair that they should participate in its cost.

We are not primarily concerned here, however, with the general philosophy back of state aid but rather with the effect of such aid on land use problems. State aid has made it possible to establish and maintain schools in localities where school facilities would otherwise have been lacking entirely or would at least have been of decidedly lower quality. Such aid is, of course, desirable where settlement and development is justified. But the provisions of legislative acts do not always permit of sufficient adaptation in the granting of aid to make it serve the ends of most desirable land use. Thus state aid may sometimes help to maintain an uneconomic school organization. Desirable reorganization may be hindered or retarded because it might result in the loss to the communities involved of some of the state aid being supplied under existing laws. Transportation aid also has sometimes encouraged the scattering of settlement and when it does so it may operate contrary to desirable land use programs. It is consequently important that state aid for schools, roads, and other purposes be granted and administered in such a way that it will support rather than interfere with the land program. Although these adjustments are still to be worked out, their importance is gaining wider recognition, and the indications are that progress will be made toward a more unified program.

[18] For further treatment of this matter the reader is referred to the recommendations and report of the Governor's Committee on Land Utilization, *Land Utilization in Minnesota : A State Program for the Cut-Over Lands* (The University of Minnesota Press, 1934). See especially pages 29–30 and chapter 12.

LAND CLASSIFICATION

Classification of lands generally has not been provided for by legislative action. The desirability of classification, however, has been recognized in various acts. Thus an act [19] passed by the 1927 legislature relating to tax-delinquent land provides that land becoming state property through tax delinquency "shall be classified and appraised by the county under the supervision of the state auditor, as agricultural and non-agricultural." This provision does not, of course, contemplate any comprehensive classification but rather a grouping of specific parcels of land into agricultural or non-agricultural as a basis of sale. In another measure passed at the same session the legislature authorized the commissioner of forestry and fire prevention "to examine, classify, and make a list or tabulation of all lands owned by the state which are suitable for afforestation or reforestation." [20] This measure likewise relates only to certain of the lands in state ownership.

The Committee on Land Utilization appointed by the Governor in 1932 recommended, in an interim report made on February 24, 1933, legislation to create a permanent State Land Use Committee and to authorize the creation of county land classification committees "with powers to consult, advise, and cooperate with the State Land Use Committee in the classification of lands and land policies." [21] This recommendation led to the passage by the legislature of an act [22] creating a Land Use Committee consisting of the governor, the chairman of the Conservation Commission, the commissioners of conservation, agriculture, education, and highways, and the chairman of the Tax Commission. The act provided in part that "it shall be the duty of said Land Use Committee to classify all public and private lands in the state with reference to the use to which such lands are adapted, but principally as to adaptability to present known uses such as agriculture and forestry." This legislation also provided, as had been suggested by the Committee on Land Utilization, for county committees in counties in which 25 per cent or more of the land was tax delinquent or in state or national ownership, such committees to consist of the county auditor, the chairman of the board of county commissioners, the county treasurer, the county surveyor, and the county superintendent of schools. The statement of the duties and powers of the county

[19] Laws of 1927, chapter 119.
[20] Laws of 1927, chapter 248.
[21] *Land Utilization in Minnesota*, pp. 258–59.
[22] Laws of 1933, chapter 436.

Classification Committee provided for cooperation between the state and the county committee, but apparently left final determination in the hands of the latter. In order to clear up the uncertainty, the Committee on Land Utilization in its final report recommended that this legislation "be amended so as to make it clear that the final and controlling voice in land classification rests in the State Land Use Committee," on the ground that "the interests of both the counties and the state demand uniformity of policy and method in land classification. This is assured only if there is united control." [23] When this point is cleared up, the necessary authority for classification will be established, although some financial support may need to be provided before much activity in classification will take place.

Another legislative act [24] having some bearing on classification is that authorizing the county board of any county to establish, with the approval of the Conservation Commission, conservation and agricultural zones for the purpose "of consolidating the holdings of land owned by the state absolutely or in trust which were acquired under the delinquent tax laws, and for the purpose of decreasing the expenses of local governmental units by reducing the number of scattered and isolated private holdings." Provisions were included to authorize the exchange of state-owned land in agricultural zones for privately owned land in conservation zones.

ZONING LEGISLATION

In many cities and villages zoning restrictions governing land use have been in force for a considerable time and have become accepted and established as a definite part of a well-ordered urban program. The application of such restrictions to rural lands, however, is still in its infancy. The first reaction of some persons to such a program is that it is unjustified interference with the use to which a man may devote his own property. While that may be a perfectly natural reaction, it overlooks the fact that the public has interests in the matter and that it has a right to see that those interests are safeguarded. Some persons refer to the pioneering spirit of those who go to the outposts of existing settlement and undertake to hew themselves a farm out of the wilderness. They are said to be following in the footsteps of the early pioneers who paved the way for the development of this country. But there is a vital differ-

[23] *Land Utilization in Minnesota*, p. 28.
[24] Laws of 1933, chapter 418.

ence that needs to be kept in mind. The early pioneers were really self-reliant. They did not expect nor receive assistance in the way of schools, roads, or other public services. Such services are part of our modern standards. We want people to have them and we seek to provide them. In order that the burden may not become too great, the public has a right to insist that the individual so adjust his program that the services can be provided for him without undue expense.

It is the growing recognition of the relationship between land use and public interest that has led to a consideration of zoning restrictions for certain rural lands. Wisconsin has passed an enabling act giving counties authority to zone land.[25] Subsection 1 of this act (Section 59.97, Wisconsin Statutes) reads in part:

> The county board of any county may by ordinance regulate, restrict, and determine the areas within which agriculture, forestry, and recreation may be conducted, the location of roads, schools, trades, and industries, and the location of buildings designed for specific uses, and establish districts of such number, shape, and area, and may also establish set-back building lines, outside the limits of incorporated villages and cities, as such county board may deem best suited to carry out the purposes of this section.

Under this law various counties in Wisconsin having problems of land use substantially similar to those of northern Minnesota are proceeding to restrict settlement and agricultural development in some districts. Such restriction does not extend to land already in agricultural use; the limitation applies to new, not to existing uses. By this process, settlement can be kept concentrated in areas best suited for agriculture. Economies can be effected in providing schools, roads, and other services. Forest fires can be reduced. Community life can be improved and settlers can be directed to better lands.

While Minnesota does not at this writing have a law providing specifically for the zoning of rural lands, a growing sentiment for such authorization is evident, and it seems likely that the needed legislation will soon be adopted. Zoning offers the means of making a program of land use effective. It is the logical accompaniment of land classification.

LOCAL POLICIES

While it is true that many aspects of land use problems can be dealt with only by state or federal action, it must not be over-

[25] For details of the program see the special circular of the Extension Service, College of Agriculture, University of Wisconsin, entitled *Making the Best Use of Wisconsin Land through Zoning.*

looked that local units of government have an important part to play. For one thing, the cooperation of local officials and citizens is necessary to the successful operation of many features of the program of the larger units. Such programs must always keep the local point of view in mind. With respect to some problems the initiative and execution of programs must come primarily if not entirely from the local units. One of the problems encountered in most localities having serious land use difficulties is the tax burden. While this is by no means solely a local matter, it is primarily that because taxes collected in such areas are expended chiefly for local purposes. The taxable wealth is usually limited because of the lack of development. The property tax for state purposes is applied at a uniform rate over the entire state, consequently the amount of the general property tax for state support is low where the taxable wealth is low. Local requirements, however, usually force the rate of taxes for local purposes to a high point, making the local expenditures of greater importance than those for the state as a whole.

Concrete illustrations of this point may easily be obtained by comparing tax bills of property in different localities. Some years ago the state auditor published illustrative tax statements from each of the counties of the state.[26] According to this publication a certain farmer owning a quarter section of land in Rock County in southwestern Minnesota had a taxable valuation of $6,445 and a total real estate tax of $103.76. Of this total, $34.42 was the state tax, $40.33 was for county purposes, $6.45 went to the township, and $22.56 to the school district. Another farmer in Koochiching County in northern Minnesota with a quarter section had a taxable valuation of $1,311. The tax bill of this second man was $227.85. Because his valuation was not much over a fifth of the first man's, his payment for state purposes was only about a fifth as large, or $7.01. His county tax, however, was $69.29, his township tax $31.20, and the school district tax $120.35. In other words, state taxes made up 33 per cent of the Rock County farmer's tax bill, whereas they represented only 3 per cent of the total of the Koochiching farmer's tax.

This comparison emphasizes the fact that adjustments in the tax burden in cut-over areas are primarily the problem of local units of government rather than that of the state. There has been a definite trend toward reduction of expenditures by local units in

[26] Ray P. Chase, State Auditor, *Your Taxes*, 1930.

recent years. Much of this reduction has come from reduction in services, improvements, and payrolls. Increasing consideration is being given, however, to the possibilities of achieving economies through reorganization of services, especially in the school system. Most of the schools throughout Minnesota are operated as local schools and the possibilities of economies without serious impairment of efficiency are limited. Where the school unit is a larger area, as in Koochiching County, for instance, greater possibilities for economies have developed. Through a coordination of schools, better school facilities are being provided at lower costs. An appreciation of this fact should gain support for the establishment of larger school districts.

Where the population is scattered and the tax base small, the township government may find it difficult to render effective service except at a relatively heavy cost. This has led to the dissolution of townships in some cases. Many people would oppose the discontinuance of townships generally, for frequently the township unit is thought of as an integral part of our democratic form of government. But this reasoning hardly applies to situations where settlement is so scattered that there is little real need for these units. There is also a growing tendency to regard certain services, such as road construction and maintenance, as the function of counties or larger units. Such rearrangements can be achieved without township dissolution where local interests are ready to take such a step.

LIMITATIONS OF PRESENT POLICIES

The preceding brief review is indicative of a need for taking stock of existing policies of land use and for developing new policies that will deal more adequately with the problem. The fact that there is a need for improvements in land use and that this need is receiving extensive consideration attests further to the inadequacy of some of the present policies in dealing with the situation. The purpose of Part II of this report is to point out some of the changes that are desirable.

PART II

PROPOSED POLICIES AND PROGRAMS
OF ADJUSTMENT

CHAPTER VI

LAND CLASSIFICATION AND ZONING *

Experience has shown that uncontrolled private initiative in the use of land may lead to many economic and social evils. Many of the problems and difficulties described in the foregoing chapters can be traced to improper or untimely use of land. To a large extent these problems and difficulties, and the human suffering they have entailed, could have been avoided if a wiser policy of land settlement had been adopted. To review the mistakes of the past or to elaborate upon a land policy which, in retrospect, would seem to have been better than the course actually pursued would be, for the present purpose, futile. We are faced with concrete problems, and the task is to develop plans of action that will enable us to cope effectively with these problems.

The problems of land use planning are in many ways analogous to those that confront the individual farmer in organizing his farm business. The prudent farmer in planning a new farm business takes a careful inventory of the various fields embraced by his farm, noting differences in the texture and fertility of the soil, topography, drainage, shape, and location. On the basis of this inventory a cropping system is adopted that provides the best combination for the utilization of the various fields, allowances being made, of course, for prospective prices, labor, power and equipment requirements, and other factors having a bearing on the choice of enterprises. An identical problem, although one of much greater magnitude, faces the nation, the states, and local units in the utilization of available natural resources. It is just as essential for governmental units to have plans for the future utilization of lands as it is for farmers to have plans for the use of the land in their farms.

Two broad lines of action are needed: first, measures of a preventive nature designed to prevent repetition of mistakes in the settlement and use of land; and second, measures of a corrective nature designed to facilitate normal economic adjustments and to conserve as much as possible the human, institutional, and material resources involved. Although in an emergency considerable re-

* This chapter has been prepared by R. I. Nowell.

liance must be placed upon remedial measures in order to meet pressing and immediate problems of relief and adjustment, for purposes of permanent land use planning, measures of a preventive sort appear to give most promise of lasting benefits. Of various preventive measures, land classification provides an essential and substantial basis for the development of plans for future land use.

LAND CLASSIFICATION

The term "land classification" is ordinarily used loosely to cover land and economic inventories, land use planning, and zoning. As a matter of fact, there are three distinct phases of the problem, and it is important that each be clearly recognized. An economic inventory is usually a distinct job of assembling essential data regarding ownership, tax delinquency, etc., and of mapping soil types, vegetative cover, topography, location of farms, and other physical features of the area. Having the inventory, the next job is to formulate plans for future land use and to classify the lands covered by the inventory into appropriate use districts. Land use planning and land classification are in a sense synonymous terms. As Lovejoy has said,[1] "classification and land planning go hand in hand, for classification is essentially purposive; it looks to the attainment of some end and hence includes planning." Zoning is a device that gives legal effect to land use plans. It is a form of social control over the use of private property in the interests of the general welfare. In the absence of zoning, control over land use must be secured by public ownership, which is a rather costly method if applied generally.

The Need for Land Classification

Land classification, given legal effect through zoning ordinances, provides a method for directing new settlement to the better agricultural lands and for effecting a rational redistribution of the population of the country. The evils of unplanned settlement, manifest in many parts of the country, are illustrated by conditions in northern Minnesota. Every year there is a trickle of new settlement into the cut-over lands of the northern counties as well as an exodus of families who, finding it impossible to obtain an adequate living from the soil, become discouraged. In years of depression the trickle of new settlement enlarges to a fair-sized stream. Unfortunately much of the new settlement is on old abandoned places

[1] P. S. Lovejoy, "Theory and Practice in Land Classification," *Journal of Land and Public Utility Economics,* 1:160–75 (1925).

or on wild land physically unfit for farming. Some of these new
settlers take up poor land because, having had no previous farming experience, they lack judgment. On the other hand, many
people buy poor rather than good land because it is cheaper and
can be purchased on easier terms. Others are led by high-pressure
salesmanship into accepting places unadapted to farming. Still
others have sometimes chosen poor isolated places deliberately,
expecting to secure remuneration from the school board for transporting their children to school or from the county or township for
work on the roads.

The costs to the locality and to the state of maintaining for
these isolated families roads and schools that might otherwise be
eliminated frequently amount to many times the tax contribution
of such families, as is shown in Table 29, which gives the figures for
twenty-eight isolated cases selected from the records of the superintendent of schools of St. Louis County. The cost to the public of
transporting the children of these twenty-eight families to school
was $185.61 per family. The assessed value of their property was
$85.64 per farm and their annual tax levy was only $10.06 per farm.
Even if the total tax levy had been collected in 1932, it would have
amounted to only 5.4 per cent of the cost of school transportation.
Actually only 61.8 per cent of the levy was collected, or 3.4 per cent
of the transportation bill incurred especially for these families, to
say nothing of the maintenance of roads and schools.

In Table 30 are presented thirteen cases in which roads are provided at public expense for the sole use of one or two families. For
this group the average annual public cost of roads amounted to
$90.88 per family, the tax levy to $19.14, and 1932 collections to
only $7.03. The levy amounted to 21 per cent of the cost of the
special service and the total tax collection to only 7.7 per cent.
Again the costs of providing transportation, schools, and services
other than roads have been omitted from consideration.

Families that are unable to earn their livelihood are a burden
on the public. By directing new settlement to productive lands, not
only is the potential relief burden reduced but the settler becomes
a prospective taxpayer, that is, an asset to the county and state
rather than a liability.

Boards of county commissioners are continually harassed by
property owners demanding extension and repair of roads in undeveloped areas where costs of construction are high and the number
to be served by such roads is extremely small. Where there are no

TABLE 29.—SPECIAL TRANSPORTATION COSTS ATTRIBUTABLE TO TWENTY-EIGHT ISOLATED FAMILIES IN ST. LOUIS COUNTY FOR THE SCHOOL YEAR 1931–32

Case No.	No. of Children	Distance to School in Miles	Special Transportation Cost Attributable to Family	Ownership Status	Assessed Value of Property*	Tax Levy	Tax Collections, 1932
1	3	3.00	$159.60	Tenant	$ 80.00	$ 9.89	Delinquent
2	2	2.50	98.80	Tenant	80.00	9.89	$9.89
3	2	4.00	154.70	Owner	80.00	9.89	9.89
4	5	2.00	193.30	Tenant	80.00	9.89	Delinquent
5	4	2.00	332.00	Tenant	....	....	Delinquent
6	2	....	} 344.00	Tenant	54.00	8.12	$2.10
7	4	....		Owner	62.00	9.32	9.32
8	4	5.50	259.00	Tenant	80.00	8.06	Delinquent
9	2	9.75	} 454.60	Owner	274.00	31.49	$31.49
10	7	2.00		Owner	319.00	39.42	39.42
11	1	11.75	78.58	Owner	113.00	11.39	5.69
12	3	11.00	228.69	Owner	78.00	7.86	7.86
13	1	11.25	77.96	Owner	103.00	10.38	Delinquent
14	2	11.50	159.39	Owner	103.00	10.38	$10.38
15	1	12.25	84.93	Owner	27.00	2.72	2.72
16	4	6.75	291.25	Tenant	115.00	13.01	Delinquent
17	2	3.00	226.26	Tenant	81.00	9.01	$9.01
18	1	2.00	75.42	Owner	52.00	5.24	5.24
19	3	2.50	240.00	Tenant	84.00	10.95	10.95
20	1	5.50	182.50	Owner	100.00	13.04	Delinquent
21	4	4.50	} 338.00	Tenant	72.00	9.89	Delinquent
22	4	4.50		Owner	144.00	18.78	Delinquent
23	3	8.00	346.00	State land	....	....	Delinquent
24	1	12.75	78.36	Tenant	27.00	2.94	2.94
25	1	12.75	78.36	Tenant	107.00	11.65	$11.65
26	1	11.50	70.95	Owner	27.00	2.94	2.94
27	1	15.50	128.80	Tenant }			
28	4	15.50	515.20	Tenant }	56.00	5.64	5.64
Average	2.6	7.00	$185.61		$85.64	$10.06	$6.22

* Represents 33.3 per cent of the true and full value.

140

TABLE 30.— SPECIAL ROAD COSTS ATTRIBUTABLE TO THIRTEEN ISOLATED FAMILIES IN ST. LOUIS COUNTY, 1932

Case No.	Road Maintenance for Family in Miles	Annual Cost			Assessed Value of Property*	Levy Tax	Tax Collection 1932
		Maintenance	Snow Plowing	Total			
1	2	$ 50.00	......	$ 50.00	$207.00	$36.48	$36.48
2	2	70.00	$50.00	120.00	{ 165.00	17.07	17.07
3					241.00	24.92	Delinquent
4	1	25.00	......	25.00	170.00	19.86	$19.86
5	2	50.00	......	50.00	234.00	18.74	Delinquent
6	1	25.00	......	25.00	157.00	17.95	$17.95
7	3½	87.50	......	87.50	165.00	16.63	Delinquent
8	3½	122.50	85.50	208.00	{ 241.00	19.36	Delinquent
9					73.00	5.86	Delinquent
10	3	275.00	93.00	368.00	{ 144.00	18.78	Delinquent
11					244.00	31.82	Delinquent
12	2	186.00	62.00	248.00	{ 136.00	10.15	Delinquent
13					150.00	11.19	Delinquent
Average	1.54	$68.54	$22.35	$ 90.88	$179.00	$19.14	$7.03

* Represents 33⅓ per cent of true and full value.

land use plans and zoning ordinances, the county commissioners either grant these requests or refuse on the basis of lack of funds, such refusal usually constituting a commitment to provide the service as soon as funds become available. Similarly, local or county school boards are frequently confronted with requests for new schools in areas where only four or five pupils reside. In such cases the annual cost of minimum facilities and teaching services ranges from $200 to $300 or more per child, as compared with perhaps $50 to $75 in areas of denser population. The extension of school transportation lines, while it is usually the cheapest plan, requires added expenditure for road maintenance and snowplowing during the winter months. Well-conceived land use plans supported by zoning ordinances provide helpful guides to county, town, and school boards in deciding upon new road and school facilities.[2]

Land use plans and zoning ordinances, in so far as they check or decrease the numbers of isolated settlers living in forested areas, are also of real benefit to the conservation movement. The isolated settler in his clearing operations constitutes one of the most serious of fire hazards. Such people are usually unsympathetic toward reforestation programs, since their most pressing need is for more cleared land for the production of crops. Although difficult to prove, there are grounds for suspecting that settlers have even started fires deliberately in order to secure employment with the state in fighting fires. Timber stealing and game poaching are also indulged in by some isolated settlers. Frequently the productivity of the settler's farm is so low that these transgressions may be the only alternatives to starvation.

If the tax delinquency law of 1927 as amended in 1933 remains unaltered, the state will gain title to perhaps seven million acres of tax-delinquent land in 1935 and to additional acreages in subsequent years. Probably the most perplexing problem facing the state is what to do with this huge acreage. Lack of an adequate answer was an important factor in having the date of reversion extended two years at the legislative session of 1933. Several colonization and homesteading plans designed to return the land immediately to the tax rolls have been advanced. Most of these plans overlook the fact that land has reverted to the state because of maladjustments in use and the prevailing system of taxation. Unless these maladjustments are corrected, attempts to return the

[2] See Chapter XI for a more complete discussion of the effects of zoning on road and school costs.

land to the tax rolls will prove futile. Land use planning and zoning point the direction in which the state must proceed to manage this huge newly acquired domain.

As evidenced by legislation now on the statute books, land classification has been recognized as an essential step in the formulation of a land use policy, but the methods of classification most appropriate and the legal instruments necessary to give force to the classification have not been clearly visualized.[3] The laws of 1927 relative to tax-forfeited lands instructed counties to appraise and classify, under the supervision of the state auditor, all parcels of forfeited land either as agricultural or non-agricultural. The difficulties of such a classification were pointed out in the interim report of the Governor's Land Utilization Committee in January, 1933.[4] The legislature then in session authorized the county boards to classify all land of the county into agricultural zones and conservation zones,[5] but did not provide authority for actual zoning.

METHODS OF LAND CLASSIFICATION

Land classification in the broad sense of the term, as explained above, involves land use planning, and therefore many factors other than the physical qualities of the land must be considered in arriving at the classification. In the first place, the classification should be on the basis of considerable areas rather than specific parcels of land. Broad land use districts, each representing the best use that could be made of a major portion of the land within it, should be established. In glaciated areas large bodies of agricultural land are interspersed with small pieces that are not adapted to agricultural use. To pick out small pieces, say of forty or eighty acres each, within an agricultural zone and classify them as non-agricultural would be a useless refinement of the plan. Administration of such small pieces as conservation areas would be most difficult. It would be equally unwise to classify as agricultural small "islands" of good land located in the midst of a forest removed from other settlement, roads, and schools. The cost of providing services to such "islands" would be far out of proportion to the advantages gained from their use for agriculture. A classification by specific legal descriptions as apparently contemplated in the tax delinquency law of 1927 would lead to many such difficulties.

[3] See the sections on classification and zoning in the previous chapter.
[4] See *Land Utilization in Minnesota*, p. 250.
[5] Session Laws, 1933, chapter 418.

In the second place, the classification should be simple, especially at first, involving no greater number of use districts than are actually necessary. Plans must be flexible, and refinements in the form of additional use districts can be added later as circumstances require. If the classification is simple, there will be much less difficulty in drawing the boundaries of the districts. Moreover, local support is more readily enlisted for a simple classification than for a complicated one, and the task of administration is simplified. The legal enforceability of zoning ordinances depends largely upon the reasonableness of the restrictions imposed. It is easier to prove a simple classification to be reasonable than a complicated one. Finally, most advantages of land use planning and zoning can be obtained as well with a simple classification as with more elaborate ones.

Land use plans must be flexible. Unpredictable future developments might easily render obsolete the best of plans predicated upon present economic and social conditions. New uses or new markets for agricultural products might conceivably change the entire land use picture. Technical improvements frequently have far-reaching effects. Plans should be sufficiently flexible to permit of refinements and revisions whenever changed conditions dictate. As needs develop for additional agricultural lands, restrictions should be removed first from the best of the unused areas. Conversely, if future events result in a continuing surplus of cultivated land, the poorest areas in cultivation should gradually be retired from production. To be workable, a land use program must include provisions for keeping the plans in balanced adjustment with changing economic conditions.

Physical, social, and economic conditions are so different in various parts of the nation that the same methods of land classification cannot be used everywhere with equal success. Factors that are very important in some states have little or no significance in others. To illustrate, in New York, where several generations of farmers have tried repeatedly to farm practically all the land, classifications may be based largely upon human experience. By the process of trial and error, appropriate land use districts have gradually emerged. In terms of human labor and effort this has been a costly method. In the land classification work of New York State the size and condition of farm buildings are regarded, among other factors, as indications of the productivity of the land and the returns from farming. Similarly, the present use of land, being the result of a long period of experimentation by farmers, is regarded as evidence of what are the most profitable uses for land of different character. These two factors, the condition of buildings and present land use, are given much weight in New York in laying out land use districts.

In the state of Washington, on the other hand, where large areas of timber land have only in recent years been cut over for the first time and settlement has never been attempted, the criteria used in New York would have little, if any, application. There the soil survey must be relied upon as the chief basis of classification. In Wisconsin, where land classification work is well advanced and where conditions are somewhat intermediate between those in New York and Washington, the following criteria are used: (1) tax delinquency by stages, (2) location of farms, both operating and abandoned, (3) landownership and land entered under the state forest crop law, (4) location of schools, school district boundaries, and school bus lines, and (5) the soils map showing main soil types.

In all states careful study must be made of the various physical, economic, and social factors involved. The office analysis must be followed by field inspection and interviews with local people. Those factors must be considered and methods used that seem most significant for the particular area being studied. In general it may be said that the greater the amount of information available about an area the easier it is to draw reasonable and workable plans for land use. The customary land use survey provides adequate information as a basis for land classification, but in the past such surveys have been comparatively expensive. While they are useful, they are by no means indispensable, and counties that do not have them need not wait to classify their land until such studies are made; land use maps can usually be prepared and zoning ordinances adopted at very small cost by drawing upon available data and adopting some short-cut methods.

A Tentative Classification of Fourteen Northeastern Minnesota Counties

In 1933 boards of county commissioners were authorized by the legislature to establish conservation zones and agricultural zones.[6] In the words of the act: "Conservation zones shall be areas which are to be devoted primarily to timber growing and other conservation purposes. Agricultural zones shall be areas devoted primarily

[6] Session Laws, 1933, chapter 418.

to agricultural purposes." One or two of the county boards appointed land classification committees which attempted to classify their respective counties. The methods used were different in each county, and little was accomplished because the legislature failed to pass a zoning act to give legal force and sanction to the established classification.

The task of preparing tentative classifications for the various counties was undertaken as a part of the present study, with a view to furnishing county boards tentative classifications all prepared on the same basis by workers qualified for the task. Figures 25–38, pages 159–172, are maps of the fourteen counties showing suggested conservation zones in cross-hatch and agricultural zones in white. The conservation zones represent either (1) lands that because of their physical characteristics appear, in the light of present and prospective economic conditions, to be unable to yield a net return from agricultural use or (2) lands so located that it would impose an undue burden upon the public to provide school, road, and other services if new settlement were permitted at the present time.

A wide range of natural conditions is found in the northern counties; at one extreme are conditions that positively exclude agriculture; at the other, conditions that are very favorable to agriculture. Between the two are numerous intermediate stages. A gradual blending from one stage to the next occurs, the transition usually being difficult to detect. The boundaries of zones must therefore be fixed rather arbitrarily. At the boundary line conditions may be essentially the same on both sides, but a short distance away rather sharp differences in natural and economic conditions may be observed.

In arriving at the zone boundaries shown on the maps the following methods were employed. All lands in farms were first mapped on township plats (scale one inch to the mile) from the township assessment books on file in the county courthouses. Each piece of land having assessed improvements was marked with a cross, and all adjoining lands under the same ownership were shaded. Working one township at a time, the settlement pattern was studied in relation to the soils map, roads, schools, and cover. A first approximation of the zone boundary was then drawn in, attempt being made to separate, so far as possible, the settled from the unsettled parts of the township. The preliminary boundaries were next transferred from the plat maps to a county base map.

In this form the map was presented to various county officials having first-hand information concerning the county for their criti-cisms and suggestions. Some of their suggestions were incorporated directly, others were noted for closer field investigation. Among the officials usually consulted were the county agricultural agent, the highway engineer, workers in charge of relief, the superintendent of schools, state forest rangers, and occasionally members of the board of county commissioners. These interviews were particu-larly helpful in locating settled areas that are too poor to support families. Of great value in this connection were the testimonies of county relief workers. These interviews also were helpful in locat-ing unsettled areas of exceptionally good agricultural land.

Following the interviews with local officials the zone boundaries were checked in the field, both by inspection and by interviews with well-informed local residents. The men working on this phase of the study were trained in farm management research and were capable of recognizing and evaluating the various soil types. In the checking work townships were again the unit of study. No check-ing was done in townships falling definitely within either the con-servation or agricultural zones. Thus the field work was limited to the townships adjacent to or including zone boundaries. Efforts were made to traverse the important roads in each township and to actually see as much of the land as possible. Limitations of time and personnel, however, prevented complete accomplishment of this objective.

The present or previous township assessor was generally found to be the best informed man in the township. He was usually the first and occasionally the only man consulted. If the assessor seemed well informed and no differences of opinion were encoun-tered in deciding on zone boundaries, the field man immediately passed on to the next township. Where the field man questioned the observations or judgments of the assessor, however, efforts were made to interview one or more other residents of the town-ship and to inspect personally the disputed boundaries.

Maps showing the location of farms, roads, schools, etc., as well as the preliminary zone boundaries for each township were carried in loose-leaf notebooks by field men. Answers to the following list of questions were usually secured in the course of interviews:

1. Is this map of settlers and their farm lands correct for your township?
2. Describe soils, topography, and stoniness of each section in the township.
3. Are there undeveloped areas in this township on which farming could now be developed with a fair degree of success?

4. Which areas of this township now developed should not have been developed? Why?

5. Which wild or undeveloped parts, if any, of this township should not be developed at the present time? Why?

6. Are the isolated settlers making as good a living as those in the better developed areas?

7. Where are the most serious relief cases in the township?

8. Describe briefly the type of farming in different parts of the township.

9. What are the principal sources of farm income?

10. Does the line on this map indicate the approximate boundary between the fairly good farm land and rather poor farm land in your township?

11. If new farm settlement were to be restricted in this poor land area, what change in the boundary line would you suggest?

Answers were not written out during interviews but occasional notes were jotted down, and a rather complete summary prepared later. Frequent conferences of the men checking boundaries were held at night to make certain that all workers were treating similar problems in a similar way.

In all questionable settled areas boundaries were drawn in favor of the agricultural zone except where such doubtful areas were located within designated state or national forests. In cases of questionable wild land, conservation zones were usually given the benefit of the doubt. Attempts were made throughout to give due consideration to factors other than soil, such as proximity to roads, schools, markets, resorts, industries, etc. Thus, for example, in central Cass County there is considerable resort development around the lakes. Vacationists furnish farmers in this locality a market for small fruits, vegetables, poultry products, and milk. With this special market farmers are able to get along fairly well, and the area is classified as agricultural even though the soil and topography are not well adapted to farming. Numerous similar cases elsewhere in the fourteen counties were treated in the same way.

Tax delinquency maps showing delinquency by stages were available for all counties but for several reasons were seldom used. In the first place, many parcels of relatively worthless land held by nonresidents were found to be tax paid. Elsewhere taxes were paid on wild lands by timber companies until such lands could be logged of cordwood or second growth material. After the land is logged, tax payments usually stop abruptly, and in such areas the delinquency map is merely a reflection of logging operations. The prevailing system of making delinquent tax abatements has led to rather widespread voluntary delinquency, with the result that important acreages of good land have become delinquent in anticipation of bargain settlements. Differences in the rates of assessment are also reflected in the amount of delinquency.

The zone boundaries in Hubbard County are based entirely upon data collected for the economic surveys in 1929 and 1930. Data for this county are so complete that field-checking of boundaries at this stage was not considered necessary.

TABLE 31. — LAND AREA IN SUGGESTED AGRICULTURAL AND CONSERVATION ZONES IN 14 NORTHEASTERN COUNTIES

COUNTY	ACREAGE IN			PERCENTAGE OF LAND IN	
	Agricultural Zones	Conservation Zones	Total	Agricultural Zones	Conservation Zones
Aitkin	523,460	641,175	1,164,645	44.9	55.1
Beltrami	628,907	976,764	1,605,671	39.2	60.8
Carlton	383,052	167,040	550,092	69.7	30.3
Cass	548,929	753,690	1,302,619	42.1	57.9
Clearwater	317,817	322,873	640,690	49.6	50.4
Crow Wing	358,493	290,386	648,879	55.2	44.8
Cook	37,652	898,507	936,159	4.1	95.9
Hubbard	264,355	332,461	596,816	44.3	55.7
Itasca	444,812	1,284,700	1,729,512	25.7	74.3
Koochiching	456,915	1,532,153	1,989,068	23.0	77.0
Lake	52,736	1,315,123	1,367,859	3.9	96.1
Lake of the Woods..	217,175	616,787	833,962	26.0	74.0
Pine	550,618	355,751	906,369	60.8	39.2
St. Louis	1,065,755	2,977,955	4,043,710	26.4	73.6
Total	5,850,686	12,465,365	18,316,051	31.9	68.1

Figure 39, page 173, a condensation of the fourteen preceding maps, shows the conservation zones of the fourteen counties in black on a greatly reduced scale. The suggested conservation zones in the fourteen counties embrace a total of 12,465,365 acres, or 68.1 per cent of the total land area. (See Table 31.)

Throughout the preparation of these zone maps great pains were taken both in the office and in the field to make them as reasonable and accurate in detail as possible; the location of every line is the result of considered judgment in the light of available information. Still there are instances in which they might be modified if more detailed information were available. Hence they must be considered as tentative and as subject to revision at all points where conditions would seem to warrant changes. They are offered as a first step toward the formulation of land use plans and the enactment of county zoning ordinances. For this purpose they are considered adequate. In the following pages the subsequent steps to be taken toward the enactment of zoning ordinances are set forth.

RURAL ZONING

The practice of rural zoning is of very recent origin, and its exact legal status is yet to be determined. The principles involved, however, are essentially the same as in urban zoning, which is well established, and there are good reasons for believing that the courts will look with favor upon the practice.

Oneida County, Wisconsin, was the first county in the United States to adopt an ordinance designed specifically to regulate the use of rural land for agriculture, forestry, and recreation. Earlier county zoning ordinances, such as the Los Angeles County Ordinance of 1923 and the Milwaukee County Ordinance of 1927, were designed to control industrial land uses within urban parts of the counties, to protect scenic areas, or to regulate the use of land in ribbon zones along highways. Since enactment of the Oneida County ordinance several other Wisconsin counties have adopted similar ordinances.

The Oneida County ordinance divides the county into two classes of use districts: forestry and recreation districts, and unrestricted districts. An official zoning map showing district boundaries is an integral part of the ordinance. In the forestry and recreation district, so far as new uses are concerned, only those specified are permitted and all unspecified uses, one of which is farming, are prohibited. Family dwellings for year-round residence are specifically prohibited. In the unrestricted district, as the name implies, there are no restrictions as to use. This ordinance represents a self-imposed restriction on the part of the local people for the purpose of decreasing public expenditures and thereby reducing taxes. It is a means whereby local residents may protect themselves against added costs for schools and roads imposed by new settlers who are unable or unwilling to bear a fair share of the costs of government.

This ordinance does not compel farmers who happen to be living in restricted zones to give up their homes or to discontinue the use of their land for farm purposes. On the contrary, a nonconforming clause in the ordinance specifically permits the continued use of any building, land, or premises existing at the time of passage of the ordinance, even though the use may be contrary to the specifications of the ordinance. If, however, the non-conforming use is discontinued, any future use of the property must be in conformity with the provisions of the ordinance. It is to be desired, however, that agricultural settlement in the conservation areas will eventually be discontinued. If there is no new settlement, natural forces will tend to depopulate these areas. The human lot would be made much easier if means were provided to facilitate the moving of families from conservation zones to more productive land. Funds made available by the federal government for the retirement of submarginal agricultural land may demonstrate the feasibility of moving families from such areas.[7]

VALIDITY OF RURAL ZONING

The validity of county zoning ordinances has not yet been tested in the courts. The first test case will be followed very closely, since it probably will have a profound influence upon the future of the rural zoning movement. Whereas city ordinances have heretofore derived their validity from the police power to protect the health, morals, safety, and comfort of the public, the county ordinances must rest more upon the power of government to control the use of private land for the purpose of conserving natural resources and of reducing public expenditures.

Views of the attorney-general's offices of Wisconsin and Minnesota may shed some light upon the probable attitude of the courts on rural zoning. Responding to a question raised by the Wisconsin Interim Committee on Forest Fires and Delinquent Taxes with respect to the use of zoning power to regulate areas within which agriculture, forestry, and recreation may be conducted, the attorney-general's department, through Mr. F. M. Wylie, gave the following opinion:

The county zoning statute is undoubtedly in the public welfare. The cut-over areas of northern Wisconsin speak as eloquently against haphazard development as any city condition. The spotting of these lands with remote or abandoned farms, resulting in sparsely settled districts with insufficient population or value to support roads and schools or to afford the comforts of living that this day should give to all, the misdirected efforts to farm lands not well suited to agriculture, with resulting personal grief and social loss, the far-reaching economic ill effects of stripping the state of timber, the fire hazard of human habitation in their midst, all cry out for planning, for social direction of individual effort. . . . I am inclined to the view, upon my limited information, that the necessity is so great, in the interest of future perhaps more than present welfare, that the court should find the absolute prohibition of agriculture in certain areas reasonable and not a taking of property without compensation, while in other areas such a prohibition might be unreasonable. Care

[7] See Chapter X for a more complete discussion of this program.

must be exercised, however, not to unreasonably discriminate between areas but to base differences in regulations upon differences in conditions. . . . I believe the judicial tendency is going to be to recognize more and more the great social evil of uncorrelated and unrestrained individual and selfish enterprise and hence to broaden its views of the power of government to plan the social and economic conditions of the present and the future.[8]

This statement suggests upon what ground the courts may be expected to uphold zoning legislation when a test case is tried. No less positive is an opinion rendered through the Minnesota attorney-general's office by Mr. Matthias N. Orfield. Replying to a question raised by Mr. G. M. Conzet, director of the Division of Forestry, Minnesota Department of Conservation, Mr. Orfield said:

You inquire whether a statute authorizing the zoning for conservation purposes of certain areas of the state especially adapted for such purposes would be valid if such statute authorized the exclusion from areas so zoned of new agricultural enterprises but permitted the continued operation of farms established at the time when such zoning measures might go into operation.

This question [zoning] has been considered by our Supreme Court in a long series of cases. . . .

In these cases the following propositions have been upheld:

1. In order to be valid a zoning ordinance must in some degree tend to prevent public injury and promote the common good.

2. It must not unreasonably impair or abridge property rights.

3. Such an ordinance need not be confined strictly to the preservation of the public health, public morals, and public peace, but *may be based upon other public interests*.[9]

4. The prevention of fires comes clearly within the scope of the police power.

5. Cities may prescribe districts within which occupations may not be carried on which are noxious or offensive in character or which tend to interfere with the comfort and prosperity of others.

6. Large discretion is vested in the legislature to determine what the public interest requires and what measures are necessary to protect it. . . .

Northeastern Minnesota contains vast areas of land admirably adapted for forestry, park, wild life refuge, and similar conservation purposes. Such areas contain occasional settlers eking out a precarious living by farming. . . . It is obvious that there are fire hazards connected with the use of land for farming purposes in an area devoted mainly to conservation purposes not only in that the burning of slashings and the starting of fires by such settlers in connection with the clearing of land tend to result in starting forest fires, but also in that with settlers living, one here, one there, and often miles removed from another, it is well-nigh impossible for fire patrolmen to convey information to them with reference to threatening forest fires and thereby protect them from being injured by such fires.

There is also the problem of providing settlers so scattered with adequate school and road facilities without prohibitive expense.

We will also call attention to the additional cost of maintaining township organizations in such areas.

In view of these matters, all of which are closely connected with public safety and public welfare, we believe that our Supreme Court would uphold a zoning statute of the character above indicated.

[8] F. M. Wylie in Wisconsin Attorney-General's Opinions, 20:751.
[9] Italics supplied.

These opinions are reassuring to those who regard the zoning movement as a means of solving many difficult problems in the cut-over counties. It must be added, however, that the courts will in all probability subject every ordinance over which the issue is raised to a rigid test of reasonableness. Poorly conceived plans of land use which tend to discriminate against certain individuals or parcels of land will probably be disapproved.

Steps Necessary for the Enactment of Zoning Ordinances

In Minnesota the following seven steps must be taken if rural lands are to be zoned:

1. Passage of a state enabling act.
2. Preparation of a proposed zoning ordinance and map.
3. A series of educational meetings.
4. A series of public hearings for receiving objections.
5. Examination of petitions and revision of ordinance and map wherever necessary.
6. Final enactment and publication of zoning map and ordinance.
7. Preparation of a list of existing non-conforming uses.

The first step must be taken by the state legislature; the other six require county action.

A State Enabling Act

Authority to classify lands is given boards of county commissioners under chapter 418, Session Laws of 1933. This act, however, confers no power on the board of county commissioners to regulate the use of land within the respective zones established. This power, which the Wisconsin county boards have, must be given Minnesota counties before zoning can be put on a sound legal basis.

The following suggested draft of a bill contains the essential points required in such legislation. This draft, which is in part patterned after the Wisconsin act, is included here to indicate more clearly the nature and purpose of zoning. The provisions of legislation that may be enacted are likely to differ somewhat in form and detail from those of the bill below.

A Bill for an Act Authorizing County Boards to Formulate, Adopt, Amend, and Enforce Comprehensive Zoning Ordinances

BE IT ENACTED BY THE LEGISLATURE OF THE STATE OF MINNESOTA:

Section 1. The board of county commissioners of any county may by ordinance regulate, restrict, and determine the areas within which agriculture, forestry, and recreation may be conducted, the location of roads, schools, trades, and industries, and the location of buildings designed for specified uses, and may establish districts of such number, shape, and area, and set-back building lines outside the limits of incorporated villages and cities, as such board of county commissioners may deem best suited to carry out the purposes of this section. For each such district, regulations may be imposed designating the trades, industries, or purposes that shall be included or subjected to special regulations and designating the uses for which buildings may not be erected or altered.

Section 2. In all counties in which the board of county commissioners desires to exercise the authority conferred by this act, there shall be a committee of land classification,[10] composed of the county auditor, the chairman of the board of county commissioners, the county treasurer, the county surveyor, and the county superintendent of schools. The chairman of the board of county commissioners shall be chairman of the land classification committee. In any county having a county agricultural agent, such agent shall meet and advise with said committee.

The county land classification committee shall first formulate a tentative zone map and county zoning ordinance and shall hold public hearings thereon before submitting a final zoning map and county zoning ordinance to the board of county commissioners. After such final map and ordinance is submitted and adopted, the board of county commissioners may from time to time alter, supplement, or change the boundaries or regulations contained in such ordinance in the manner herein set forth, but not less than thirty days' notice of any such proposed changes shall first be published in the official newspapers for publication in such county, and a hearing be granted to any person interested, at a time and place to be specified in the notice. Each such notice shall be published at least three times during the thirty days prior to the date of hearing. All proposed changes, amendments, or supplements to either the official zone map or county zoning ordinance shall be made upon a two-thirds vote of the board of county commissioners.

Section 3. The board of county commissioners shall prescribe such rules and regulations as it may deem necessary for the enforcement of the provisions hereof, and of all ordinances enacted in pursuance thereof. Such rules and regulations and the districts, set-back building lines, and regulations specified in section 1 shall be prescribed by ordinances which shall be designed to promote the public health, safety, and general welfare. Such ordinances shall be enforced by appropriate fines and penalties. Compliance with such ordinances may be also enforced by injunction or mandamus at the suit of the board of county commissioners, or the owner or owners of real estate within the district affected by such regulations. Such ordinances shall not prohibit the continuance of the use of any building or premises for any trade or industry for which such building or premises are used at the time such ordinances take effect, or the alteration of, or addition to, any existing building or structure for the purpose of carrying on any prohibited trade or industry within the district where such buildings or structures are located.

Section 4. The powers herein granted shall be liberally construed in favor of the county exercising them, and this act shall not be construed to limit or repeal any powers now possessed by any such county.

Section 5. All previous laws or parts of laws relative to county zoning inconsistent or in conflict with this act are hereby repealed.

This proposed bill is in effect a delegation of authority from the state legislature to the boards of county commissioners. It constitutes a grant of additional power to the counties for the purpose of regulating the use of land. Zoning under the suggested bill would

[10] This committee corresponds to that created for certain counties by chapter 436, Session Laws of Minnesota, 1933.

be optional with the board of county commissioners rather than mandatory.

PREPARATION OF A PROPOSED ZONING ORDINANCE AND MAP

Under an enabling act such as that suggested above the task of formulating a zoning ordinance and map would rest with a county land classification committee. This local committee would have the responsibility of deciding how many classes of zones to propose and the uses to be permitted in each, and to show on a base map the boundaries of each of the proposed zones. The broader features of the zoning ordinance are outlined in the enabling act, but the details must be formulated by the local committee to fit the particular requirements of each county. As a guide to county land classification committees in formulating county ordinances the following tentative draft is presented.[11]

ZONING ORDINANCE FOR ――――― COUNTY, MINNESOTA

An ordinance regulating, restricting, and determining the areas within the county in which agriculture, forestry, and recreation may be conducted, the location of roads, schools, trades, and industries and of buildings designed for specified uses, and the establishment of zones for such purposes and of set-back building lines outside the limits of incorporated villages and cities, pursuant to
Minnesota Session Laws, ―, Chapter ―.

The Board of County Commissioners of ――――― County does ordain as follows:

SECTION I. ZONES AND ZONE MAPS

For the purpose of promoting public health, safety, and general welfare and regulating, restricting, and determining the areas within which agriculture, forestry, and recreation may be conducted, and establishing zones which are deemed best suited to carry out such purposes, outside the limits of incorporated villages and cities, and in accordance with the provisions of Minnesota Session Laws, 1935, Chapter ―, the land area of ――――― County is hereby divided into two classes of use zones as follows, to wit: (1) conservation zones, and (2) unrestricted zones.

The boundaries of the aforesaid two (2) use zones are shown upon the official map of ――――― County, attached hereto, being designated the "Zoning Map Showing Use Zones," ――――― County, Minnesota, dated ―――――, and made a part of this ordinance. All notations, references, and other things shown upon said zoning map showing use zones shall be as much a part of this ordinance as if the matter and things set forth by said map were all fully described herein.

No land or premises shall be used except in conformity with the regulations herein prescribed for the use zones in which such land or premises is located.

No building shall be erected or structure altered or used except in conformity with the regulations herein prescribed for the use zones in which such building is located.

SECTION II. CONSERVATION ZONES

In the conservation zones no buildings, land, or premises shall be used except for one or more of the following specified uses:

――――――――――

[11] Adapted in the main from provisions relating to the Oneida County Zoning Ordinance.

1. Production of forest products.
2. Forest industries.
3. Public and private parks, playgrounds, camp grounds, and golf grounds.
4. Recreational camps and resorts.
5. Private summer cottages and service buildings.
6. Hunting and fishing cabins.
7. Trappers' cabins.
8. Boat liveries.
9. Mines, quarries, and gravel pits.
10. Hydroelectric dams, power plants, flowage areas, transmission lines, and sub-stations.
11. Harvesting of any wild crop, such as marsh hay, ferns, moss, rice, and berries.
12. Trails, highways, and landing fields.
13. Stores and stations for dispensing supplies for hunters, trappers, campers, and travelers, and for the purchase of furs.

(Explanation: Any of the above uses are permitted in the conservation zones, and all other uses, including family dwellings, shall be prohibited.)

SECTION III. UNRESTRICTED ZONES

In the unrestricted zones any land may be used for any purpose whatsoever, not in conflict with law.

SECTION IV. NON-CONFORMING USES

The lawful use of any building, land, or premises existing at the time of the passage of this ordinance, even though such use does not conform to the provisions hereof, may be continued, but if such non-conforming use is discontinued for a period of more than two years, any future use of said building, land, or premises shall be in conformity with the provisions of this ordinance.

The lawful use of a building, land, or premises existing at the time of the passage of this ordinance may be continued even though such use does not conform with the provisions hereof, and such use may be extended throughout such building, land, or premises.

Whenever a use zone shall be hereafter changed, any then existing non-conforming use in such changed zone may be continued or changed to a use permitted in the new use zone, provided all other regulations governing the new use are complied with.

Whenever a non-conforming use of a building, land, or premises has been changed to a conforming use, such use shall not thereafter be changed to a non-conforming use unless the zone in which such building, land, or premises is located is changed to an unrestricted zone.

Immediately following publication of this ordinance by the county board, the committee of land classification shall prepare a list of all instances of established non-conforming uses of land and publish the same to permit appeal on errors and omissions. Thirty days after publication of this list a final and official copy shall be filed in the office of the register of deeds.

Nothing in this ordinance shall be construed as prohibiting forestry and recreation in any of the use zones nor a change from any other use to forestry and recreation.

SECTION V. INTERPRETATION AND APPLICATION

The provisions of this act shall not apply to buildings, land, or premises belonging to and occupied by the United States, the State of Minnesota, the county, or any town or school district.

(Explanation: Restrictions as to the use of land for farms in conservation zones shall not apply to lands owned by Indians.

SECTION VI. CHANGES AND AMENDMENTS

The Board of Commissioners of ———— County may from time to time amend, supplement, or change by ordinance the boundaries of zones or regulations herein established. Any proposed changes shall first be submitted to the committee of land classification for its recommendation and report.

SECTION VII. ENFORCEMENT AND PENALTIES

The provisions of this ordinance will be enforced by and under the direction of the Board of County Commissioners. Any person, firm, company, or corporation who violates, disobeys, omits, neglects, or refuses to comply with or who resists the enforcement of any of the provisions of this ordinance shall be subject to a fine of not less than ten dollars ($10) nor more than two hundred dollars ($200), together with the costs of action, and, in default of payment thereof, to imprisonment in the county jail for a period of not less than one (1) day nor more than six (6) months, or until such fine and costs be paid. Compliance therewith may be enforced by injunction or mandamus at the suit of the county or the owner or owners of land within the district affected by the regulations of this ordinance.

SECTION VIII. VALIDITY

Should any section, clause, or provision of this ordinance be declared by the courts to be invalid, the same shall not affect the validity of the ordinance as a whole or any part thereof, other than the part so declared to be invalid.

SECTION IX. DEFINITIONS

Certain terms and words used in this ordinance are defined as follows:

Words used in the present tense include the future; words in the singular number include the plural number, and words in the plural number include the singular number; the word "building" includes the word "structure" and the word "shall" is mandatory and not directory.

Forest products. Products obtained from stands of forest trees which have been either naturally or artificially established.

Forest industries. The cutting and storing of forest products, the operation of portable sawmills and planer, the production of maple syrup and sugar.

Public and private parks, playgrounds, camp grounds, and golf courses. Areas of land with or without buildings designed for recreational uses.

Recreation camps and resorts. Areas of land improved with buildings or tents and sanitary facilities used for occupancy during part of a year only.

Private cottages and service buildings. Buildings designed for seasonal occupancy only and normally used by the owner together with additional structures to house materials, equipment, and services.

Hunting and fishing cabins. Buildings used at special seasons of the year as a base for hunting, fishing, and outdoor recreation.

Trappers' cabins. A building used as a base for operating one or more trap lines.

Boat liveries. Establishments offering the rental of boats and fishing equipment.

Building. A structure having roof supported by columns or walls for the shelter, support, or enclosure of persons, animals, or chattels.

Non-conforming use. A building or premises occupied by a use that does not conform with the regulations of the use zone in which it is situated.

Family dwelling. Any building designed for and occupied by any person or family establishing or tending to establish a legal residence or acquiring a legal settlement for any purpose upon the premises so occupied.

SECTION X. WHEN EFFECTIVE
This ordinance shall be in effect upon passage and publication.

Adopted ....

Published...

Signed:..

Chairman, Board of County Commissioners

——— *County, Minnesota*

(Seal) Signed: ....

County Clerk, ——— *County, Minnesota*

In the preparation of the official county zone map, which is an integral part of the county ordinance, the committee of land classification has an important responsibility. The success of the entire ordinance depends largely upon the care and judgment exercised in preparing the zone map. Poor zoning is worse than none. The maps shown in Figures 25–38, the first drafts of zone maps for the fourteen counties, are by no means in final form and must be very carefully checked and revised by the local committees. Natural areas and land use districts occur without regard to political boundaries, and land classification cannot be limited or distorted by such boundaries. Zoning, which is after all a method of giving legal effect to classification, should recognize this, and adjacent counties should coordinate their zoning programs. Cooperation with state agencies will be highly desirable because such agencies have assembled considerable information bearing on the problem of classification and zoning. Committees in counties not included in the fourteen must start from the very beginning in the collection of the data needed for the preparation of the zone map. The official county map should be on a rather large scale (preferably one inch to the mile) and should show accurately every listed description of land in the county.

Having prepared the preliminary map and zoning ordinance, the sponsoring committee should next hold a series of educational meetings at strategic points throughout the county.

Educational Meetings

These meetings are for the purpose of explaining to the public the nature and purpose of the proposed regulations. They should be announced well in advance and should be preceded by carefully prepared discussion in the local press. It is highly desirable that the tentative ordinance and map be published in local papers so that residents of the county may study the proposals and know exactly what is being suggested. This will tend to prevent ill-

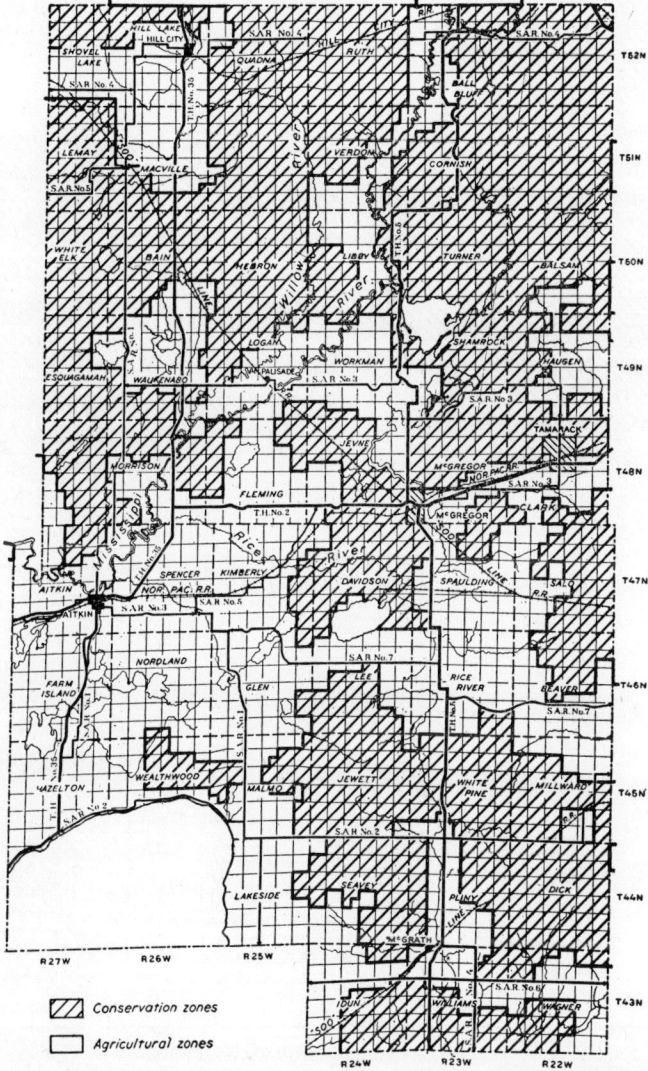

FIGURE 25. — SUGGESTED CONSERVATION ZONES IN AITKIN COUNTY

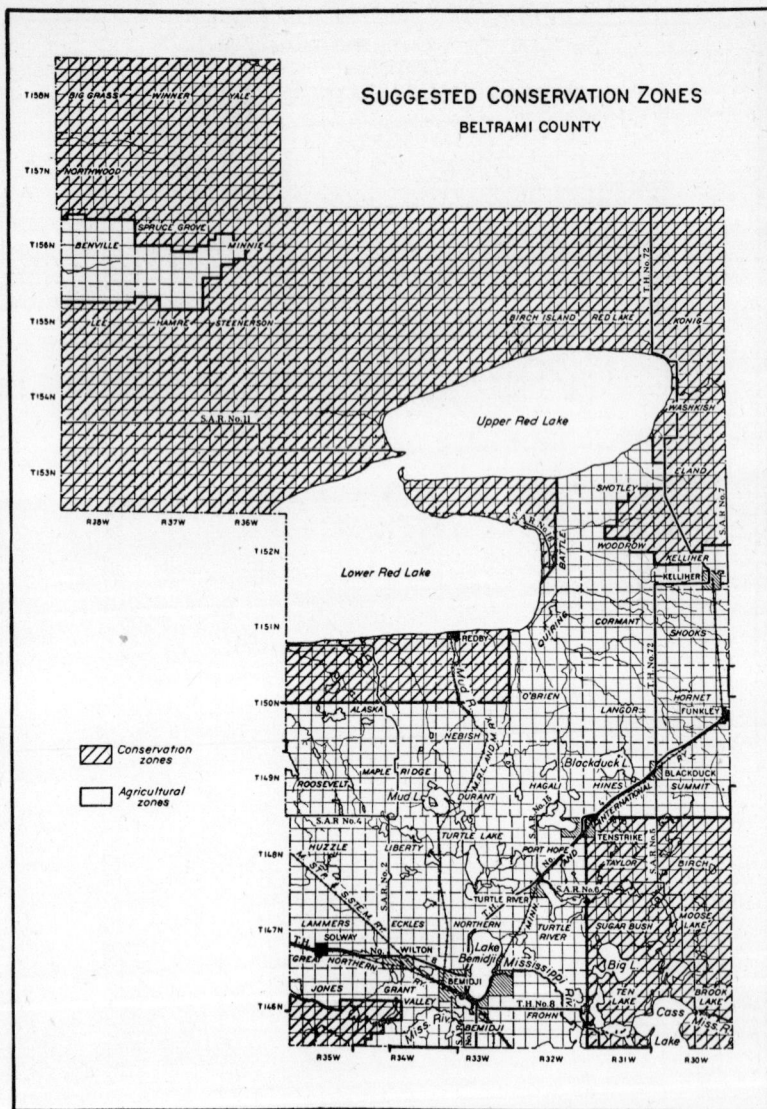

FIGURE 26. — SUGGESTED CONSERVATION ZONES IN BELTRAMI COUNTY

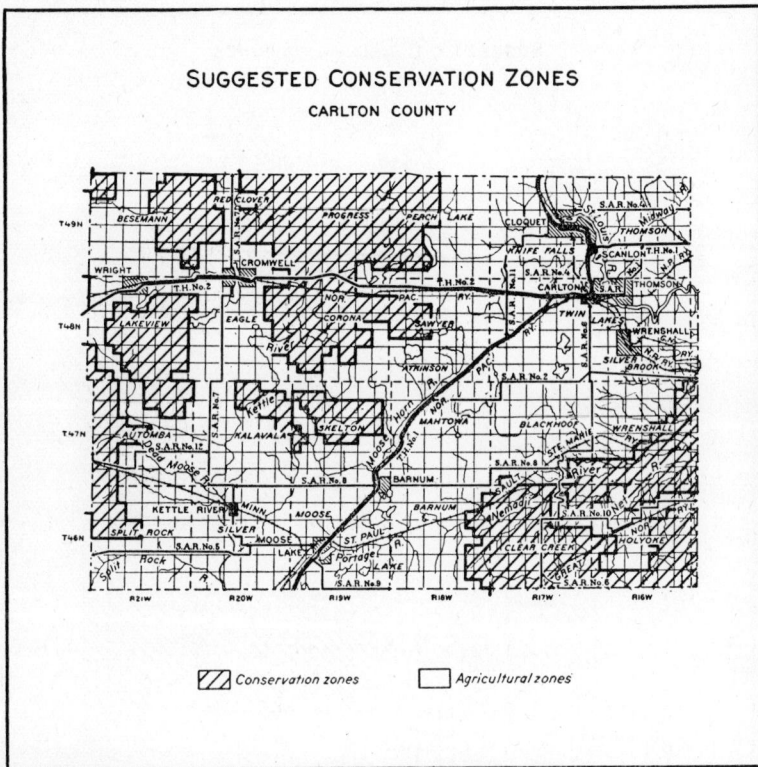

FIGURE 27. — SUGGESTED CONSERVATION ZONES IN CARLTON COUNTY

conceived and unwarranted objections from consuming valuable
time at the first meetings. Persons conducting these meetings
should be well fortified with data on tax delinquency, school costs,
transportation costs, road costs, and relief costs for the various
parts of the county. Arguments for zoning can be most forcefully
presented in terms of the dollar and cents savings involved. Following the educational meetings a series of public hearings should
be held.

PUBLIC HEARINGS

To permit property owners or others affected by the proposed
ordinance to voice objections or offer constructive suggestions, a
series of public hearings should be held. These meetings may well
be held in the same places as the educational meetings, and should
likewise be advertised well in advance of the dates set. All objections to either the proposed zone map or to the proposed ordinance

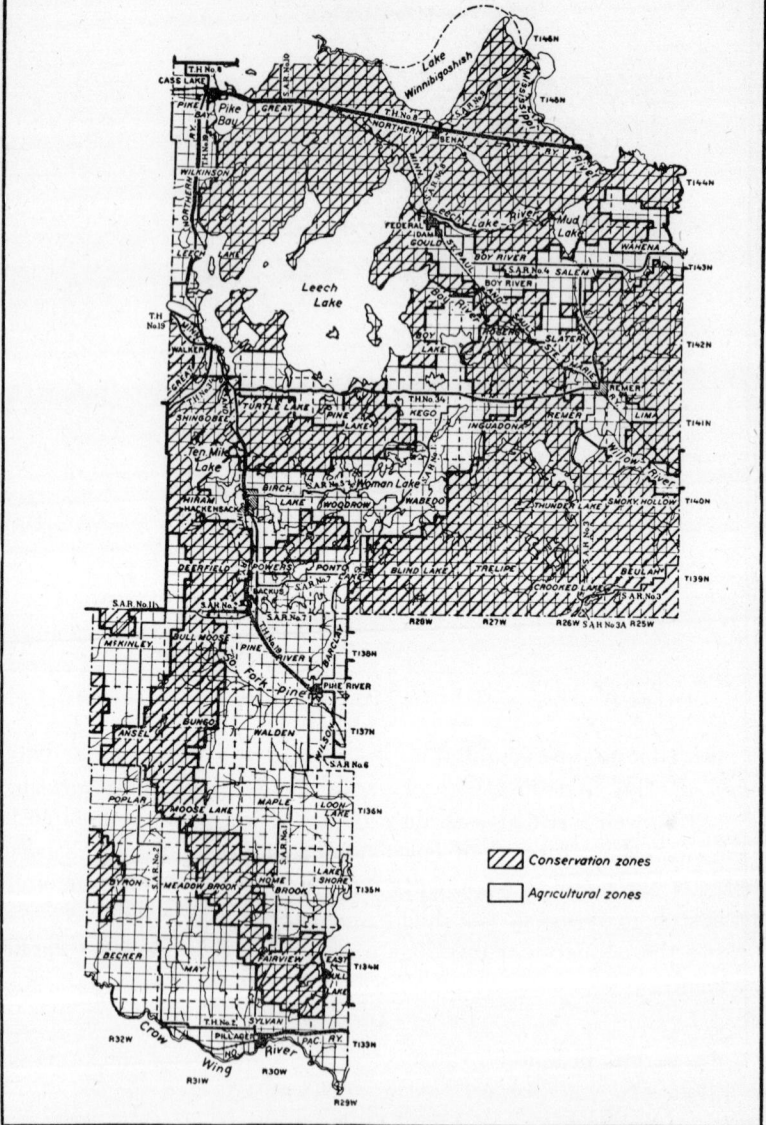

SUGGESTED CONSERVATION ZONES

CASS COUNTY

Legend:
- Conservation zones
- Agricultural zones

FIGURE 28. — SUGGESTED CONSERVATION ZONES IN CASS COUNTY

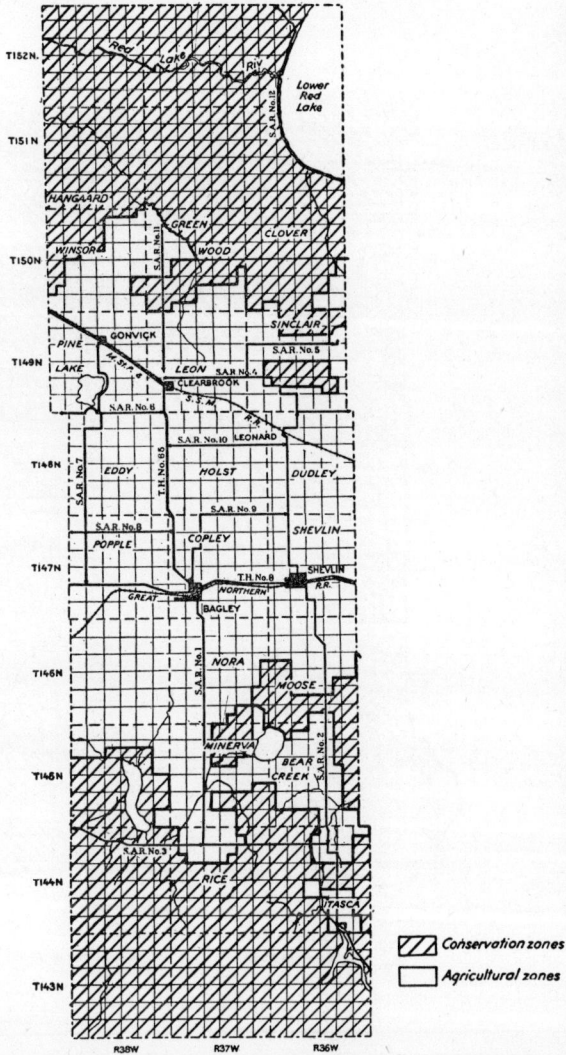

SUGGESTED CONSERVATION ZONES
CLEARWATER COUNTY

Conservation zones

Agricultural zones

FIGURE 29. — SUGGESTED CONSERVATION ZONES IN CLEARWATER COUNTY

163

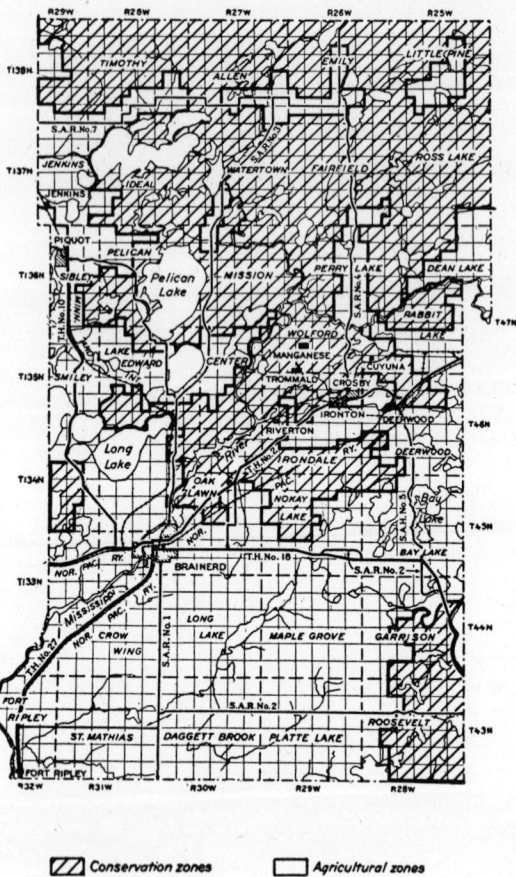

FIGURE 30. — SUGGESTED CONSERVATION ZONES IN CROW WING COUNTY

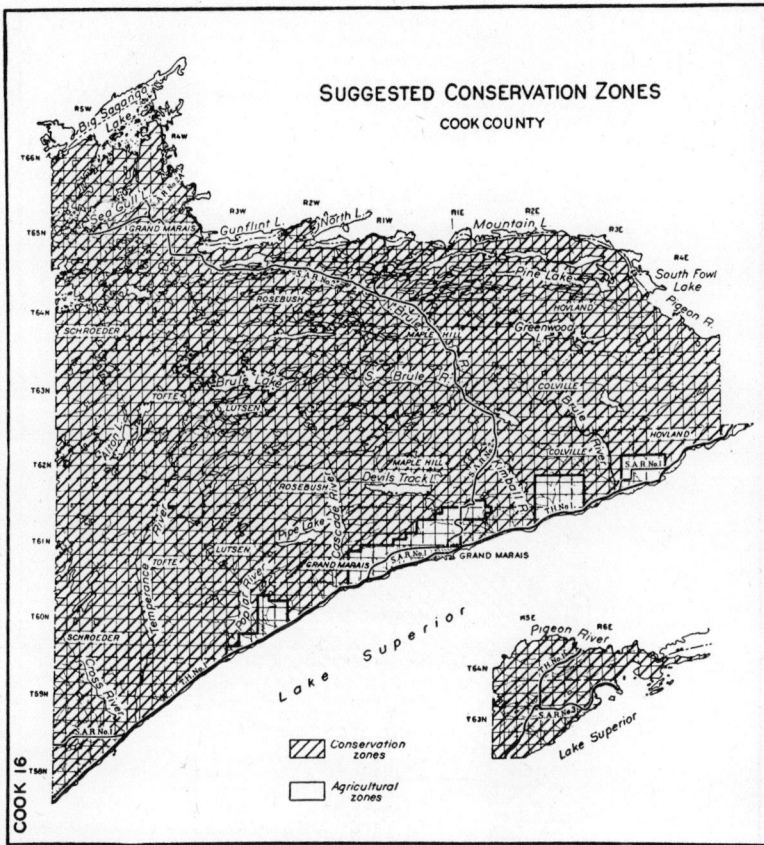

FIGURE 31. — SUGGESTED CONSERVATION ZONES IN COOK COUNTY

should be filed in writing with the committee at the time of the public hearing. Such petitions should state the proposed changes, set forth clearly the reasons for such changes, and should be signed by the parties recommending them. Complete records of all public hearings should be kept by the committees.

EXAMINATION OF PETITIONS

The two series of local meetings should give the committee a good picture of the public reaction to the proposed ordinance and map. The next move by the committee should be to examine carefully the petitions filed and make such revisions in map and ordinance as appear warranted. In addition to re-examining available data on the questionable areas, the committee may find it neces-

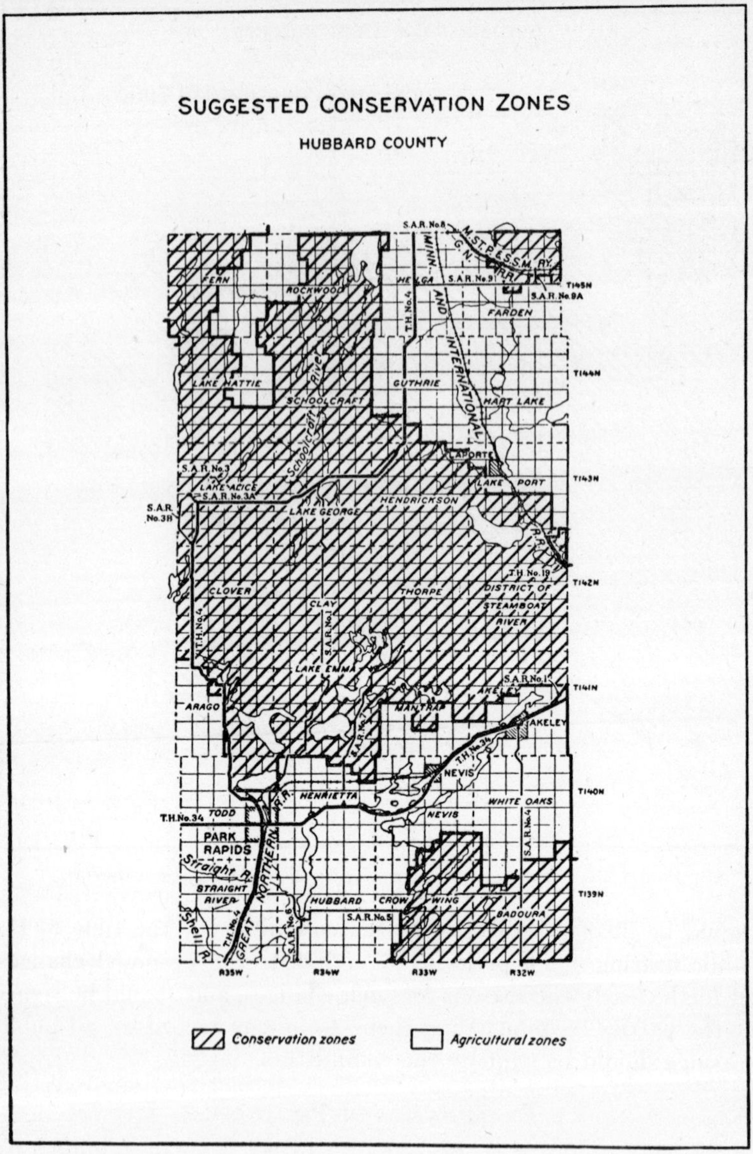

FIGURE 32. — SUGGESTED CONSERVATION ZONES IN HUBBARD COUNTY

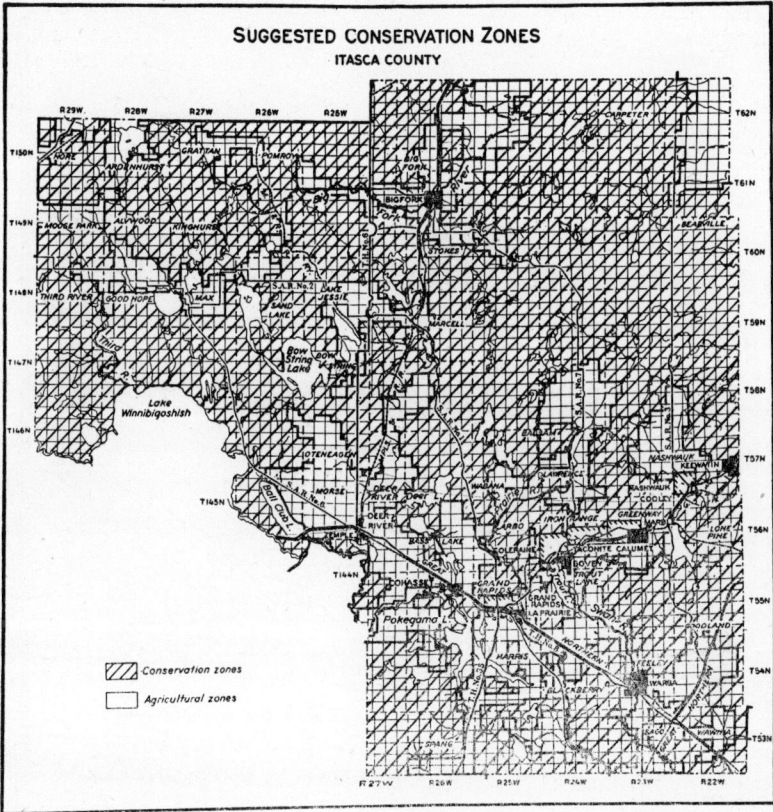

FIGURE 33. — SUGGESTED CONSERVATION ZONES IN ITASCA COUNTY

sary to make some field examinations. As each petition is disposed of, the petitioners should be notified of the action taken, the reason for granting or denying the request being stated.

ENACTMENT AND PUBLICATION OF A ZONING MAP AND ORDINANCE

After the land classification committee has completed final revisions of the map and ordinance, a resolution should be drawn outlining in brief the objectives of the proposed zoning ordinance, summarizing the work of the committee, and recommending adoption of the proposed map and ordinance by the board of county commissioners. Upon adoption the official map should be filed with the county register of deeds. Small-scale copies of the official zoning map, along with the text of the zoning ordinance, should be published for public distribution.

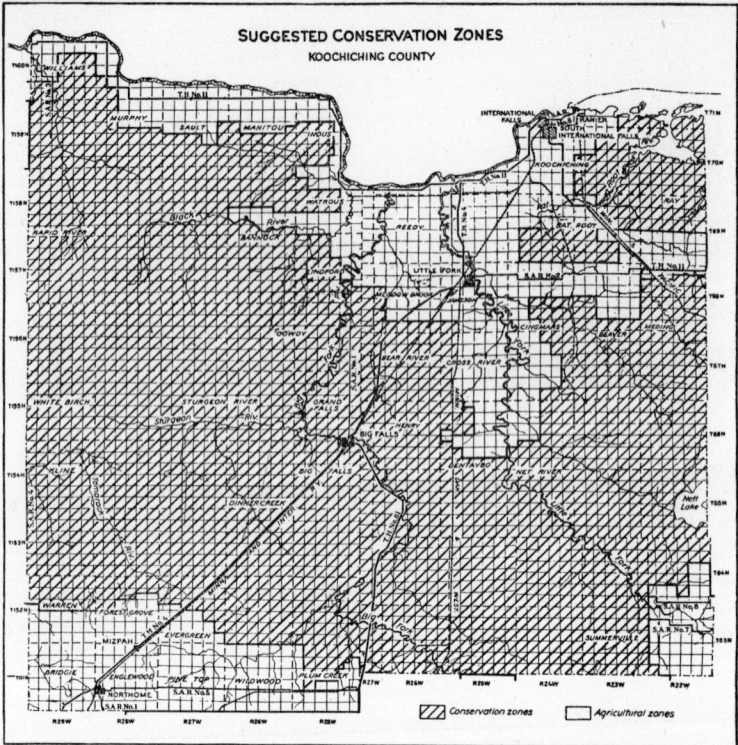

FIGURE 34. — SUGGESTED CONSERVATION ZONES IN KOOCHICHING COUNTY

PREPARATION OF LIST OF NON-CONFORMING USERS

After enactment of the ordinance a list of existing non-conforming users should be prepared by the land classification committee.
This list should be published to permit the checking of errors or
omissions. Thirty days after publication the official copy of this
list should be filed with the register of deeds. Names included on
it should be deleted whenever the non-conforming use shall have
been discontinued for a period of more than two years.

The results accomplished will depend largely upon how well the
ordinance is enforced and administered. If exceptions are permitted
and enforcement becomes lax, the work of the land classification
committee will have been largely wasted. Problems will constantly
arise to challenge the ingenuity of the county officers. Adjustments
must be made; changes in assessments and rates of taxation may
be necessary to encourage reforestation in conservation zones; isolated settlers will need to be given assistance in moving into the
good agricultural areas.

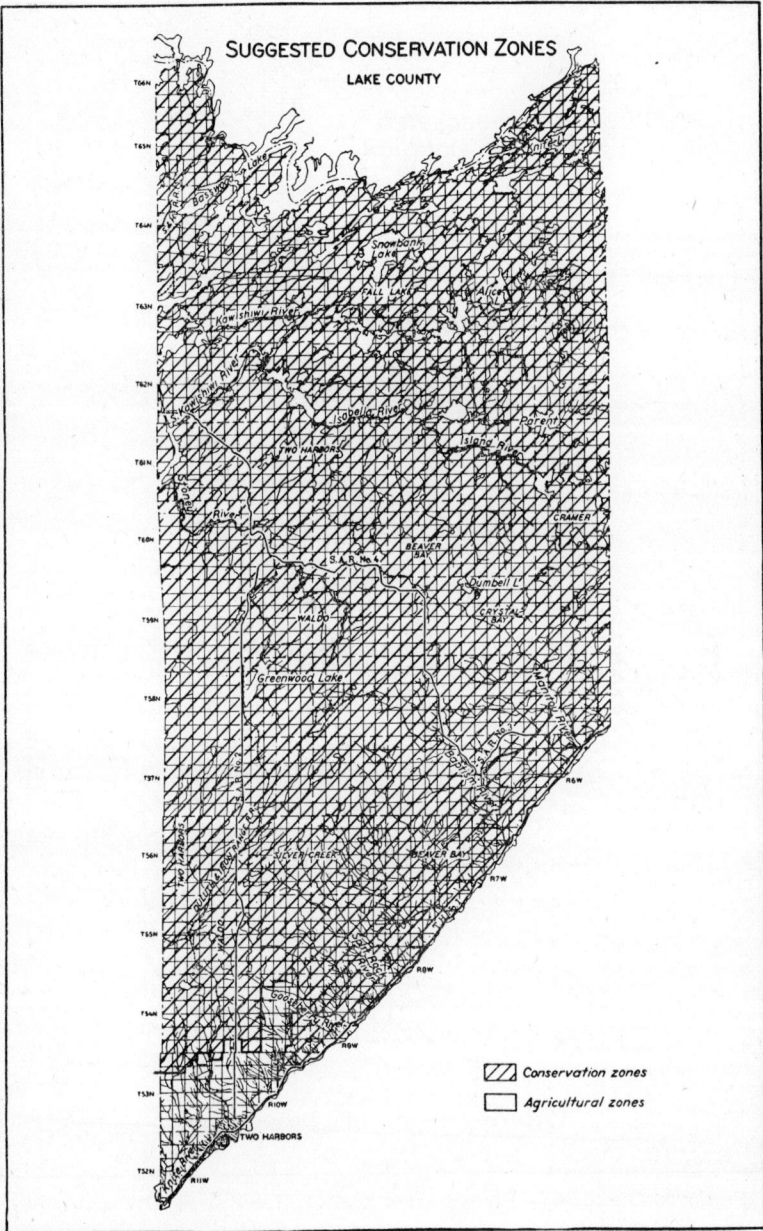

SUGGESTED CONSERVATION ZONES
LAKE COUNTY

Conservation zones
Agricultural zones

FIGURE 35. — SUGGESTED CONSERVATION ZONES IN LAKE COUNTY

169

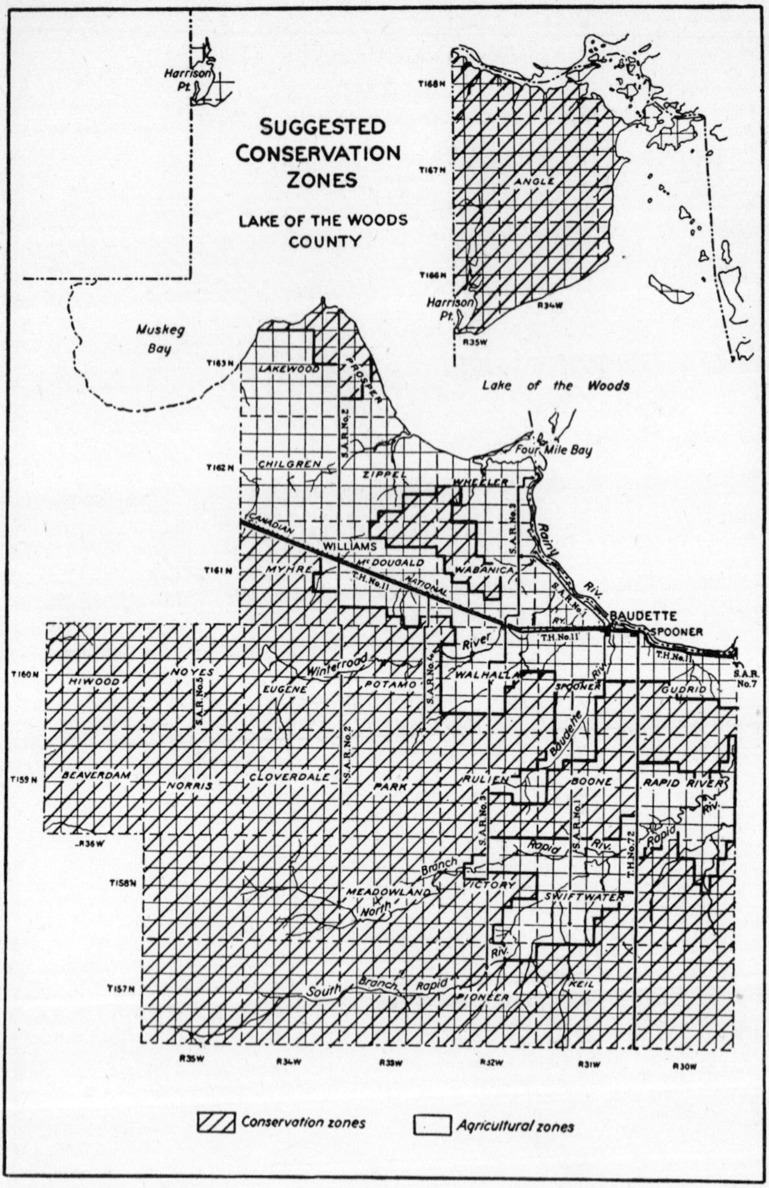

FIGURE 36. — SUGGESTED CONSERVATION ZONES IN LAKE OF THE WOODS COUNTY

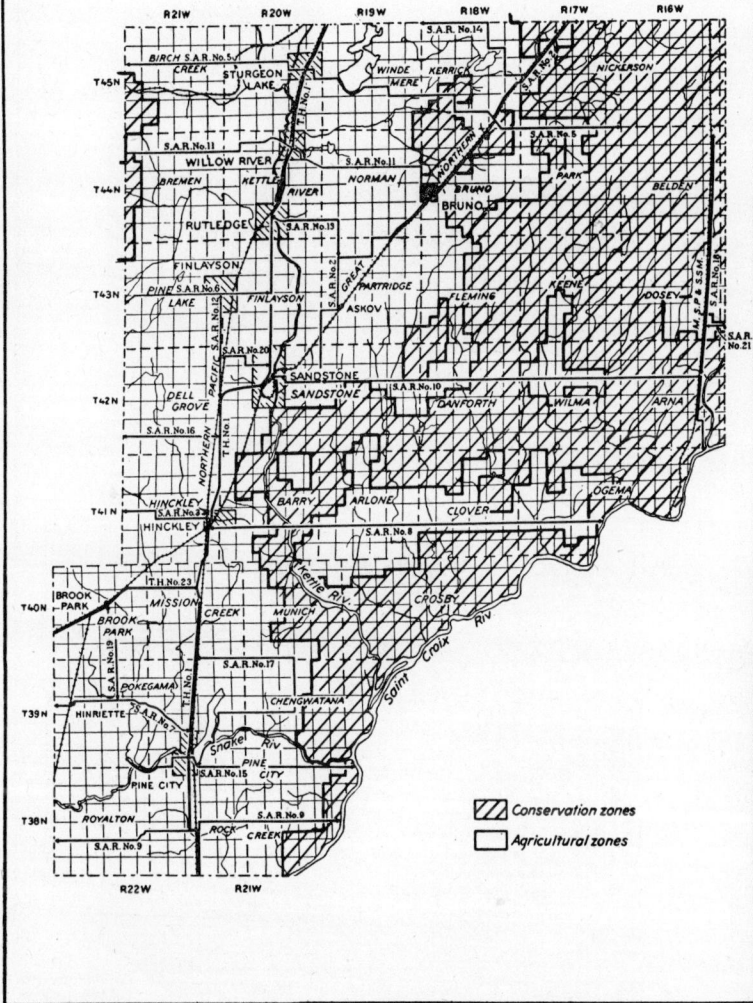

SUGGESTED CONSERVATION ZONES

PINE COUNTY

Conservation zones

Agricultural zones

FIGURE 37. — SUGGESTED CONSERVATION ZONES IN PINE COUNTY

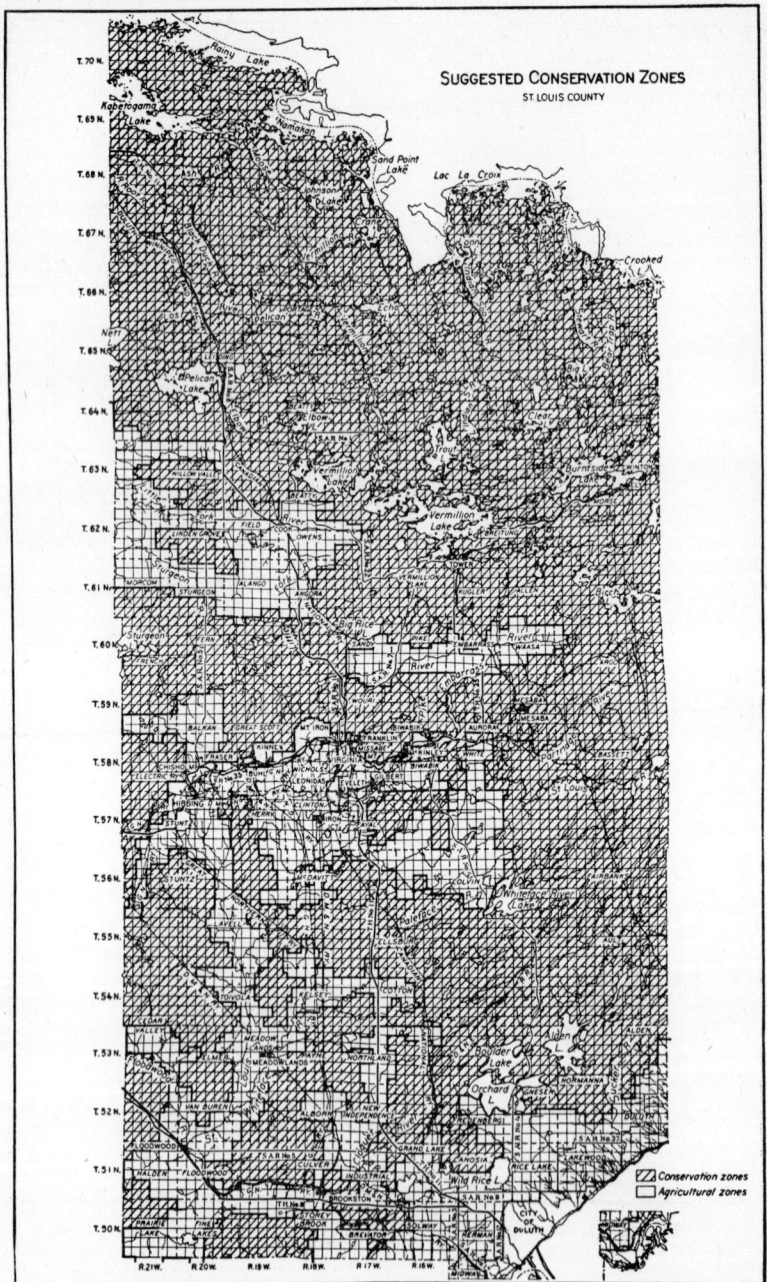

FIGURE 38. — SUGGESTED CONSERVATION ZONES IN ST. LOUIS COUNTY

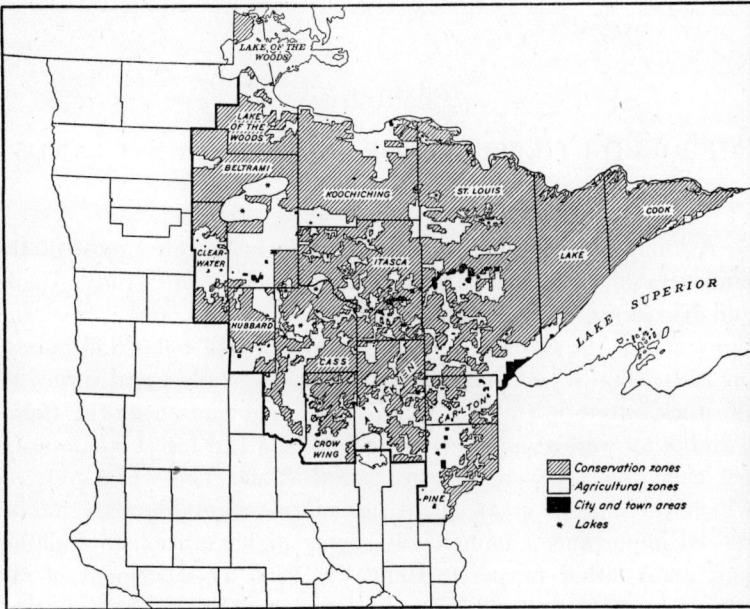

FIGURE 39. — SUGGESTED CONSERVATION ZONES IN FOURTEEN
NORTHEASTERN COUNTIES

CHAPTER VII

IMPROVED UTILIZATION OF PRIVATE FOREST LANDS *

The Forest

A hundred years ago a magnificent forest covered most of the land area of the fourteen counties included in this study. White and Norway pine predominated on the highland, and spruce and tamarack in the lowland forest. Northern white cedar and balsam on the lowlands, jack pine on the sandier highlands, and spruce on the rock outcrops and the heavier clay highlands near the Canadian border were also important members of this forest community. All these species were of commercial value. The white pine, of which there were great quantities of merchantable size, was of special importance commercially, being highly prized for building and many other purposes. Hence, as soon as settlement of the country to the south and west of this forest became well started, the pine-spruce forest of the counties under discussion became one of the state's most valuable assets.

Logging began on the St. Croix River in 1838. At first these operations were small and cut into the forest slowly. But as time passed, the operations greatly increased, both in numbers and in size, and there was a corresponding increase in the volume of lumber and other products removed from the forest. The old growth pine stands which predominated on the highlands within this area were relatively even-aged. This circumstance, combined with a relatively dry climate which created a great fire hazard as compared with that in the Atlantic Coast forests, soon brought about the adoption of clear cutting as the standard method followed by the logger in removing the timber. Most of the logging was done in the winter time. Late summer and fall fires were much more destructive to the old growth timber than were spring fires. Unless destroyed, the slash resulting from each winter's logging became, by midsummer, a serious threat to adjoining stands of old growth timber. To protect themselves, at least partially, from this danger, the loggers soon began to burn, during the first dry weather in the spring, the slash produced by the previous winter's operations.

* This chapter has been prepared by J. H. Allison.

174

Very little pine or other coniferous young growth survived these fires. Weeds, followed by aspen ("popple") and birch, or by brush succeeded the pine. While the loggers made some effort to keep slash fires out of their old growth timber, they made no effort to keep them out of the lands already logged. Hence these were burned repeatedly. The common belief was that most of these lands would ultimately be used for agriculture and burning was regarded as an aid in making land available for farming. As a consequence most of the cut-over forest lands have been subjected to repeated burning, with the result that much of the formerly forested area is now non-restocking, or is covered with poor reproduction.

Below are estimates[1] of the distribution and condition of the forest lands in the fourteen counties studied:

Sawtimber		10 per cent
Cordwood		44 per cent
Reproduction		
Good	10 per cent	
Fair	19 per cent	
Poor	10 per cent	
Total		39 per cent
Non-restocking		7 per cent

More recently the United States Forest Service has undertaken a timber survey in which survey lines are run and the trees in plots at frequent intervals checked. All trees in these plots having a diameter of five inches or more breast high are measured and tallied. Tree species less than five inches in diameter are recorded and density indicated. This survey when completed will supply much more accurate information on the condition of the present cover on forest lands. An analysis of the records of 6,439 of these plots indicates that the estimates presented above are too liberal in regard to the amount of sawtimber, cordwood, and good reproduction lands and too low in regard to poor reproduction and non-restocking lands.

It is evident that the forest cover over much of the fourteen counties is not encouraging for private forestry. The proportions of the area covered with sawtimber and cordwood are much too small and the proportions that are not restocking or are restocking very poorly are much too large. To be reasonably attractive to the owner for the practice of forestry, approximately 20 per cent of

[1] The rangers and a number of patrolmen of the Minnesota Forest Service in the fourteen counties assisted in the development of these estimates by sketching in on maps of their districts the acres falling within each of the different classes.

the land should be in sawlogs and about 50 per cent in cordwood. The portion of the area in fair and good restocking is reasonably satisfactory from the point of view of its proportionate area, but it is entirely unsatisfactory from the point of view of distribution of species. Altogether too much, namely, two thirds, of it is aspen, while only about a twenty-fifth is upland conifers (white, Norway, and jack pine). About a third of the fair to good reproduction is lowland conifers. This proportion is reasonably satisfactory.

A few private owners hold limited areas of timber where the class distribution is reasonably favorable to the practice of forestry. In stands in which the proportion of the area covered by merchantable sawtimber and cordwood is excessive, holdings may be balanced by the retention or acquisition of near-by cut-over lands. Aside from the relatively small areas just referred to, the Superior and the Chippewa National Forest include those forest areas in which the class distribution is most favorable to the practice of forestry. The forest cover on state lands, because of severe cutting and burning in the past, is much less favorable than that on the national forest lands. Most privately owned forest lands are in very poor shape for the practice of forestry; they contain far too small an area of sawlogs and cordwood and far too large an area of poor reproduction and non-reproducing lands now mostly covered with hazel or alder brush.

Prospective Market for Timber

Plans for private forestry naturally must take into consideration the prospects for market outlets. To forecast the probable future market for a long-time crop like timber is much more difficult than in the case of annual crops. Because of the many unknown factors in the problem it is impossible to specify just what the outlets for Minnesota forest products will be fifty, a hundred, or a hundred and fifty years hence. Certain facts throw some light on this matter, however, and they are worth consideration by private owners of forest lands.

Among the uncertainties of the situation may be mentioned the long-time dependence upon wood. There are those who predict that substitute products will replace wood to so great an extent that future demand will be much reduced. Technical improvements which are unpredictable might easily change the prices of substitute products materially. Price is, of course, an important factor in the selection of material. The extent of wood replacement in the future will be affected somewhat by the availability of suitable timber. If the production of timber is inadequate, prices will be high and more substitution will take place than if supplies were more plentiful and prices more favorable to the use of timber. Wood is used in so many ways that it seems logical to expect that it will remain an important product and to plan accordingly.

Still another question arises, and that is with respect to the source of the needed supply. Are Minnesota and neighboring states to recover an important place in the timber market or will other regions constitute the chief sources of supply? By and large the determining factor is the comparative advantage of the various producing regions. The area that can place products on the market at the lowest cost will naturally have the advantage in competition. Included in the complex of costs are conditions of soil and climate that affect the species grown, the rate of growth, and the quality of the product. Another important factor is location with respect to markets and the costs of transportation. Still another factor is the production methods employed.

It does not necessarily follow that a forest region will command the markets in its section of the country merely because it is nearer those markets than are competing regions. The latter may overcome the handicap of distance by the availability of other transportation facilities or by superior production conditions or methods. Considerable fruitless calculation has been engaged in to demonstrate the savings possible in Minnesota's lumber bill if its requirements were produced in the state instead of being shipped in from a distance. Presumably, so long as products need to be shipped in, transportation is one of the costs that must be covered. This cost will tend to be a factor in price without regard to place of production unless the region reaches the point where it produces an excess over its own requirements and becomes dependent upon outside markets rather than upon outside sources of supply.

Recognizing these factors, it is still of interest to note the market requirements of Minnesota and adjacent territory, since it is in this market that Minnesota producers will have the best opportunities. The latest available information, covering the year 1928, indicates an annual consumption in Minnesota of about 725,000,000 feet board measure of lumber [2] and 1,650,000 railroad ties.[3] Much

[2] *A National Plan for American Forestry* (73d Congress, 1st Session, Senate Document No. 12, 1933), p. 963.
[3] Computed from information in Senate Document No. 12, p. 271, based on mileage data furnished by State Railroad and Warehouse Commission.

of this came from other states. North and South Dakota, Iowa, and Wisconsin brought in a total of 1,374,000,000 feet board measure of lumber and large numbers of railroad ties during that year. Minnesota used about 265,000 cords of pulpwood [4] in 1929 and supplied plants in Wisconsin with 210,000 cords.[5] About 1,150,000 cords of firewood [6] and considerable quantities of posts, poles, piling, lath, shingles, cooperage stock, mine timbers, veneer logs, excelsior, and novelty and match stock were used in the state. Only pulpwood, fuel wood, posts, mine timbers, excelsior, and match stock are produced in sufficient quantities within the state to satisfy the requirements of its consumers. Only pulpwood and posts are shipped out in considerable quantities.

These figures indicate that there is a considerable market near at hand for products that can be produced in Minnesota forests. As suggested above, location alone does not assure Minnesota forests a prominent place in these markets. Location is undoubtedly an important advantage, however. The West, which is now supplying these markets with large quantities of timber products, by no means possesses inexhaustible resources. It will take many years of careful management and successful protection from fire and other destructive agencies to place the forests of this state in such condition that they will become an important source of timber. By that time it is likely that competing areas in the West will be in a less favorable condition to supply these markets because by then much of the present distress stocks of old growth timber will probably have been consumed.

While the trend in consumption of lumber, both national and local, has been downward for many years, the slope is very gradual; so gradual that it must be greatly accentuated during the next twenty years if it is to bring consumption down to the present annual growth. Even the greatly reduced lumber consumption of 1932 and 1933, as compared with the 1925–29 five-year average, was nearly double the estimate of sawtimber growth currently taking place in the forests of the country. Although the consumption of forest products in the future will be determined by the needs of the nation for the various things that may be fabricated out of wood and the relative abundance, suitability, and cheapness of the woods available, as compared with those of substitute materials, it

[4] United States Census.
[5] *Forest Land Use in Wisconsin* (Report of the Committee on Land Use and Forestry), p. 51.
[6] United States Census.

appears almost certain that the market for forest products will continue to be much larger than the rate of production currently taking place in the forest.

There is enough land in the suggested conservation zones and in farm woodlots in the suggested agricultural zones to produce the probable requirements of forest products if these lands are made to produce a reasonable portion of the timber growth of which they are capable. Information regarding the forest growth now taking place within the state is very inadequate. Much more will be available after the United States Forest Service Timber Survey is completed within this state. A preliminary examination of data obtained from several thousand plots within the fourteen counties indicates a smaller total stand of timber and a lower rate of growth than has been indicated by the less reliable previous estimates. That both the volume of the merchantable timber and the growth were small over the greater part of the fourteen counties had been suggested by the conditions found in Hubbard County by the Land Economic Survey of that county. This survey found only 0.9 per cent of the area of the county covered with sawtimber and 7.9 per cent of the area covered with merchantable pulpwood. The growth taking place upon all forest lands within this county averaged only 0.18 cords per acre annually. Well-stocked stands were found to be putting on growth at the average rate of 0.62 cords per acre per year.[7]

If the Hubbard County average rate of growth, which was determined with considerable precision, is applied to the total productive area of the conservation zones, there is now a current annual growth within these zones of about 2,000,000 cords, over half of which is aspen. Of this growth, less than 100,000 cords (equivalent to approximately 50,000,000 feet, board measure) is upland conifers, about 600,000 cords is lowland conifers, and the remainder, about 300,000 cords, is various upland and lowland hardwoods. This estimate is probably too high for lowland conifers and too low for the growth of aspen, much of which will not become merchantable, however, for any use except fuel wood. The rate of growth now taking place appears to be sufficient to meet the requirements of the present paper and fiber products industries and leave a surplus of perhaps a hundred thousand cords or more for shipment to Wisconsin mills, which need this material badly. The supply also seems amply sufficient to meet all the com-

[7] Data from Hubbard County Land Economic Survey, 1930.

mercial uses thus far developed for aspen except possibly the very high-grade aspen required for matches. But there is a very great shortage in the volume growth of upland conifers (chiefly the pines) available to satisfy the markets for these species. The annual growth of these species totals only about 50,000,000 feet board measure a year, whereas the annual consumption of coniferous (softwood) lumber in this state for the five years 1925–29 totaled over twelve times that amount.

Cost of Growing Timber

There are no definite records that can be used as a check upon the estimated cost of growing a stand of timber. But the cost can be estimated with a reasonable degree of accuracy. It consists of several parts, namely, of an annual rental corresponding to interest on the capital value of the land used for growing the timber; the taxes and the annual cost of protection and administration; the cost of establishing the crop by planting where nature has not already established it, or will not do so in the near future; an allowance to cover the risk of loss from fire, insects, or other destructive agencies; and the interest upon these various items or parts of items from the dates when such payments are made to the date when the forest crop is marketed. Interest is perhaps the most important of these items, because of the long time it takes to grow a forest crop. Risk is the item most difficult to estimate because it varies so much in different parts of the area under consideration. It varies from a minimum of 3 mills an acre annually in the Superior National Forest to a maximum of about 14 cents an acre in certain parts of Beltrami, Koochiching, and Lake of the Woods counties. The average for that portion of the fourteen counties outside the national forests is at present about 4 cents an acre per year.[8]

With a reasonably adequate protective organization and with reasonable care and cooperation on the part of the local population and the general public who travel through these counties and fish and hunt within their confines, the average annual loss should be cut to about a cent an acre. Assuming a value of a dollar an acre for the conservation zone lands, 14 cents an acre per year for taxes (approximately half of the average per acre tax burden resting upon all "wild" land located within these counties in

[8] J. A. Mitchell, *Forest Fires in Minnesota* (Minnesota Forest Service in cooperation with the United States Department of Agriculture, Forest Service, 1927, p. 36.

1926),[9] 1 cent an acre for risk of fire loss, and 5 cents an acre for protection and administration, the estimated per acre cost of growing a crop of timber, using certain specified rotations and interest rates, is as shown in Table 32.

TABLE 32. — ESTIMATED COSTS OF PRODUCING A CROP OF TIMBER WITH INDICATED ROTATIONS AND INTEREST RATES *

Rotation (number of years required to grow crop)	Interest Rate (per cent)	Sum of Rentals for Use of Land	Sum of Annual Expenses	Per Acre Cost with Natural Re-production (no planting cost)	Cost of Planting at $7.50 per Acre Carried to End of Rotation †	Per Acre Cost When Land is Planted
50 years.....	3	$ 3.38 ‡	$22.53 §	$25.91	$25.35 ‡	$51.26
	4	6.11	30.54	36.65	45.80	82.45
	5	10.47	41.88	52.35	78.52	130.87
	6	17.42	58.07	75.49	130.65	206.14
60 years.....	3	4.89	32.61	37.50	36.69	74.19
	4	9.52	47.60	57.12	71.40	128.52
	5	17.68	70.72	88.40	132.60	221.00
	6	31.99	106.63	138.62	239.93	378.55
80 years.....	3	9.64	64.27	73.91	72.30	146.21
	4	22.05	110.25	132.30	165.38	297.68
	5	48.56	194.25	242.80	364.20	607.00

* These estimates are based on land valued at $1.00 per acre, cost of planting at $7.50 per acre, and annual expenses of taxes at $0.14, loss at $0.01, and protection and administration at $0.05, making a total annual expense of $0.20 per acre. The per acre cost of growing the forest crop for other values than those assumed in this table may be calculated easily by multiplying the value given in the table by the proportion which new basic value bears to the one used in the calculations for the table. For instance, if it is desired to estimate the cost of growing timber upon land valued at $1.50 per acre, for a 50-year rotation, using a 4 per cent interest rate, multiply $6.11 by 1.50 and substitute this value for the $6.11. Similarly, if the annual expenses of taxes, protection, administration, and loss totaled only $0.15 per acre per year, multiply, for a 50-year rotation, using a 4 per cent rate, $30.54 by 0.75.

† According to Kittredge, this is approximately the average planting cost for the Lake States region. However, such a large proportion, four-fifths, of the non-restocking productive forest land is covered with brush that the actual average cost for mass planting of the non-restocking productive forest lands of the fourteen counties here under consideration will probably run a great deal higher than the $7.50 per acre used in these calculations. The average cost of successful planting on brush-covered lands may easily run up to $10.00 or more per acre. Joseph Kittredge, *Forest Planting in the Lake States* (United States Department of Agriculture Bulletin No. 1497, 1929).

‡ Calculated by using the formula $1.00\ (1.03^{50}-1) = \$1.00\ (3.38) = \$3.38$ or $7.50\ (1.03^{50}-1) = \$7.50\ (3.38) = \$25.35$; etc.

§ Calculated by using the formula $\dfrac{\$0.20\ (1.03^{50}-1)}{.03} = \dfrac{\$0.20\ (3.38)}{.03} = \$22.53$.

Make the proper substitutions in the other columns.

---

[9] Herman H. Chapman, *Tax Base Continued, Tax Rates, and the Tax Burden on Wild Lands* (Forest Taxation Inquiry, United States Department of Agriculture, Forest Service Progress Report No. 5, November 1, 1929), Table 9.

INCOMES EXPECTED FROM GROWING TIMBER

Aspen is the species most extensively represented in the second growth. In the conservation zones fair to good aspen cordwood covers about 300,000 acres.[10] Another 1,750,000 acres is covered with fair to good aspen restocking of less than cordwood size. About 500,000 acres more are covered with aspen cordwood stands that are too open to justify commercial logging operations and another 2,000,000 acres with aspen restocking that is classified as "poor." These acreages greatly exceed those covered by any other species, or groups of species. The income-producing capacity of aspen will be considered first in this discussion.

On good soils, aspen reaches satisfactory merchantable size for match stock, sawlogs, or pulpwood at about fifty years of age. But even at that comparatively young age, 11.4 per cent of the merchantable volume of the average tree has become worthless because of heart rot. Because this rot develops very rapidly thereafter,[11] aspen should be cut at about this age. Fully stocked stands on good soils should yield about 55 cords of peeled pulpwood per acre, well-stocked stands from 35 to 40 cords, and fair stands about 20 cords. With aspen stumpage at $1.00 a cord, a price at which good quality aspen has been sold, a well-located forest on suitable land will yield a gross income at fifty-year intervals of $20.00 per acre for stands of fair density, from $35.00 to $40.00 per acre for well-stocked stands, and $55.00 per acre for fully stocked stands. On the basis of costs presented in Table 32, these gross incomes would yield a return equivalent to a compound interest rate of a little less than 3 per cent on the investment in land and production costs from stands of fair density, a rate of 4 per cent from stands of good density, and a rate of 5 per cent from fully stocked stands. In the future stumpage prices running as high as $1.50 to $2.50 per cord for good quality aspen are anticipated.[12] Such prices would appreciably increase the compound interest rate earned on the investment.

Fair to good stands of lowland conifers, mostly black spruce, of reproduction and cordwood size, cover approximately 1,175,000

[10] This and subsequent estimates of acreages are based on preliminary results of the Forest Service Timber Survey.

[11] Henry Schmitz and Lyle W. R. Jackson, *Heartrot of Aspen* (University of Minnesota Agricultural Experiment Station Technical Bulletin No. 50, 1927).

[12] Joseph Kittredge, Jr., and S. R. Gevorkiantz, *Forest Possibilities of Aspen Lands in the Lake States* (University of Minnesota Agricultural Experiment Station in cooperation with Forest Service, United States Department of Agriculture, Technical Bulletin No. 60, 1929).

acres within the suggested conservation zones. This acreage equals about 9.5 per cent of the total area of these zones. Next to aspen this is the type of forest cover which is at present most extensive on the area under consideration. It takes about eighty years for this type to grow merchantable pulpwood. The yield averages only 12 cords per acre.[13] For the six-year period 1925–30, the state of Minnesota received an average stumpage price of $2.12 per cord for spruce pulpwood from state lands.[14] At that price, this type of forest would produce a gross income of about $25.00 an acre at eighty-year intervals. This is equivalent to a compound interest rate of one per cent. A possible future stumpage price of $5.00 per cord for spruce pulpwood is suggested by Kittredge.[15] At such a price the better spruce swamps would produce a return equivalent to about a 3 per cent compound interest rate for the eighty-year period required to produce the crop. While lowland conifers are widely scattered over all the fourteen counties, they are of greater importance in Areas II and X, described in Chapter III, because of the marked concentration of this type in those areas.

Only about 2.25 per cent, or less than 300,000 acres, of the suggested conservation zones are covered with second growth upland conifers, jack pine being the dominant species on about five-sixths of this area. At fifty years of age, the poorer jack pine soils yield about 20 cords and the better ones about 40 cords of pulpwood per acre.[16] With stumpage prices for good, well-located jack pine ranging between $1.00 and $2.00 a cord,[17] one may expect from these stands a gross income of between $20.00 and $80.00 an acre at fifty-year intervals. Such incomes are equivalent to a return of the direct crop costs plus compound interest at rates varying from 2.5 per cent for the poorer situations to 6.0 per cent for the best ones.

Non-restocking areas cover 25.6 per cent of the total forest lands, or approximately 2,875,000 acres, within the conservation zones. About 1,650,000 acres of this area is covered with lowland brush (alder and willow). These lands can be restocked only with difficulty and at great expense. The expenses involved are not justified by the prospective returns to be obtained from the sale of

---

[13] Raphael Zon, *Timber Growing and Logging Practice in the Lake States* (United States Department of Agriculture Bulletin No. 1496, 1928).

[14] Data furnished by the Timber Department, Office of the State Auditor.

[15] Joseph Kittredge, Jr., *Forest Planting in the Lake States* (United States Department of Agriculture Bulletin No. 1497, 1929).

[16] Zon, *Timber Growing and Logging Practice in the Lake States.*

[17] Kittredge, *Forest Planting in the Lake States.*

the timber. This area should be given fire protection, but no attempt should be made at present to convert it into productive forest. Another 650,000 acres is covered with highland brush. Upon this area also it will be difficult and expensive to re-establish the forest. Only experimental reforestation should be attempted here for the present. The remaining 575,000 acres is sufficiently brush-free so that the re-establishment of the forest may be accomplished by planting. White pine, Norway pine, and white spruce are the species that should be used most extensively, the one to be selected for any specific area depending upon the soil moisture conditions, the character of the soil, and the requirements of the forest owner.

On average soils, planted white and Norway pine should yield 20,000 feet per acre at the end of eighty years. Such a yield at $15.00 per thousand feet would return the costs involved in growing the crop and compound interest at the rate of 4 per cent. Similarly planted white spruce, which should yield 30 cords per acre on a sixty-year cropping period, with stumpage at $2.00 a cord would return the investment in crop expenses plus compound interest at the rate of 2.5 per cent per annum. With stumpage at $3.00 a cord, the compound interest rate earned would be increased to 3.5 per cent. If a $5.00 per cord stumpage rate should materialize, a stumpage rate that Kittredge considers within the range of possibilities, the compound interest rate paid would be increased to about 5.5 per cent.[18]

The advisability of planting jack pine is open to question, except perhaps on very sandy lands. Planted jack pine should yield at least 25 cords of pulpwood per acre at the end of fifty years. With stumpage at $2.00 a cord, such a yield would be equivalent to about a 3 per cent compound interest rate.

Two paper-manufacturing companies in Wisconsin are planting jack pine on sandy land and spruce on heavier soils. These plantations are being established for the purpose of protecting a large investment in paper-manufacturing plants, which now must bring in their pulpwood from a considerable distance.

The underplanting of the 2,500,000 acres of aspen cordwood and restocking lands which are classified as "poor" should be given serious consideration. It is probable that a considerable area of these lands could be transformed into spruce or pine stands, yielding a compound interest rate of 3 per cent or more, as against a probable current yield of less than nothing.

[18] *Ibid.*

Perhaps too much emphasis has been placed in the preceding pages upon the rates of compound interest that stands of various commercial species might earn under certain specified conditions. It should be remembered that it is only for the period during which the sustained-yield forest is being established that compound interest can reasonably be injected into the picture. If a forest owner is able to start with a forest having reasonably well-stocked stands of trees ranging in age from very young stands to merchantable mature ones, he should be able to pay out of current income all his expenses, such as taxes, protection, administration, loss, and planting (if planting is necessary). Whatever income the forest yields in excess of the amount required to meet these annual expenses is income on the capital invested in the land and the growing timber standing upon that land. To illustrate, suppose a paper company requiring 60,000 cords of spruce a year was able to acquire a forest property covered, in approximately equal amounts, with stands ranging from one to sixty years of age; that the land was of such character and the stands of such density that each of them would produce 30 cords of pulpwood an acre when it was sixty years old; and that the forest was run on a sixty-year cropping period. To meet the pulpwood requirements of this company, this forest would need to cover 120,000 acres. Every year 2,000 acres would be cut over. This 2,000 acres would yield 60,000 cords, which, at $2.00 a cord, would produce a gross income of $120,000. Assume that taxes, protection, administration, and loss totaled 40 cents an acre annually, or a total of $48,000 for the tract. Assume that replanting the area cut each year would cost $8.00 per acre, or $16,000 for the total area cut over each year. Then the net income received from the forest would equal $120,000 minus ($48,000+$16,000) or $56,000. This $56,000 would be the income upon the capital invested in the 120,000 acres of land and the timber growing on that land. The rate earned would equal $56,000 divided by the capital invested in the forest. Compound interest would not and should not appear in this calculation.

About 1,300,000 acres of the total area included in the suggested conservation zones is nonproductive forest land, that is, muskeg, bare rock outcrop, etc. The greater part of this is found in Areas II and X. These lands should be protected from fire, but economic conditions do not justify any other forest management at this time.

The greater part of this area is now in private ownership,

mostly clouded with tax delinquency. Although many of the larger owners, and probably the smaller ones as well, feel that no financial return from forest ownership is in prospect, still they are faced with the likelihood that neither the state nor the federal government will buy all the available lands. This is one of the reasons why many are permitting their lands to become tax delinquent.

So far the state has not forced private owners to choose between paying taxes or losing title to lands, but it may do so. It should do so to clear up definitely the forest landownership situation. Assuming that it does, there probably will remain a considerable acreage of forest lands in private ownership, particularly if the tax burden resting upon them is adjusted to their prospective income-producing capacity, either by administrative reforms in our tax-levying mechanism or by special forest taxation laws.

In Europe, outside of Russia, large-scale private ownership of forests still persists. In Sweden 76 per cent, in Finland 65 per cent, in Poland 70 per cent, in France 63 per cent, and in Germany 47 per cent of the forest area is in private ownership. Under the conditions existing in those countries, forests have proved to be a relatively safe investment, and consequently a relatively low return upon the investment is accepted as normal. In this country, largely because of the great volume of old growth that in the past has always been available in some part of the country and a transportation system that has made this timber accessible to market, there has been little current need for second growth timber. Consequently stumpage values for such timber have been so low that they have not yielded a satisfactory income on the investment. Also the risk of loss, especially from fire, has further tended to keep the private owner from making timber production his chief object in land management. Old growth, now very largely confined to the Pacific Coast, will take care of our timber requirements for perhaps another twenty years. Thereafter we will rapidly become more and more dependent upon our second growth. With the exhaustion of the commercially available old growth timber and the great reduction in volume of the second growth available to take its place, the price of stumpage should then rise to a point that will make the growing of timber attractive to the private owner of forest lands. As that time approaches, the public, as an owner of timber and timber lands, will probably be able to advance the price of publicly owned stumpage to the point where it will cover all the costs involved in growing the timber crop.

Assuming that forestry can be practiced on private lands covered with sawtimber or with fair to good cordwood or with fair to good young growth of less than cordwood size, the forest management problem divides itself into two distinct parts, namely, (1) farm forestry and (2) non-farm forestry. The forest management problems of each are distinctly different and will be discussed separately.

FARM FORESTRY

In the fourteen northeastern counties of Minnesota woodlots cover 1,533,874 acres, or 50.5 per cent of the total farm area. The proportion of land in woodlot ranges from a minimum of 32.2 per cent of the land in farms in Natural Area VIII to a maximum of 61.7 per cent of the land in farms in Natural Area III. These percentages indicate clearly the great importance of woodlot management in this region. A form of use involving 50.5 per cent of the total land in farms of a region is important to the farmers even though it is undeveloped, as it is on most of these farms.

Even if the portion of the present woodlot area that could be used for crop and improved pasture land were to be converted to these uses, there would still be a large area in woodlots. How large this area would be is perhaps suggested by Swedish experience. There, where glacial soils, topography, climate, and forest cover are somewhat similar to those of northeastern Minnesota and where relatively intensive agriculture has been carried on for several hundred years, the woodlot today occupies 66.5 per cent of the average farm in southern and 72.5 per cent of the average farm in central Sweden.[19]

According to the 1930 federal census, the farms located within the fourteen counties used or marketed in 1929 about 50,000,000 feet board measure of saw and veneer logs, 330,000 cords of firewood, 140,000 cords of pulpwood, 800,000 posts, 200,000 railroad ties, 80,000 poles and piling, 1,700 gallons of maple syrup, and 3,000 pounds of maple sugar. These products were valued at about $3,900,000, which compares favorably with the value of potatoes and other vegetables in the same area. These woodlots are being given practically no attention by their owners. With management they could be made to produce a gradually increasing volume of products.

[19] G. S. Perry, *Forestry in Sweden* (published by the author at Mont Alto, Pennsylvania, 1929). Percentages are computed from data given on page 127. The figures given are unweighted averages and somewhat below the real averages.

Ordinarily the woodlot should not be pastured. A good wood-lot provides little in the way of useful forage for cows or sheep, and these animals pack the soils by tramping and destroy much of the undergrowth that is necessary to the continued health of the woodlot, thus bringing about a marked reduction in its wood productivity. Where the fire hazard is high, the woodlot may be pastured moderately for the purpose of removing grass and weeds.

The woodlot should be protected from fire, which is the most destructive enemy of the forest. The farmer can greatly reduce losses by being careful himself and by cooperating with the Minnesota and United States forest services in their fire prevention and control work.

Insects or fungi (wood rots) sometimes threaten serious damage to the woodlot. As soon as such a threat is recognized, the owner should call it to the attention of the Agricultural Experiment Station at the University Farm, St. Paul.

Under intensive management it would take twenty acres of woodlot per farm to produce the firewood, posts, poles, piling, and sawlogs now coming from the farms in this region. If no effort is made to improve the woodlots, the volume and value of the products obtained from them will gradually decrease. With a moderate degree of forest management, the annual yield of marketable products could be materially increased, and the needed amount of firewood and fence posts could be obtained from the unmerchantable parts and from thinnings.

Will there be a market for the materials grown? The large saw-mills at Cloquet and International Falls are likely to become increasingly dependent upon farm woodlots. They are already or soon will be in the market for any sawlogs they can obtain. The smaller mills at Virginia, Deer River, and Cass Lake and the portable mills scattered over this portion of the state will always require sawlog material.

Spruce is the most important kind of pulpwood used by the mills of both Minnesota and Wisconsin. These mills consume about 1,500,000 cords a year, of which about half is spruce, the remainder being divided between hemlock (not native to the state), jack pine, balsam, and aspen. Most of the spruce pulpwood cut in this state comes from lowlands. Only about 7 per cent of the woodlot area of this region is lowland, so there probably will be a good market for all the spruce that can be grown on these lowlands as well as for upland spruce. White spruce grows well upon the heavier upland soils. Because of its relatively early marketability as pulpwood, it should be encouraged in woodlots with satisfactory soil requirements. There is and probably will continue to be a satisfactory market for jack pine and balsam fir as pulpwood or as rough lumber. There also will be a satisfactory market for sound, good-form paper birch of railroad-tie or match or toothpick-bolt sizes. A large portion of the woodlot area covered by stands classed as "cordwood" or "good restocking" is aspen. There is an oversupply of poor and medium quality aspen and an insufficient supply of the better grades. There is now a ready market for high-grade logs for match bolts and lumber for finishing purposes and for crating.

In marketing woodlot products, farmers must recognize that forest products are sold according to grade. Lumber, paper, match, and railroad companies have formulated very definite specifications covering the species and the minimum sizes they will accept. These specifications also state the maximum amount of defect (rot, crook, shake, etc.) acceptable in any particular class of product and the deductions that will be made for defects within the maximum limits specified. For instance, in 1933 one paper company specified that "rough" (unbarked) spruce pulpwood must be free from rot, that each stick must be 100 inches long and not less than 4 inches in diameter inside the bark at the small end. As this class of pulpwood was delivered, they deducted from the full scale of each pile an amount equal to the total space occupied by all rotten or undersized sticks plus an amount equal to the open space found in the pile.

To obtain the best financial results, the woodlot owner must obtain the specifications of the purchaser to whom he intends to sell, and then see to it that the material he delivers meets these specifications. He should leave in the woods, or place in his woodpile, all the material that does not meet these specifications. He ought to leave to grow to larger size all healthy, good-form spruce, birch, and aspen that will not make a full minimum-sized stock under the specifications, and also all vigorous well-formed trees of these species that will cut only one stick per tree of specification size.

The cut taken out of the woodlot annually should not exceed the annual growth. This relation can be determined from time to time, say at five-year intervals, by recording the diameters of all trees on strips covering a certain portion, say 10 per cent, of the area of the woodlot. If, according to this record, the number of trees in each diameter class is being maintained or if the number of trees in the larger diameter classes is increased, the annual cut is being limited to the annual growth or to somewhat less than the annual growth. A cumulative record of the volume of all material removed from the woodlot should also be kept; it is of great assistance in determining how much can be taken out in the future.

Cooperatives organized for the purpose of giving the woodlot owner technical advice on the management of his woodlot and the marketing of its products could be made of great assistance to the woodlot owner. Cooperatives could assist both the seller and the buyer of forest products. Until very recently the larger lumber and paper companies could not buy from the farmer for two reasons: (1) the small quantity and irregular delivery of the material offered for sale and (2) the uncertainty of the ownership of the material offered. Lumber companies were particularly wary of purchasing sawlogs from farmers because the real owner of these logs, if they were cut in trespass, might seize the whole of each yard pile of lumber into which material had gone from the logs cut in trespass. This problem is sufficiently serious to make it seem advisable to many companies purchasing from farmers and small jobbers to employ field men to check the ownership and tax delinquency status of the lands from which farmer and small-jobber material is coming. Cooperatives could assume the responsibility of obtaining for the mill much larger volumes of raw material and of checking ownership and tax status of the land from which the material was coming. In this way it could deal more favorably with the various purchasers than the individual woodlot owner. It could also keep its members informed as to specifications currently in force, and see that products shipped met these specifications. Thus it could save its members considerable sums of money and much irritation.

Privately Owned Forest Land Not in Farms

There are about 10,500,000 acres of privately owned forest land outside of farms in the fourteen counties, the greater part of which is located within the conservation zones. The owners can be divided into two groups, small and large. Classifying individual ownership of less than 400 acres as small, the Forest Taxation Inquiry [20]

[20] H. H. Chapman and Daniel Pingree, *Tax Delinquency in the Forest Counties of the Lake States* (Forest Taxation Inquiry, United States Department of Agriculture, Forest Service, mimeographed Progress Report No. 10, August 1, 1930), Table 9.

found that in Beltrami, Cass, Hubbard, Itasca, Koochiching, and Lake counties the small owners held 57 per cent and the large 43 per cent of the non-farm forest acreage. Applying these percentages to the fourteen counties, small owners hold about 6,000,000 acres and large ones about 4,500,000.

Nearly all the small forest owners acquired their holdings after the original merchantable timber had been removed, in most cases for speculative purposes. These owners are usually so far away that they cannot personally supervise their holdings, which are not large enough to justify hired supervision. Such owners have no interest in the use of these lands for forest production, and cannot be expected to practice even the most extensive forms of forest management. Tax delinquency is high among them, and probably only a very small acreage will be redeemed. The rest will ultimately pass into public ownership. This process should be speeded as much as possible in order that these lands may be given proper care.

The size of the ownership, 400 or more acres, used by the Forest Taxation Inquiry as a basis for their "large" class of owners is not at all satisfactory from the point of view of forest management because a minimum holding of about 20,000 acres is required to justify the degree of supervision called for by forest management. Probably less than 3,000,000 acres is in holdings of sufficient size to justify the employment of the trained personnel necessary for proper management.

Privately owned old growth timber is mostly in the possession of owners possessing over 20,000 acres. In 1926 the old growth timber then remaining in the fourteen counties was estimated at 8,837,000,000 feet board measure.[21] Perhaps a quarter of this timber has been cut since that date. The old growth merchantable stands of timber now left in large ownerships probably approximate a million acres, or about a third of the total acreage in such ownerships.

The remaining 2,000,000 acres in holdings large enough for effective forest management is cut-over land. On the basis of estimates prepared by the United States Forest Service Timber Survey, these 2,000,000 acres of cut-over land probably include about 200,000 acres of fair to good cordwood, about 700,000 acres of fair to good restocking, and about 1,100,000 acres of non-commercial cordwood, poor restocking, and nonproductive land. This distri-

[21] Fred R. Fairchild, Director of the Forest Taxation Inquiry, United States Department of Agriculture, Forest Service, mimeographed Progress Report, September 5, 1928, Table 12.

bution is not satisfactory for sustained-yield management. It is too late to convert these holdings into sustained-yield sawlog-producing forests, but some of them could be converted into sustained-yield forests for the production of pulpwood, box-crating, and match bolts.

The larger owners of forest property in Minnesota have accepted the provisions of Article 10 of the "Code of Fair Competition for Lumber and Timber Products Industries," approved by President Roosevelt on August 19, 1933. This code binds the forest industries "in cooperation with public and other agencies, to carry out such practicable measures as may be necessary for the . . . conservation and sustained production of forest resources." [22] A subsidiary code applying only to the Lake States region has been agreed to by the larger operating owners in this region. Under this subsidiary code these operators are required to give their forest lands considerable more fire protection than in the past, and to protect young growth and immature trees, so far as possible, from injury or destruction during logging operations. This subsidiary code recognizes sustained yield as the basic objective of forest management. Its adoption is a step forward in the conservation and management of forest resources held by the larger private owners.

Certain problems are involved in placing these large holdings on a sustained-yield basis. The size classes and species found on the holdings are not suited to such a program. The large sawmill capacity encourages greater cutting of sawtimber than is permissible at present under a sustained-yield plan. In the case of pulpwood, box material, and match bolts there are greater opportunities for adopting a sustained-yield program. There are several factors limiting such development, however, among them problems of taxation and credit.

The taxation problem is an important one, and one difficult to solve. After a prolonged study of forest taxation problems, Fairchild states:

It can be shown that, even though all other conditions might be favorable, the present property tax involves such ruinous possibilities as to present a serious obstacle to investment in forest growing on cut-over lands. Whatever may be the other difficulties, it is certain that annual interest in forest growing in the cut-over and second growth regions cannot be expected as long as the unmodified property tax prevails. . . . If the forest tax problem is ever really to be solved, it must yield to attack from three directions: (1) reduction or check of the heavy and growing

[22] Franklin Reed, "The National Lumber Code," *Journal of Forestry*, 31:644–48 (1933).

cost of state government, (2) improvement in the assessment and collection of the property tax, and (3) such modification of the property tax as will adapt it to the peculiarities of forest investment.[23]

The Forest Taxation Inquiry has proposed two plans for meeting the forest tax problem, namely: (1) the "adjusted property tax" and (2) the "partial timber exemption tax."[24] The proposed adjusted property tax will not be discussed here because the procedure called for under its tentative provisions appears to be unsuitable for use by the untrained assessors now responsible for the assessment of rural property.

The second plan, the "partial timber exemption" plan, involves merely the exemption from the property tax of a part of the value of the timber. "Separate assessment of land and timber values would . . . be required. The amount of the exemption should be definitely stated in the law as a percentage of the value of the timber."[25] For second growth timber the exemption proposed would range from nothing, for cutting cycles of four years or less, to 50 per cent, for cutting cycles of twenty-five years or more. Old growth timber in operated forest properties would be taxed as at present. But the assessed value of old growth timber held for future sale or as a reserve supply for future operation would be reduced 5 per cent of the timber value annually until this reduction amounted to 50 per cent. Thereafter 50 per cent of the value of the timber would remain exempt from taxation until the timber became part of the operated property, after which it would be taxed under the general property tax.

This plan offers a simple method of modifying the property tax system so as to make it fit fairly well the peculiar conditions pertaining to forest properties in this state. Its adoption would probably cause no serious disruption in the flow of local revenue.

A third plan, the "differential timber tax" plan, has been proposed more recently by Fairchild.[26] This plan would leave "the land subject to the regular property tax but it would offer to second growth forests a differential tax on timber. The assessed value of timber, determined in the ordinary way, would be reduced by a

[23] Fred R. Fairchild, "Suggestions for the Solution of the Forest Tax Problem," *Journal of Forestry*, 32 : 130 (1934).

[24] Fred R. Fairchild, Director of the Forest Taxation Inquiry, United States Department of Agriculture, Forest Service, *Changes in the Tax System Relating Especially to Forests : Conclusions and Recommendations* (mimeographed Progress Report No. 18, May 1, 1933).

[25] *Ibid.*, p. 32.

[26] Fairchild, "Suggestions for the Solution of the Forest Tax Problem," *Journal of Forestry*, 32 : 138 (1934).

specified rate known as the 'reduction factor.' This factor would usually be uniform throughout the state and would be so calculated as to give forest properties subject to a standard or typical degree of income deferment a tax burden equivalent to that of a net-yield tax. The reduction factor would be prescribed by law, 50 per cent being regarded as the maximum. Forests subject to a deferment greater than normal would be obliged to bear a somewhat heavier tax burden than that of a net-yield tax, but much less than that of the property tax. On the other hand, forests which were so regulated as to receive a substantial income at shorter intervals than indicated by the standard income cycle would enjoy a lighter tax burden than that of a net-yield tax."

After the "reduction factor" or "factors" had been fixed by law, this plan would be simple in operation and would require practically no extra work on the part of the regular taxation administrative machinery. It could be applied to old growth timber as well as to second growth timber. If applied to old growth timber, it is suggested that the authorized reduction in assessed value be made on a sliding scale in order to prevent a sudden reduction in local revenue.

None of the yield taxes as enacted into law are approved by the Forest Taxation Inquiry.[27] The purpose of the yield tax is to fix rather definitely the amount of taxes the owner of a forest property will be required to pay from year to year until the forest is placed on a sustained-yield basis, and to postpone the payment of a considerable portion of the taxes until cash income can be secured from the sale of the timber produced.

The Minnesota Auxiliary Forest Law is of this type.[28] This law authorizes a specific annual property tax of five cents an acre, plus a tax of three cents an acre for fire protection (which does not apply to farm woodlots), plus a 10 per cent yield tax, payable at the time of cutting, on the full and true stumpage value of the timber cut except that which was merchantable at the time of classification or that cut for the owner's use.

To have his lands classified as auxiliary forests under this law the forest owner must first get the approval of the county commissioners and then that of the state commissioner of forestry. To be eligible for classification, commercial forest tracts must have an area of at least 160 acres and a full and true value of not less than

[27] Fairchild, *Changes in the Tax System Relating Especially to Forests.*
[28] See Roy G. Blakey and others, *Taxation in Minnesota,* pp. 147–69, for a more detailed discussion of forest taxation and of the Minnesota act referred to here.

$3.00 nor more than $10.00 an acre. The lands approved must contain or immediately be planted to young growth of merchantable species in sufficient quantity to produce a commercial forest. This forest must be managed under a definite plan approved by the commissioner of forestry and the chief of the Division of Forestry of the University of Minnesota. A fifty-year contract covering the specified tax levies and the plan of management must be entered into between the owner and the state. Cutting is permitted only with the permission of and in accordance with regulations laid down by the commissioner of forestry. Declassification of approved auxiliary forests is provided for.

No forest land has been classified under this law, chiefly because of the opposition of taxpayers living in the county within which classifiable lands are located. It might now be possible to bring about the establishment of auxiliary forests because of the great increase in tax delinquency that has taken place since 1929 and the consequent need of even the small amount of revenue that the land included within these forests would provide. The support that forest conservation is now receiving from the national government might also aid forest owners in getting auxiliary forests established. Successful use of the auxiliary forest law would lighten materially the tax burden now resting upon much of the second growth forest land and would stabilize this burden for the period required to transform these unmerchantable second growth forests into merchantable ones to which the sustained-yield form of management could be applied.

The substitution of a gross income or a sales tax for the general property tax, either wholly or partially, should add to the attractiveness of forest property as an investment. Such a method of taxation would shift forest property taxes wholly or in large measure, in corporation accounting, from an overhead expense to a current operating expense. The greater part of the forest property taxes would then appear to fall on the manufacturing end of the business instead of on the forest end. Such a change would make the practice of forestry more attractive to the private owner than it is now, and would encourage the establishment of privately owned sustained-yield forests.

None of the changes in the routine of taxation suggested here should relieve the property owner from watching the proposed budget of the communities in which his property is located. Watching these budgets and attempting to keep them within reason should be one of the chief responsibilities of forest ownership. After the local budget is adopted, then the only phase of the tax administration in which the forest owner can legitimately interest himself is the equitable distribution of the tax burden among the different property owners or groups of property owners. In certain parts of Europe the watching of local budgets and of the equitable distribution of the tax burden between forests and other property constitutes an important duty of the forester in private employment.

The practice of sustained-yield forestry, including selective logging, requires the investment of additional funds in forest property. After several years of unsatisfactory commercial operations, many large forest owners are without the necessary reserves to establish the foundations of sustained-yield forests. Often the forest lands are covered by mortgages, which must be paid as the timber is cut. In order to pay these debts it frequently becomes necessary for the owner to strip the land of everything that can be turned into cash.

Many forest owners need low-cost credit in order to practice sustained-yield forestry. They would be aided if they could be given credit similar to that available to farm owners through the federal land banks. One solution would be to authorize federal land banks to make this type of loan. The primary purpose of such loans should be to establish and maintain sustained-yield forest units that would bring about an increase in the forest wealth of the United States through building up and protecting the forest growing stock and providing for its orderly utilization.[29] Amortization of these loans should be provided for in the usual way, due consideration being given to the time when the forest can be expected to produce income. The establishment and maintenance of sustained-yield forests would probably add a considerable amount of taxable property to that now found in many of the communities in this part of the state. Such forests would also require the use of much local labor in their development and maintenance.

Control over units of 20,000 acres or more is necessary to the development of sustained-yield forest properties. The simplest and most satisfactory form of control is direct ownership. Lands may be exchanged to consolidate scattered holdings into solid blocks.

[29] Burt P. Kirkland, "Federal Aid in Organizing Forest Credit Facilities," in *A National Plan for American Forestry* (73d Congress, 1st Session, Senate Document No. 12, 2 vols., 1933), pp. 1125–34; "A Forest Credit System," *American Forests*, 40:203–04 (1934).

Authority for the state to exchange lands with private owners would serve this end. Leasing to private owners state-owned forest lands outside the boundaries of state forests might be authorized by law.[30]

Sustained-yield management units should be accessible to the mills that are the chief markets for their products. The cost of transporting forest products from the woods to the manufacturing plant is always an important factor in determining the stumpage value and the profitability of sustained-yield forest units.

There is a difference of opinion among forest owners as to whether it is more desirable to concentrate in single units all lands under one ownership or to divide them into units of from 20,000 to 30,000 acres at considerable distances from each other. In order to provide reasonably effective protection from fire and trespass, the units must be compact as to ownership and of sufficient size to justify the maintenance of at least one man on each unit. The risk of fire is reduced by dividing a large ownership into several units separated by considerable areas of other land, but the larger the unit above the minimum economic size the more intensive can be the protection and supervision. Some owners will prefer to reduce the conflagration hazard, whereas others will prefer to provide more intensive protection and supervision. Topography, soil, and forest cover, together with density of settlement, attitude of settlers, and actual landownership will have much to do with the owner's decision in this matter.

Protecting forests from injury or destruction by fire must be the joint undertaking of the owner and the state. The state should assume the responsibility for the educational work necessary to make the public conscious of forest values and the importance of fire prevention. Private forest owners should support this work. The detection and suppression of fire must be a state function to a large extent, but the private owner should assume part of this responsibility. In northeastern Minnesota the distribution of responsibility between the private owner and the state should be definitely arranged by the parties at interest. Some owners will prefer to assume most, if not all, of the responsibility of handling fires within and adjacent to their property. If they are prepared, they should be allowed to do so under state supervision. Owners should

[30] E. W. Hartwell, "Views on Utilizing State and Tax Delinquent Lands outside of the State Forests for Forest Production," unpublished manuscript, Minneapolis, dated March 15, 1934.

be required to maintain specified equipment always ready for use and should be required to provide men for fire fighting whenever called upon to do so. Equipment and men should be furnished free of charge by owners whose property is threatened.

With reference to the adequacy of protection offered by the Minnesota Forest Service, Mitchell comes to the conclusion, after very careful study, that the protection now provided is inadequate but that adequate protection could be provided at a cost of about $650,000 per year, an increase of $350,000 over present expenditures.[31]

Trespass prevention is another form of protection of which more is required by the private forest owner. Timber thieves have specialized in Christmas trees and firewood, but considerable amounts of sawlogs and pulpwood are cut in trespass from year to year. The small absentee forest owner is usually the victim of such operations, but the large owner is also subject to rather frequent loss.

The protection of large holdings from fire and trespass could be improved markedly by substituting local part-time farm and village labor for transient labor and by providing laborers with enough work so that the forest would become an important and regular source of income. Such workers could aid greatly in preventing fire and trespass, since every fire and every trespass would reduce the amount of work available to them. Sustained-yield forests may become an important factor in the success of part-time farming in the forested regions.

The owners of all forest property should have the right to regulate hunting, fishing, and trapping on their property. The sale of these rights could be made to yield an appreciable amount of revenue to the forest owner during periods when the forest is yielding very little. Many a highly productive European forest has been developed out of an area originally set aside for hunting purposes.

Some private forest landowners feel that there should be no further expansion of state and national forests or forest-purchase areas until the state and federal governments have completed the acquisition of most of the land within the present units and until these public organizations have demonstrated what they can do in the way of growing timber and converting it into public revenue. Also, some private owners feel that further increases in the area of state forests and national forest purchase units will involve a dan-

[31] Mitchell, *Forest Fires in Minnesota.*

gerous reduction of the property base available for taxation to meet the needs of the local communities for revenue.

After making ample allowances for the probable expansion of public forest units and the passage into public ownership of scattered areas of forest land lying outside these units, a considerable area of forest will still remain in private ownership. Improved utilization of these lands must be brought about. Present and prospective economic factors connected with the utilization of these lands justify their owners in applying to them either extensive or intensive forestry, depending upon the local circumstances surrounding each tract. The elimination of the various obstacles to sustained-yield forest management discussed in this chapter should go far toward bringing about a gradual but ultimately noteworthy improvement in the utilization of privately owned forest lands within and outside of farm ownership.

CHAPTER VIII

ACQUISITION AND UTILIZATION OF LAND FOR PUBLIC PURPOSES *

According to estimates presented in Table 31, there are in the fourteen northeastern counties approximately 12,465,365 acres of land which because of physical characteristics or location is not adapted to agricultural use under prevailing economic conditions. Perhaps an additional million acres of such land is located in adjoining counties on the south and west of the fourteen studied. This total acreage is greater than the land area of Denmark, and over half as large as that of Ohio. In the interests of public welfare it should be dedicated to the most profitable uses. Some of it possesses excellent recreational qualities. All will support game cover. Most of it is admirably adapted to the production of timber, and in view of the national timber situation, the use of considerable land for forestry appears to be an economically feasible long-time undertaking.

THE NATIONAL TIMBER SITUATION [1]

Since we enjoy free interchange of processed commodities, goods, and persons between the various states of the Union and presumably shall continue to do so, the timber outlook for Minnesota is greatly influenced by the timber outlook for the nation. That outlook may be briefly summarized as follows: remaining old growth sawtimber in the United States amounts to approximately 1,346 billion board feet, or about 26 per cent of the original virgin stands. Old growth sawtimber makes up 80 per cent of the total. About four-fifths of all sawtimber and about nine-tenths of the old growth are on the Pacific Coast. The total timber stand in the United States, including sawtimber, cordwood, and restocking areas, amounts to about 487 billion cubic feet and is distributed by regions approximately as follows: New England, 5.2 per cent; Middle Atlantic, 4.7 per cent; Lake, 4.4 per cent; Central, 6.3 per cent;

---

* This chapter has been prepared by R. I. Nowell.
[1] *A National Plan for American Forestry* (73d Congress, 1st Session, Senate Document No. 12, 2 vols., 1933) has furnished much valuable data and many suggestions used in this chapter.

Southern, 23.4 per cent; Pacific Coast, 39.4 per cent; North Rocky Mountain, 9.8 per cent; and South Rocky Mountain, 6.8 per cent.

The timber resources of the nation are being consumed at the rate of about 16⅓ billion cubic feet annually — one-tenth by fire and other losses and nine-tenths by cutting. Of the total cut, lumber constitutes about half and fuel wood about a third.

The trends of many factors, all of which are difficult to forecast, will determine our future timber requirements. Estimates prepared by the United States Forest Service are probably the best available and indicate a normal annual consumption of about 16½ billion cubic feet. The estimated annual growth is about 9 billion cubic feet of timber of all sizes. The normal drain, therefore, is almost double the annual growth. In the case of sawtimber, annual growth is estimated at somewhat less than 12 billion board feet and annual drain at about 59½ billion board feet. The ratio of annual consumption to growth of sawtimber is therefore about 5 to 1. If the present rate of consumption is to continue, the national problem is to double annual growth of all sizes and increase sawtimber growth five times. This is easily within the realm of possibility but is not likely to be attained without considerable increases in annual expenditures for forest management.

There are in the nation about 509 million acres of land available for commercial timber production. The United States Forest Service has estimated that with 100 million acres under intensive management, 339 million acres under extensive management, and 70 million acres given simple protection, this land would produce, sixty or eighty years hence, an annual growth of about 21½ billion cubic feet of timber, perhaps 5 billion cubic feet more than normal requirements. A less intensive plan of land use, which would approximately balance the national timber budget, would require intensive management of about 70 million acres, extensive management of about 279 million acres, and simple protection for 111 million acres. This plan would leave about 49 million acres idle and would produce an annual growth of about 17½ billion cubic feet after the plan became fully operative. At present a negligible acreage is given intensive management, perhaps 110 million acres are managed extensively, and fire protection is given about 321 million acres.

With only this meager beginning, a total expenditure in 1932 of about $43,475,000 (86.5 per cent public and 13.5 per cent private) was required. Annual expenditures of about five times that amount would be necessary to establish the nation's forests upon a long-time producing basis with a yield sufficient to balance the national timber budget. Much of the outlay would be in the nature of capital investments during the initial period, after which the annual expenditures would be materially reduced.

Since much of the forest land has little or no valuable timber, many years must elapse before income will be large enough to off-set current expenses. For this reason such forests represent financial liabilities until they reach advanced stages of development. Private capital usually shuns such investments.

It seems highly improbable that private initiative will assume much of the responsibility for developing forestry to a point that will insure an adequate future timber supply for the nation. Public agencies, therefore, must assume the major burden of this responsibility. Ownership and management of a relatively large percentage of the forest lands by public agencies appear unavoidable because of the characteristics of the investment.

By far the most important factor favoring public rather than private ownership of forests is the fact that a considerable portion of forest income is a social return apart from that obtained from the sale of timber products. The effect forests have in preventing rapid run-off with resulting soil erosion and silting of streams, waterways, and harbors is of high social value; but individuals practicing private forestry are unable to show these items on income statements. Again, the esthetic value of green forests may justly be considered a social asset. Also, the production of game and the provision for public recreation are rightly social responsibilities. Individuals and corporations, however, experience difficulty in capitalizing on these by-products of the forest.

That the difficulties of private forest ownership here enumerated are not mere philosophical abstractions may be amply illustrated by examining the records of public and private forestry.

PRIVATE OWNERSHIP RESPONSIBLE FOR EXPLOITATION OF FOREST LANDS

The lumber industry, which represents by far the most important form of timber utilization, has in nearly every region and probably at all times been overbuilt and overcapitalized. The resulting heavy fixed charges on logging equipment, manufacturing plants, standing timber, and lands have forced operators to adopt a "cut out and get out" policy. Pressure has always been exerted to liquidate investments as rapidly as possible. Instead of ceasing operations during periods of slack lumber demand, production has continued as long as lumber prices were sufficiently high to cover the variable operating costs.[2] Timber owners have correctly taken the position that they lose less by operating under such circumstances than by permitting plant and equipment to lie idle. Gross overproduction of lumber has resulted.

The fault lies not with the timber owners but with the form of ownership. Timber owners have operated exactly as other private interests of the population would have operated under similar circumstances. The grave mistake was made in originally permitting forest resources to pass from public to unrestricted private ownership.[3]

Approximately four-fifths of the commercial forest lands of the nation and about nine-tenths of the potential growing capacity are held by private owners. Most of this area, which includes much of the most highly productive of our forest lands, is being badly managed from a social point of view. About 10 million acres are being cut over annually, 98 per cent of which is in private ownership. Fully 95 per cent of the private cutting is made with complete disregard of future possibilities of growth, whereas practically all cutting on public forests is selective, designed to place the forests on a sustained-yield basis.

There are about 83 million acres of denuded or poorly stocked forest lands in the nation. Of this total, 74 million acres, or 90 per cent, is in private ownership and a large part of the balance became denuded under private management. About 95 per cent of the annual forest devastation is on lands in private ownership.

Approximately 98 per cent of the forest area burned annually during the last few years is privately owned. The ratio of actual to allowable burn on lands in private ownership is about 11 to 1, whereas the ratio on the national forests has been held to about 1.07 to 1. Almost half of the privately owned forest lands needing fire protection are neglected, and the public pays five-sixths of the cost of protecting the balance of the privately owned lands.

With one-fifth of the forest lands publicly owned, intensive sustained-yield management on public lands is ten times as great as on private, and the acreage replanted is double that on private lands.

[2] Including the drain on standing timber inventory as a variable cost.
[3] The same may be said of coal, mineral, and oil resources.

Wasteful Operations Responsible for Much Social Loss

Private ownership of the forests must take the blame for much social loss. Millions of young trees are destroyed annually through carelessness in logging operations. Immature trees that produce poor grades of lumber are cut and dumped on the market for whatever price they will bring. Prudent social economy dictates that such trees be left until mature, when they will produce the high grades of lumber. The urge for economy in the use of labor in logging operations has led to methods of cutting that have been wasteful of timber. Forest surveys on the west coast indicate an annual waste of over 6 million cords of sound wood. In the coast states material suitable for conversion into 1.7 billion board feet of lumber is wasted annually, an amount equal to nearly one-sixth of the 1926 cut.

Industries dependent upon forest products have suffered losses amounting to untold millions. The advancing front of virgin timber exploitation has left in its wake stranded industries and stranded populations. Lumbering towns that have "cut out" and then gradually died are far too numerous throughout the nation. As explained previously, the logging operations have usually been badly over-expanded. This has tended to give a boom atmosphere to urban development. Schools, roads, stores, and service establishments have been overbuilt, only to be abandoned or partially used when the timber supply has dwindled. In contrast, forests on a sustained-yield basis afford a perpetual source of raw material for the support of dependent industries. They also provide continuous employment for labor and continuous revenue for the support of roads, schools, and other public services.

In order to dispose of land holdings some timber companies have sponsored inadvisable land settlement schemes after having stripped the land of its timber resources. This is not true of all companies nor of all settlement projects, but far too often lands have been sold to settlers for agricultural purposes that were entirely unsuited to such use. These cut-over colonization schemes have frequently entailed tremendous public expense and unwarranted human suffering and loss.

Another unfortunate consequence of the way in which our forest resources have been exploited is extensive tax delinquency. Millions of acres of cut-over land have been long delinquent for the nonpayment of taxes, and during the depression annual additions to the delinquency list have been greatly increased. Throughout the entire country, privately owned cut-over forest lands are reverting to public ownership for nonpayment of taxes.

In fourteen northeastern Minnesota counties approximately 48 per cent of the total taxable land area was delinquent for general property taxes in 1931. Delinquency has not been summarized according to different land uses, but a cursory examination indicates that upwards of two-thirds of the undeveloped lands were delinquent in 1931.

Legislatures of various states have passed forest crop laws to stimulate private forestry and to stem the rising tide of tax delinquency. Despite the various inducements offered, the results have not been markedly successful. As indicated in the previous chapter, Minnesota has a forest crop law, which was passed by the legislature in 1927.[4] At the present writing (November, 1934) not a single acre has been set aside in an auxiliary forest.

In Wisconsin, where forestry conditions are essentially the same as in Minnesota, the forest crop law provides for a limited assessment of ten cents per acre and a 10 per cent severance tax, but in addition the state pays the township ten cents per acre annually to offset the loss in tax revenue. About 1,387,419 acres have been entered under this law, of which 252,507 acres are privately owned, and 1,134,912 acres, or 82 per cent, county owned.[5] Because of the payment by the state the Wisconsin law has special appeal to local taxing units, whereas the Minnesota law meets resistance locally.

Private ownership aided by forest crop laws probably can be made to work on lands having some merchantable virgin timber or on well-stocked second growth lands that can immediately be placed on a sustained-yield basis; but for the vast areas of cut-over or burned-over lands there appears no alternative to public ownership and management. Of course, if subsidies were made sufficiently lucrative, private ownership could be induced to reforest such lands, but the costs to the public would be prohibitive. Outright public ownership and direct expenditures probably will prove to be the cheapest method of reforesting devastated areas.

The Wisconsin Governor's Committee on Land Use and Forestry has raised serious questions about the Wisconsin forest crop law after scarcely three years' operation. The committee says: [6]

[4] Session Laws, 1927.
[5] As of June 26, 1934. In Wisconsin land reverting through tax delinquency passes into county ownership.
[6] Forest Land Use in Wisconsin, 1932, p. 112.

The present law is thus more in the nature of a state subsidy than a forest-management measure. The counties have already entered 460,521 acres of their tax-delinquent land under the forest crop law. When these are established as county forest reserves, the counties and the townships may be entitled to draw $92,000 annually from the state. If all counties follow this procedure, the annual burden upon the state would be many times this amount and there would nevertheless be no assurance that the land will be in a productive condition. . . .[7]

Similarly, Professor Wehrwein of the University of Wisconsin has remarked:

Probably enough time has elapsed to test the efficiency of this form of taxation not only from the standpoint of a taxation scheme but its effect on reforestation and the importance of forest crop tax money to towns and school districts. In many towns the income from this source has done much to stabilize revenues, but perhaps it has also tended to keep alive marginal towns which should be eliminated.[8]

Whether we like it or not, the trend toward public ownership of the denuded lands is unmistakable. The wild land in northern Minnesota on which taxes are now being paid is usually in nonresident speculative ownership. These lands are being held with the ultimate object of sale for agricultural purposes.

In this discussion of some of the apparent advantages of public as opposed to private ownership of forest lands, the arguments are not to be construed as recommending complete public ownership and management of all forest lands. There are far more lands in need of management than public agencies — county, state, and federal — can conceivably take care of for years to come. Private ownership should be encouraged within reasonable limits to assume as much of the task as possible. Perhaps the better-stocked areas can be placed upon a sustained-yield basis and with the aid of reasonable tax adjustments remain permanently in private ownership. Considerable production of timber may continue on woodlots included in farms. Paper companies and manufacturers of wood fiber products having heavy investments in plant and equipment have a much greater incentive to practice forestry as a means of securing a perpetual supply of raw material than do the sawmills. It takes only about half as long to produce pulpwood as to produce good sawlogs, a factor of no little importance as an inducement to private ownership. It is probably true, however, that even paper mill operators would prefer to have public agencies assume the burden of producing their necessary raw materials.

If public agencies come quickly to recognize the new responsi-

[7] As of June 26, 1934, the annual county and township drain on the state for county forests was about $227,000.
[8] G. S. Wehrwein, "Research in Public Finance Arising from Land Zoning," *Journal of Farm Economics,* January, 1934, p. 125.

bility that is being thrust upon them, much time can be saved in initiating programs of forest acquisition, consolidation, and management. The task is a big one, and during the development period heavy and continuing appropriations will be necessary. The granting of these appropriations is no doubt contingent upon public support. These appropriations should be looked upon as public investments which if properly husbanded will return dividends to be enjoyed by future generations.[9]

County, State, or Federal Ownership of Forest Lands

The objectives of county, state, and federal ownership of forest lands are in most cases essentially the same. All seek to promote, by means of education, a better public appreciation of the conservation movement. The production of timber products and the propagation and protection of wild life are common objectives. The development of public recreational opportunities, the prevention and control of fire and erosion, the reduction of loss from insects and diseases, and the curtailment of governmental expenditures for roads, schools, relief, etc., are all fundamental parts of public ownership programs, regardless of whether they be county, state, or federal.

It would seem that the choice of public agencies for forest management should rest upon the financial ability and readiness of the respective agencies to carry the program to fulfillment. In this respect the counties are probably the least qualified. Lack of continuity in the policy of county administration may be a handicap to a long-time undertaking such as forestry. In the parts of Minnesota where the greatest acreage is in need of management, counties have difficulty in meeting the financial needs of ordinary functions of government. Many are so heavily in debt that it is impracticable for them to assume additional responsibilities. In some states where title to tax-reverted lands rests with counties, large areas of county forests have been created. In Minnesota, however, where title to delinquent lands rests with the state, there appears little if any occasion for having county forests. While there are no serious objections to county forests, it would seem that in Minnesota the state and federal forest services are much better equipped to own and manage forest lands than are the counties.

[9] For an impassioned argument for nationalization of the forests read Robert Marshall, *The People's Forests* (1933).

As between state and federal ownership the case is less clear-cut, but fortunately a choice between the two need not be made, since there are more lands in the state than both organizations are capable of administering intensively for years to come.

The two national forests, Chippewa and Superior, were created before the state forestry program was well under way. The sites of these two forests are both very desirable. The Chippewa National Forest was created from Indian lands located around Lake Winni-bigoshish and contains some very fine Norway and white pine stands.[10] The Superior Forest is located in northern St. Louis, Lake, and Cook counties, in the rock outcrop and lake region. The timber is mostly mixed hardwoods and conifers, jack pine, and spruce; but the forest includes some of the finest wilderness canoe routes in the nation. Unfortunately, from a management stand-point, the forest is divided into two parts, separated by a long narrow strip of land. (See Figure 40.) Plans for a third national forest in the state were started in 1931, when the Mesabi purchase area, located immediately north of the Iron Range in St. Louis County, was created.

For purposes of economy in supervision and management the United States Forest Service has endeavored to consolidate and enlarge the federal holdings around these original forest areas. Meanwhile the State Division of Forestry has aggressively sponsored the creation by legislative acts of a number of small forest units. These forests are well distributed over the northern part of the state, and two of them, Grand Portage and Kabetogama, embrace some of the choicest border waters of the state. Both the state and national forests have been so located as to be available to large numbers of people and thereby enlist public support. By coming in direct contact with the forests people are better able to appreciate the full value of the conservation program.

In the establishment of these forests there has sometimes been conflict between state and federal programs. For example, in the case of the George Washington Memorial State Forest and the Mesabi National Purchase Unit, an overlapping of designated boundaries occurred. Conferences between the state and federal agencies are bringing about a coordination of programs that will prevent future differences.

[10] About eleven sections of virgin Norway pine on the shores of Cass Lake in addition to some 12,000,000 board feet on Star Island have been reserved, while the rest of the merchantable timber has been cut. E. G. Cheyney and Alfred L. Nelson, *Forestry in Minnesota* (1929), p. 32.

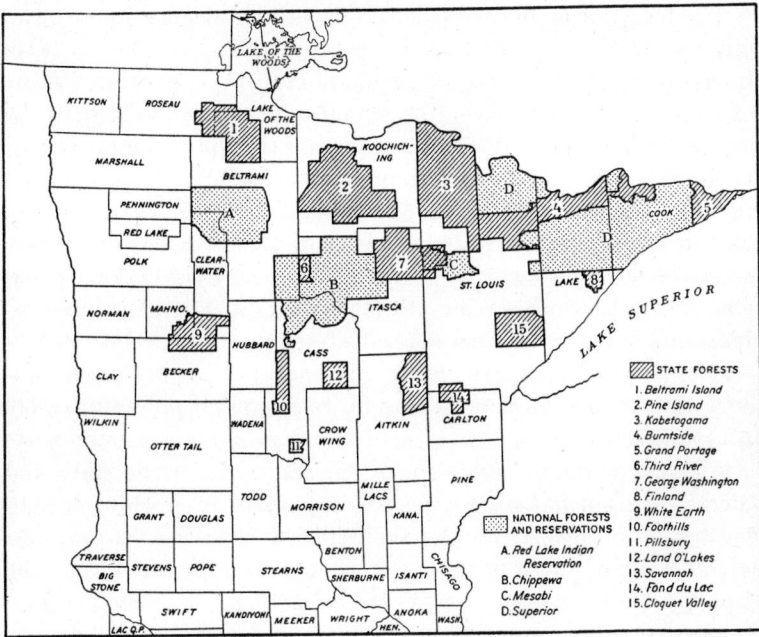

FIGURE 40. — STATE AND NATIONAL FORESTS AND RED LAKE INDIAN RESERVATION

Appropriations available to the State Division of Forestry have heretofore been required for fire protection of both private and state forest lands, and it has been impossible to engage in very much active forest improvement within state forests. Moreover, most of these are of relatively recent establishment with only a small amount of land in state ownership. The United States Forest Service, on the other hand, having established the forests earlier and having more funds, has provided some employment for local men on improvement work and has made a somewhat better showing in the national forests. As a result local sentiment in various places has favored placing lands in federal rather than state forests. Another factor that has added to the appeal of the federal forests is that 25 per cent of all gross receipts from national forest lands are turned over to the counties in which the receipts originate to help defray general county expenses. In 1933, however, the state legislature largely removed this advantage by passing a law authorizing the state to pay counties 50 per cent of all gross receipts from certain state lands located within state forests.[11]

[11] Session Laws, 1933, chapter 313.

The national Forest Service can obtain forest lands in only two important ways — by purchase and by exchange; the state in three ways — by purchase, exchange, and tax reversion. Future expansion and consolidation of national forests will be chiefly by purchase and exchange, while expansion of state forests will be accomplished largely by the addition of tax-reverted lands. Owners of lands that are to be added to the national forests will therefore probably receive small cash considerations, whereas in state forests little money will be spent for land purchases. This situation, which is rather obvious to landowners and largely unavoidable, causes owners and local residents to prefer national to state forests. In recent years the State Division of Forestry has encountered considerable local resistance to its expansion program largely on this account.

An understanding needs to be reached between the state and federal governments with respect to the areas in which each is to develop its forests. At present there is local agitation favoring one or the other of these agencies. It should be recognized that the areas available for public forests are larger than the federal service is prepared to take care of, consequently the entire task need not be turned over to the federal government. Moreover, such a step would be unthinkable in view of the excellent progress that the state is making in the establishment of state forests. A coordinated plan of acquisition and expansion showing unity in objective and plan of action should be developed for the future.

Proposed National and State Forest Acquisition Areas

Representatives of the state and federal forest services have within recent months held a series of conferences to eliminate differences and to agree upon long-time forest-expansion areas. The chief topics of these discussions have been the division of lands adjacent to the border waters and the ultimate boundaries of national forests within the state. Concerning the broader features of the division mutual agreement has already been reached.

In brief, this understanding contemplates state retention of all established state forests except certain state forest lands located between the two parts of the Superior National Forest. The Superior Forest may absorb these lands and expand southward and westward so as to merge with the Mesabi Purchase Unit. Room for expansion of the Chippewa National Forest in all direc-

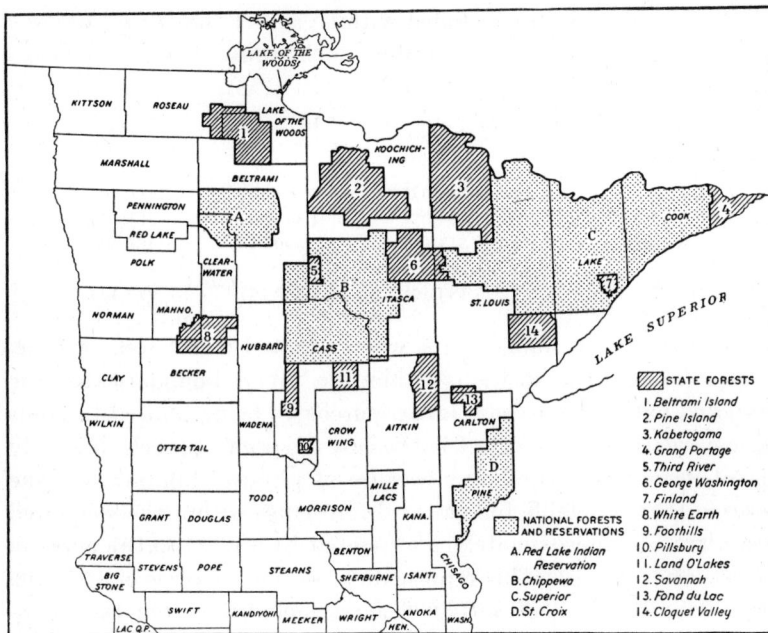

FIGURE 41. — PROPOSED PURCHASE AREAS IN MINNESOTA

tions is provided, and a new national forest, the St. Croix, in eastern Pine and Carlton counties is established. Except for the Red
Lake Indian Reservation, which is under federal control, all other
forest lands in the cut-over counties are to be subject to state
acquisition and management.

Figure 41 shows the tentative boundaries of the proposed national forest purchase areas and boundaries of the authorized state
forests. This figure is based largely upon a map prepared in con-
ference by representatives of the federal and state forest services
with refinements and extensions of the national purchase areas
suggested by the tentative zoning map which serves as a base for
the figure.[12] (See Figure 39, page 173.) Two state forests, the Third
River and Finland, are completely encompassed by the proposed
federal purchase areas. Present plans are for state retention of
these forests, but eventually the state might relinquish them in
favor of the national forests.[13]

[12] See Chapter VI for a discussion of the zoning map.
[13] After Figure 41 had been prepared and estimates of the areas made, a joint
committee representing the federal Forest Service, the State Department of Conservation, the State Planning Board, and other interested agencies made slight
modifications, but the revised map differs in only a few minor details.

The gross land area included within each of the three proposed national forests classified according to land-use zones is approximately as follows:

Forest	Total Land Acreage	Acreage in Conservation Zones	Acreage in Agricultural Zones
Superior	3,345,075[14]	3,184,167	160,908
Chippewa	1,594,087[15]	1,414,077	180,010
St. Croix	547,459	390,953	156,506
Total	5,486,621	4,989,197	497,424

Official county zoning maps when adopted might well serve as guides for land acquisition within the broad boundaries of the proposed national purchase areas, purchases being limited to lands in conservation zones except in the case of specific parcels definitely unsuited to agricultural use because of physical limitations. The acreage then available for national forest use within the suggested boundaries is approximately represented by the 4,989,197 acres in conservation zones.[16] This represents a possible increase of 3,916,209 acres over the present 1,072,988 acres included within the boundaries of the Superior and Chippewa forests and the Mesabi Purchase Unit. Official designation of the proposed national forest purchase areas and the formulation of long-time acquisition plans at an early date would be highly desirable.

The chief responsibility for managing and protecting the conservation zones outside the proposed national purchase areas will have to be assumed by the state. Outside these areas there are approximately 7,500,000 acres in the suggested conservation zones of the fourteen northeastern counties. In initiating a state management program, efforts might well be concentrated first in putting lands now in state forests on a productive basis. Then, as the conservation program grows in scope and momentum, cultural practices might gradually be extended to cover other suitable forest lands within the remaining conservation zones. All the proposed conservation zones should ultimately be placed under some kind of management, private, state, or federal.

Figure 42 [17] indicates the intensity of technical management of permanent forest areas that has been proposed by representa-

[14] Exclusive of 47,563 acres in the Finland State Forest.
[15] Exclusive of 46,354 acres in the Third River State Forest.
[16] See page 219 for ownership of lands in purchase areas.
[17] This map necessarily represents a first approximation and is subject to modification and refinement on the basis of future study.

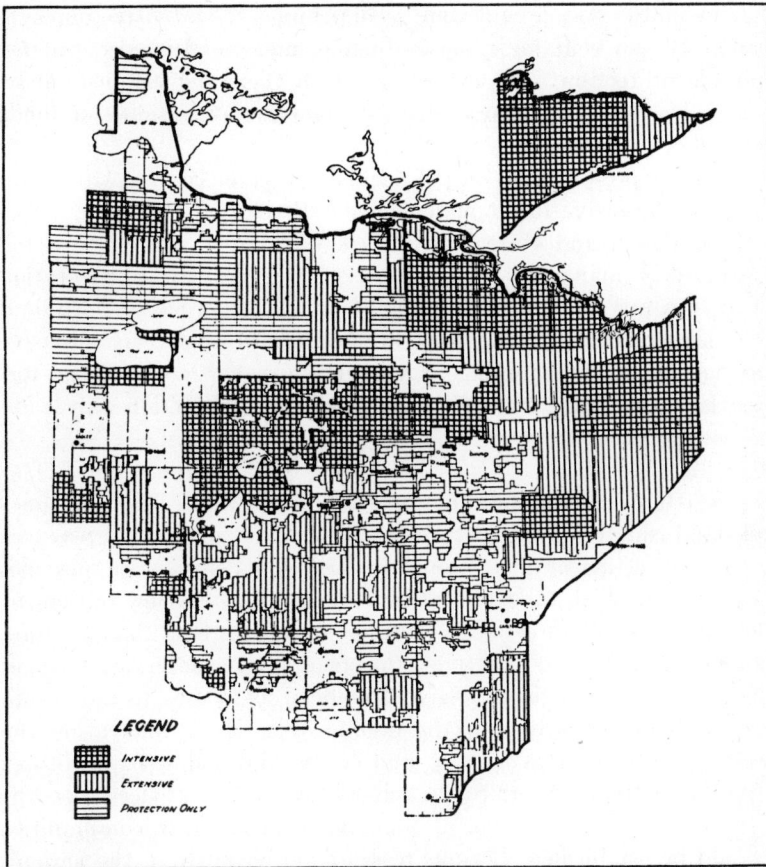

FIGURE 42. — SUGGESTED INTENSITIES OF MANAGEMENT OF PERMANENT
FOREST AREAS

tives of the state and federal agencies concerned. Three degrees of
intensity of management are indicated: (1) intensive, (2) extensive,
and (3) protection only. In deciding upon the areas suitable for intensive management, the recreational possibilities as well as the
quality of the soil for timber production and the proximity of
wood-using industries were considered. Areas having somewhat
less favorable soil types or less favorably located with respect to
wood-using industries but located in convenient administrative
units were recommended for extensive management. Lands distinctly inferior for forest production, such as bogs, muskegs, etc.,
or lands located outside the proposed administrative units were
recommended for protection only. Of the forest lands in the four-

teen counties 35 per cent were recommended for intensive management, 38 per cent for extensive management, and 27 per cent for simple protection. The extent to which these suggestions will be carried out will, of course, depend upon the availability of funds for such purposes.

At the present time only a negligible area of land in Minnesota is given intensive forest management. Perhaps the Chippewa National Forest and Itasca State Park have come nearest to being intensively managed. The advent of the Civilian Conservation Corps camps has provided labor for much constructive work, and the sites of the various camps are temporarily receiving intensive management. Prior to the CCC work, however, most of the forest lands of the state were given simple fire protection only.

FARM-FOREST COMMUNITIES

Scattered throughout the forest lands are small irregular zones of land suitable for agricultural use. Most of these areas are sparsely settled and offer only limited opportunities for new development. With the adoption of zoning ordinances new settlement can probably be directed to these regions. As a long-time program the isolated settlers scattered throughout the conservation zones should be encouraged and given financial assistance to move into the agricultural areas for the double objective of increasing the settler's returns from farming and of reducing public expenditures for the maintenance of roads, schools, and other services.

Thus the foundations of permanent farm-forest communities would be established. Persons residing permanently in the agricultural zones could work part time in the woods on logging operations as well as in planting, thinning, slash disposal, fire prevention, and other cultural operations. Small permanent wood-manufacturing establishments, which would furnish additional opportunities for part-time employment, presumably could be attracted by comparatively cheap raw materials and labor. In areas having productive soils the small part-time farms could be made to contribute substantially toward the maintenance of respectable standards of living for the population.

The essential elements, it would seem, are present for the establishment of stable, well-balanced permanent communities within the forests. These communities must necessarily be rather small, but perhaps not smaller than fifty families, the number required to furnish children for an efficient school unit. In the light of present and prospective economic conditions the natural resources in the cut-over counties, except on the Range, appear to be far too meager to support a dense population. There are probably enough permanent residents in the fourteen counties now to supply the labor necessary for the operation of farms and forests on a permanently sustained-yield basis.

With such a reorganized social-economic pattern in the cut-over counties the population could probably be maintained on a much higher standard of living than now prevails. A prime requisite, however, for such a reorganization is that funds for forestry, wild life, and recreational development be forthcoming from outside sources. Returns from this investment would be obtained in the future from the harvesting of timber and from the social benefits provided by the forests.

METHODS OF FOREST CONSOLIDATION AND EXPANSION

Most important for the unification of the state and federal forest programs in Minnesota is the consolidation and blocking up of the landholdings of the respective agencies. Supervision and management of small scattered pieces is unsatisfactory and expensive. Cooperative arrangements for the management of lands may be worked out where pieces of state lands are interspersed among national forest lands and federal lands are scattered through state forests. Cooperative arrangements are not as desirable, however, as outright ownership, and in places where public lands are scattered among lands predominantly in private ownership, cooperative management is quite unsatisfactory if not impossible.

Unmanaged privately owned lands scattered in or adjacent to state and national forests frequently create serious fire and disease hazards and in other ways militate against low-cost forest management. Scattered isolated settlers constitute distinct handicaps to efficient forest management.

As remarked above, consolidation and expansion of public forest areas may be accomplished in three principal ways: by purchase, by reversion through tax delinquency, and by exchange.

Federal purchases. — Purchases of land for national forests are authorized under the Weeks Act passed in 1911 and subsequently amended by the Clark-McNary Act of 1924.[18] Under these laws the secretary of agriculture is "authorized and directed to examine, locate, and recommend for purchase such forested, cut-over, or

[18] U. S. C. A. — T 16, S 513 to 519.

denuded lands within the watersheds of navigable streams as in his judgment may be necessary to the regulation of the flow of navigable streams or for the production of timber." [19] However, authority is not granted in these laws for the acquisition of farm properties within forest purchase areas.

From March 1, 1911, to July 1, 1933, a total of 4,532,698 acres of forest lands were acquired by the United States Forest Service in states east of the Great Plains at a total cost of $20,578,410.51, an average of $4.58 an acre.[20] Purchases have been made only in states east of the Great Plains because in the West there are huge areas of unreserved public domain that may best be converted to national forest lands by exchange. In the national forests of Minnesota a total of 130,580 acres were purchased during the period at an average price of $1.61 per acre.

In recent depression years there has been a strong tendency to liquidate private holdings in forest lands. Much more land was offered, at greatly reduced prices, than could be bought with the diminished land acquisition appropriations of the federal Forest Service. The president, however, by executive order of May 20, 1933, allotted $20,000,000 for the purchase of lands from funds made available by the act of March, 1933. This additional appropriation made it possible to accelerate land purchases greatly, but the amount is still far too small to effect all the desirable consolidations, and continuing annual appropriations may be used to good advantage.

Federal funds for land acquisition have also been made available from another source. A fund of $83,000,000 has been set aside by the President for the retirement of submarginal agricultural lands. It is planned to buy up farm lands that are obviously too poor to support farm families and to assist the farmers financially and otherwise to become established in new locations on productive soils near good roads and schools. The fund is to be used in setting up comparatively small experimental projects which may serve as models for larger projects in the future.

If the feasibility of the program can be definitely established, the administration has indicated a willingness to make much larger sums available in succeeding years for this purpose. The plan is to convert lands acquired under the program to their best alternative uses. With this in view the original fund has been tentatively

[19] *Ibid.*
[20] Annual Report of the United States Forester, 1933, p. 15.

allotted to the following four types of projects: first, for purchases of lands in areas where the agricultural problem is the most pressing one in need of solution, such lands to be used for forestry or grazing or be left idle, depending upon the most satisfactory alternative use; second, for lands that may be converted into parks or recreational areas, necessarily located comparatively near large centers of population; third, for purchases of poor farm lands in Indian reservations, the plan being to return to the Indians lands that at one time were unwisely opened to homestead entry; and fourth, for the purchase of specialized waterfowl refuges along the Mississippi flightway.

Titles to all lands purchased will be in the name of the United States government, but such lands may be turned over on a long-time arrangement to various agencies qualified and willing to administer them, such as the federal Indian Service, the National Park Service, state divisions of forestry, etc. An opportunity is thus provided to further the consolidation of public lands, to concentrate settlement on land suitable for agriculture, and to remove the isolated settler from forests. From this original grant of funds two projects in northern Minnesota have been tentatively approved, for which probably 100,000 acres or more of farm lands will be purchased.

State purchases. — It is expected that state forests will be developed primarily on cut-over land which is reverting to public ownership through the process of tax delinquency. Present indications are that the state will in this way gain title to far more land than it will be able to manage intensively for years to come. Consequently, extensive purchases will not be required in order to build up state forests. However, some land will need to be acquired, such as certain key properties that control important rights of way, tower sites, timbered areas, and lands needed to consolidate holdings. Such lands must necessarily be acquired with state funds. The state has appropriated money for land acquisition from funds accumulated from the sale of fish and game licenses and from state taxes on intoxicating liquors and beers.[21] At the end of the fiscal year, June 30, 1934, a total of 22,714 acres of land within state forests had been purchased with fish and game funds at a total cost of $32,750, or $1.44 per acre.

Tax-reverted lands. — The process of tax reversion offers by

[21] See Session Laws, 1929, chapter 332; 1933, chapter 419; Extra Session Laws, 1933, chapter 67.

far the most important method of acquiring lands for state forests. Unfortunately an apparent contradiction in the law as to whether reverted lands belong to the state or to the counties has led to much confusion. In part the law reads as follows: [22] "All parcels of land hereafter duly . . . bid in for the state as provided by law, shall at the expiration of five years . . . become and be the absolute property . . . of the state . . . or its assigns." In the same section the act continues, "The title to each and every parcel of land thereby acquired by the state shall be held by it in trust for each and all of the taxing districts." Thus in a single paragraph tax-reverted lands are given in absolute title to the state at the same time that they are defined as being merely held in trust by the state. The original reversion law was passed in 1927 and was to have become operative in 1933, but the legislature then in session extended the date on which it should take effect to 1935. Unless modified by the legislature, the act will become effective this year.

The lenient policy of the legislature in granting tax abatements and extending the date of reversion has aggravated the tax situation by encouraging voluntary delinquency. It would be a mistake to postpone the reversion date longer, particularly on wild lands. An exemption on farm homesteads for another two-year period would not be particularly objectionable from the standpoint of making land use adjustments, and conditions by that time might possibly improve enough to permit resumption of tax payments in some cases. If the tax-reversion law were amended to provide, first, for reversion to the state in absolute title of all wild lands located in conservation zones [23] that have been delinquent for five years or more and, second, for reversion to the state in trust for the various taxing districts of all wild lands located in agricultural zones that have been delinquent for five years or more, the situation would be greatly clarified. Reverted lands in conservation zones could then be turned over to the Department of Conservation for permanent management, while suitable lands in agricultural zones could be resold for agricultural settlement. Proceeds of sale from such lands should be distributed among the various taxing districts according to their respective interests, to be used for the retirement of bonded indebtedness. The local taxing districts might also receive 50 per

[22] Session Laws, 1929, chapter 415.
[23] As established by county boards of commissioners and the Department of Conservation.

cent of gross receipts from all reverted lands in conservation zones placed under state forest management.[24] These funds should also be used for debt retirement.

Consolidation by exchange. — Exchange of lands could sometimes be employed to advantage in rounding out tracts in public ownership. Thus, if suitable exchanges can be made, the state would be able to obtain title to privately owned land within the confines of state forests in return for lands located elsewhere that may be better adapted to private ownership. There are also opportunities for the exchange of state-owned land within national forests for federal lands more suitably located for state development. Unfortunately constitutional limitations have restricted the state in making exchanges of this kind. A constitutional amendment to remove the restriction has been up for consideration but up to the present has failed to secure the affirmative vote needed for approval. When this barrier is removed, the state will be in a better position to make desirable exchanges of land with the federal government and private owners.

Details of transfers remain to be worked out, and the legislature must formulate the general terms of exchange. The acreage in federal, state, and private ownership in the three proposed national forests is about as follows:

Forest	Federal	State	Private	Total
Superior	949,939	430,102	1,965,034	3,345,075
Chippewa	245,986	203,857	1,144,244	1,594,087
St. Croix	547	2,737	544,175	547,459
Total	1,196,472	636,696	3,653,453	5,486,621

In addition to the state-owned lands in these forests there were in 1931 an additional 1,729,967 acres of land delinquent for general property taxes. Much of this delinquency was of long standing, and a large percentage of the lands will revert to the state in 1935. In legally designated state forests there are about 88,000 acres of federally owned lands. Many of the federal lands are held in trust for Indians, and before exchanges of these lands can be effected the United States Forest Service must secure clear title, either by purchase or transfer with the Indian Service. A few of the federal lands available for transfer are remnants of the old public domain which are distinctly inferior to most state lands within the federal

---

[24] Laws, 1933, chapter 313, would need to be amended to designate all conservation zones established by the adoption of county zoning ordinances as state forest areas eligible for participation in gross income from such lands.

forest areas. Such lands would have to be appraised and traded on the basis of their value, due allowances being made for timber values.

One of the limiting factors, it would seem, in effecting wholesale consolidations will be to find enough suitable federal lands for transfer. Of course, it is not anticipated that the state will transfer to the government all state lands in the proposed national forests for years to come. In the Superior Forest there are several townships that are almost entirely state-owned at the present time. The state presumably will wish to consolidate these blocks. The federal government probably will be able to secure title to these large blocks of state land only through exchanges involving changes in boundaries. Federally owned lands in the Superior National Forest adjacent to either the Grant Portage or the Kabetogama State Forest could always be used for trading purposes. Perhaps submarginal agricultural lands purchased by the federal government in its newly inaugurated land retirement projects may be used as trading stock for making forest consolidations. In some states the federal Forest Service has declared state forests as federal purchase areas for the purpose of acquiring trading stock. The undertaking has many challenging ramifications, but the objective sought — a simplification of forest ownership — is worthy of great effort.

CHAPTER IX

IMPROVED USE OF AGRICULTURAL LAND *

The improved utilization of agricultural land in northern Minnesota involves both factors outside the farm business and factors inherent in the organization of the individual farm. Among the external factors is the present sparsity of settlement, which militates against the most effective use of the land. Marketing units are often too small to function economically or are at a prohibitive distance from many farms. Where settlement is scattered, public facilities can be supplied only at relatively high costs, with the result that taxes are bound to prove a severe burden to agriculture.

This chapter, however, deals with the internal problems of farm organization and operation. The authors recognize fully that unless some of the external handicaps are removed, even the most carefully planned and carefully executed farm organization can be only partially successful in effecting better land use and a better standard of living for the farmer.

In planning a better utilization of land two types of development must be considered. The first involves the reorganization of existing farms and the second the development of new farms on wild land. In this chapter chief emphasis will be placed on the improvement of present organizations. The discussion does not apply primarily to part-time and self-sufficing farms, of which there are a large number in this section of the state. The operators of the former are often interested primarily in other occupations than farming, and many of the latter would rather take a moderate return, even though it provides only a meager standard of living, than exert themselves to better their situation. The suggestions here given are not primarily intended for these classes of operators, but for men who are willing to apply themselves, mentally as well as physically, to using their resources to best advantage in maintaining a fair standard of living.

TYPE OF FARMING

Dairying is the chief farm enterprise in northeastern Minnesota. According to the 1930 federal census, 55 per cent of the farms

* This chapter has been prepared by G. A. Pond and C. W. Crickman.

were classed as dairy farms; 23 per cent were classed as general farms, on the majority of which dairying was undoubtedly the largest single source of income; 7½ per cent were classed as crop specialty farms, and on these potatoes and hay were the principal crops; poultry farms made up 1.6 per cent of the total; and 11 per cent were classed as self-sufficing. Even in those localities where considerable specialization in poultry and in vegetable growing has taken place, these lines of production are minor as compared with dairying. Potatoes are the principal cash sale crop in the area, clover, alsike, and alfalfa seed being of local importance in some sections. According to the 1930 census the average value of farm production per farm on the dairy farms was 46 per cent greater than the average for all farms in the fourteen counties, and considerably greater than the average for any other important type of farming. All indications point to dairy farming as more generally adapted to this area than any other type.

SIZE OF FARM

The average size of farms in the fourteen northeastern counties as reported by the 1930 federal census was 117 acres. Thirty-two per cent included from 100 to 174 acres, 29 per cent from 50 to 99 acres, and 20 per cent from 20 to 49 acres. Only 14 per cent exceeded 175 acres. These figures are a little misleading, since a considerable number of small part-time and self-sufficing farms are included. The average size of dairy farms was 131 acres and of general farms 141 acres. The area in harvested crops was 41 acres and 36 acres, respectively, for these two types.

An analysis of farm accounting records indicates that the size of the farms is one of the important factors limiting farm earnings in this section of the state. The small acreage of tillable land per farm limits the size of business and therefore the earning power. Most settlers in northern Minnesota came here because their capital was limited, and they could buy more acres of land with a given amount of money than elsewhere. Usually after making an initial payment on the land, erecting simple, inexpensive buildings, and providing the necessary stock and equipment, they had little, if anything, left to spend in clearing land. Sometimes outside work provided funds for land clearing, but too often the settler was forced to resort to hand labor. This was a slow, tedious process as compared with what he might have done if funds had been available for the purchase of explosives. Land development, therefore, progressed slowly, and a considerable proportion of the farms still have too small an acreage of cleared land to provide an adequate earning basis.

It is difficult to say just how large a farm should be in this territory. It varies, of course, with the type of farm. For a poultry or a truck farm one would not need nearly so large an acreage as for a dairy or general farm. The size of farm should also be governed by the managerial ability of the operator and the capital and labor supply he can command. In general it may be said that 80 acres should be considered the minimum size of a dairy farm and that 40 acres of this should be crop land; 120 acres is a more desirable size, and for the man to whom family labor is available 160 acres or more offers much more assurance of satisfactory earnings. On the other hand, the man with limited funds and a limited labor supply should avoid buying more land than he can develop within a reasonable period of time. Raw land will in some cases contribute sufficient income from pasture and timber products to pay the taxes and other carrying costs, but unless there is some such income, idle land, even though it may be potentially productive, is likely to be a serious burden to the owner.

Factors Affecting the Selection of Crops and Livestock

Climate and soil. — Climate and soil are two of the most important factors affecting the farm organization in any area because they determine very largely the crops that can be grown, and the choice of livestock is to a considerable extent dependent on the feed crops available. The climate of the fourteen counties included in this study is favorable to the production of small grains, forage crops, root crops, and potatoes. The growing season in much of this area is too short and too cool to grow corn for grain. It can be grown as a forage crop in the southern and western part of the area, but in the northeastern counties sunflowers largely take its place as a silage crop. Late spring and early fall frosts limit the production of tender crops on peat land. Both root and leaf vegetable crops are well adapted climatically and do well on most of the peat land, although commercial fertilizer may be needed if the peat is deficient in certain essential elements.

The choice of livestock is affected to some extent by climate. The short pasture season necessitates a long period of dry feeding. The long cold winters make necessary more warmly constructed shelter for stock than in a milder climate.

Soils are highly variable in this section of the state, but on most of the mineral soils the crops mentioned can be grown. Potatoes are grown on practically all soil types. Root crops are better adapted to the heavier soils. Much of the area, especially in the eastern counties, is deficient in lime; and alsike is the only legume roughage that can be grown. Alfalfa and sweet clover can be grown on the mineral soils in the western counties without liming, but in much of this area a heavy application of lime is necessary if these crops are to be grown and even then winter killing frequently occurs on the heavier soils. Some soil types have a hard substratum that prevents the alfalfa roots from going sufficiently deep to withstand dry weather. Wherever it is adapted, alfalfa will produce more digestible feed per acre of a quality suited to feeding needs than will any other crop in this area. Sweet clover, likewise, where it is adapted, has a higher carrying capacity as a pasture crop than any other commonly grown.

Over a considerable part of these fourteen counties it is necessary to keep a fairly large proportion of the crop land seeded to legume hay or pasture in order to maintain the humus and nitrogen supply, especially if intensive cultivated crops such as potatoes are to be grown.[1] This is especially true in the eastern counties. This in turn necessitates a sufficient acreage of small grain to serve as a companion crop for the seedings. Fortunately most of the soils are well adapted to legume crops. Legumes and grasses, in addition to being grown on tillable land, may be seeded on land too stony for cultivation or land from which the stumps have not been removed. They are often seeded on newly brushed land under a system of delayed clearing. Both soil and climate in this area are such as to give hay and pasture crops a prominent place in cropping systems.

Labor supply. — Most of the labor used on farms in northern Minnesota is supplied by the farmer and his family. Indeed, on many farms the acreage of tillable land is so small that it is difficult to use all the available supply of family labor advantageously in crop and livestock production. On farms in the process of development some of this labor can be used in clearing land or in cutting and marketing timber products. Sometimes outside work, such as lumbering, mining, or road construction and maintenance, can be secured to employ family labor. The income from such work is

[1] M. J. Thompson, *Field Crops at Duluth* (Minnesota Agricultural Experiment Station Miscellaneous Bulletin, 1930).

especially valuable in the early stages of development, when income from the farm is insufficient to maintain the family.

Because the labor supply is large in relation to the area of tillable land, such crops as potatoes, roots, and the more intensive vegetable crops have an important place in the cropping system. Four times as much labor is used in raising an acre of potatoes as in raising an acre of oats. Six times as much is used for an acre of rutabagas. These intensive crops make possible a fuller ultilization of the available family labor. Likewise such livestock enterprises as dairy cows and poultry use more labor in proportion to feed consumption than beef cattle, sheep, and swine. Dairy cattle have a special advantage in that they furnish much employment in winter, when there is no crop work to be done.

Feed supply. — Hay and pasture are the principal feed crops produced in the area. Good legume hay and pasture are assured except in periods of extreme drouth. The pasture season is shorter than in southern and western Minnesota and on the lighter soils has a somewhat lower carrying capacity. Where sweet clover is adapted it provides pasture comparable with that grown elsewhere in the state. Legume hay can be produced at a cost comparable with production in other parts of the state. Corn for either grain or silage cannot be advantageously produced because of the climate. Small grain yields are comparable with those in other parts of the state, but the costs are relatively high because of the small fields and the small acreage per farm. Root crops can be produced at as low a cost as in any part of the state, but they have an unimportant place in livestock feeding because the cost of nutrients in root crops is high as compared with those in grain or hay or in such succulent roughages as corn or sunflower silage.

All these fourteen counties are in a distinctly deficit area as regards corn and small grain. Even in years of high yields, large quantities of cereal and cereal by-products are shipped in from outside the area for livestock feeding. Hay, except in occasional dry years, is produced in sufficient quantities to supply farm feeding needs, with some surplus for local cities and lumber camps. As a result the prices of grain and grain feeds are higher than in any other part of Minnesota, whereas hay prices correspond very closely to those in other sections of the state. The relatively high price of grain in these counties is due both to the cost of transportation from surplus areas and to the high cost of handling small quantities. Where farms are small and scattered, the individual sales are small and the volume of business per dealer is so low as to make the expense per unit high.

Since grain feeds are high in price as compared with roughage, livestock that can utilize large quantities of roughage relative to concentrates have an advantage. Dairy cattle are well adapted for this reason and because they provide productive employment for labor, especially in winter. Sheep can be maintained largely on roughage, but they have a disadvantage on the small farm in that they do not provide productive employment for any considerable amount of labor. The lack of sheep-tight fences and of the capital with which to build them limits sheep production, and in many sections dogs and wolves are a menace. The high price of concentrate feeds makes unprofitable the feeding of beef cattle, and they, too, offer a small market for family labor. There may, however, be a place for the production of feeder and stocker cattle on some of the larger farms. Both hog and poultry production are handicapped as compared with dairying by the high price of concentrates, since neither can use roughage in any quantity. Poultry have an advantage over hogs in that they provide employment for more labor. The operator who has sufficient skill in handling poultry to secure high production may thus offset the disadvantage of high feed costs.

Another element that affects the selection of livestock in this area is the availability of certain by-products that may be used for livestock feeding. Most important of these are skimmilk, cull potatoes, and roots. The principal dairy product sold is cream for butter manufacture, and the skimmilk is retained on the farm. Some is fed to young dairy cattle and even to cows, but most of it is fed to hogs and poultry, and on many farms considerable quantities are thrown away during part of the year. The availability of skimmilk often makes profitable the raising of hogs or poultry, although they would involve a loss if all the feed consumed by them was purchased on the market. In years of very low prices even marketable potatoes and roots may be fed to livestock more profitably than they can be sold for cash. Livestock offers some insurance against severe losses from unusual declines in crop prices.

Available capital. — The availability of capital is an important factor in the choice of crops and livestock. In general, less capital is available for farm loans and the cost of obtaining capital is greater in northern Minnesota than elsewhere in the state. The cost of making and servicing loans is greater in an area of small farms and low values because of the small size of the loan, and it is further increased by the sparsity of settlement. The risk is greater in a newly settled region, and there is usually little accumulation of locally owned or locally controlled capital available. The credit situation limits livestock production. Not only is capital needed for the purchase of livestock, but because of the severe climate warmer shelter is required. Sheep, hogs, and beef cattle may be maintained in relatively inexpensive sheds, but the livestock otherwise best adapted, dairy cattle and poultry, require more substantial building equipment. Likewise certain crops, such as potatoes, which are well adapted from the standpoint of soil and climate, can be handled much more advantageously by the use of such expensive equipment as planters and diggers. Silo fillers and threshing machines are other examples of expensive equipment needed in this section. None of the machines can be used to capacity on small farms. Cooperative ownership and use of high-priced pieces of equipment are a means of reducing the capital needs of the individual settler. The rental of machines from others who are not using them to capacity will accomplish the same purpose. The exchange of horse work between farms will reduce the number of horses needed per farm. Cooperative ownership of sires or the hiring of the services of sires owned by other farmers helps to keep down the livestock investment.

Market outlets. — Market outlets are another important factor in the selection of crops and livestock. In most of this area there are regular markets for cream at prices comparable with those in the rest of the state. The market for whole milk, on the other hand, except near a few of the larger cities, is very limited. Eggs are salable anywhere, but the quality of the market varies widely. In some regions cooperative marketing of graded eggs has resulted in sufficient price advantage to offset the handicap of high-priced feeds.

The cash crops that may be grown depend largely on the local market. Potatoes are the only cash crop for which a market is generally available practically anywhere in the area. In some sections the grading of potatoes and the use of local brand names have created a better market outlet for this crop. In a few localities, such as northern Pine County, a special market for rutabagas has been developed. The same is true of other vegetables. In several of the western counties a fairly dependable market for clover, alsike, and alfalfa seed is being developed. The selection of cash crops for an individual farm is largely dependent on the special market outlets available.

Planning the Farm Organization

More careful planning of the organization of farms will result in a better utilization of land in northern Minnesota. It is not possible, however, to draw up standard farm organizations that will be generally applicable even within a single county. Both farms and farmers differ widely, especially in this section of the state. Each farm is an individual problem. In general, the objective of farm planning is so to utilize the factors of production as to bring in the largest net return to the farmer and his family. Obviously this involves a combination that will change from time to time, particularly if a farm is in the process of development. The following discussion will deal with the principles of farm organization and with the considerations involved and the information needed to develop a farm plan and adjust it to the conditions on a particular farm.

Selecting Crop Rotations

The first step in planning a farm organization is the development of a cropping system. This system should provide the optimum quantity and quality of sale crops adapted to the market outlets, and of feed crops adapted to the livestock planned for the farm. In order to maintain soil fertility, to control weeds, and to utilize fully the various factors of production available on the farm, a fairly definite succession or rotation of crops is necessary. A good rotation for this part of the state includes a grain crop, a legume hay or pasture crop, and an intertilled crop grown in regular succession. The comparative advantage of forage crops, especially legumes, in this part of the state has already been mentioned. Small grain is advisable as a companion crop in seeding the hay crop. The intertilled crops are useful in controlling weeds and the more intensive ones help to increase the size of business.

The common rotation in the past has been a three-year succession of these three classes of crops. Since there is usually nontillable land to provide pasture, the legume crop is cut for hay. Experimental work at the Northeast Experiment Station indicates that at least for the livestock farms in the eastern counties a four-year rotation with one year of small grain, two years of hay, and one year of intertilled crops has certain definite advantages over the three-year system, as is indicated by the following statement:

> In the light of these findings, what rotation should be adopted on the reasonably developed northern livestock farm? There was a time when the three-year rotation was universally recommended, and with reason. The hay would contain more clover, and clover was easy to raise. Times have changed. Failures to "catch" and winter-killing have become more frequent with the passing years and the opening of the country. On the assumption that an abundant supply of roughage must at all times be assured, this station is disposed to favor the lengthened rotation of four years, and sometimes at certain places, five years, once the farm is cleared and stocked. The reasons advanced in favor of the four-year as compared with the three-year rotation are:
>
> 1. One-half the land instead of one-third is engaged in growing a crop that is relatively sure, cheap to grow, and native to the country — hay.
>
> 2. It is a more normal division of the plow land. One-third of the land in cultivated crops is usually too heavy a proportion; a fourth is ample.
>
> 3. With 50 to 60 per cent of the land in hay, the market problem is lessened, for this crop is marketed through the farm livestock.
>
> 4. The slightly reduced hay yield and clover content is more than compensated for by the reduced annual plowing or breaking cost; the better, thicker sod developed; the lower growing cost as compared to cultivated crops; the greater net return as compared to grain.[2]

Obviously the length of the rotation for any particular farm will depend on such factors as the quality of soil, the market outlets, the size of the farm, and the available labor and capital.

The selection of crops within each of the three rotation groups, like the selection of the rotation itself, is also an individual problem for each farm and farmer. The data in Table 33 indicate some of the factors involved in the selection of cash crops. The crops to

TABLE 33. — CASH VALUE PER ACRE OF POTATOES AND RUTABAGAS
IN NORTHERN MINNESOTA

	Potatoes	Rutabagas
Standard yield, bushels or tons......	150	12
Number of bushels seeded...........	15	..
Net yield, bushels or tons...........	135	12
Relative sale price.................	$ 0.40	$6.00
Gross cash value....................	$54.00	$72.00
Hours of man labor................	48.7	75.4
Hours of horse work..............	63.3	62.2

be selected for such a comparison as well as the prices to be used depend on local markets. In this case, rutabagas yield a larger cash value per acre. The direct cash costs of production, which cover spray materials in the case of potatoes and seed in the case of rutabagas, are about equal. The expense of fertilizers is the same for the two crops. Potatoes require less man labor than rutabagas,

[2] Thompson, *Field Crops at Duluth.*

but involve the use of more specialized equipment, such as planters and diggers, if considerable acreages are to be produced. The cost of this special equipment required for the potato crop may not be a factor of immediate importance in determining the relative profitability of these two crops for the farmer who already has the potato machinery. It must, however, be considered by him when making replacements and also by other farmers who are considering the expansion of this enterprise or its introduction into their cropping systems. The seasonal distribution of labor for the two crops must also be considered in determining how each crop will fit into the labor program. This same method may be used in comparing other crops.

The selection of feeding crops may be based in part upon the method of comparison shown in Table 34. The individual farmer making this comparison should use yields that may reasonably be expected on his farm. Other crops may be included in this comparison. Wherever barley yields as well as oats in this tabulation,

TABLE 34. — FEEDING VALUE YIELDED PER ACRE BY VARIOUS CROPS IN NORTHERN MINNESOTA

| Crop | Yield per Acre (minus seed) | Pounds of Feed | Pounds of Digestible Matter Available * | | Production Costs | | |
			Total Digestible Nutrients	Digestible Protein	Hours of Man Labor	Hours of Horse Work	Direct Cash Costs
	Bushels						
Oats	42.5	1,360	957	132	12.6	24.0	$1.75
Barley	28.0	1,344	1,066	121	12.6	24.0	1.30
Oats and barley.......	36.75	1,470	1,101	137	12.6	24.0	1.65
	Tons						
Corn fodder †	2	4,000	1,443	111	19.1	40.2	1.05
Corn silage	6	12,000	1,596	120	26.1	50.2	2.85
Sunflower silage	8	16,000	2,016	160	30.1	55.2	3.85
Rutabagas	12	24,000	2,280	240	75.4	62.2	0.06
Alfalfa hay ‡	2.50	5,000	2,550	530	12.2	17.4	1.20
Alsike hay §	1.75	3,500	1,656	277	7.3	9.6	0.65
Alsike, clover, and timothy hay	1.75	3,500	1,726	179	7.3	9.6	0.70
Wild hay	1.20	2,400	1,157	72	4.7	7.0	...

* Based on average analyses given in Henry and Morrison, *Feeds and Feeding*, and in Eckles and Schaefer, *Feeding the Dairy Herd* (Minnesota Agricultural Experiment Station Bulletin No. 218).

† Original feeding value has been reduced one-fourth to compensate for losses by weathering and by failure of animals to consume the whole plant.

‡ Seed cost based on the assumption of a two-year stand.

§ Seed cost based on the assumption of a three-year stand.

it will produce more digestible feed per acre at practically the same cost. The percentage of protein is somewhat smaller, but the total quantity is approximately the same. A mixture of oats and barley yields slightly more digestible food per acre than barley alone and has a higher protein content.

Among the roughages, alfalfa produces the most digestible feed per acre and contains the highest percentage of protein. Wherever it can be grown successfully, this increased production much more than offsets the additional labor and cash costs. However, alfalfa does not fit into a rotation as well as clover and timothy, and in part of this area it is so difficult to secure and maintain a stand that the crop is not generally adaptable. Rutabagas are second in the production of digestible feed per acre, but they require large amounts of rather tedious hand labor. Sunflowers produce more digestible feed per acre than does corn silage, but the labor, power, and cash costs are somewhat higher. The two crops require practically the same tillage and harvesting machinery. As compared with rutabagas, they require relatively less hand labor but more machinery. On the small farm, therefore, succulent feed can be produced to better advantage in a root crop such as rutabagas, but on the larger farms either corn or sunflower silage has an advantage from the standpoint of labor requirements.

Alsike produces slightly less total digestible feed per acre than does mixed alsike, red clover, and timothy hay, but produces considerably more protein. The costs are similar, but the mixed hay is somewhat easier to cut and cure, and it is easier to secure a good stand with the mixed seeding. Both these hay crops produce more digestible feed of a much higher protein content than does either corn fodder or corn silage and the costs are lower. The latter crops, however, may be desirable in a rotation in order to provide a sufficient area of intertilled crops to control weeds. This is likely to be the case on the larger farms, where the labor supply is insufficient to care for the desired acreage of intertilled crops if only such intensive crops as potatoes and rutabagas are grown. The digestible feed obtained from an acre of wild hay is so small and of such poor quality that this crop is grown only on land that is too wet or too stony or is otherwise unfit to be included in the rotation.

In selecting from each group the feed crops to be included in the rotation, the farmer must consider the seasonal distribution of labor on the crop, the labor supply on the farm, the machine equipment, and especially the kind and amount of livestock to be kept.

The crop by-products also affect the selection. The small grain crops produce straw that may be used for either feed or bedding. Oats usually produce more straw per acre than barley, and oat straw is more valuable as feed. Rutabaga tops provide considerable succulent feed for dairy cattle. The aftermath of the meadows may be used as pasture. All these factors must be weighed in determining the crops best adapted to the rotation for a particular farm.

Balancing Crops and Livestock

After developing the cropping system of the farm organization, the next step is to combine with it such livestock enterprises as will utilize effectively the feeds available. The main problem is to secure such a combination of the different classes of livestock that the farmer will receive the maximum return from the resources available. Some of the functions performed by livestock are:

1. To increase the volume of business, thus making for less overhead expense per unit of product.

2. To convert both salable and unsalable farm products into salable products with a higher market value.

3. To aid in maintaining the productivity of the soil and in this way the returns to the farm operator.

4. To concentrate salable feed products into less bulky products, thus reducing shipping costs.

5. To distribute the demand for labor, power, and equipment over a greater part of the year than could be done with crops alone, thus aiding in the reduction of these direct costs.

For the small farms of northern Minnesota, which have ample labor supply but a limited crop area and higher cash outlays for materials, it is especially important (1) that the volume of business be increased so far as possible with a given overhead, (2) that everything that can be produced on the farm be used to advantage, (3) that the fertility of the soil be maintained, (4) that the bulk of shipped products be reduced to decrease shipping charges, and (5) that the available family labor supply be utilized effectively.

As already noted, dairy cattle are admirably fitted to serve as the chief livestock enterprise on farms in this area. They use to advantage, both absolutely and relatively, large quantities of the rough feeds that are necessary in the cropping system and that otherwise could be marketed only with difficulty, if at all. Further, they permit the return to the soil of much of the crop fertility removed. The concentration of bulky feeds into marketable products of higher unit value, the addition of volume to the business, and the more effective utilization and distribution of labor are additional advantages of this type of livestock. The opportunity to market productively the otherwise unused family labor and the unsalable rough feeds is an important advantage to the small farmer in this region.

In contrast, the high price of grain for feeding beef cattle, the difficulties of carrying on this enterprise on the small farm, and the all-too-limited opportunity to market productively the labor of the family, rule beef cattle out of major consideration. Sheep similarly, are not important, although on larger farms with surplus roughage, ample finances, and freedom from dogs and wolves, some sheep may find a place. Hogs in small numbers are useful primarily to consume the otherwise waste skimmilk and some of the cull potatoes. In utilizing such by-products it is necessary to reduce the use of concentrates to the minimum consistent with satisfactory gains. Since feed constitutes such a large proportion of the total cost of hog production (at times from 75 to 80 per cent), and since this feed must be composed very largely of concentrates, northeastern Minnesota cannot produce hogs exclusively on purchased or marketable feeds in competition with the marketing of these feeds through dairy cattle, which can at the same time utilize productively the available family labor. Poultry, like hogs, can use little other than concentrated feeds. Poultry offer an effective opportunity to market much of the skimmilk, which, with some cull potatoes, cull roots, and some added grain, represents a large proportion of the cost of poultry production. The labor used on poultry is largely family labor for which there is less productive opportunity on the other and larger farm enterprises.

BUDGETING PRODUCTION PROGRAMS

The final step in planning a farm organization is the comparison of returns that may be expected from various possible combinations of crops and livestock selected on the basis of the considerations just discussed. This process is known as budgeting. It involves the computation of the physical costs involved to determine whether these plans can be handled with the feed, labor, power, and equipment available. The probable production under each plan is then estimated and the approximate return over cash expense is computed. In this way the estimated returns from various combinations of crops and livestock may be compared.

A knowledge of the labor and material costs of crops and live-stock, of the yield of crops, and of livestock production methods is needed in applying the budgeting method. These data should apply to the individual farm under consideration. Detailed records kept by a group of Pine County farmers in cooperation with the University Department of Agriculture have supplied a basis for setting up standards that serve as useful guides to farmers in northeastern Minnesota in budgeting their farm business.[3]

In preparing a farm budget it is necessary to know the approximate yield of crops that will be obtained. Obviously crop yields vary widely with varying weather and soil conditions. They also vary with varieties grown, quality and treatment of seed, and cultural practices. Corn for grain cannot be matured satisfactorily in the northern and eastern portion of the area. In considerable areas it will not even produce forage regularly. In other sections alfalfa is not adapted. Yield figures must be adapted to the individual farm.

To determine the probable returns from different crop and livestock combinations it is necessary to estimate costs and sales prices. These should represent the farmer's best estimate of the prices that are likely to prevail in the future. Present prices are useful only to the extent that they are likely to prevail for some years to come or as they indicate a relationship between different prices that is likely to continue for some time. In the budgeting analysis it is more important that the various prices used bear the same relationship to each other that they are likely to bear in the future than that the actual money values be accurately forecast. In comparing different plans it is often desirable to use different price combinations in order to find the one that offers the greatest stability of income under changing price conditions.

Wherever possible, figures from the farm in question should be used in budgeting. Where no records are available, as when a new farm is being developed, records from other farms may be used as guides, but they should be adjusted to meet conditions on the particular farm studied. In the case of a farm in the process of development it is well to plan, at least in a general way, an organization for the farm after it is fully developed. A program of devel-

[3] See G. A. Pond and C. W. Crickman, *Planning Farm Organization for the Northeast Cut-Over Section of Minnesota* (Minnesota Agricultural Experiment Station Bulletin No. 295, St. Paul, 1933). This bulletin includes a number of tables showing crop yields and standard requirements of labor, power, and materials for the production of different crops and livestock. Readers are referred to that source for detailed information.

opment can be laid out to fit the supply of labor and capital available for the operations. The plan should provide for the expansion of crop and livestock production as the development proceeds. Much time and effort will be saved if the whole process has been planned in advance.

It should not be inferred from this discussion that once a budget plan has been made, it should be followed rigidly. Prices and other conditions affecting farm profits are continually changing. Some of these changes are temporary, others are relatively permanent. The farmer must be ever alert to these changing conditions and adjust his production plan to them as rapidly as possible. The reader is referred to the bulletin cited in footnote 3 for a further discussion of the budgeting method of farm planning and for illustrations of the method as applied to farms in northern Minnesota.[4]

MANAGEMENT PRACTICES

A well-planned crop and livestock organization will not in itself insure satisfactory returns. There must also be a reasonable degree of efficiency in the conduct of the various operations involved in the plan and an adaption of farm practices to local conditions. The use of good seed of the best-adapted varieties, careful seedbed preparation, weed, insect, and disease control, and the proper selection and breeding of livestock, balanced rations, disease control, and sanitation are all essential to success. The efficient use of labor, power, and equipment increases farm earnings. All are important elements in farm success anywhere and should be given full attention in the operation of a farm in northern Minnesota. There are in addition certain good practices particularly applicable to northern Minnesota that deserve special mention.

Delayed clearing. — One of the big problems in northern Minnesota is that of land clearing. Successful settlers have found that the most economical method is what is known as "delayed clearing." Instead of removing the green stumps immediately, the settler cuts the underbrush, fences the land, and seeds it to alsike or clover and timothy. He then pastures for five or six years with sufficient cattle or sheep to keep down new growth of brush. At the end of this time the small stumps can be jerked out with a team and the larger ones will require less dynamite than when green. Furthermore, during the pasturing period the clover sod supplements the thin layer of leaf mold on the virgin soil in storing

[4] *Ibid.*, pp. 73–101.

humus-forming material. The roots and refuse decay and the land settles. This simplifies the job of breaking and preparing a seedbed and insures a good crop on the new breaking. Wherever it is possible to follow this practice, a very material saving over the cost of "green clearing" can be effected.

Seeding meadows and pastures. — The comparative advantage of meadows and pasture in northern Minnesota farming has already been discussed. One problem involved is that of seeding the crop without undue expense for seedbed preparation or without sacrificing the use of crop land. Usually small grain is used as a companion crop for the seedings. In many cases the return from small grain is low, or equipment for harvesting and threshing is not available. At the Northeast Experiment Station at Duluth fair success has been achieved in seeding alsike and timothy with sunflowers. The sunflowers are planted in rows eighteen inches apart, and the grass seed is broadcast about two weeks later.[5] Grass seed may also be planted in corn at the last cultivation. These methods are worthy of trial as a means of reducing the acreage of small grain.

Alsike and timothy may also be seeded on newly brushed land before the stumps and stones have been removed. The use of a spring-tooth harrow before and after seeding aids in securing a stand. A good stand of grass and legumes can be obtained on freshly burned-over land with little or no preparation of a seedbed. From three to five pounds of timothy and alsike are sufficient for a satisfactory stand in most cases.

Reducing labor, power, and machinery expense. — On most farms in northern Minnesota the cleared area is not large enough to permit of using much of the crop machinery to capacity. As already mentioned, economies can be effected by cooperative ownership and use of the more expensive machines. The rental or exchange of machines may accomplish the same result. For example, one farmer may have a grain drill that he uses only a day a year. He may rent it to his neighbors for the balance of the seeding season or he may exchange its services for the loan of a grain binder or some other implement. Since oats are used exclusively for feeding purposes, threshing costs can be saved by feeding them on the sheaf. The use of a grain binder can also be saved by cutting the oats with a mower while it is still green enough so that the straw will make a palatable roughage.

[5] Thompson, *Field Crops at Duluth.*

A number of farm operations, such as haying, require the services of more than one man for short periods. By exchanging work with his neighbors the operator of a small farm is able to handle peak loads. Likewise there are many farms on which two horses can handle all the work except certain operations, such as harvesting grain or digging potatoes, for which three or four are required. These peaks can be handled by the exchange of horses between neighbors. Considerable time can be saved by neighborhood cooperation in haying, harvesting, and threshing, in marketing cream, eggs, and similar products, and in purchasing supplies. This type of cooperation is especially important in an area of small farms.

Maintaining dairy cattle largely on roughage. — Pasture and roughage, as compared with concentrates, are cheap in northern Minnesota. By breeding cows to freshen in the spring it is possible to maintain them on pasture through the summer, the period of heavy production. During the winter they can be fed largely on good legume hay with little use of concentrates. While the total production for the year will be less than if the cows had freshened in the fall and received a full ration of concentrates through the winter, the costs are likely to be decreased much more than the income. It increases the labor load during the summer months, but labor is not the important limiting factor on many farms in this section. This practice is worthy of more general adoption in northern Minnesota.

Utilizing skimmilk. — Considerable skimmilk is available on most dairy farms in northern Minnesota, since the milk is usually separated on the farm and only the cream is sold. It is commonly used for feeding calves, hogs, and poultry.[6] The largest return is obtained when skimmilk is fed to young animals, although it can be used to replace grain for mature animals. A calf from two to six months of age can use from sixteen to eighteen pounds daily to advantage. Beyond that quantity and for older cattle it must be considered a substitute for grain. One hundred pounds of skimmilk thus used is equivalent to ten or twelve pounds of farm-grown grains. Up to a certain point skimmilk can be substituted for grain in the ration for hogs. Three pounds of skimmilk to one pound of grain is usually a satisfactory proportion. If this ratio is greatly exceeded, the results are unsatisfactory. Skimmilk can be used both for growing chicks and for laying hens. Two gallons of skimmilk

[6] C. H. Eckles, E. F. Ferrin, and A. C. Smith, *Using Skimmilk on the Farm* (Minnesota Agricultural Extension Division Special Bulletin No. 143, 1931).

are equal to one pound of meat scraps for poultry. When poultry are fed skimmilk, it is necessary to withhold water from them so that they will consume enough skimmilk to balance their ration. The consumption of skimmilk by poultry is often increased by feeding it in the form of cottage cheese, though in this case the whey is often wasted. On many northern Minnesota farms there is more skimmilk that can be fed to advantage to the limited number of calves, hogs, and poultry. With both hogs and poultry, concentrates must be fed in addition to the skimmilk. The high price of concentrates may make it unprofitable to increase these classes of stock sufficiently to utilize effectively all the skimmilk available. In such cases the skimmilk may profitably be fed to the cows. This will eliminate some of the expenditures for high-protein concentrates. One gallon of skimmilk is equal to one pound of linseed meal as a source of protein for dairy cows.

Keeping farm records. — Farm records are a valuable source of data in farm planning. They also serve as a check on the success of the plan and the efficiency with which different operations are performed. They are especially important on a farm in the process of development in a new country. Conditions are constantly changing. These changes necessitate alterations in the farm plan, for which the records furnish a useful guide. The high price of concentrates in this section handicaps dairy and poultry production unless it is offset by increased efficiency in production. Records of milk and egg production are an invaluable basis for breeding and culling for high production. Farmers in these counties have a special advantage in keeping farm records, namely, the cooperative accounting service offered to farmers in this section by the University Department of Agriculture. For a nominal fee farmers are supplied with farm-record books and are assisted in keeping them. At the end of the year these records are carefully summarized by farm management specialists and the farmer is supplied with a very complete analysis of his business. For an additional fee a mail-order cow-testing service is furnished. This service makes the keeping and use of farm records much easier for the farmer and much more useful.

CHAPTER X

PROBLEMS INVOLVED IN MOVING FARM FAMILIES *

Attention has been called in various places in this report[1] to the tragedy of farm families trying to eke out an existence on land that because of poor soil, the presence of stone, or location is not capable of supplying an adequate living. Attempts to use such land for farm purposes is unfortunate, not only for those located on it but also for local units of government. Families on unproductive soil tend to be the first to go on rural relief rolls. Many of these families consist of industrious people who would be self-supporting on more productive soil, and it is consequently in the public interest to work out programs for establishing them in more favorable situations.

Isolated settlement, too, even if the settlers are on good soil, may place an inordinate burden upon governmental units in providing roads, schools, and other services. Such settlers should be relocated so that settlement may be concentrated on good soil in established communities that are already serviced by good roads and schools.

Two lines of action are involved in the attack upon this problem. First, measures should be taken to prevent mistakes of settlement in the future. The discussion of zoning in Chapter VI was devoted to this subject. Secondly, there is need for the adoption of measures to correct past mistakes. The present chapter considers the possibilities of moving families to better locations. The two are related because it is important that other settlers be prevented from going into the relocation areas.

Economic forces in time will tend to correct the situation by forcing abandonment of farms in the poorest areas. This is a very slow process, however, and, in terms of human sacrifice, very expensive. Once a farmer has invested his savings or equities in a piece of land, change may be difficult. A buyer for poor land is hard to find and, being unable to restore his capital to mobile form, the owner is tied down to his location. If he does succeed in selling, the problem is merely shifted to the shoulders of another. Then, too, settlers are often reluctant to abandon unsuitable locations because

* This chapter has been prepared by R. I. Nowell.
[1] See especially Chapters IV and VI above.

239

of their strong attachment to the home, the church, the school, the cemetery, and relatives and friends. For these reasons abandonment is the step taken only when no other alternative presents itself. Families usually will put forth every effort to remain and will accept a low standard of living as one of the consequences. A remnant of the population will probably remain until removed by death.

If desirable relocation is to be accomplished with any expedition, public agencies must participate in the program. The use of public money for such a purpose is quite justifiable. For one thing, it must be recognized that in the past public policy has permitted and even encouraged settlement on lands that now are recognized as being unsuited to successful farming. It may therefore be said that public agencies are under a moral obligation to assist in correcting an undesirable condition that public policy has helped to create. But the case need not rest on moral grounds alone. The use of public funds to bring about a proper relocation of settlers represents a financial investment that will bring returns in the form of a substantial reduction in the cost of governmental services.[2] Among the farmers on poor soil there are some who will remain permanent relief cases if left where they are. Relocation expenditures may serve to rehabilitate such families and to eliminate the relief problem of caring for them in their present unfavorable location. Even those who are not dependent upon direct relief for sustenance usually require more public services than their present circumstances enable them to support.

RELATIONSHIP OF QUALITY OF MEN TO QUALITY OF SOIL

Dr. Henry C. Taylor states that "it is a matter of common observation that competition tends to distribute the farmers on the different grades of land in accordance with their efficiency, the A-grade farmer on the first-grade land, the B-grade farmer on the second-grade land, and so on."[3] This is, of course, intended merely as an expression of a trend resulting from the fact that efficient farmers can make good land yield a greater return than the inefficient and are therefore able to outbid the latter and thus gain possession of the better grades of land. Many exceptions to this trend occur, however. The immobility of the population, its habits and customs, and other factors prevent a nice adjustment between the

[2] See page 267 for an estimate of possible savings involved in settler relocation in the fourteen counties studied.
[3] *Outlines of Agricultural Economics*, p. 244.

different grades of men and land. The principle works out more perfectly in an established, well-settled region where land values reflect differences in productivity. In parts of northern Minnesota some land poorly adapted to agriculture is being farmed while considerable areas of better agricultural land are unoccupied.

The tendency above referred to cannot be ignored. It has practical significance in settler relocation because of the fact that some of the submarginal land is being occupied by submarginal farmers. The more alert and ambitious settlers who locate on poor land are probably among the first to realize their mistake and to go elsewhere, leaving behind the less efficient. Some would say that this was not altogether unfortunate, for these people may lose less on poor soil than they would if they attempted to operate on good land with a larger investment in land, improvements, and equipment. But this is a short-sighted view. Continued isolation with high-cost public services is not justified merely because settlers are inefficient. The point that needs to be recognized is that in any relocation program it is necessary to consider the quality of the farmers as well as that of the land. It would be a mistake to treat all alike. Some are capable of working out a very satisfactory solution if they are helped to acquire better lands. At the other extreme are those who are likely to remain relief cases permanently. Even these it may be desirable to relocate because of the lower cost of providing relief assistance to people in compact communities.

It is desirable that cases requiring rehabilitation be so handled that the individual's self-respect is maintained and cultivated. Intelligent assistance may help doubtful cases to work out their own solution. Even those who are near the lower end of the scale may contribute substantially to their own support if they are located in better surroundings and provided with work at some supervised employment.

The care of families who are incapable of assuming the financial and managerial responsibilities involved in the development of new farms in better areas constitutes a very difficult phase of the relocation program. It is a relief problem rather than one of land use and must be approached from that viewpoint. It is important that each case be studied and that families offering slight prospect of succeeding on farms be designated for special treatment by appropriate relief agencies. The success of a relocation project would be jeopardized if such families were placed on farms to care for themselves.

Self-sufficient farms have been suggested as a solution for problems such as these. A self-sufficient type of agriculture in this area is possible only with a very low living standard. Some cash income is necessary. Part-time farming, in which the operator relies upon the farm to supply part of his living and obtains a cash income from other employment, is therefore more satisfactory. Such a combination is limited mainly to areas relatively close to population

TABLE 35. — SUMMARY OF AVERAGE CASH INCOME FOR DULUTH PART-TIME FARMS, YEAR ENDING JUNE 30, 1933 *

Size of Farms	No. of Farms	Crops	Live-stock	Dairy Pro-ducts	Poul-try and Eggs	Wood Pro-ducts	Labor off Farm	Miscel-laneous	Total
2.5 acres or less......	16	$16	$8	$33	$ 80	..	$479	$57	$673
2.6– 7.5 acres	12	40	2	11	90	..	472	33	648
7.6–12.5 acres	7	56	..	9	155	$7	446	43	716
12.6 acres or more † ..	2	500	..	..	10	..	...	..	510
All farms	37	$57	$4	$20	$94	$1	$445	$43	$664

* From E. C. Johnson and T. B. Manny, *Minnesota Farm Business Notes,* No. 131.
† These workers were unemployed.

centers and consequently cannot be extensively used in northern Minnesota. In time, greater opportunities for part-time work in the forests may increase the possibilities.

A survey has been made of a number of part-time farms in the vicinity of Duluth to obtain specific information on possibilities in this area. Table 35 summarizes the cash income of thirty-seven farms, and Table 36 gives additional information on the family living furnished by such farms and the farm expenses involved. As

TABLE 36. — SUMMARY OF AVERAGE INCOME AND EXPENSES FOR DULUTH PART-TIME FARMS, YEAR ENDING JUNE 30, 1933 *

Size of Farms	No. of Farms	Total Cash Receipts	Total Value of Family Living Furnished by Farm	Total Cash and Non-Cash Income †	Total Farm Expenses
2.5 acres or less...	16	$673	$222	$895	$234
2.6– 7.5 acres.....	12	648	271	919	185
7.6–12.5 acres.....	7	716	315	1,031	219
12.6 acres or more	2	510	201	711	168
All farms.......	37	$664	$254	$918	$212

* From E. C. Johnson and T. B. Manny, *Minnesota Farm Business Notes,* No. 131.
† Cash value of use of house, estimated at $154 per farm, not included.

suggested by these tables, outside employment and markets for surplus products are important to the success of part-time farms.

FARM RECORDS SECURED TO DEMONSTRATE FEASIBILITY OF MOVING FARM FAMILIES

During the summer of 1933 several areas in northern Minnesota where farming conditions are relatively unfavorable and settlers have made little financial progress were selected for special study. These were designated as "relocation areas." Others were selected in the same counties which were well developed and represented the more successful agricultural portions of these counties. These were designated as "development areas." Survey records were obtained on 83 farms in the relocation areas and on 188 farms in the development areas. In addition to other purposes these records were secured to test the feasibility of moving farm families from poor to good agricultural lands.

The location of farms studied, their distribution by counties, the type of information secured, and numerous significant contrasts between farms in the two kinds of areas were presented in detail in Chapter IV. So far as the data presented in that chapter bear on the question of moving farm families, the following are perhaps the most salient contrasts. Cash income was more than three times as great in the development as in the relocation areas. Net cash farm income for the year ending June 30, 1933, was $247 per farm in the development areas and only $9 per farm in the relocation areas. Net farm income, which includes non-cash items of income in addition to cash income, was $591 and $212 per farm, respectively, for the development and relocation areas. Farm income during the depression years probably has declined much more in development than in relocation areas. Over a period of years the difference in farm income between the two types of areas probably would be much greater than is indicated by these data. Income for labor off the farm was $149 per farm in the relocation areas as compared with $89 in the development areas. This item reflects the dependence of settlers in relocation areas upon outside sources of income. Much of this outside work was on public roads and was given to the settlers to avoid carrying them on regular county relief rolls.

The limited number of bona fide sales of farms during depression years makes it difficult to establish market values of the farms studied. However, in order to provide some measure of the financial progress that had been made, estimated values were placed on lands and improvements, the values reflecting the settlers' opinions of present values. It is recognized, of course, that these estimates are not necessarily accurate, but they may be used as a basis for making some comparisons of net worth. Whereas the net worth of farms in development areas at the time of settlement averaged one-third greater than that of farms in relocation areas, on July 1, 1933, it was three and one-third times as large. The gain in net worth in the development areas was $3,259, or $155 a year, since settlement, while the gain per farm in the relocation areas totaled only $80, or $5 a year since settlement.

One must not conclude that if families were moved from relocation to development areas their incomes would immediately rise to the higher brackets. Soil differences and locations are not the only factors responsible for differences in earnings. The managerial ability of settlers is an important factor and undoubtedly accounts to some extent for the higher earnings on the farms in the development areas. The development of new farms is a difficult task and requires years to accomplish. During the first few years current earnings on newly developed places might easily be lower than the former earnings on the abandoned farms. It is safe to conclude, however, that average earnings would eventually be higher than on farms in relocation areas.

Comparisons suggest that it would not be unreasonable to assume that the average net farm incomes of relocated families could be increased by as much as $200 annually. This would represent an increase of almost 100 per cent over average earnings in 1932 on the relocation areas studied, and would amount in total to about 70 per cent of average earnings in 1932 on farms in development areas. Against this anticipated increase in annual farm earnings must be balanced the estimated costs of moving, and consideration must be given to the question of how new farms are to be acquired and developed. But before considering these questions let us examine first the possibilities of improving the productivity of farms now occupied.

In general, the poor farms of northern Minnesota are those located on sandy soils that are infertile and drouthy, stony soils, or soils having considerable areas of peat bogs. On the sandy soils heavy applications of commercial fertilizers are required to produce ordinary field crops and pasture. The profitableness of this practice is subject to question, and in dry years crop failures result regardless of fertilizer expenditures. A stable farm income under such conditions is quite impossible. On stony soils it is usually the limited acreage available for crop production that limits farm incomes. A special study was made of clearing costs on seventeen farms in the vicinity of Brimson in St. Louis County, which is located about thirty-five miles north and east of Duluth, to determine the possibilities of enlarging the cultivated area.

Estimated Clearing Costs in the Brimson Area *

The data on the Brimson farms were included in the averages for relocation areas presented above and in Chapter IV. Because of the prevalence of stone, lands are cleared and put under cultivation only with the greatest of effort. (See Figures 43 to 45.) There is a total of 2,000 acres in the seventeen farms studied, or an average of 117.6 acres per farm. The farms have been settled from five to twenty-eight years, the average time since settlement being seventeen and a half years. At the end of this long period the land actually under cultivation averaged only 5.3 acres per farm, and only 4.6 acres per farm of the undeveloped land was listed as potentially suitable for agriculture. The quantity of stone on 84.5 acres of the undeveloped land is so great that removal costs were listed as "prohibitive" and on seventeen acres as "heavy." The tillable acreage on these farms probably will never average over 10 acres per farm, or less than 9 per cent of the land in farms.

Detailed records of the costs of stone removal in the Brimson area are not available, but estimates based on interviews with settlers indicate that to clear an acre requires about 360 hours of man labor, 340 hours of horse labor, and $8.50 worth of explosives, caps, and fuse. The value of the settler's labor depends upon what alternative opportunities there are for cash employment. Much of the stoning work is done when the settler and his team have nothing else to do, so there is usually no cash cost involved for labor items. It must be recognized, however, that settlers on stone-free land would have much more time for productive work on crop and livestock enterprises and that indirectly some labor costs might be imputed to the clearing operations. If unit costs of 20 cents per hour for man labor and 10 cents per hour for horse labor were assumed, the cost of removing the estimated 4,375 cubic feet of stone per acre at Brimson would aggregate the preposterous figure

---

* This section and the next are based on data gathered by D. G. Miller, N. A. Kessler, and L. H. Schoenleber.

of $117 an acre. In addition, on this presumably cleared land there were counted an average of 281 surface boulders per acre. By boulder is meant a stone that without blasting would require at least two men to handle. The presence of visible surface boulders indicates that the clearing job is still far from complete.

In the above estimates nothing is included for other land clearing operations, such as brushing, stumping, breaking, etc. In this area these items, with man and horse labor at 20 and 10 cents per hour, respectively, might well run from $25 to $75 per acre, depending upon many variables. On the basis of these assumed unit costs of man labor, horse labor, and materials, the clearing and stoning costs in the vicinity of Brimson are probably in excess of $150 per acre. The difficulties of land clearing at Brimson may be somewhat further emphasized by pointing out that the above estimates are based on lands already cleared, and the tendency is to clear the easiest lands first and to leave the most difficult to the last.

The Brimson area was selected for this study to demonstrate the difficulties of land clearing under which some settlers are struggling. In this locality there are approximately 150 settlers, all of whom have essentially the same stone problem. Elsewhere throughout the fourteen counties are hundreds of other settlers who have a stone problem just as bad as exists at Brimson. For settlers whose cleared area is too small to support farm families and who cannot clear additional acreages except at excessive costs, the logical solution of the problem is relocation on land better suited to farming.

Salvage of Buildings

A study was also made to determine the salvage value of the buildings in the Brimson area. Figures 43 to 45 show farmsteads of three of the seventeen farms included in this study. The buildings on these farms are rather typical of those found throughout the Brimson area. They were constructed at a time when the settlers were able to secure outside employment in the woods and on road construction work, consequently they are somewhat better than one would expect to find in an area so little suited to agriculture. Some of the settlers also had merchantable timber on their places, which provided cash with which to finish their buildings. For the most part the buildings were constructed from timber found on the farms and finished with funds from outside sources. The people who populate the Brimson area are skillful axemen and are able to construct very serviceable buildings from rather crude materials.

FIGURE 43. — AN INVESTMENT IN FARM BUILDINGS AMID
UNFAVORABLE SURROUNDINGS

FIGURE 44. — A FARM RESIDENCE OUT OF KEEPING WITH ITS SURROUNDINGS

The buildings on farms in relocation areas elsewhere throughout the fourteen counties are somewhat inferior to those at Brimson. Exceptions, of course, occur in many places, as for instance in
eastern Pine County, where mortgage loans obtained from banks
and various investment companies have supplied funds to construct fairly elaborate buildings on soil unsuited to agriculture.

Since parts of practically all the buildings examined on the
Brimson farms were of log construction, it would be impracticable
to move them as units. Salvage values depend upon the size, construction, and condition of the building, the distance it is to be
moved, and whether the settler is to do his own construction. The
mill work — windows, doors, etc. — and some of the hardwood
flooring could be salvaged to advantage from most buildings regardless of the distance to be moved, but it would hardly pay to
move the heavier log materials very great distances. If the settler
were to construct his new buildings himself, according to his own
plans, far more of the old material could be used to advantage than
if the buildings were to be constructed from new plans with hired
labor.

Moving Costs

The task of moving farm families is a comparatively simple one.
The volume of machinery, tools, livestock, and household effects is
small on relocation farms. Most settlers have an old car of some
description or a team and wagon with which they could assist, and
in some cases, if the distance were not too great, the settler could
handle the moving job himself. If the settler was not equipped to
move, a large truck could probably move everything, including salvage material from the buildings, in three trips.

Cost of Acquiring New Land

It is assumed that most settlers will prefer to relocate somewhere in the northern cut-over counties. There are certain distinct
advantages in their doing this, and it probably should be encouraged. Of greatest importance is the fact that settlers have had experience in the prevailing type of farming. If they were to move
elsewhere, the Red River Valley, for instance, most of them would
feel quite lost and would have difficulty in adjusting themselves to
the new conditions. In the northern country a free fuel supply is
available, and fish, game, and wild berries are abundant. These
items are of no little importance in helping to support the farm
family while the new farm is being improved. Local boards of

county commissioners would probably prefer to have settlers relocate in the same county, but if a settler had some distant place in mind to which he would like to move, the county boards probably would not interfere.

In most of the fourteen counties good lands are available comparatively nearby. The fact that these lands have not been settled previously is to be explained by three principal reasons. On some lands the timber has within recent years been cut over for the first time, making them available for farm settlement. Other lands, and these in the aggregate form a large acreage, have been held in speculative ownership at prices so high as to preclude farm settlement. The economic depression has made much of this land available at more reasonable prices. A third group of lands have been covered by a layer of peat and a dense vegetation, which have made clearing expensive. During the recent series of dry years fires have burned the peat cover from many acres, exposing good mineral soils. These are among the most promising lands of all for purposes of resettlement.

Prices of wild lands suitable for resettlement will vary from five to ten dollars an acre, depending upon location, amount of stone, and ease of clearing. Long-time contracts are usually available at these prices. Some of the burned-over peat lands are owned by the state and may be purchased for five dollars an acre on a forty-year contract.

When wild lands are purchased, an additional investment of materials and labor is necessary to clear them ready for the plow. The settler always has the alternative of buying improved lands. In recent years improved properties in the northern counties have been available at from ten to twenty-five dollars per acre. While these prices may seem low in comparison with farm land values in other parts of the state, they are too high to be within reach of the majority of farmers living in relocation areas. Furthermore, while the purchase of improved farms may be preferable to buying wild land for some individual settlers, this method cannot be recommended for any considerable number of farmers because of the problem it would raise of caring for the displaced farm operators. Most relocation families must be placed on wild lands. The only other alternative is the subdivision of existing farms. This is inadvisable in most cases because it involves either a change in the type of farming or the operation of units of improper size. In either case possibilities of profitable operation would be limited.

Cost of Clearing Wild Lands *

Wild lands were examined in considerable detail in two areas in St. Louis County to determine clearing costs. Examinations were made near Cook, a small town located about twenty-five miles north and six miles west of Virginia, and near the town of Floodwood, which is located about twelve miles north and thirty-five miles west of Duluth. Both of these are comparatively good agricultural areas and were studied as suitable locations for the development of new farms. About a thousand acres in seventeen tracts were examined in five townships lying between Cook and the Itasca county line,[4] and about thirteen hundred acres in thirty-one tracts were examined in three townships near Floodwood.[5]

Units of eighty acres each were examined as suitable farm sites. Lands showing excessive stone were not included. All tracts were on cut-over lands covered with green, second growth timber. Counts of tree sizes and species and brush height and density were made on quarter-acre sample plots, aggregating about 10 per cent of the total area of each tract. It has been assumed that standing merchantable timber on each tract would pay for cutting and removing all trees. Costs were estimated for the remaining clearing operations, such as brushing, stumping, breaking, and root picking.

Clearing costs are dependent upon many variable factors, including species, age, and size of stumps, type and moisture conditions of the soil, and the efficiency of methods employed. Green stumps are very difficult to remove, and the amount of labor and explosives required may be greatly reduced if root decay is permitted to take place. Stumps of deciduous trees decay rapidly, but pine stumps decay very slowly. There were few pine stumps on the tracts studied. It is evident that clearing costs may be greatly affected by the way clearing operations are planned. Normally a settler moving onto a piece of uncleared land will clear and break a small area for subsistence crops the first year and will also brush a few additional acres for pasture. Each succeeding year he will extend his operations, until finally most of the stumps when blasted are four or five years old. Stump removal delayed as long as possible materially reduces land clearing costs, provided green shoots and brush are kept down by pasturing or other means.

Estimates of labor and materials required to clear an acre have

* The discussion of clearing costs in the Cook and Floodwood areas is based upon material gathered by D. G. Miller, N. A. Kessler, and L. H. Schoenleber.
[4] T. 61, R. 19, 20, and 21, and T. 62, R. 20 and 21.
[5] T. 51, R. 20 and 21, and T. 52, R. 20.

been prepared for alternate plans of green clearing delayed to the second, third, fourth, and fifth years. (See Table 37.) Tree diameters were slightly smaller at Cook than at Floodwood, but the Cook area has 2.6 times as many stumps per acre, which makes the costs of clearing considerably greater. The estimated cost of the materials needed to clear an acre in each of the areas and the average of the two follow:

Area	Delayed to 5th Year	Delayed to 4th Year	Delayed to 3d Year	Delayed to 2d Year	Green
Cook	$2.01	$3.47	$6.73	$14.64	$21.79
Floodwood	2.45	2.97	4.07	7.14	9.74
Average......	$2.23	$3.22	$5.40	$10.89	$15.76

Unless delayed until the fourth or fifth year, the cost of materials alone makes the clearing of new land, from an economic point of view, a very questionable undertaking. This is especially true in the Cook area, where the cost of material for clearing green timber approximates the market price of improved farms.

As explained previously, clearing operations are usually sandwiched in between other farm tasks and are often performed when

TABLE 37. — ESTIMATES OF LABOR AND MATERIALS REQUIRED TO CLEAR AN ACRE OF LAND, GREEN OR DELAYED TO FIVE YEARS, IN COOK AND FLOODWOOD AREAS OF ST. LOUIS COUNTY *

Age of Clearing	Hours of Man Labor	Hours of Horse Labor	Pounds of Explosives	Number of Caps	Feet of Fuse
COOK AREA					
Green	150	104	101	205	308
Delayed to 2d year	129	99	57	205	308
Delayed to 3d year	106	95	26	95	143
Delayed to 4th year.......	97	95	14	45	68
Delayed to 5th year.......	94	95	8	27	40
FLOODWOOD AREA					
Green	94	69	46	86	130
Delayed to 2d year	84	67	30	86	130
Delayed to 3d year	74	65	19	37	56
Delayed to 4th year.......	72	65	14	26	40
Delayed to 5th year.......	70	65	12	19	29
AVERAGE OF COOK AND FLOODWOOD AREAS					
Green	122	87	74	146	219
Delayed to 2d year	107	83	43	146	219
Delayed to 3d year	90	80	23	66	100
Delayed to 4th year.......	85	80	14	36	54
Delayed to 5th year.......	82	80	10	23	34

* These quantities of materials and labor required were estimated on the basis of several years of clearing operations in northern Minnesota as reported in Minnesota Agricultural Experiment Station Bulletin 299.

the settler can make no other profitable use of his time, and therefore assumed labor costs may be misleading. The hourly wages a settler earns in clearing operations may be illustrated with the data in Table 37. If we assume that wild land can be purchased for five dollars an acre and cleared land for twenty-five, then after deducting material costs the following hourly rates for labor would be obtained:

Area	Delayed to 5th Year	Delayed to 4th Year	Delayed to 3d Year	Delayed to 2d Year	Green
For Man and Horse Labor Combined (in cents)					
Cook	19.1	17.0	12.5	4.2	—1.1
Floodwood	25.1	23.7	21.5	15.3	10.9
Average......	21.7	19.7	16.2	8.5	3.5
For Man Labor Alone (in cents, assuming one hour of man labor to equal in value two hours of horse labor)					
Cook	12.7	11.4	8.6	3.0	—0.8
Floodwood	17.1	16.3	14.9	10.9	8.0
Average......	14.6	13.4	11.4	6.1	2.6

If a public agency undertook to clear land with hired labor as part of a program of settler relocation, the labor item would stand out very prominently. With man labor at 20 cents an hour and horse labor at 10 cents, the following clearing costs are estimated:

Area	Delayed to 5th Year	Delayed to 4th Year	Delayed to 3d Year	Delayed to 2d Year	Green
Labor Costs					
Cook	$28.30	$38.90	$30.70	$35.70	$40.40
Floodwood	20.50	20.90	21.30	23.50	25.70
Average....	$24.40	$24.90	$26.00	$29.60	$33.05
Labor and Material Costs					
Cook	$30.31	$32.37	$37.43	$50.34	$62.19
Floodwood	22.95	23.87	25.37	30.14	35.44
Average....	$26.63	$28.12	$31.40	$40.49	$48.61

Moreover, agricultural engineers suggest that even a conservative estimate must include an additional item of 15 per cent to cover miscellaneous items of labor, materials, etc. These data are for the costs of brushing, stumping, breaking, and root picking only, no allowance having been made for stoning. Stone in varying quantities will be found on practically all lands in northern Minnesota, but by careful selection areas on which the stone problem is not a serious one may be found for the development of new farms.

If hired labor were used to clear green timbered lands for new farms and the costs were added to the settler's mortgage indebtedness, it would in most cases be impossible for the settler to succeed and retire his obligations. Such a project could never become self-liquidating, and a loss of government funds would probably result. Despite the tremendous costs involved, proposals are being made repeatedly that CCC labor or federal relief labor be used to develop new farms for settlers now residing in submarginal agricultural areas.

This consideration of the cash costs of clearing leads to the conclusion that the successful development of a farm on wild, timbered land in northern Minnesota is dependent upon the willingness of the settler to put in a tremendous amount of work at a relatively low wage rate. The settler who is well enough established on the land to obtain his living from it may be justified in devoting considerable labor that would otherwise not be utilized. That is quite a different matter from incurring heavy cash costs when improved land is available at present figures.

As previously remarked, there is a considerable acreage of burned-over peat land in northern Minnesota on which farms can be developed with comparatively little expense and labor. These lands are located principally in Koochiching, Lake of the Woods, and Roseau counties. The clearing costs involved in putting such lands under the plow are dependent upon the thoroughness of the burning, which in turn was influenced by the wind, the moisture, and the depth of the peat covering. In some places the fires were very hot, and an excellent job of clearing was accomplished. In such fires the brush, trees, and stumps were totally consumed. On other lands the trees and brush were merely uprooted by the fire, and are now lying on the surface. On many lands the peat burned in spots and patches and left standing clumps of trees and hummocks of peat. In dry years the clearing could be completed on such lands at practically no cost by the judicious use of fire. Stones occur on the burned peat lands in varying amounts, usually as large boulders lying completely exposed on the surface.

In addition to the clearing problem the peat lands present a drainage problem. While it is important to provide adequate drainage in wet years, this is not necessarily a difficult or expensive undertaking, because lands having the best drainage have usually been the ones to burn first and hardest. Clearing costs on these lands will obviously range all the way from a negligible amount to figures approximating those for the tracts examined at Cook and Floodwood.

Careful examination of the burned areas with a view to using them for resettlement has not been made, and therefore no estimate has been made of the number of families that can be accommodated.

It is highly essential that clearing and development costs be kept to an absolute minimum if families are to be relocated successfully. For this reason it seems that experimental projects might properly be started on the best of the burned-over lands where little clearing is required.

Suggested Procedure for a Settler Relocation Project *

Plans for a relocation project in northern Minnesota are in the course of preparation. Numerous details remain to be worked out, but the broader features are well defined. The details must be adapted to the local conditions, and a special procedure must be worked out for each individual project. A plan that would work well for one project probably would not work in another state, nor perhaps even in another county of the same state.

Important for the success of any project is the cooperation and support of local officials and the settlers concerned. This can best be obtained from local officials by giving them some responsibility in the formulation of plans. Because of their intimate knowledge of local conditions and the people within the project area, they can be of material assistance in putting the project into operation. If they feel that it is their project and that responsibility as well as credit will rest partially on their shoulders, they will fight for its success.

Settlers must also be given responsibility if they are to cooperate effectively. Their self-respect must be cultivated. They cannot be approached and treated as charity cases and be expected to cooperate on a business basis.

The question of how paternalistic the government should be in re-establishing farm families in new locations is one on which there are differences of opinion. At one extreme are those who argue that the government should buy the land, give the settler his check, and permit him to shift for himself. But if this were done, some might repeat the mistake of selecting an unfavorable location and fail to improve their situation. Others argue that the use of federal money

* Helpful suggestions have been received from A. D. Wilson in the preparation of this and the following section.

on such projects should be very carefully supervised. Lands should be selected by experts, buildings constructed according to well-conceived plans, and the type of farming and choice of enterprises worked out in detail for each individual settler. The recognized danger of this latter approach is that initiative would tend to be stifled. Settlers might become leaners. They would place responsibility on the director of the project for everything that went wrong. They would probably take the attitude that the government was responsible for getting them onto the new place and that it was the government's responsibility to carry them through. It would seem that the two extremes are about equally dangerous and that a middle course probably should be pursued, one giving sufficient latitude to permit adaptation to the qualifications and desires of each individual settler.

A procedure for executing a project in northern Minnesota which appears feasible would be about as follows: First secure options on lands suitable for developing new farms. Option if possible more lands than are actually needed so as to allow settlers a wide range of choice. These lands should be examined in detail, special attention being given to the amount of stone, the types of soil, the probable clearing costs, and the drainage requirements. Resale prices should be set on the various forty- and eighty-acre tracts in accordance with their respective qualities.

Having secured the lands, the next step should be to study the families that are prospects for relocation. They should be interviewed by a competent man, and the government's program explained to them. Their attitude toward moving, their family history, and their special training, experience, desires, and aptitudes should be ascertained. No attempt to secure options on the submarginal farm should be made on the first visit. On the basis of information secured, the families that are apparently unable to manage for themselves should be segregated from those who appear capable of developing and operating new farms. Then the settlers should again be visited, and this time a careful appraisal of the farm should be made. On the basis of the appraisal a purchase price should be set and a concrete proposal of a new farm should be made. If this is acceptable to the settler, the program can then be carried through.

The settler should be given the opportunity to choose a new tract at a specified price per acre from the lands on which the government holds options. Having selected his new farm site, the settler should next be given a choice of methods of improvement. Several alternatives might be suggested. For a specified sum, part of the acreage might be cleared, a house and barn erected, fences and other necessary improvements made, and the farm turned over to the settler ready for occupancy and operation. The cost of development in such case would be added to the price of the land and the difference between the new farm and the settler's equity in the old place would be covered by a mortgage, to be held by the government. The advantage would be that the settler would be established quickly; the disadvantage would be the heavier financial burden imposed upon him.

Another alternative might be to provide only a temporary home which might later be used as a granary, poultry house, or garage. The settler could move into this immediately with his family and himself assume the responsibility of developing his place. He might be loaned a specified sum for improvements, land clearing, etc., to be advanced as rapidly as the work was completed. For every dollar saved in developing his farm by the use of labor supplied by him and his family or by the use of salvage material or timber cut on the farm the government might agree to advance sixty or seventy cents as a loan to be added to the mortgage. In this way a settler could be assured of a "grub stake" or enough income for a family living while he was developing his new farm. Under this arrangement the settler would be given freedom in the planning of buildings, etc., under prescribed limitations to safeguard against the use of government money for the construction of unsuitable buildings. The principal difference between this method of development and the first one suggested is that in the latter case the government would in effect hire the settler to develop his own farm instead of using outside relief labor. Various combinations of the two methods might be proposed, depending upon special circumstances affecting individual cases.

The balance of argument seems to favor having the settler develop his own farm so far as possible. The more responsibility he can be made to assume the more likely is he to stand on his own feet after the farm is developed. If a man has participated in making the plans and selecting the materials for improvements, he is less likely to criticize and object to the finished job than if it were all prepared in advance for him.

By using the latter of the two development methods outlined above, many border-line families could be placed on the land for a trial period without a heavy investment of government funds. If such families were able to make a favorable showing during the first year, the government could then proceed with the development with some assurance that the family would succeed, whereas if they were placed upon fully developed and improved farms the trial period might prove very expensive to the government.

A danger in government development of the farms is that administration and labor costs may mount so high that the settler cannot carry the burden. The earlier discussion of clearing costs may be recalled at this point. There the conclusion was reached that the only way a settler can successfully develop a farm on wild timbered land in northern Minnesota is to put in a tremendous amount of labor and be prepared to accept a very low hourly wage rate. An exception might be made of the farms developed on peat burns requiring little clearing, but in general it will be very difficult to make a financial success of developing and operating a new farm if labor must be paid at prevailing wage rates.

ESTIMATED COSTS OF ESTABLISHING SETTLERS ON NEW FARMS

Table 38 presents estimated costs of establishing a settler on eighty acres of burned-over peat land. For the initial project, which involves moving about three hundred families, these estimates are believed to be adequate. On many pieces of land little or no clearing material will be needed. Clearing costs will depend much upon how many families are moved. Land almost entirely clear could probably be found for many families, but as the number is increased, lands on which the clearing problem becomes inceasingly difficult must be used.

The estimates of building costs assume that full use will be made of salvage material from old buildings and that fence posts and considerable log material will be cut from the land. Figure 46 shows an inexpensive serviceable barn of log construction. All relocation farms now have some machinery, and the machinery item in Table 38 represents the cost of additional equipment needed. The estimates contemplate that the settler will perform much of the labor and that the remuneration he receives for this will pay cash living expenses during the development period. With this money available, the settler can devote his full time to the improvement of the farm instead of working on the roads or in the woods and neglecting the farm, as has commonly been done by unaided settlers.

Most settlers have enough livestock to start with. On the

FIGURE 45. — STONE REMOVAL ON THIS FARM HAS MEANT MUCH HARD LABOR

FIGURE 46. — AN INEXPENSIVE BARN OF LOG CONSTRUCTION

TABLE 38. — ESTIMATED COSTS INVOLVED IN ESTABLISH-
ING A SETTLER ON 80 ACRES OF BURNED-OVER PEAT LAND

Land, 80 acres at $7.50			$ 600
Land clearing			
	Materials	$ 50	
	Labor	150	
			200
Buildings			
House			
	Materials	550	
	Labor	250	
Barn			
	Materials	150	
	Labor	150	
Other buildings			
	Materials	50	
	Labor	50	
Fencing			
	Materials	50	
	Labor	50	
Well			
	Materials	50	
			1,350
Farm machinery			150
Seed and feed			200
Total			$2,500

seventy-seven relocation farms studied there were an average of
5.9 dairy cows, 2.8 heifers, and 1.3 horses.

The total investment of $2,500 represents the estimated average
investment. Some men may want more land, larger buildings, etc.,
which will run the investment over $2,500, while others may prefer
to keep their investment below that figure. In every case the mortgage will be reduced by the amount of equity the settler owns in
the old place. Unfortunately this will be very little in most cases.
Practically all the farms on poor soil are tax delinquent. In many
cases the tax claim will be greater than the appraised value of the
land. There are other mortgages and liens against many of the
places which also are greater in many instances than the appraised
value of the land. If the taxing districts and mortgages were paid
in full, many settlers would get nothing for their property. It may
be possible, however, to secure tax abatements, and many creditors
would probably consent to a scaling down of debts for a cash settlement. Regardless of the various adjustments the settler's equity is
very small, perhaps not over $250 per farm on an average.

The estimates in Table 38 contemplate that the farmer will devote his time at the outset to land clearing. An industrious settler probably could clear up forty acres of peat burn in two years, and by the third or fourth year the farm should be producing enough to enable him to begin paying interest and amortization payments on the loan. The data in the following section indicate that from then on such payments should be carried with little difficulty.

BUDGETARY ANALYSIS OF PROSPECTIVE FARM INCOMES

After the settler gets about forty acres cleared, a cropping system similar to that presented in Table 39 might be adopted. This provides for four ten-acre fields in a three-year rotation, the alfalfa

TABLE 39. — DISTRIBUTION OF ACREAGE AND PRODUCTION AND DISPOSAL OF CROPS ON 80 ACRES

CROP	ACRE-AGE	PRODUCTION		DISPOSAL		
		Per Acre	Total	Seed	Feed	Sales
		Bushels or tons		Bushels	Bushels or tons	
Oats and barley..............	10	35	350	30	320	..
Oats and barley straw........	..	1	10	..	10	..
Alfalfa hay	10	2	20	..	20	..
Clover and timothy hay......	10	1.75	17.5	..	17.5	..
Clover seed	5	3	15	1	..	14
Clover straw	..	1	5	..	5	..
Wild hay	5	1	5	..	5	..
Potatoes	5	135 *	675	75 †	100	500
Garden	1	..	..	..	..	..
Wild pasture	34	..	..	..	..	..

* Includes 20 bushels of culls and no. 2 potatoes.
† Includes 20 bushels used in house.

seeding being carried three years on the fourth field and one five-acre field of clover held over. The crop sequence on each field would be oats or barley, clover and timothy, potatoes and clover, with alfalfa for a three-year period once every twelve years. At least a five-acre natural meadow will be found on each of the wild forties, from which about five tons of wild hay can be cut annually for the horses. The acreage of potatoes may vary from three to five acres, either rutabagas or fodder corn being substituted on the remaining acres. If fodder corn is substituted for some of the potatoes, then more of the clover or alfalfa may be left for seed as a substitute cash crop. Depending upon the prospective seed sets, five acres of either the clover or alfalfa may be left for seed, and in the case of alfalfa either the first or second cutting may be left, depending upon moisture conditions and the resulting seed pollination.

Livestock numbers and the production and disposition of livestock products are presented in Table 40. If this number of livestock are carried, it is highly important that approximately 37 tons of legume hay be produced each year. (See Table 41.) For this reason it is necessary to sacrifice somewhat the alfalfa and clover

TABLE 40. — NUMBER, PRODUCTION, AND DISPOSAL OF LIVESTOCK AND LIVESTOCK PRODUCTS ON 80 ACRES

KIND OF LIVESTOCK	NUM-BER	PRODUCTION		DISPOSAL		
		Kind	Amount	Fed to Livestock	Used in Home	Sold
Dairy cows..	8	Butterfat	1,600 lbs.	50 lbs.	135 lbs.	1,415 lbs.
		Skimmilk	48,500 lbs.	42,000 lbs.	6,500 lbs.	....
		2 cull cows	2,200 lbs.	....	....	2,200 lbs.
Young Cattle	5	4 veal calves	500 lbs.	....	....	500 lbs.
		1 yearling	300 lbs.	....	300 lbs.	....
Brood sow ..	1	6 hogs	1,200 lbs.	....	400 lbs.	800 lbs.
Hens	100	Eggs	850 doz.	....	85 doz.	765 doz.
		Meat	230 lbs.	....	105 lbs.	125 lbs.

seed enterprises. Dairy cows provide a more stable and dependable source of income and are therefore to be given preference over the more hazardous seed crop. The assumed standards of crop yields and livestock production are conservative and should be easily obtained as an average by all settlers on the project. In Table 42 are presented the returns that may be expected from the proposed

TABLE 41. — ESTIMATED LIVESTOCK FEED REQUIREMENTS

KIND OF LIVESTOCK	HOME-GROWN FEEDS		PURCHASED FEEDS	
	Kind	Pounds	Kind	Pounds
2 horses	Oats and barley	3,500		
	Legume hay	4,000		
	Wild hay	10,000		
	Clover straw	5,000		
8 cows	Oats and barley	4,500	Mill feeds	3,200
	Legume hay	58,000		
5 young dairy cattle	Legume hay	13,000		
	Clover straw	5,000		
	Skimmilk	15,800		
1 brood sow and litter	Oats and barley	2,200		
	Cull potatoes	6,000		
	Skimmilk	16,200		
100 hens	Oats and barley	2,600	Poultry feeds	4,800
	Skimmilk	10,000		

TABLE 42. — ESTIMATED RETURNS FROM PROPOSED ORGANIZATION

INCOME

Crop sales

Potatoes	510 bu. at $.40	$204.00	
Alsike clover seed.........	14 bu. at 6.00	84.00	
Total crop sales................................			$288.00

Livestock and livestock product sales

Butterfat	1,415 lbs. at	.20	283.00	
2 cows	2,200 lbs. at	.02	44.00	
4 veal calves	500 lbs. at	.06	30.00	
4 hogs	800 lbs. at	.04	32.00	
Eggs	765 doz. at	.15	114.75	
Poultry	125 lbs. at	.075	9.38	
Total livestock sales...........................			513.13	
Total crop and livestock sales...........................				$801.13

CASH EXPENSES

Cost of materials and services for crops

Containers		25.00	
Twine	30 lbs. at .08	2.40	
Threshing small grain.....	350 bu. at .03	10.50	
Threshing and cleaning clover seed	15 bu. at 1.50	22.50	
Fertilizer	500 lbs. at 1.75	8.75	
Paris green	10 lbs. at .40	4.00	
Garden seed		5.00	
Total cash crop costs...........................		78.15	

Cost of materials and services for livestock

Veterinary and medicine..................		30.00	
Bull service	8 cows at 2.00	16.00	
Dairy feed	32 cwt. at 1.25	40.00	
Poultry feed	48 cwt. at 1.50	72.00	
Total cash livestock costs.......................		158.00	
Machinery and building expense, parts, repairs, etc.....		50.00	
Insurance on buildings.............................		10.00	
Taxes		40.00	
Interest and amortization on indebtedness of $2,500 at 6 per cent....................................		150.00	
Total cash costs		486.15	
Net cash farm income...			$314.98
Non-cash income			225.00
Net farm income......			$539.98

farm organization on the basis of average prices prevailing in the northern part of the state in 1933 and 1934. During those years prices of farm produce in relation to production cost items were much lower than they had been for ten years. Any favorable change in price relations would be reflected immediately in higher farm earnings.

It will be observed from Table 42 that on the basis of the various assumptions involved, a net farm income of about $540 would result after all cash operating costs, interest, and amortization charges had been covered. The estimated net farm income in 1932 on the seventy-seven farms in relocation areas which were studied was $212 per farm. The difference of $328 between the two figures presumably represents the possible annual gains available to individual settlers. However, conditions on the burned-over peat lands of the state are admittedly very favorable for such a relocation project, and it is questionable if as promising results could be anticipated elsewhere in the northern counties, particularly in places where heavy clearing costs are involved.

POSSIBLE SAVINGS IN THE COST OF GOVERNMENTAL SERVICES ARISING FROM THE RELOCATION OF FARM FAMILIES *

Reference has repeatedly been made throughout this report to the savings in governmental costs that would be possible if isolated settlers were relocated on good soil near settled communities. In Chapter VI data were presented to show that the public was paying from 93 to 97 per cent of the cost of special road and transportation services received by certain families. By relocating such families most of the public outlay could be saved. Occasionally an entire community receives more from the county and state in the way of services than it contributes in taxes. The difficulties of moving such communities are much greater than moving scattered and isolated settlers, although the need may be just as pressing, for it involves moving dependent business establishments, such as stores, garages, service stations, etc.

With full recognition of the many difficulties involved in moving an established community, a special study was made to illustrate the savings in governmental expenditures that could be accomplished thereby. As a basis for the study it was assumed that 135 families living in three townships [6] in the Brimson area were to be moved out and relocated on good soil in eight townships [7] in the Cook area.

---

* The savings presented in this section are based on data assembled by field workers under the direction of Roy G. Blakey, particularly Gerhard J. Isaac and Mark Regan.

[6] T. 55, R. 12, T. 56, R. 12, and T. 57, R. 12.

[7] T. 61, R. 18, 19, 20, and 21, and T. 62, R. 18, 19, 20, and 21.

Roads and schools are the most important public facilities maintained in the Brimson area. There are 18 miles of township roads and 31.75 miles of county roads in the three townships. During the school year 1931–32 four schools were maintained, one of which was discontinued at the beginning of the 1932–33 school year. In the four schools 109 pupils were enrolled, and 7 teachers were employed. In addition to these facilities, there were three telephone lines, two town halls, and three cemeteries. Since there are approximately 135 families located in the area, there is less than one child of school age per family.

If the settlement were completely evacuated, practically all the school operating expenses in this area could be saved. For the school year 1931–32 these amounted to $17,748. It is estimated that all the operating costs, with the exception of one item of $884, representing expenditures for textbooks, could be saved.

The total cost of maintaining roads in the area amounts to $11,846, which is divided as follows:

County roads
   Maintenance ....$ 9,470
   Snow clearance 1,008
Town roads
   Maintenance   918
   Snow clearance   450
                                             _____
      Total $11,846

Not all the road facilities could be withdrawn. For recreational purposes about 8.5 miles of county roads would be necessary, although the maintenance cost on this stretch would be considerably reduced. Traffic on the remaining road would be much lighter. To offset the cost of continuing this road, snow-clearing costs on ten miles of county road outside this area could be saved. Thus the net savings in the maintenance of roads would amount to $11,246.

Practically the entire cost of township government could be dispensed with. This saving would amount to $2,206.

There is little doubt that all the general or revenue expenditures could be saved. If there were no settlers in the area, fire costs would be practically eliminated, also town halls and telephones. The cemeteries would probably be maintained, but very little is spent on their upkeep.

The fourth item of saving would be in public relief. Although direct relief in the area amounted to only $498 in 1932, indirect relief in the form of payrolls for road construction amounted to

$7,797. The total amount of relief in this district is measured more accurately by the addition of the direct and indirect sums, or $8,295. It is difficult to estimate how much of this would be saved.

The assured savings, based on 1932 costs, would amount to $30,316, divided as follows: schools, $16,864; roads, $11,246; and township government, $2,206. These savings would revert to the governmental agencies in approximately the following amounts:

	Local	County	State	Total
Schools	$2,174	$ 8,978	$5,712	$16,864
Town roads	918	450	.....	1,368
County roads	....	9,878	.....	9,878
Town government	2,206	.....	.....	2,206
Total	$5,298	$19,306	$5,712	$30,316

St. Louis County carries a large share of the burden of maintaining roads, schools, and relief for the community and would profit most from the relocation. The state would save the next largest amount, all in state aid to schools, and the savings of local units would almost equal those of the state.

The local contributions made to the state and the county have not been deducted from the savings of these agencies in this analysis. These are rather insignificant items, however. In 1932 the Brimson area paid only $411 to the county and $247 to the state. The net contributions of each of the governmental agencies to the support of public services in this area were as follows: local, $5,956; county, $27,190; and state, $5,465. The Brimson area paid $411 to the county and received from the county $27,601 — $19,306 in public services and $8,295 for road employment. It paid $247 to the state in taxes and received $5,712 in school aid. Considering relief also as a cost and giving the locality credit for its payments to the county and the state, the area contributed only 15.4 per cent of the funds required for its support; the state contributed 14.1 per cent, and the county 70.5 per cent.

Thus far we have considered only gross savings. It is obvious, of course, that these settlers will increase the governmental expenses in the area into which they move. Let us consider what these additional costs will amount to.

Apparently the schools in the Cook area can care for a considerable increase in enrollment. There are thirteen schools, valued at $160,230 and having equipment valued at $20,944. Their capacity, without enlarging the buildings or increasing the number of teachers, is 1,176 pupils. The total enrollment in 1931–32 was 842, or 334 less than capacity. Since only 109 pupils are to be moved from the Brimson area, the Cook schools can take care of the increase without any additional expense except for transportation.

But since the first consideration in selecting sites for the incoming settlers is the productiveness of the land, the full capacity of the schools cannot be utilized, because the better tracts do not all fall within reach of the schools in which the unused capacity is greatest.

With two exceptions (schools no. 114 and no. 167), school facilities are adequate to handle the contemplated increase in settlement within the area. In all the school areas except these two the factor limiting additional settlement is the lack of suitable land rather than the size of the school. Thirty-two families can be added with no increase in transportation or other costs because the facilities are available or the tracts are within walking distance of the schools.

The transportation cost for the rest of the families has been estimated at $3,025. In addition, it is suggested that a room might be added to school no. 167, at an estimated cost of $5,000. This is an almost new brick building, the plans for which permit such additions to be made. The estimated cost of operation and maintenance for this added room would total $1,700, including $225 for interest on the investment, $1,035 for one more teacher, $415 for janitor, fuel, and supplies, and $25 for increase in maintenance costs. Thus the maximum additional school cost would approximate $4,725. Since the possible savings in the Brimson area amount to $16,864, the net saving on schools would be $12,139.

Under the present regulations there would be a slight increase, amounting to $118, in regular state aid because of the additional room in school no. 167. The increase in transportation aid for the area would also be slight, amounting to $265. The increase in supplemental state aid, however, amounting to approximately $4,317, would almost offset the total increased cost. State aid would thus provide $4,700 of the $4,725 additional cost, or all but $25. The county would bear this slight difference. There would be no additional cost to the taxpayers of the Cook area through this increase of settlers. Of the $12,139 saved in school costs the state would gain $1,011, the Brimson locality $2,174, and the County of St. Louis $8,954.

The road facilities in the Cook area are adequate to care for this increase in settlement. There is an extensive system of county roads,

most of which are graveled and in good repair, and the suitable locations are all on these roads.

Nor is there any reason to believe that township government
costs would increase. The most important single cost is the construction and maintenance of town roads, and since this item
would not be increased, there is little likelihood that there would
be any increase in general revenue costs, fire fighting, telephone,
etc. All the town governments are working far below capacity, and
a much larger increase of settlement than has been suggested would
be necessary to increase the costs of town government.

It is difficult to estimate possible savings in relief. The main
purpose of the move would be to make settlers more self-sufficing.
Farm schedules show that the settlers in the Cook area are less
dependent upon outside work as a source of income than those in
the Brimson area. Assuming that the new settler will eventually
reach approximately the same standards of productivity, it is almost certain that there will be a considerable saving in relief. The
savings in this item are much more difficult to estimate than are
the others. In order to arrive at a reasonable estimate of relief savings, it would be necessary to make a study of the personal ability
of the settlers to be relocated. When given the opportunity to obtain a good piece of land, many settlers will become self-supporting.
Others less able, even though on better land, will still need aid, although not as much as before. It is perhaps enough if the saving in
relief is recognized as one of the factors favoring the move, even
though the definite amount of saving cannot be estimated.

Though the well-being of the individuals may be the primary
justification for such a movement of settlers, the units of government would save a very considerable amount, the estimated sum
being $25,591 in this instance. The following summary shows where
the savings would be made.

	Local	County	State	Total
Schools................................	$2,174	$ 8,954	$1,011	$12,139
Town roads......................	918	450	.....	1,368
County roads	....	9,878	.....	9,878
Town government..............	2,206	.....	.....	2,206
Total	$5,298	$19,282	$1,011	$25,591

Since practically all these savings would accrue to the taxpayers of the county, the county could well afford to take the initiative
in assisting farm families poorly located to move. The average estimated annual savings in government costs amount to $190 per

TABLE 43. — ANNUAL ESTIMATED SAVINGS ARISING FROM LOCAL GOVERNMENT
REORGANIZATION AND SETTLER RELOCATION IN 14 NORTHEASTERN
MINNESOTA COUNTIES

County	County Savings	Town Savings	School Savings	Total Savings
Aitkin				
Reorganization	$10,200	$15,000	$ 8,500	$33,700
Reorganization and relocation....	10,200	22,000	22,000	54,200
Beltrami				
Reorganization	10,600	2,000	27,400	40,000
Reorganization and relocation....	10,600	10,600	47,400	68,600
Cass				
Reorganization	9,400	16,600	15,100	41,100
Reorganization and relocation....	9,400	22,300	42,700	74,400
Koochiching				
Reorganization	7,700	5,200	*	12,900
Reorganization and relocation....	7,700	9,700	21,800	39,200
Lake of the Woods				
Reorganization	2,900	−2,400	*	500
Reorganization and relocation....	2,900	2,100	8,700	13,700
Clearwater				
Reorganization	2,900	3,000	5,200	11,100
Reorganization and relocation....	2,900	7,500	14,200	24,600
Hubbard				
Reorganization	5,400	−2,800	10,700	13,300
Reorganization and relocation....	5,400	3,900	28,100	37,400
Carlton				
Reorganization	9,000	30,000	14,000	53,000
Reorganization and relocation....	9,000	40,200	33,000	82,200
Pine				
Reorganization	5,800	25,800	15,000	46,600
Reorganization and relocation....	5,800	30,200	35,000	71,000
Crow Wing				
Reorganization	*	28,000	18,000	46,000
Reorganization and relocation....		36,200	37,000	73,200
Itasca				
Reorganization	*	17,200	34,000	51,200
Reorganization and relocation....		32,800	61,000	93,800
St. Louis				
Reorganization	*	36,400	*	36,400
Reorganization and relocation....		55,100	155,000	210,100
Lake and Cook consolidated				
Reorganization	28,200 †	25,100	4,500	57,800
Reorganization and relocation....	28,200	34,800	18,000	81,000
Total : Reorganization.............	92,100	199,100	152,400	443,600
Total : Reorganization and relocation	92,100	307,400	523,900	923,400

* No reorganization contemplated.

† $7,800 savings due to reorganization of county offices, balance of $20,400 to consolidation.

family in the group we have used as an illustration, of which the county's share would amount to $144. It is admitted that possible savings per family are much greater in the Brimson community than they would be, on the average, in the fourteen counties as a whole. The effects of settler relocation on costs of government have been presented chiefly to illustrate the numerous aspects of the problem. In the following chapter similar estimates have been prepared to demonstrate possible savings in other localities, assuming that settlers in all conservation zones were relocated on good land.

In order to take maximum advantage of settler relocation, certain reorganizations of local government are necessary. Accordingly estimates are presented in the following chapter to show, first, savings from reorganization only and, second, savings from reorganization combined with settler relocation. In the fourteen counties the reorganization of local government would result in annual savings of $443,600, and reorganization combined with settler relocation would result in savings of $923,400. (See Table 43.) The additional savings from settler relocation thus amount to $479,800. The director of the Division of Forestry of the State Department of Conservation has estimated that annual fire fighting costs could be reduced by $40,000 if settlers were removed from the forests, which would bring the total estimated public savings from relocating settlers to about $519,800 per year.

There are approximately five thousand occupied farms in the suggested conservation zones of the fourteen counties. The estimated savings resulting from relocating settlers, providing evacuation is complete, would amount to about $100 per family annually. This is equal to interest on an investment of $2,000 at 5 per cent. In other words, at an interest rate of 5 per cent public agencies could afford to spend a maximum of $2,000 per family in assisting settlers to become relocated. If settlers could be re-established at a net cost to the public of less than $2,000, a public saving would result from the undertaking. On the Beltrami Island project, where the public expenditure for the purchase and administration of poor farms will probably amount to $1,000 per farm, the return in savings will approximate 10 per cent on the public investment. It should be understood that these estimates of possible savings to be derived from relocation of settlement will not be achieved unless all the settlers now in conservation zones are relocated. If only part of them move, or if new settlement takes place, roads, schools, and other services must continue in these areas.

CHAPTER XI

ADJUSTMENTS IN LOCAL GOVERNMENT *

Attention has been called to the relationship between land use and the cost of local government. In this chapter consideration will be given to the financial condition of individual counties and the possibilities for improvement. In many parts of the area local units are facing a very difficult situation. Revenues have been declining. The returns from the tax on general property have been decreasing both because of the fall in assessed valuations and because of the increase in tax delinquency. Expenditures have decreased less rapidly, with the result that the burden on the property that remains on the tax rolls has increased, and this in turn has led to further delinquency. Another effect has been an increase in the net public indebtedness.

There are limits to the reduction of expenditures. Beyond a certain point expenses cannot be curtailed if government is to be maintained, because there are certain fixed items, such as interest and principal payments upon debt, salaries fixed by legislative acts, and the maintenance of certain standards as a qualification for state aids. The need for a reduction in the burden is only too apparent, however. In many counties the tax rates on general property are almost confiscatory, and with declining trends in property value, there is little prospect of increased revenues from the tax on property. The receipts from miscellaneous fees and earnings, which at best are only minor sources of revenue, have likewise been declining. Many units cannot borrow much longer, for they are approaching the limits set upon the floating of bonds and warrants.

Subventions and grants from the state could conceivably be increased to assist local units. In many counties these have increased absolutely and in all counties relatively. How far the state should go in increasing aids to local units is a question of policy that has not been definitely settled,[1] but it seems reasonable to

---

* The phase of the study on which this chapter is based was conducted under the direction of Roy G. Blakey. This chapter was prepared by Mark Regan. Gerhard J. Isaac and Sylvan Warrington assisted in the field work and, with K. B. Heggenhaugen, in the analysis.

[1] See *Land Utilization in Minnesota* (Report of the Committee on Land Utilization, University of Minnesota Press, 1934), Chapters 9 and 10, for a more extended discussion of state aid.

expect that no considerable extension of state aid will take place without assurances that the results will tend to further policies in the interest of the state as a whole.

School districts are more dependent upon state aid than are towns and counties, consequently they feel the effects of increasing property tax delinquency somewhat less than the other units of local government in the cut-over area. As a result of lower property valuations, the claims of the schools for state aid under existing law have increased. Funds available for this purpose have been insufficient, however, to increase the aid to the full amount of the claims.

School districts that are faced with the difficulty of maintaining revenues from local taxes may regard state aid as the source of revenue in which the possibilities for expansion are greatest. The state regards education as one of the services to which all its citizens are entitled and from which the people generally derive benefit. This is an inducement to increase its support of schools. But if state school aids are to be increased, it should be upon the condition that the added support will be used to make desirable adjustments in the organization of the school system. Presumably the state has no desire to increase aid in order to subsidize a school system that is inefficiently organized. Consequently it is important that the most effective organization possible be established and that this be promoted by a proper land use program.

A similar situation occurs in connection with county and state aid roads. If the state is to participate in road building and upkeep, it is justified in requiring that county road systems be so organized that the maximum of service will be derived from such financial assistance.

It must not be inferred that the state alone is interested in the efficient organization of local government. On the contrary, it is the people living in the units in question who are primarily concerned in having their local government so organized that it will render effective and economical service. It is only when these units demand aid in carrying on their functions that the state becomes directly interested.

As has been suggested, units of local government in the cut-over area have been forced to curtail expenditures because of the decrease in receipts from the property tax, particularly those towns whose revenue is almost entirely derived from that source. In Minnesota the towns receive no state aid, and their receipts from miscellaneous earnings and fines are of little consequence. The counties, though many of them receive enough road aid to finance their highway construction and maintenance program, as well as substantial aid for the payment of interest and principal on ditch bonds, are also heavily dependent on the property tax as a means of financing the other county activities. On the other hand, the schools in this part of the state, outside of those in St. Louis County, obtain a major portion of their revenue from state aid. But even for the schools the property tax is an important source of revenue.

Local government units have reduced costs of government in three of four ways. They have reduced salaries where these are not set by legislative statutes; in Cass County, in pursuance of a special act passed by the legislature in 1933, the salaries of all elective officers were reduced.[2] Many of the counties have decreased their personnel, especially the number of office assistants. Several counties have curtailed or eliminated particular services. Expenditures for conservation and the development of natural resources have been drastically reduced; in many counties roads have been maintained at a lower standard; some school districts have reduced the length of the school term; and towns have reduced road service to the point where many roads are almost impassable part of the year. A fourth possible method of reducing costs, that of increasing the operating efficiency of the various offices, has been used only incidentally, though in a few counties there have been substantial increases in efficiency with the election of more capable officers.

As methods of curtailing expenditures, the first three have little to commend them, although they are applicable to special cases where offices are overmanned or overpaid and services exceed requirements. The unfortunate thing is that the reduction in salaries has taken place in the appointive offices, where the salaries often were already at or below the minimum necessary to attract competent personnel. With the present governmental organization, possible reductions in personnel are also limited. The curtailment of services can be only a temporary method of reducing costs if the standards of the community are to be maintained.

But the reduction of costs through more efficient operation of local government merits further attention. This may involve not only an improvement in the functioning of the present organization but a change in the organization itself or a realignment of functions. At present the law provides for about the same set of offi-

[2] Session Laws, chapter 166.

cials in each county, though there are great variations among counties with respect to area, population, and assessed valuation. Though townships are more nearly the same size, they vary greatly in population and resources. School districts vary in size, in valuation, and in number of children of school age. The experiences of two counties, Koochiching and Lake, with larger school districts indicate what advantages may be obtained from organization changes.

If settlement in areas unsuited to agriculture is restricted and settlers are concentrated on the better lands, there will be much less need for a stereotyped form of local government organization. In some areas the relocation of settlers, if completely achieved, will eliminate entirely the need for town and school organizations and will considerably reduce the work load of some county offices, particularly those of the sheriff, the superintendent of schools, the highway engineer, and the relief and welfare agencies, whose work loads are affected by the location of settlement. The effect on the work load of the auditor, the treasurer, and the register of deeds would depend on the ownership of the evacuated areas. Settler relocation programs cannot produce the largest possible savings if the existing local government set-up remains intact. In some regions whole townships and school districts may be evacuated, in others parts of townships and school districts. The savings through a settlement concentration program alone would be limited to governmental costs of the particular town and school organizations eliminated and of a few county roads for which lower maintenance standards might suffice.

REORGANIZATION OF LOCAL GOVERNMENT

In the light of the preceding discussion, some of the suggestions that have been made for the reorganization of counties, townships, and schools will be considered and evaluated as to their applicability to the northeastern counties. The changes possible in the organization of each of the types of local units will be considered first. Then estimates of the effect on governmental costs arising out of the application of some of the possible changes will be made.

THE COUNTIES

Among the factors affecting the cost of county administration are population, area, assessed valuation, the extent to which primary improvements have been completed, the quantity and quality of services rendered, and the efficiency of the officials. With a given type of organization, uniform services and methods of operation, and fixed salaries, per capita overhead costs of county operation decline rapidly as population numbers increase to the 10,000 level. Studies of local government expenditures have shown that per capita overhead costs continue to decline up to a point somewhere between the 28,000 and the 35,000 level. The conclusion is that a county of from 30,000 to 35,000 population can have as low a per capita overhead expense as larger ones, but counties with a smaller number must expect to have higher costs.[3]

The per capita cost figures of the northeastern counties appear to agree in general with this conclusion. The highest are found in Cook County, with a population of only 2,400 persons. Lake and Lake of the Woods counties, also small in population, likewise have high per capita costs. St. Louis and Itasca counties are exceptions to the general rule; though they have considerably larger populations, their per capita costs are higher than either Lake or Lake of the Woods. This is accounted for by the large taxable resources of these two counties and the more extensive services they render.

Assessed valuation is another factor affecting cost of administration. The tax base of a county should be large enough so that the burden of supporting the necessary services will not be unduly high. Nine of the fourteen cut-over counties had an assessed valuation of less than $5,000,000 in 1932. The net cost of county government in these nine counties averaged $58 for each $1,000 of assessed valuation in 1932 as compared with $24 for the five counties having a valuation in excess of $5,000,000. Cook County, with an assessed valuation of slightly over $1,000,000, had a cost of $125 per $1,000 of assessed value, while the cost for St. Louis County, with a valuation of nearly $300,000,000, was only $16. In only two of the nine counties was the cost less than $45 per $1,000, while in none of the five with a valuation in excess of $5,000,000 was it over $35 and in only one was it over $30. The indications are that whenever assessed valuations fall much below the $5,000,000 level, the cost of maintaining a county organization tends to become a heavy burden.

If a population of 10,000 and an assessed valuation of $5,000,000 represent the minimum requirements for the maintenance of a satisfactory organization, Cook, Lake, and Lake of the Woods counties fall below minimum requirements by a considerable margin; and Clearwater and Hubbard, with populations approaching 10,000, are near the margin. One solution that suggests itself is that the counties

[3] *Land Utilization in Minnesota,* p. 191.

falling far below the minimum requirements merge or consolidate with an adjoining county. Many considerations must be taken into account, however: accessibility of the county seat; the office capacity of the courthouse if new capital outlays are to be avoided; the effectiveness with which the county organization is operating and its ability to cope with the situation. Cook and Lake counties appear to offer the best possibilities for effecting savings through consolidation; estimates have therefore been made for those counties.

While consolidation, properly worked out, should be effective in reducing the cost of county government, other methods are open to counties with less than the optimum population. One is to alter the governmental organization to fit the situation by joining with other counties in performing certain services such as law enforcement, criminal prosecution, construction and maintenance of highways, and administration of poor relief. This method might be applied to any function that could be carried on more effectively by units larger than the present counties. In highway building and maintenance, for example, the necessary overhead could serve a larger area and the equipment could be used more nearly to capacity. Another possibility is to combine certain county offices in which there may be some duplication of work or which do not require the full time of the official in charge. Estimates of possible savings in each county are indicated below.

The first suggestion offered for consideration is that the treasurer's office be eliminated and the work be cared for by a cashier attached to the auditor's office. There is probably more duplication in the work of these two offices than in any others in the courthouse. Aside from the duties of collection and payment of revenues, which would be taken over by a cashier, most of the treasurer's duties could be performed in the auditor's office with little or no added cost. However, some changes would need to be made in the methods of keeping books and making out receipts, a consequence of which would be a lessening of the check upon the work of the auditor. But this would be overcome in a measure by the yearly audit by the state public examiners.

The second change suggested is that the office of the probate judge and that of the clerk of court be combined. Except in unusual years, the administrative work of neither of these offices is heavy enough to require the full time of the elected officials. In the smaller counties these officials often do their own clerical work. If the offices were combined, a clerk could be hired to do the clerical work, and the official's time made available for the administrative duties of both offices. Since the Constitution [4] requires the election of a probate judge and a clerk of the district court, an amendment is necessary before such a combination can be effected.

A third proposal is to reduce the number of county commissioners to three. Considering the limited legislative functions of the counties, the smaller number of commissioners probably could handle the load satisfactorily. Counties with less than 10,000 population might consider electing only one commissioner and designating two other county officials to serve as members of the county board.

A fourth suggestion is that all fees be paid to the county and that offices now operated on a fee basis be placed on a salary basis. This might have the effect of reducing some salaries, but the added compensation given in the form of fees is not always justified. Such offices as that of the register of deeds, which is generally on a fee basis, requires more and more time for work of a non-fee type as a county matures. A much more equitable relationship of salaries and work could be attained if all officials were on a salary basis.

THE TOWNS

The functions of the towns as units of local government are limited. The major responsibility of the town is to construct and maintain roads. In addition, it has the responsibility of assessing property and supervising elections. Some towns also render such services as poor relief, fire protection, and the maintenance of a town hall, cemeteries, and telephone lines.

Except for a few towns in mining areas in St. Louis and Itasca counties, most of the northern towns have low assessed valuations and limited populations. Hence their revenues are insufficient to carry on their limited functions effectively without levying high taxes.

The number of townships in the fourteen counties falling within given population classes according to the 1930 census are as follows:

Population	Townships
49 and under	22
50–99	66
100–199	142
200–299	97
300–399	72
400 and over	99

[4] Constitution of Minnesota, Article 6, Sections 7, 13.

Of the organized towns in the cut-over counties, 46 per cent have a population of less than 200, 18 per cent a population of less than 100, and 4 per cent a population of less than 50.

As in the counties, the per capita cost of government is closely related to population. The town organization involves certain minimum costs regardless of population and if only a few people reside in the area, these costs may represent a heavy per capita burden. If six towns in Itasca County and eleven in St. Louis County, which have high taxable valuations because of mineral deposits, are excluded, the per capita costs of town government in towns of various sizes were as follows in 1932:

Population	Per Capita Cost
49 and under	$8.26
50– 99	5.42
100–199	4.22
200–299	3.44
300–399	2.77
400 and over	3.29

Per capita costs declined markedly up to a population of 400. The higher costs in the group with the largest population are probably due to higher standards of service.

Per capita costs of the seventeen towns excluded from the tabulation because of iron ore deposits average $38.54. The average for the six towns in Itasca County is not much higher than the rest of the towns in the northeastern counties. For the eleven towns in St. Louis County the per capita cost in 1932 was $62.25, which is an indication of the elaborate services rendered by the towns in the iron range area of this county.

It is a question whether an organized town is needed in sparsely settled areas and whether many areas are not unable to support a town government. The number of towns falling within given valuation classes in 1932 is shown in the following distribution:

Assessed Valuation	Number of Towns	Percentage
Less than $25,000	15	3
$25,000– $50,000	94	19
$50,000– $75,000	87	18
$75,000–$100,000	100	20
$100,000–$150,000	111	22
Over $150,000	91	18

Of the towns in the fourteen cut-over counties 59 per cent have an assessed valuation of $100,000 or less, 39 per cent $75,000 or less, and 22 per cent $50,000 or less. Seventy-two per cent of the towns in Koochiching County, 67 per cent in Beltrami County, 48 per cent in Lake of the Woods, 45 per cent in Itasca, and 26 per cent in St. Louis have assessed valuations of $50,000 or less. Just as per capita costs tend to be unduly high with sparse populations, the town costs per $1,000 of assessed valuation are high with low valuations.

The inadequacy of town services is not entirely due to the lack of revenues. The ordinary town is too small a unit to render the maximum of service with the revenues that are received. Expensive machinery is necessary for adequate road service. Even if the town were financially able to purchase such machinery, it cannot utilize it to full capacity because of its limited road mileage. Consequently methods that have long been obsolete are still used by many of the towns in the cut-over counties. It is needless to say that the condition of most town roads reflects the methods used.

Another function performed by towns that can be improved upon is property assessment. There have been numerous demonstrations of inequalities in property assessments by the township assessor.[5] Attempts have long been made to change the system by replacing the local assessors with county assessors. The Tax Commission in its report of 1928 recommended "that a law be enacted providing for the appointment of a county assessor in each county of the state by the county board thereof, such county assessor to take the place of and perform all of the duties now imposed on local assessors."[6] The Tax Commission advocated such a move as early as 1912 and has frequently repeated the recommendation since. Among the reasons given for the failure of the local assessor system is that the size of the average assessment district is much too small to require the full time of an assessor. He devotes only from three to eight weeks a year in assessment work and consequently does not become expert. Each assessor exercises his individual judgment in making assessments, and with more than 650 assessors in the fourteen northeastern counties, great inequalities appear, both in personal property and in real estate assessments.

The inequalities in property assessment are illustrated by the number and high percentage changes made by county boards of

[5] For instance, see Jens P. Jensen, *Property Taxation in the United States* (University of Chicago Press, 1931), Table 54, p. 230; Roy G. Blakey and others, *Taxation in Minnesota* (University of Minnesota Press, 1932), p. 157 and Chapter 3; G. B. Clarke and O. B. Jesness, *A Study of Taxation in Minnesota with Particular Reference to Assessments of Farm Lands* (Minnesota Experiment Station Bulletin No. 277); and "Minnesota's Tax Problem," an unpublished study of the Minnesota Taxpayers' Association.

[6] Report of the Minnesota Tax Commission, 1928, p. 1.

equalization. It is of interest to note the percentage changes in assessments of real and personal property made by county boards of
equalization in 1926 for those northeastern counties on which reports are complete. (See Table 44.) For instance, in Aitkin County
changes in the real estate assessment were made in 55 of the 61

TABLE 44. — PERCENTAGE CHANGES IN ASSESSMENTS OF REAL AND PERSONAL
PROPERTY MADE BY COUNTY BOARDS OF EQUALIZATION *

| COUNTY | REAL ESTATE | | | | PERSONAL PROPERTY | | |
| | Number of Districts | Number of Districts Changed | Percentage Changes | | Number of Items Changed | Percentage Changes | |
			Mini-mum	Maxi-mum		Mini-mum	Maxi-mum
Aitkin......	61	55	10	150	407	10	300
Clearwater..	30	25	4	108	139	10	300
Crow Wing .	44	24	10	30	67	10	100
Hubbard ...	33	33	1	122	511	3	400
Koochiching	49	22	10	50	23	10	50
Pine	47	29	10	200	138	10	600
St. Louis...	109	None	..	...	244	5	386

* Compiled from the Report of the Minnesota Tax Commission, 1928, p. 48.

districts, 54 of which were increases and one a decrease. Of the
increases, 7 were from 10 to 20 per cent; 11 from 20 to 30 per cent;
19 from 30 to 50 per cent; 9 from 50 to 70 per cent; 5 from 70 to
100 per cent; 8 from 100 to 150 per cent.

The inequalities in personal property assessment were even
more numerous and extensive than in real estate. In the northeastern counties the maximum change varied from 50 per cent in
Koochiching to 600 per cent in Pine. In addition to the changes
made by the county boards, changes were made by the State Tax
Commission. These inequalities are not limited to the cut-over
counties; they are equaled or exceeded in many of the southern
counties. It is merely an illustration of the inadequacy of the town
as the unit for the performance of this important function.

Relief administered by the towns operates under marked handicaps. Trained relief investigators cannot be employed, there are
constant difficulties over local residence rules, and relief costs often
fall heaviest on towns least able to bear them. State and national
relief administrations favor the county as the smallest competent
unit for handling poor relief.

In spite of the fact that a good case can be established for the
transfer of town functions to the county, little or no progress in

this direction has been made. The moves toward dissolution of towns have arisen almost entirely out of a stringent financial situation, which in turn is due to declining tax revenues.

Two laws providing for dissolution of towns were passed by the 1933 legislature. One of these[7] provides that "whenever the tax delinquency in any town exceeds 70 per cent in any one year, the board of county commissioners of the county wherein such town is situated on its own initiative may by resolution dissolve such town." The other[8] provides that "whenever the assessed valuation of any duly organized civil township drops to less than $50,000 or whenever the tax delinquency of any such township amounts to 50 per cent of its assessed valuation, or when the state has acquired title to 50 per cent of the real estate of such township . . . the county board by resolution shall declare any such township . . . duly dissolved."

The first law makes the dissolution optional with the county board when current delinquency exceeds 70 per cent of the levy. The second law provides that the county board shall dissolve the town organizations if the assessed valuations fall below $50,000, or the accumulated delinquency reaches half of the assessed valuation. Using the $50,000 valuation as the minimum based upon 1931 assessments, 109, or 22 per cent of all the towns in the fourteen counties, would be dissolved if the county boards took action. One hundred and seventy could be dissolved because of tax delinquency in excess of 70 per cent. On the two grounds it would be possible to dissolve 228 towns, or 46 per cent of all towns in the northeastern counties.

On the basis of this legislation, Lake of the Woods County has dissolved all its towns. In January, 1933, twenty-four of its towns had a delinquency of over 70 per cent of the current levy. For the levy due in 1932, fourteen towns had a valuation of less than $50,000. A decision of the district court in Itasca County held that these laws were unconstitutional on the ground that no provision was made for the performance of such town functions as the maintenance of town telephone lines.

One way of reducing town costs is the consolidation of adjoining towns. Four or more towns can be merged, one town board directing all the functions carried on by the consolidated unit. The economies resulting from such a step would be limited, however, because the area would still be too small for efficient operation. Road ma-

[7] Session Laws, 1933, chapter 235.
[8] Ibid., chapter 377.

chinery would still be under-utilized and a full-time assessor could not be employed. It is questionable whether any unit smaller than the county can maintain roads or assess property efficiently.

Since all the fourteen counties have areas not yet organized into towns or have organized towns likely to be dissolved, the logical step might be to dissolve all towns and turn their functions over to the counties. A general move of this kind, however, encounters opposition from those who for one reason or another see in the town an essential unit of government. Because of this feeling, many areas will want to maintain the town. But even if the organization is continued, services that can be performed more effectively by the county, such as road construction and maintenance, property assessment, and others, can be assigned to a larger unit. This will leave the town to take care of functions peculiar to it and to serve areas in which the local situation warrants such a unit. For instance, in a town such as Stuntz in St. Louis County, which had a population of 4,345 in 1930 and an assessed valuation of over $27,000,000, greater than the combined valuations of eight of the fourteen counties, there is probably need for some such local unit.

The major savings from town dissolution would result from the elimination of the overhead expenses of maintaining town boards. Savings over former outlays for town roads could also be expected in most of the counties if such roads were placed under county direction. By 1932, however, the decline in revenue had forced drastic curtailment of town expenditures for roads to the point where the benefits to be derived from the transfer of road maintenance to the counties would in many instances come largely through an improvement in the quality of the service performed. In the case of towns that have continued to expend sufficient money on roads to maintain them in good condition, a reduction in outlay could be expected.

THE SCHOOLS

The present school system includes a large number of small districts, resulting in a considerable number of schools with enrollments considerably below the capacity of even one teacher. Inasmuch as each district has its separate school board, it is difficult to arrive at satisfactory adjustments between schools. The system tends to result in heavy maintenance costs, especially when the limited educational opportunities are considered.

In spite of the progress that has been made in several of the northeastern counties toward the development of larger school districts, there are still 652 school districts in the area, including 11 unorganized districts varying in size from 2 to 3 congressional townships to over 50. Pine and Aitkin County each has over 100 districts, and Crow Wing has 97. Lake County has only one district, while Koochiching has 3, Cook 6, and Itasca 9.

Probably as a result of the movement toward larger schools and more extensive use of transportation, the enrollment per teacher in the ungraded schools of the cut-over counties is equal to the state average. Four of the counties were below the state average, nine were above. Lake County, which has no ungraded schools, was excluded from the above comparisons. Itasca had the lowest enrollment per teacher of the fourteen counties, 17.8, while Koochiching had the highest, 26.2. While there may be a fair average enrollment per teacher in the cut-over counties, the range is considerable, some schools having an enrollment of fewer than five pupils. If Lake, Koochiching, and St. Louis counties are excluded, all of which have either a large unorganized district or a county district, the percentage distribution of schools with given enrollments is as follows:

Number of Pupils per School	Percentage of Schools
5 or fewer........	1
6–10	11
11–15	17
16–20	24
More than 20......	47

Of the common schools in the northeastern counties, 53 per cent have an enrollment of 20 or fewer, 29 per cent have 15 or fewer, and 12 per cent have 10 or fewer pupils. Since a comparatively small proportion of the school costs varies directly with the number of pupils, with a given standard of service, the cost per pupil falls rapidly as the number of pupils increases up to the point where expansion in the plant becomes necessary or the decline is more than offset by the increase in transportation cost.

Based upon average daily attendance, the following distribution shows the cost per pupil for the various enrollments in the common schools in the northeastern counties. Koochiching, Lake, and St. Louis counties are again excluded:

Average Daily Attendance	Cost per Average Daily Attendance	Percentage
5 or fewer...................	$183	4
6–10	105	18
11–15	69	27
16–20	58	20
More than 20................	57	31

Costs declined substantially as the average daily attendance increased through the 16–20 group. There was only a slight decrease in the costs of schools with an average daily attendance of 21 or more. Undoubtedly this is due to the fact that as schools become larger, more services are given, such as transportation, libraries, and specialization by grades, and that, on the whole, higher educational standards are maintained. The increased costs of added services and facilities are sufficient to offset the decrease in overhead costs per pupil.

In view of the limited school services offered by small school districts, and the high cost per pupil of even these limited services, extensive changes appear to be necessary in many of the northeastern counties if the benefits of a higher standard of educational service are to be obtained at a cost that is not prohibitive. Judging by the experiences of Lake and Koochiching counties, both of which have made considerable progress in the reorganization of their school systems, the adoption of some form of county school district, either organized or unorganized, appears to be the solution. The results achieved in these counties are presented in some detail to suggest possibilities in this field.

The Lake County plan provides one district for the entire county. In spite of low valuations and other difficulties, such as scattered settlement, reorganization has enabled this county to improve the entire educational system, giving the rural children high school as well as other advantages and at the same time decreasing the total school costs. As a result of this reorganization, savings were effected in every department with the exception of "auxiliary expenses," which were increased about 10 per cent because of the transportation and board and room provided for additional rural pupils attending high school.

During the first year of operation under the county district, costs were reduced slightly over 5 per cent. During the second year costs were reduced 11 per cent. By 1932–33 costs had been reduced 14 per cent, though not all this saving could be attributed to reorganization, because by that time salaries and the prices of supplies were lower.

At the same time the rural children of Lake County were receiving greater educational opportunities than under the old system. In most schools the length of term had been increased by approximately two months. A high school education was made available for all rural pupils in the county. All pupils living two miles or more away were either transported to school or boarded. Other advantages include a school nurse, a traveling library, and higher requirements for the elementary teachers.

The number of schools operating in the rural area was reduced from 37 to 11. The total number of schools now operating in Lake County, including the urban schools, is only 14. Twenty-five busses are used for transportation, seven of which transport children to Two Harbors and eighteen to the rural schools. Three hundred and fifty-one pupils, 22 per cent of the entire school population, are transported in busses which travel 3,699 miles a day, or slightly over 10 miles a day per pupil. In addition to those transported, 46 pupils are given board and room, of whom all but 3 are attending high school. Fifty-nine per cent of the pupils in the rural area are either transported or given board and room aid.

Transportation and board aid account for 14.9 per cent of the total — $24,953.55 — expended for school maintenance. This is less than the cost of maintaining numerous small schools throughout the county.

As a result of the improvement in transportation service and the increase in the length of the school term, the average daily attendance at rural schools increased from 130 days to almost 170. The increase in attendance, combined with other improvements in the educational facilities, resulted in 85 per cent of the rural pupils in Lake County passing the state board examinations in 1933, as compared with 64 per cent of those in the rural schools of the state as a whole. The Lake County school district has made no expenditures for the construction of new buildings. This is perhaps one of the more important reasons why it has been possible to operate so efficiently and at the same time reduce costs.

The procedure followed in Koochiching County has been somewhat different. Instead of combining the school districts into a single county district, all but two school districts have been dissolved and added to the unorganized county district, which is under the supervision of a board consisting of the county superintendent of schools, the county treasurer, and the chairman of the county board.

The enlargement of the unorganized district made it possible to reduce the number of schools from 39 to 21 during the first year of operation (1931–32), and to 20 the second year. In the first year of the unorganized system, maintenance costs were reduced from $223,249, the amount expended in the last year of the district system, to $145,698, a saving of 35 per cent. This saving was increased to 37 per cent the second year. The cost per pupil was reduced from $147 in 1930–31 to $94 in 1931–32 and to $87 in 1932–33. As in Lake County, a high school education is now available to every pupil in the unorganized district in Koochiching County.

While low per-pupil costs may be obtained in rural schools with an enrollment of about thirty pupils, such a system is still far from being complete without high schools. About 20 per cent of all pupils in the public schools in Minnesota are enrolled in high schools. A district supporting a high school with a necessary minimum of approximately one hundred pupils would need over ten times the optimum enrollment of the ordinary common school in the graded and ungraded elementary schools. This in turn would require one high school and from ten to twenty ungraded schools for an approach to maximum efficiency.[9]

A great advantage of the larger district is its flexibility. Poorly located buildings can be closed and the pupils transported to neighboring schools. If the enrollment drops temporarily, a building can be closed for a year or two until the number of children of school age increases and makes reopening advisable. There is also greater flexibility in the use of available facilities. The better buildings can be used to capacity, and supplies and equipment transferred as the need arises. In addition, economies through quantity buying are possible.

As the size of the district increases, the system tends to become more flexible, and the benefits from expert supervision are obtained at lower cost per pupil or per capita. Although the minimum requirement of a complete school system is a population of about 2,500, the maximum efficiency is not reached short of 10,000 or 15,000 population. With few exceptions the logical school unit in the cut-over counties appears to be the county.

A county unit school district is in a better position to make adjustments when redistribution of population takes place. As certain areas are depopulated, the schools can be closed and the equipment and supplies moved to other areas where the population is being concentrated. The county district is flexible enough to operate efficiently during the transition period as well as after the completion of the movement.

[9] For a general discussion of the size of the school district, see William Anderson, *The Reorganization of Local Government in Minnesota,* p. 16 (reprint from *Minnesota Municipalities,* vol. 18, nos. 2 and 3, February and March, 1933), and Blakey, *Taxation in Minnesota,* Chapter 14.

SAVINGS FROM REORGANIZATION

Suggestions for reorganization of local government have been discussed above. Below are some estimates of the savings that would result if these reorganizations are made. Aitkin County has been used as an illustration. Estimates are also given for Lake and Cook counties because of the opportunities for county consolidation they present. Summary tables presenting estimates of possible savings from the reorganization of other counties are given in Tables 86–89 at the close of the chapter.

It will be recalled that the changes suggested for county reorganization included combining the treasurer's office with that of the auditor, consolidating the offices of the clerk of court and probate judge, reducing the number of county commissioners to three, and requiring all fees to be paid to the county and fee offices placed on a salary basis. In the case of the towns, transfer of their functions to the county, except where a real need for the town unit exists, was suggested. The functions transferred to the county would include road maintenance, assessment of property, and supervision of elections. Where towns perform other functions, such as the operation of telephone lines, town halls, fire protection, and cemeteries, these would be assumed by non-governmental agencies. The suggestion with regard to schools is that with some exceptions county units replace local districts.

In earlier chapters, especially Chapter VI, suggestions have been made for the zoning of land and for relocation of existing settlement on lands unsuited to such use. If zoning regulations are adopted and settlers are relocated, it will be possible to effect additional savings, and estimates of these savings are presented. These estimates are based on the assumption that school and road services will be eliminated in conservation areas, work in the county assessor's office reduced, and the maintenance costs on certain county and state aid roads will be decreased. It should be appreciated that the attainment of these savings is dependent upon the adoption of effective zoning and the complete removal of settlement from nonagricultural areas.

AITKIN COUNTY

The financial condition of Aitkin County is revealed by a brief survey of its financial records. On December 31, 1932, the outstanding obligations of all governmental units in the county were equal to 43 per cent of the assessed valuation of all real and personal property. In other words, for each $1,000 of assessed valuation [10] there were outstanding obligations of $430. The indebtedness was $129 per capita and $1.69 per taxable acre. Table 45 shows the outstanding obligations of each governmental unit on December 31 of each year from 1929 to 1932.

TABLE 45. — COUNTY, TOWNSHIP, CITY AND VILLAGE, AND SCHOOL INDEBTEDNESS OF AITKIN COUNTY, 1929–32 *

	December 31, 1929	December 31, 1930	December 31, 1931	December 31, 1932
County bonds	$1,331,362.00	$1,165,962.00	$1,135,162.00	$ 981,300.00
County warrants	223,215.36	173,329.34	230,498.00	277,179.38
Total	$1,554,577.36	$1,339,291.34	$1,365,660.00	$1,258,479.38
Township bonds	$ 133,950.00	$ 152,173.45	$ 146,650.00	$ 143,265.00
Township warrants	68,632.05	58,545.58	53,595.59	46,679.98
Total	$ 202,582.05	$ 210,719.03	$ 200,245.59	$ 189,944.98
City and village bonds	$ 105,550.00	$ 102,500.00	$ 80,000.00	$ 73,800.00
City and village warrants	23,654.03	13,060.14	10,681.04	9,104.59
Total	$ 129,204.03	$ 115,560.14	$ 90,681.04	$ 82,904.59
School bonds	$ 390,830.00	$ 369,870.00	$ 363,360.00	$ 381,057.54
School warrants	24,683.69	43,799.92	44,188.63	34,470.72
Total	$ 415,513.69	$ 413,669.92	$ 407,548.63	$ 415,528.26
Total bonds	$1,961,692.00	$1,790,505.45	$1,724,172.00	$1,579,422.54
Total warrants	340,185.13	288,734.98	338,963.26	367,434.67
Grand total	$2,301,877.13	$2,079,240.43	$2,063,135.26	$1,946,857.21

* County obligations taken from public examiners' reports. They include trunk highway reimbursement bonds. Township, city and village, and school data taken from *Interest Bearing Debts of the State of Minnesota*, compiled by the Minnesota Tax Commission.

Over this four-year period the total obligations of governmental units in the county were reduced 15 per cent. However, if the payment of trunk highway reimbursement bonds by the state [11] is excluded, the reduction was only 6 per cent. The obligations of the county constitute the major portion of the indebtedness, amounting in 1932 to 65 per cent of the total. The county has been responsible for 83 per cent of the decrease in the total debt of governmental units during the period.

[10] Under the classified assessment law, different classes of property are assessed for tax purposes at various percentages of their true and full value. Thus unplatted real estate is assessed at 33⅓ per cent of its true and full value.

[11] These payments were to reimburse the county for bonds issued for state trunk highway construction. Session Laws, 1921, chapter 522.

The total outstanding obligations of the county on December 31, 1932, amounted to $1,258,479.38, of which $277,179.38 consisted of warrants and $981,300.00 of bonds. These totals include the bonds and warrants outstanding against all county funds. Where the county acts as an agency for towns, cities and villages, and schools, the funds are classified as trust and custodial. The ditch fund is handled as a trust and custodial fund. Of the total warrants listed as county obligations in 1932 only $873.02 were against trust and custodial funds. Of the bonds $632,200.00 were the direct obligation of the county; $349,100.00 were the direct obligation of the ditch fund and an indirect obligation of the county.

Since December 31, 1929, the total obligations against all county funds have decreased $296,097.98, or 19 per cent. The bonds outstanding have been reduced $350,062.00; the warrants have increased $53,964.02. Ditch bonds were reduced $190,462.00 as compared with a reduction of $159,600.00 in bonds that are a direct obligation of the county. The reduction in total county bonded indebtedness is less significant when it is realized that it includes payment by the state of $214,169.45 of trunk highway reimbursement bonds. The reduction in obligations as a result of payments made by the county out of its usual receipts, against both county and trust and custodial funds, is $135,891.55. The major part of the reduction was made possible by state payments of principal and interest on ditch bonds of $132,212.90. The payment by the state of trunk highway bonds reduced county obligations. Otherwise the direct obligations of the county would have increased $54,569.45, largely because of the direct assumption by the county of ditch obligations.

While the total warrants outstanding against all funds increased by $53,964.02, the outstanding warrants against trust and custodial funds were reduced $53,352.98; the increase in warrants against the county funds amounted to $107,327.00. Thus, with a reduction of $159,600.00 in the bonds that are a direct obligation of the county and an increase of $107,327.00 in warrants against the county funds, the outstanding obligations of both forms were reduced only $52,273.00. If allowance is made for the state payment of trunk highway bonds, the result is an increase in county obligations of $161,896.45 over the four-year period.

The gross direct indebtedness of Aitkin County on December 31, 1932, was $908,506.36, including $276,306.36 in warrants and $632,200.00 in bonds. Allowing for the cash on hand of $52,942.54,

TABLE 46. — NET DEBT OF AITKIN COUNTY, 1929–32

	1929	1930	1931	1932
Net debt at beginning of year	$687,395.08	$829,215.93	$738,646.38	$801,819.39
Net debt at end of year..	829,215.93	738,646.38	801,819.39	855,563.82
Increase or decrease	+$141,820.85	−$ 90,569.55	+$ 63,173.01	+$ 53,744.43

the net debt of the county on that date was $855,563.82. The net debt in each year from 1929 to 1932 is shown in Table 46. The changes in net debt arise directly out of the relationship between net revenue receipts and net governmental cost payments [12] as well as the transfers to and from county funds. (See Table 47.)

TABLE 47. — NET REVENUE RECEIPTS, GOVERNMENT COST PAYMENTS, AND TRANSFERS IN AITKIN COUNTY, 1929–32

Item	1929	1930	1931	1932
Net revenue receipts	$270,410.43	$486,323.05	$295,864.38	$211,738.19
Net government cost payments	281,010.19	298,322.39	288,974.48	255,251.34
Difference	−10,599.76	+188,000.66	+6,889.90	−43,513.15
Betterments	139,525.68	....	....	....
Net transfers to county	8,304.59	....	....	....
Net transfers from county.	....	97,431.11	70,062.91	10,231.28
Net excess or deficit	−141,820.85	+90,569.55	−63,173.01	−53,744.43

The greatest increase in net debt occurred in 1929. A small part of this increase was due to the fact that costs exceeded revenue by $10,599.76, but chiefly it was due to the building of a new courthouse. A transfer of $8,304.59 to the county from trust and custodial funds offset to some extent the excess of costs over revenue. In 1930 there was a very considerable reduction in debt. Revenue exceeded costs by $188,000.66 as a result of the fact that the state supplied funds for the retirement of trunk highway bonds. Only about half of this excess was used to reduce net debt because of the transfer from county funds to the ditch fund. In 1931, while net revenue exceeded costs by $6,889.90, a transfer of $70,062.91 to the ditch fund caused an increase in net debt of $63,173.01. In 1932 costs exceeded revenue by $43,513.15. This, with a transfer to the ditch fund of $10,231.28, brought about an increase in net debt of $53,744.43.

[12] The term "governmental cost payments" refers to the payments for operating expenses including interest but excluding payments on principal of bonded indebtedness.

As has been pointed out, the change in net debt is dependent upon the relationship of revenue to costs as well as upon the transfers to and from county funds. The heavy transfers in Aitkin County are somewhat exceptional. They arise out of the responsibility of the county for meeting the ditch obligations, a fund which is very far from being on a self-sustaining basis.

It is obvious that net debt can be reduced over a period of years only by an excess of revenues over costs, this in turn being dependent either on an increase in revenue or a decrease in costs. It is hardly to be anticipated that the county will have any substantial increase in revenues, particularly when it is realized that the county levy is already 131.84 mills and that assessed valuation is decreasing and delinquency is increasing. Table 48 shows the revenue receipts of Aitkin County in each of the four years.

TABLE 48. — REVENUE RECEIPTS OF AITKIN COUNTY, 1929–32

Source	1929	1930	1931	1932
Property tax.............	$190,671.80	$165,167.69	$189,302.57	$101,670.59
Subventions and grants...	56,022.08	307,467.22	88,068.92	94,137.81
Miscellaneous receipts and earnings..............	24,004.06	15,802.82	18,572.15	16,324.17
Total revenue receipts..	$270,697.94	$488,437.73	$295,943.64	$212,132.57
Receipts refunded	287.51	2,114.68	79.26	394.38
Net revenue receipts..	$270,410.43	$486,323.05	$295,864.38	$211,738.19

By 1932 the revenue from the property tax was only 53 per cent of that in 1929, and subventions and grants from the state were almost as important a source of revenue as were property taxes. Whereas in 1929 the property tax contributed 70 per cent of the revenue, by 1932 it contributed only 48 per cent. On the other hand, subventions and grants constituted only 21 per cent of the revenue receipts in 1929 as compared with 44 per cent in 1932. As has been explained, the pronounced increase in subventions and grants in 1930 was due to the payment of trunk highway bonds by the state. The regular aid from the state for that year was $93,297.77. Miscellaneous receipts and earnings of the general departments are of comparatively minor importance, although they have maintained their volume better than has the property tax.

It is possible that receipts could be enlarged by an increase in subventions and grants, but in view of the size that this item has already attained, large increases are unlikely. On the whole it would appear that the possibilities of increasing revenues with the prevailing system of taxation are very limited. It is more likely that expenditures will be further reduced. Governmental cost payments have declined less rapidly than revenues. Table 49 shows the classification of governmental cost payments for the period. The

TABLE 49. — GOVERNMENTAL COST PAYMENTS OF AITKIN COUNTY, 1929–32

Item of Expenditure	1929	1930	1931	1932
County revenue fund.....	$ 74,817.45	$ 73,556.95	$ 68,134.46	$ 59,953.80
Road and bridge fund....	138,164.81	155,820.21	142,913.03	128,735.84
Poor relief..............	19,575.29	16,500.38	17,975.36	15,789.93
Interest	44,361.55	48,397.77	54,728.39	45,121.86
Sanatorium	4,936.55	5,195.38	6,358.79	6,157.62
Total	$281,855.65	$299,470.69	$290,110.03	$255,759.05
Payments refunded	845.46	1,148.30	1,135.55	507.71
Net cost payments ...	$281,010.19	$298,322.39	$288,974.48	$255,251.34

largest item of expenditure is that for the road and bridge fund, which decreased comparatively little over the four-year period. The expenditures from the county revenue fund, which are second in importance, declined 20 per cent. Interest on bonds and warrants remained practically constant over the period. Expenditures for the poor declined somewhat. Further decline in the demands upon this fund may be expected as a result of state and federal relief aid. Almost no decreases were made in any of the funds until 1932, when expenditures for all purposes were reduced.

Total receipts include funds from the sale of bonds as well as revenue. Table 50 shows the total county receipts from all sources.

TABLE 50. — TOTAL COUNTY RECEIPTS OF AITKIN COUNTY, 1929–32

Source	1929	1930	1931	1932
Gross revenue receipts....	$271,543.40	$489,586.03	$297,079.19	$212,640.28
Sale of bonds	....	147,000.00	100,000.00	....
Total	$271,543.40	$636,586.03	$397,079.19	$212,640.28

In only two of the four years, 1930 and 1931, were funds received from the sale of bonds, such funds being used largely for the retirement of other bonds that were due. Similarly, total payments include, in addition to governmental cost payments, payments on bond principal and betterments. Table 51 shows the total expenditures of county funds for the period. In addition to the receipts and

TABLE 51. — TOTAL EXPENDITURES FROM COUNTY FUNDS OF
AITKIN COUNTY, 1929–32

Item of Expenditure	1929	1930	1931	1932
Government cost payments	$281,855.65	$299,470.69	$290,110.03	$255,759.05
Betterments	139,525.68	....	....	....
Bond principal	33,200.00	285,000.00	67,400.00	54,200.00
Refunds................	287.51	2,114.68	79.26	394.38
Total	$454,868.84	$586,585.37	$357,589.29	$310,353.43

expenditures which the county handles in its own behalf, it receives
revenues for other agencies. These trust and custodial receipts are
then apportioned to the fund or agency for which they have been
collected. The total receipts for both county and trust and custodial funds are given in Table 52. The two most important sources

TABLE 52. — TOTAL RECEIPTS OF AITKIN COUNTY FROM ALL SOURCES, 1930–32

Source	1929	1930	1931	1932
Property tax.............	$552,351.88	$ 478,498.37	$466,366.30	$299,104.71
Subventions and grants ...	162,058.98	438,483.78	231,332.45	329,705.06
Taxes and fines..........	27,965.90	20,413.23	22,283.59	20,844.84
Other trust collections	58,346.16	26,536.85	16,939.92	19,184.14
Refunded payments	845.46	1,148.30	1,135.55	507.71
Sale of bonds............	....	147,000.00	100,000.00	....
Total	$801,568.38	$1,112,080.53	$838,057.81	$669,346.46

of receipts are again subventions and grants and the property tax.
Whereas the property tax accounted for 69 per cent of the total receipts in 1929, in 1932 it accounted for only 45 per cent. Subventions and grants have increased both proportionately and absolutely. By 1932 they were larger than the property tax, accounting
for 49 per cent of the total receipts.

The total warrants issued from all funds and their distribution
between county and trust and custodial funds are given in Table
53. The purposes for which the county funds were expended have
already been discussed. The warrants issued on the trust and custodial funds in turn become the receipts for the particular agency involved. The purposes for which school and town expenditures were
made are discussed later in this section. Reductions in expenditures
are difficult because of the indebtedness and the heavy fixed charges
accompanying it.

The reductions accomplished in Aitkin County since 1929 were
made by reducing the personnel, by lowering the salary scales of

TABLE 53. — TOTAL WARRANTS ISSUED FROM ALL FUNDS IN AITKIN COUNTY, 1929–32

	1929	1930	1931	1932
County funds............$	454,868.84	$ 586,585.37	$357,589.29	$310,353.43
Trust and custodial funds.	602,643.68	521,212.31	496,523.56	484,272.24
Total.................$	1,057,512.52	$1,107,797.68	$854,112.85	$794,625.67

the appointive offices, and by curtailment and elimination of services. Over 80 per cent of the reduction in expenditures from the
county revenue fund arose out of the reduction in two funds, that
for the development and conservation of natural resources and that
for charities and corrections. Road services were curtailed through
the reduction of road maintenance and construction. Further reductions in road costs could probably be accomplished if the entire responsibility for road expenditures were turned over to the
highway engineer. In the past, responsibility has been divided between the county commissioners and the engineer according to the
decision of the commissioners.

All of the recommendations for the reorganization of county
government that were proposed earlier in this chapter appear to be
applicable to Aitkin County. If the treasurer's office were combined
with the auditor's, the offices of probate judge and clerk of court
merged, the number of county commissioners reduced to three, and
all fees paid to the county, the estimated yearly reduction in costs
would be over $10,000. The sources of these savings are shown in
detail in Table 54. In 1932 the treasurer's salary was $2,000.00 a
year, the deputy treasurer was paid $1,134.00, and clerk hire
$577.50, a total of $3,711.50.

At present there is considerable duplication in the work of the
treasurer's and auditor's offices. Warrants issued by the auditor
could be registered by him at the time of issue instead of by the
treasurer. The handling of statements and receipts for school land,
state swamp land, delinquent taxes, mortgage registry, private re-
demptions, teachers insurance and retirement, and miscellaneous
collections could be consolidated in one office. The monthly reports
supplied by each to the public examiner could likewise be combined. With certain changes in bookkeeping methods these duties
could be handled by the auditor's office. That part of the treasurer's work connected with the issuance of checks, the redemption of
warrants, the collection of taxes and other receipts, and the apportionment of these funds among the various units for which the

TABLE 54. — ESTIMATED SAVINGS OVER 1932 COSTS TO BE DERIVED FROM A
REORGANIZATION OF COUNTY OFFICES IN AITKIN COUNTY
(rounded to the nearest $100)

1. Elimination of county treasurer's office
   Present cost of county treasurer's office.................. $3,700.00
   Less cost of cashier................................... 1,200.00 $ 2,500.00

2. Merger of offices of judge of probate and clerk of court
   Present cost of clerk of court......................... 1,200.00
   Present cost of probate judge......................... 2,400.00

                                                          3,600.00
   One officer at $2,000.00
   Clerk hire   400.00............................. 2,400.00

                                                          1,200.00   1,200.00

3. Reduction in number of county commissioners to 3.......   1,600.00

4. Return of all fees to county
   Auditor.. 800.00
   Treasurer.. 100.00
   Sheriff.. 500.00
   Register of deeds.................................... 2,500.00
   Registrar... 400.00
   Clerk of court...................................... 2,000.00
   Probate judge....................................... 300.00
   Surveyor.. 300.00

                                                          6,900.00
   Less register of deeds.............................. 2,000.00   4,900.00

         Total savings $10,200.00

county acts as a trust and custodial agent could be taken care of by a cashier or clerk under the supervision of the auditor. Public funds should be adequately protected by proper bonds and state audits.

In 1932 the judge of probate received a salary of $1,700.00 and clerk hire cost $720.00, a total of $2,420.00. The clerk of court received a salary of $800.00 and $354.50 for clerk hire, bringing the total to $1,154.50. In addition to his salary the clerk of court received $1,976.99 in fees, bringing his total compensation to $2,776.99. The judge of probate received an additional $296.00 in fees.

In 1932 the probate judge performed 6 marriages, issued 17 waivers of notice of marriage, had 15 mother's pension cases under his supervision, and had approximately 100 hearings of juvenile cases not of record. In addition he had 75 estate, 24 insanity, 35 guardianship, 3 feeble-minded, 2 dependency, and 7 delinquency cases that were active.

The clerk of court issued 85 marriage licenses, entered 5,405 delinquent tax judgments, 279 civil actions, and 13 criminal actions in his records. Forty days of court were held in Aitkin County, and 5 naturalizations were completed. Neither of these offices requires the full time of the officials in charge.

In reducing the number of county commissioners to three the salaries and expenses of two would be saved. If responsibility for highway maintenance were turned over to the highway engineer, the work of the commissioners as well as their expenses would probably be reduced.

The suggestion that all fees be paid to the county involves placing the register of deeds on a salary basis and adding the work of the surveyor to that of the county engineer. Since a large part of the work of the register of deeds is of a non-fee type, and the amount of non-fee work is continually growing, this appears to be a logical move. The duties of the registrar would be added to those of the register of deeds. Many counties the size of Aitkin have no registrar. For the offices that are on a salary and fee basis a regular salary scale commensurate with the work of the office would be a more equitable basis of compensation.

Offices that would be affected by the payment of fees which have not otherwise been considered in the reorganization program include those of the auditor and the sheriff. In 1932 the auditor received a salary of $2,000.00 and the sheriff $2,250.00.

See Table 86, page 317, for estimates of savings through reorganization of counties other than Aitkin, Cook, and Lake.

THE TOWNS

On December 31, 1932, the total town indebtedness in Aitkin County was $189,944.98, a decrease of $12,637.07 from that of 1929. The decrease of $21,952.07 in warrants was partly offset by an increase of $9,315.00 in bonds, a large part of the increase in bonds in 1930 having been used to liquidate warrants. Since 1930 both bonds and warrants have decreased each year.

Since the town boards are not required to report to a superior authority and the methods of keeping accounts vary greatly between towns, it is very difficult to obtain comparable records of town expenditures. Records were obtained from 28 of the 48 organized towns in Aitkin County. The average receipts for those reporting and the classification of expenditures for a three-year period are shown in Table 55.

TABLE 55. — AVERAGE RECEIPTS AND EXPENDITURES OF 28 TOWNS IN
AITKIN COUNTY, 1930–32

YEAR	RECEIPTS	EXPENDITURES			
		Total	Road and Bridge	General Revenue	Other
1930	$1,639.34	$1,435.47	$889.31	$336.46	$209.70
1931	1,204.66	1,002.93	644.67	219.94	138.32
1932	779.77	856.10	490.72	275.14	90.24

Practically all the town receipts are from the property tax. The taxes levied and payable in 1932 were 9 per cent less than in 1930, but receipts declined much more than that — over 52 per cent, largely because of an increase of 33 per cent in tax delinquency. Seventy-two per cent of the state, county, school, and town taxes levied in the towns of Aitkin County and payable in 1932 were delinquent on the first Monday of January, 1933. Six towns had a delinquency greater than 90 per cent, 17 had a delinquency of more than 80 per cent, and 28 of more than 70 per cent. In only one town was the delinquency less than 30 per cent, and in only 4 was it less than 50 per cent.

In both 1930 and 1931 receipts exceeded expenditures. The excess was used either to build up balances or to pay off warrants. In 1932 receipts amounted to only 91 per cent of expenditures; in some towns the excess of expenditures reduced existing balances and in others it resulted in an increase in the amount of outstanding warrants.

The largest item of town expense is the maintenance and repair of roads. Over the four-year period road costs accounted for 62 per cent of the total expenditures, those from the general revenue fund 25 per cent, and other expenditures 13 per cent. In 1932 the proportions expended for these three items were 57, 32, and 11 per cent, respectively.

Expenditures from the general revenue fund consist largely of election costs, cost of assessment, payments to the town board members for attending meetings, and fees paid to the treasurer and the clerk. Other expenditures include payments for fire protection, telephones, and cemeteries, although a comparatively small number of towns render these services. Interest payments on bonds are levied, collected, and paid by the county auditor instead of being apportioned back to the town treasurer for payment.

Information was obtained from the offices of the county auditors on apportionments to all the towns. This information, with the

ratio of apportionments to expenditures for the towns that reported the latter, furnished the basis for estimates of total expenditures by the towns and their distribution for various purposes. The
total estimated expenditure was $39,550, of which $22,700 was for
roads and bridges, $12,700 from the revenue fund, and $4,150 for
other expenses. There was a marked tendency to expend for items
in the revenue fund and other purposes the funds that were levied,
collected, and apportioned for road and bridge purposes. Thus apportionments for revenue fund purposes were only 46 per cent of
expenditures and those for "other purposes" only 53 per cent of expenditures for such purposes, whereas road and bridge apportionments amounted to 123 per cent of actual expenditures on roads
and bridges.

In accordance with recommendations suggested earlier in this
chapter, the costs of county performance of necessary town functions are estimated in Table 56. The functions that the county
would take over would be the maintenance of roads, supervision of
elections, and the assessment of property. An additional estimate
is made of the cost to the county of performing these functions, assuming that the county were zoned and population assisted in
moving from the conservation areas as suggested in Chapters VI
and X.

As a basis for estimating the cost of county maintenance of
town roads, they were classified into three groups according to the
number of families utilizing the road in question. Class 1 included

TABLE 56. — ESTIMATED COST OF COUNTY PERFORMANCE OF TOWN FUNCTIONS,
AITKIN COUNTY

FUNCTION	PRESENT SETTLEMENT		RESTRICTED SETTLEMENT	
	Miles of Road	Cost	Miles of Road	Cost
1. Maintenance of town roads				
Light traffic roads............	489	$ 9,700	320	$ 6,400
Medium traffic roads.........	244	7,320	184	5,580
Heavy traffic roads..........	13	520	13	520
Total cost.................		$17,540		$12,500
2. County supervision of elections		3,060		1,800
3. County assessor				
Salary......................		2,000		2,000
Expenses and assistants.......		1,900		1,200
Total cost.................		$24,500		$17,500
Present cost..............		39,500		
Estimated savings..........		$15,000		$22,000

those roads upon which more than fifteen families lived and those connecting other important traffic routes; class 2 included roads upon which from six to fifteen families lived, and class 3, roads upon which five or fewer families lived. It was estimated that class 1 roads would be maintained at substantially the county aid or state aid standard; class 2 at three-fourths, and class 3 at half of such a standard. Some town roads would require considerable rebuilding in order to put them in shape for maintenance at the standard suggested. Capital outlays of this nature were not included as a part of the estimated maintenance cost.

Were the county to take over the town roads on this basis, it is estimated that it would be necessary to maintain 489 miles of light traffic roads, 244 miles of medium traffic roads, and only 13 miles of heavy traffic roads in addition to the present state aid and county aid roads. The estimated cost of maintaining this added road mileage approximates $17,540. This is somewhat less than the present cost of town road maintenance, estimated at $22,700 for 1932.

The organization for conducting elections would be comparatively simple. Polling places could be established about the county with reference to population, area covered, and accessibility. It is estimated that the cost of county supervision of elections would not exceed $3,060, which would provide fifty-one polling places at an average annual cost of $60 each. Frequently one voting place would be adequate for at least two towns. In areas that are more densely settled, there could be two voting places in each town. Since there would be a reduction in the number of elective offices, and elections would be necessary only every other year, this appears to be an adequate allowance for the costs of election supervision.

The initial cost of installing the county assessor's office would probably run higher than the $3,900 estimated as the maintenance cost of this office. After a complete description of all properties has been made, the yearly cost of assessing real property would involve little expense. Cities and villages are not included in the proposed work of the county assessor. Unquestionably under a general reorganization of local government cities and villages would be placed under the county assessor; but these units of local government are not within the scope of this study.

The estimated cost of maintaining roads, supervising elections, and making property assessments by the county totals $24,500. If these functions were transferred to the county, a substantial portion of the revenue costs as well as a part of the road costs of towns would be saved. It is estimated that the annual savings over present expenditures for town government would amount to approximately $15,000.

If the area were zoned as shown above in Figure 39, page 173, and the population in the conservation zones were relocated, further economies in the performance of town functions could be realized. The mileage of light traffic roads could be reduced to 320, and medium traffic roads to 184. The estimated cost of county maintenance of town roads would be reduced to $12,500. The cost of election supervision would also be reduced, since only thirty polling places would be necessary, and the cost of assessing would be reduced because of the reduction in area. With zoning and the relocation of population the cost of performing the major town functions need not exceed $17,500, a saving of $22,000 over 1932 costs. At the same time there should be an improvement in the services rendered; town roads could be maintained at a higher standard, and the quality of assessment work could be improved considerably.

THE SCHOOLS *

The school indebtedness of Aitkin County on December 31, 1932, totaled $415,528.26, of which $381,057.54 was in bonds and $34,470.72 in warrants. Over the four-year period there was little change in the total indebtedness, a reduction in bonded indebtedness being offset by an increase in warrants. A reduction in bonds in 1930 was accompanied by an increase in warrants, while an increase in bonds in 1932 was used to reduce warrants. The net receipts of the Aitkin County schools during a five-year period are shown in Table 57.

State aid provided 43 per cent of the total receipts in 1928–29 and 56 per cent in 1932–33; 53 per cent of the receipts were from local taxes in 1928–29 as compared with 31 per cent in 1932–33. Other receipts rose from 5 per cent in 1928–29 to 13 per cent in 1932–33. Comparing absolute receipts at the beginning of the period with 1932–33, it is found that state aid remained about the

* T. C. Engum has given valuable assistance in the preparation of the suggested reorganization of schools outlined in this section, and his unpublished "Study of the School Organization of Aitkin County" (April, 1932) has supplied valuable data and suggestions as to methods of procedure. As in the case of other reorganizations outlined in this report, the purpose is merely to suggest possible ways of effecting savings.

TABLE 57. — RECEIPTS OF AITKIN COUNTY SCHOOLS FROM VARIOUS SOURCES

Source	1928–29	1929–30	1930–31	1931–32	1932–33
Local taxes	$156,921.45	$143,813.61	$ 86,457.55	$104,878.48	$ 70,550.50
Rural	97,180.61	95,756.68	61,267.56	73,423.34	47,736.11
Graded and high	59,740.84	48,056.93	25,189.99	31,455.14	22,814.39
State aid	127,177.75	127,048.27	140,023.11	147,197.39	128,810.28
Rural	65,096.12	60,751.59	65,521.96	75,456.64	64,469.67
Graded and high	62,081.63	66,296.68	74,501.15	71,740.75	64,340.61
Other sources	13,978.04	32,057.70	25,073.20	40,283.81	29,113.81
Rural	10,118.60	15,171.12	17,848.44	24,888.10	6,549.23
Graded and high	3,859.44	16,886.58	7,224.76	15,395.71	22,564.58
Grand total	$298,077.24	$302,919.58	$251,553.86	$292,359.68	$228,474.59

same, receipts from local taxes fell more than 55 per cent, and receipts from other sources, although doubled, were still minor.

The rural schools have been less dependent upon state aid than the graded and high schools. Over the period 42 per cent of the receipts of the rural schools and 57 per cent of the receipts of graded and high schools came from state aid. Forty-eight per cent of the rural school and 32 per cent of the graded and high school receipts were from local taxes. In 1932–33, however, because of the sharp decline in local tax collections, 54 per cent of the rural receipts were from state aid, whereas 59 per cent of the graded and high school receipts were from this source. The total receipts of the rural schools dropped 31 per cent over the period, those of the graded and high schools 13 per cent.

The general decline in receipts, caused particularly by high property tax delinquency, has in turn forced a reduction in school expenditures. The net operating costs of Aitkin County schools for the same five-year period are shown in Table 58.

After the school year 1929–30 there was a marked decline in the net operating costs, principally in the rural schools. From the beginning of the period the operating costs (excluding debt charges)

TABLE 58. — NET OPERATING COSTS OF AITKIN COUNTY SCHOOLS

Item	1928–29	1929–30	1930–31	1931–32	1932–33
Rural					
Maintenance cost	$152,351.56	$150,490.19	$143,206.52	$113,218.31	$ 90,985.69
Transportation	26,085.85	24,730.70	25,724.84	21,160.65	20,137.26
Graded and secondary					
Maintenance cost	96,670.82	101,721.00	90,117.89	85,743.16	86,102.64
Transportation	15,265.75	14,905.00	15,075.82	16,002.12	11,764.22
Total operating cost	$290,373.98	$291,846.89	$274,125.07	$236,124.24	$208,989.81

of the ungraded schools decreased 40 per cent, those of the graded schools 12 per cent. In both cases costs declined somewhat more than revenues. The distribution of operating expenditures during the five-year period is shown in Table 59.

TABLE 59. — PERCENTAGE DISTRIBUTION OF SCHOOL OPERATING
EXPENDITURES, 1928–29 TO 1932–33

Item of Expenditure	Graded and Secondary	Rural
General expenditures......................	4.0	4.1
Teachers' salaries.........................	58.5	56.5
Other expenses of instruction *............	6.7	5.5
Operation	10.3	9.2
Maintenance............................	2.3	5.1
Transportation..........................	13.7	15.3
Other expenditures	4.5	4.3
Total	100.0	100.0

* Includes such items as textbooks, supplies, and library expenses.

Teachers' salaries are by far the largest item of expense, accounting for 58 per cent of the costs in the graded and high schools and 56 per cent in the ungraded schools. The second most important item of expense is that of transportation, which accounts for 15 per cent of the ungraded school costs and 14 per cent of the graded and high school costs. Reduction in teachers' salaries accounted for 53 per cent of the $61,365.87 decrease in maintenance costs, the amount paid out for this purpose being reduced 33 per cent. Other maintenance costs were reduced 52 per cent and transportation 23 per cent. These reductions were made with little or no change in the school organization.

There were 108 school districts in Aitkin County in 1932, in which were located 112 schools, employing 177 teachers. If Aitkin County schools were reorganized along the lines suggested earlier, all the 108 districts would be brought under unified control, and it would be necessary to maintain only about 60 schools. The number of teachers could be reduced to 129, the average number of pupils per teacher being increased from 25 to 33.

The estimated costs of a county unit school system, both with and without settlement relocation, are given in Table 60, with estimated savings over present costs. Through reorganization all the schools with low enrollments could be closed and the pupils transported to nearby schools where adequate facilities are available. The maintenance costs of the graded schools and high schools

TABLE 60. — ESTIMATED COSTS AND SAVINGS UNDER SUGGESTED REORGANIZATION OF
AITKIN COUNTY SCHOOLS

	Cost 1932–33	Estimated Cost under Reorganization	Estimated Cost under Reorganization and Settler Relocation
Rural maintenance cost	$ 91,000.00	$ 48,900.00	$ 46,400.00
Graded and secondary school mainte-nance	86,100.00	106,600.00	106,600.00
Transportation......................	31,900.00	45,000.00	34,000.00
Total maintenance and transportation	$209,000.00	$200,500.00	$187,000.00
Saving	....	8,500.00	22,000.00
State aid	128,800.00	165,500.00	157,000.00
Net cost to local taxpayers...........	80,200.00	35,000.00	30,000.00
Savings to local taxpayers............	....	45,200.00	50,300.00
School districts......................	108	1	1
Number of schools...................	112	60	57
Number of teachers..................	177	129	126

would increase as a result of the transfer of rural pupils to the
graded schools and the anticipated increase in the number of pupils
attending high school, which would make twelve additional teachers necessary.

Transportation costs would also increase because more pupils
would be transported and the average distance would increase. The
length of bus routes would be increased from 458 to 700 miles. But
the reduction in rural school costs would more than offset the increases in transportation. The estimated net saving arising out of
reorganization alone is about $8,500.

Further economies could be achieved if zoning resulted in the
relocation of present settlers. Three additional schools could be
closed and three fewer teachers would be needed. The largest saving
through relocation would be in transportation costs. Since settlement would be more concentrated, it would be possible to reduce
the length of bus routes by 175 miles. It is estimated that if isolated settlement were fully concentrated and the school system reorganized, the annual savings in school costs would be slightly
over $22,000.

Under reorganization without settler relocation, the savings to
the taxpayers of the county would be considerably in excess of the
total savings to be realized, because there would be an increase in
state grants in the form of transportation and supplemental aid.
There would be an increase in the number of pupils eligible for isolated pupil aid, and supplemental aid would be increased because
more pupils would be associated with a given assessed valuation.

If the county were zoned and settlers were relocated, the amount of state aid would be reduced by $8,500, because there would be fewer isolated pupils and a reduction in transportation aid. There would also be a slight reduction in supplemental aid.

Under reorganization alone the savings in costs and the increase in state aid would combine to reduce the cost to the taxpayers of the county from $80,179.53 to approximately $35,000, a saving of over $45,000. If the county were zoned and settlers were relocated, the cost to the local taxpayers of operating the schools would approximate $30,000, a saving of over $50,000. This reduction in costs could be used either to reduce levies for maintenance costs or to retire bonds and warrants. In addition to a reduction in expenditures, reorganization will provide educational advantages resulting from better school organization.

The total estimated savings to be realized from all types of reorganization in Aitkin County would approximate $34,000. If in addition zoning were adopted and settlement fully relocated, the savings would amount to about $54,000. The sources of these savings are given in Table 61.

TABLE 61. — ESTIMATED SAVINGS POSSIBLE IN AITKIN COUNTY
THROUGH REORGANIZATION

	Reorganization	Reorganization and Relocation
County offices.......	$10,200	$10,200
Towns	15,000	22,000
Schools	8,500	22,000
Total	$33,700	$54,200

COOK AND LAKE COUNTIES [13]

The obligations of all local units of government in Cook and Lake counties as of December 31, 1932, are shown in Table 62. With the exception of cities and villages, all units decreased their indebtedness over the period 1929–32. Four thousand dollars of the $47,000 decrease in bonds in Cook County was principal payment by the state on trunk highway reimbursement bonds. In Lake County $250,000 of the total decrease of $324,500 was from this source. Allowing for these payments and deducting bonds assumed by the state, the percentage decline in Cook County's bonded in-

[13] A review of the financial condition and governmental organization of Cook and Lake counties similar to that given for Aitkin County is presented in order that the possibilities of county consolidation may be considered. The data for the other eleven counties appear in Tables 86–89.

TABLE 62. — COUNTY, TOWNSHIP, CITY AND VILLAGE, AND SCHOOL INDEBTEDNESS IN
COOK AND LAKE COUNTIES, DECEMBER 31, 1932

CLASS OF OBLIGATIONS	COOK COUNTY		LAKE COUNTY	
	Amount	Percentage Increase or Decrease, 1929–32	Amount	Percentage Increase or Decrease, 1929–32
County bonds...........	$205,000.00	−18.64	$207,613.16	− 60.98
County warrants........	148,476.36	+ 6.22	33,534.33	− 57.90
Total	$353,476.36	− 9.77	$241,147.49	− 60.58
Town bonds	$ 41,000.00	−19.61	$ 10,658.38	− 16.83
Town warrants..........	2,085.56	−49.94	26,003.21	− 17.94
Total	$ 43,058.56	−21.90	$ 36,661.59	− 17.62
City and village bonds...	$ 20,500.00	− 2.38	$ 30,926.76	− 28.80
City and village warrants	4,223.68	+97.38	88,793.60	+123.92
Total	$ 24,723.68	+ 6.84	$119,720.36	+ 44.08
School bonds............	$ 81,200.00	−31.11	$ 12,591.01	− 13.07
School warrants	....	....	....	−100.00
Total	$ 81,200.00	−33.11	$ 12,591.01	− 17.34
Total bonds.............	$347,700.00	−21.93	$261,789.31	− 56.58
Total warrants	154,785.60	+ 5.95	148,331.14	− 2.24
Grand total........	$502,485.60	−15.04	$410,120.45	− 45.65

debtedness becomes 29 per cent, in Lake 27 per cent. Including
warrants, the total county reduction in Cook was only 11 per cent,
as compared with a reduction in Lake County of 26 per cent. The
total reduction of all units in Cook County was 17 per cent, as
compared with 23 per cent in Lake County. The distribution of obligations between county and trust and custodial funds is given in
Table 63. Allowing for cash on hand of $14,372.85 in Cook and

TABLE 63. — DISTRIBUTION OF VARIOUS CLASSES OF OBLIGATIONS AGAINST COUNTY
FUNDS OF COOK AND LAKE COUNTIES, DECEMBER 31, 1932

Class of Obligations	Lake County	Cook County
County bonds	$207,613.16	$205,000.00
County warrants	33,534.33	147,581.71
Total	$241,147.49	$352,581.71
Trust and custodial warrants	....	894.65
Grand total	$241,147.49	$353,476.36

TABLE 64. — NET DEBT OF COOK AND LAKE COUNTIES, 1929–32

	1929	1930	1931	1932
COOK COUNTY				
Net debt at beginning of year	$328,506.67	$351,182.59	$355,071.10	$338,772.20
Net debt at end of year	351,182.59	355,071.10	338,772.20	338,208.86
Increase or decrease	+$ 22,675.92	+$ 3,888.51	—$ 16,298.90	—$ 563.34
LAKE COUNTY				
Net debt at beginning of year	$623,286.45	$583,308.54	$542,142.81	$484,165.84
Net debt at end of year	583,308.54	542,142.81	484,165.84	231,012.71
Increase or decrease	—$ 39,977.91	—$ 41,165.73	—$ 57,976.97	—$253,153.13

$10,134.78 in Lake County, the net debts of these counties on December 31, 1932, were $338,208.86, and $231,012.71, respectively.

The changes in net debt that have taken place over the period are shown in Table 64. The large decrease in Lake County in 1932 was due almost entirely to the principal payment made by the state in highway bonds.

The sources of the change in net debt are shown in Table 65. Receipts exceeded expenditures in Lake County each year. In both 1929 and 1930 expenditures exceeded receipts in Cook, while in 1931 and 1932 there was an excess of revenues, although it was very small in 1932. The amount of revenue receipts received from vari-

TABLE 65. — NET REVENUE RECEIPTS, GOVERNMENTAL COST PAYMENTS, AND TRANSFERS IN COOK AND LAKE COUNTIES, 1929–32

	1929	1930	1931	1932
COOK COUNTY				
Net revenue receipts	$122,299.46	$147,809.05	$150,469.33	$131,381.05
Net government cost payments	148,315.24	154,697.57	133,701.29	130,020.26
Difference	— 26,015.78	— 6,888.52	+ 16,768.04	+ 1,360.79
Net transfer to county	+ 339.86			
Net transfer from county			— 469.14	— 797.45
Bonds paid by state	+ 3,000.00	+ 3,000.00		
Net increase or decrease	— 22,675.92	— 3,888.52	+ 16,298.90	+ 563.34
LAKE COUNTY				
Net revenue receipts	$211,932.81	$220,421.29	$258,373.29	$455,289.68
Net government cost payments	172,550.87	179,255.56	200,033.03	202,105.49
Difference	+ 39,381.94	+ 41,165.73	+ 58,340.26	+253,184.19
Net transfer to county	595.97			
Net transfer from county			— 363.29	— 31.06
Net increase or decrease	+ 39,977.91	+ 41,165.73	+ 57,976.97	+253,153.13

ous sources is shown in Table 66. The decline in property taxes and increases in subventions and grants are as pronounced in these counties as in any of the northeastern group. The increase in Lake County in 1932 is explained by the trunk highway reimbursement bonds.

TABLE 66. — REVENUE RECEIPTS FROM VARIOUS SOURCES IN COOK AND LAKE COUNTIES, 1929–32

Source	1929	1930	1931	1932
COOK COUNTY				
Property tax....................	$ 66,450.26	$ 66,526.54	$ 49,105.29	$ 36,473.21
Subventions and grants..........	37,982.82	67,393.41	93,085.86	87,201.85
Miscellaneous receipts and earnings	17,901.64	13,946.13	8,278.18	7,705.99
Total revenue receipts........	$122,334.72	$147,866.08	$150,469.33	$131,381.05
Less receipts refunds..........	35.26	57.03	....	....
Net revenue receipts..........	$122,299.56	$147,809.05	$150,469.33	$131,381.05
LAKE COUNTY				
Property tax....................	$127,379.07	$131,951.25	$130,760.77	$ 89,296.86
Subventions and grants..........	67,004.77	73,710.10	95,752.30	338,134.92
Miscellaneous receipts and earnings	18,290.81	14,759.94	31,860.22	27,857.90
Total revenue receipts........	$212,674.65	$220,421.29	$258,373.29	$455,289.68
Less receipts refunds..........	741.84	....	....	....
Net revenue receipts..........	$211,932.81	$220,421.29	$258,373.29	$455,289.68

TABLE 67. — PAYMENTS FOR GOVERNMENTAL COSTS IN COOK AND LAKE COUNTIES, 1929–32

Item of Expenditure	1929	1930	1931	1932
COOK COUNTY				
County revenue fund.....	$ 33,129.33	$ 36,436.47	$ 30,928.16	$ 26,271.98
Road and bridge fund.....	87,478.68	94,646.22	72,910.50	80,869.57
Poor relief..............	5,699.83	5,778.17	6,760.91	4,685.96
Interest	22,948.50	18,377.04	23,265.25	18,519.38
Total	$149,256.34	$155,237.90	$133,864.82	$130,346.89
Less payments refunded	941.10	540.34	163.53	326.63
Net cost payments......	$148,315.24	$154,697.56	$133,701.29	$130,020.26
LAKE COUNTY				
County revenue fund.....	$ 53,399.60	$ 63,936.38	$ 63,520.24	$ 58,893.58
Road and bridge fund.....	66,542.56	67,102.44	88,245.03	104,995.80
Poor relief..............	14,701.57	15,577.39	17,993.48	18,332.42
Interest	38,782.81	35,084.24	31,202.51	21,144.86
Total	$173,426.54	$181,700.45	$200,961.26	$203,366.66
Less payments refunded	875.67	2,444.89	928.23	1,261.17
Net cost payments.....	$172,550.87	$179,255.56	$200,033.03	$202,105.49

Payments for governmental costs in the two counties are classified in Table 67. The decline in costs in Cook County, though not so marked as in many counties, is typical of the trend in the cut-over counties. Total costs have increased in Lake County, largely as a result of increased road and bridge expenditures, as well as increased expenditures from the county revenue fund.

The total receipts going to the county, including both receipts from the sale of bonds and revenue receipts, are given in Table 68. Lake County floated no bonds during the period, and Cook County issued bonds in only one year, 1929.

TABLE 68. — TOTAL COUNTY RECEIPTS OF COOK AND LAKE COUNTIES, 1929–32

Source	1929	1930	1931	1932
COOK COUNTY				
Gross revenue receipts....	$123,275.82	$148,406.42	$150,632.86	$131,707.68
Sale of bonds.............	50,000.00	....	....	....
Total	$173,275.82	$148,406.42	$150,632.86	$131,707.68
LAKE COUNTY				
Gross revenue receipts....	$213,550.32	$222,866.18	$259,301.52	$456,550.85
Sale of bonds.............	....	....	....	....
Total	$213,550.32	$222,866.18	$259,301.52	$456,550.85

The total payments from county funds are given in Table 69. Both counties paid off some bonds each year. Over the period Cook County retired $5,954.09 more in bonds than it issued, $4,000 of this being received from the state for highway bonds. Lake County paid off $335,000, of which $250,000 represented payments from the state.

The total receipts from all sources are shown in Table 70. Here

TABLE 69. — TOTAL EXPENDITURES FROM COUNTY FUNDS IN COOK AND LAKE COUNTIES, 1929–32

Expenditure	1929	1930	1931	1932
COOK COUNTY				
Gross government cost payments	$149,291.60	$155,294.93	$133,864.82	$130,346.89
Bond principal................	12,000.00	12,000.00	15,954.08	16,000.00
Total	$161,291.60	$167,294.93	$149,818.90	$146,346.89
LAKE COUNTY				
Gross government cost payments	$174,168.38	$181,700.45	$200,961.26	$203,366.66
Bond principal................	10,500.00	10,500.00	45,500.00	268,500.00
Total	$184,668.38	$192,200.45	$246,461.26	$471,866.66

TABLE 70. — RECEIPTS FROM ALL SOURCES, COOK AND LAKE COUNTIES, 1929–32

Source	1929 Amount	1929 Per Cent	1930 Amount	1930 Per Cent	1931 Amount	1931 Per Cent	1932 Amount	1932 Per Cent
COOK COUNTY								
Property tax	$191,805.36	60	$185,871.47	64	$133,336.31	52	$101,532.38	47
Subventions and grants	52,009.90	16	82,818.81	29	109,031.49	43	103,440.75	48
Miscellaneous receipts and earnings	18,116.78	6	14,251.48	5	8,963.47	4	7,776.86	3
Other trust collections	4,898.14	2	6,574.93	2	3,272.01	1	3,490.05	2
Sale of bonds	50,000.00	16						
Refunded payments	941.10	*	540.34	*	163.53	*	326.63	*
Total	$317,771.28	100	$290,057.03	100	$254,766.81	100	$216,566.67	100
LAKE COUNTY								
Property tax	$349,264.95	67	$327,613.41	66	$319,844.73	60	$223,990.93	33
Subventions and grants	133,366.90	26	150,460.63	30	180,389.01	33	424,149.15	62
Miscellaneous receipts and earnings	22,272.54	4	16,007.34	3	32,124.46	6	28,282.09	4
Other trust collections	12,443.34	3	5,159.30	1	4,374.91	1	8,021.15	1
Sale of bonds								
Refunded payments	875.67	*	2,444.89	*	928.23	*	1,261.17	*
Total	$518,223.40	100	$501,685.57	100	$537,661.34	100	$685,704.49	100

* Less than 0.5 per cent.

again the declining trends in property tax receipts as well as the increasing trends in state aids are very marked.

The total warrants issued from all funds, distributed between county and trust and custodial, are given in Table 71. The major portion of the total warrants issued in Cook County was on county funds, the trust and custodial funds being of secondary importance. Cook is the only one of the counties covered in which this is the usual situation. It shows that the county organization is the major unit in collecting and expending moneys.

TABLE 71. — TOTAL WARRANTS ISSUED IN COOK AND LAKE COUNTIES, 1929–32

	1929	1930	1931	1932
COOK COUNTY				
County funds............	$161,291.60	$167,294.93	$149,818.90	$146,346.89
Trust and custodial payments	137,969.81	152,892.89	109,067.53	75,088.14
Total	$299,261.41	$320,187.82	$258,886.43	$221,435.03
LAKE COUNTY				
County funds	$184,668.38	$192,200.45	$246,461.26	$471,866.66
Trust and custodial payments	300,887.02	278,869.81	275,889.85	232,396.33
Total	$485,555.40	$471,070.26	$522,351.11	$704,262.99

Because conditions in Cook and Lake counties are favorable to county consolidation, estimates have been made of the economies that might be expected to result from such a move. In counties in which the assessed valuation and the population are as small as in these, such a move strikes at the very heart of the problem. In 1932 the per capita costs of county government alone were $53 in Cook County and $29 in Lake County; the costs per thousand dollars of assessed valuation were $126 in Cook County, $78 in Lake. These two counties have the highest costs, judged by these measures, of all the fourteen northeastern counties, Lake of the Woods County ranking third with a per capita cost of $19 and costs of $48 per thousand dollars of assessed valuation. It is apparent that when the assessed valuation falls to the $1,000,000 level or below, the minimum costs of supporting a county organization are greater than the valuation can bear, regardless of the efficiency of county officials. This is the situation in which Cook County finds itself.

No new buildings would be necessary, for the courthouse at Two Harbors can provide the additional office space required. The counties have already joined in utilizing the jail space of Lake County. Although the distance from many parts of Cook County to Two Harbors may be a handicap, it is offset to a considerable extent by the excellent road facilities.[14]

In order to check the reasonableness of the estimated costs of the combined offices, a third county, Aitkin, fairly comparable in assessed valuation, area, and population, was selected for comparative purposes. The comparisons appear in Table 72. Aitkin County

TABLE 72. — COMPARATIVE MEASURES FOR COOK, LAKE, AND AITKIN COUNTIES *

Item of Comparison	Cook	Lake	Lake and Cook	Aitkin
Assessed valuation	$1,034,083	$2,587,552	$3,621,635	$4,542,244
Taxable acres	504,162	792,506	1,296,668	1,145,433
Population	2,435	7,068	9,503	15,009
Number of personal property assessments	532	2,226	2,758	3,470
Miles of county aid roads	63	129	192	200
Miles of state aid roads	72	103	175	220

* All are 1932 figures except those for population, which are for 1930.

TABLE 73. — COMPARATIVE WORK LOAD IN THE AUDITOR'S OFFICE IN COOK, LAKE, AND AITKIN COUNTIES

Item of Comparison	Cook	Lake	Total Lake and Cook	Aitkin
Board meetings	12	14	26	12
Trial balance	12	12	24	12
Warrants issued	2,168	3,827	5,995	6,036
Vouchers filed *	1,860	3,500	5,360	5,000
Delinquent tax statements	210	218	428	782
Mortgage registry tax statements	40	91	131	194
Miscellaneous collection receipts	137	301	438	272
Private redemption statements	1	8	9	6
Teachers' retirement fund receipts	2	6	8	11
Notices of redemption	4	9	13	5
Game and fish licenses	2,409	3,344	5,753	6,962

* Estimated by the auditors of the respective counties.

is somewhat larger in all respects except taxable acreage, which is about 11 per cent less. Costs were estimated for each of the consolidated offices, based upon the work done in each in 1932. The corresponding offices studied in Aitkin County were used as a check on these estimates. In Table 73 the auditor's office is given as an example of the procedure followed in each of the offices. It will be noted that the work load in Aitkin County is practically equivalent to that in Lake and Cook. The salaries and clerk hire of

[14]Adjustments should be made in the present methods of providing state aid for roads so that these will not act as a barrier to desirable consolidation. Exisiting public debts would, of course, remain a claim against the taxable property in the area affected.

the auditor's office in the three counties, rounded to the nearest $100, and the estimated cost of a consolidated office, are shown in the following tabulation:

	Cook	Lake	Cook and Lake	Aitkin	Consolidated Office
Salary	$2,100	$2,400	$4,500	$2,000	$2,400
Clerk hire......	1,700	2,500	4,200	3,000	3,100
Total	$3,800	$4,900	$8,700	$5,000	$5,500

The estimate allows the auditor the same salary as the Lake County auditor now draws, with $600 additional for clerk hire, making a total of $500 more than the present cost of the Aitkin office. The estimated saving through consolidation of the auditor's office is $3,200, all in salaries and clerk hire. Since overhead costs, such as supplies, lights, fuel, telephone, water, insurance, etc., are not allocated to the different offices, the estimated savings in each of these items are for all the offices in the two courthouses. All offices and items of expense for which it is estimated that consolidation might result in a saving are given in Table 74.

TABLE 74. — PRESENT COSTS AND ESTIMATED SAVINGS THROUGH CONSOLIDATION OF COOK AND LAKE COUNTIES
(all costs rounded to nearest $100)

Item of Cost	Costs in 1932				Estimated Cost of Consolidated County	Estimated Savings
	Cook	Lake	Total	Aitkin		
County offices						
County commissioners...	$2,300	$2,500	$4,800	$3,000	$3,000	$1,800
Auditor	3,800	4,900	8,700	5,000	5,500	3,200
Treasurer	2,900	4,100	7,000	3,700	4,500	2,500
Probate court..........	700	2,100	2,800	2,400	2,400	400
Clerk of court..........	1,700	2,300	4,000	3,100 *	3,000	1,000
Register of deeds	2,500	2,800	5,300	2,800 *	3,100	2,200
County attorney	900	2,100	3,000	1,900	2,100	900
Highway engineer	5,300	3,100	8,400	2,800	4,400	4,000
Operation, maintenance, and overhead						
Janitor	1,100	1,800	2,900	1,000	1,800	1,100
Courthouse and jail maintenance	200	1,000	1,200	800	1,000	200
Printing and publishing..	1,700	2,300	4,000	3,100 †	2,500	1,500
Insurance	300	800	1,100	500	800	300
Official bonds	600 †	200 †	800	300 †	500	300
Water, lights, and fuel..	800	900	1,700	2,800	900	800
Telephone and telegraph	400	400	800	700	600	200
Total	$25,200	$31,300	$56,500	$33,900	$36,100	$20,400

* Fees added to clerk hire.   † Three-year average.

The offices of the sheriff, county agent, and superintendent of schools do not appear in the above table because it is unlikely that economies could be effected by consolidation of these offices. The sheriff of the consolidated unit would require a deputy, whose salary and expenses would be as great as those of the present Cook County sheriff. The agricultural agent in Cook County received approximately $1,000 from the county in 1932, which amount would be necessary to cover the salary and expenses of an assistant in the consolidated unit.

It is estimated that the entire salary of the Cook County attorney could be saved. In all other offices an allowance is made for additional clerk hire. The salary scale in all offices is equal to or higher than the Lake County scale for 1932. With respect to operation and maintenance, it is probable that all the Cook County expenditures for janitor, courthouse maintenance, insurance, water, light, and fuel could be saved. The estimated savings in the offices listed amount to 36 per cent of the 1932 costs of these offices in the two counties.

Were such a consolidated county in turn to reorganize along the lines suggested for other northeastern counties the estimated additional savings would be $7,800. The sources of these savings are given in Table 75. This would bring the total savings through reorganization and consolidation to $28,200.

TABLE 75. — ESTIMATED ADDITIONAL SAVINGS THROUGH
REORGANIZATION OF COUNTY OFFICES IN
CONSOLIDATED UNIT

Treasurer	$2,800
Probate judge and clerk of court...............	1,800
County commissioner..........................	1,200
Return of fees	2,000
Total......................................	$7,800

THE TOWNS

The indebtedness of the towns of the two counties is given in Table 76. The town indebtedness was reduced 22 per cent in Cook and 18 per cent in Lake County during the period 1929–32.

The average receipts and expenditures for the towns reporting are given in Table 77. Receipts in Cook County have declined much more rapidly than expenditures. Receipts exceeded expenditures in both counties in 1930 and 1931; in Cook County, however, there was a considerable deficit in 1932.

TABLE 76. — TOWN INDEBTEDNESS, COOK AND LAKE COUNTIES, 1929–32

Class of Obligations	1929 *	1930	1931	1932
	COOK COUNTY			
Town bonds	$51,000.00	$48,500.00	$44,000.00	$41,000.00
Town warrants............	4,166.52	4,511.11	4,652.06	2,085.56
Total	$55,166.52	$53,011.11	$48,652.06	$43,085.56
	LAKE COUNTY			
Town bonds	$12,814.82	$11,750.00	$11,387.42	$10,558.38
Town warrants............	31,687.34	28,486.50	26,848.83	26,003.21
Total	$44,502.16	$40,236.50	$38,236.25	$36,661.59

* As of December 31 of each year.

All the towns in both Cook and Lake counties had a tax delinquency of over 40 per cent of the current levy in 1932, but none were more than 70 per cent delinquent. The average township tax delinquency in Cook County was 50 per cent and in Lake 48 per cent.

The total expenditures of all towns in the two counties are estimated in Table 78.

The estimated costs of a consolidated county performing the town functions in Cook and Lake counties are given in Table 79. The largest savings would be effected in road costs, on which the towns in the two counties spent $30,400 in 1932. The estimate is based on the assumption of one assessor for the consolidated county at a salary of $2,000 and an allowance of $2,000 for clerical help and expenses. If settlement were restricted and relocated, it is estimated that the clerical help and expenses could be reduced to approximately $900.

TABLE 77. — AVERAGE TOWN RECEIPTS AND EXPENDITURES, COOK AND
LAKE COUNTIES, 1930–32 *

	Cook County			Lake County		
	1930	1931	1932	1930	1931	1932
Receipts	$3,591.81	$2,606.07	$1,297.02	$5,737.88	$5,763.29	$3,602.09
Total expenditures	3,447.82	2,356.85	2,614.75	5,763.18	5,114.77	4,260.21
Road and bridge	2,244.06	1,541.97	1,412.54	4,318.86	4,049.03	3,038.36
General revenue	556.46	382.45	309.82	1,232.27	936.94	1,066.20
Other	647.30	432.43	892.39	212.05	128.80	155.65

* Based on reports from 75 per cent of the towns in Cook and 87 per cent of those in Lake County.

TABLE 78. — ESTIMATED TOWN EXPENDITURES IN COOK AND LAKE COUNTIES, 1932

County	Total	Road and Bridge Fund	Revenue Fund	Other
Cook	$19,000	$10,100	$ 2,300	$6,600
Lake	29,700	20,300	8,300	1,100
Total	$48,700	$30,400	$10,600	$7,700

TABLE 79. — ESTIMATED COSTS OF COUNTY OPERATION OF TOWN FUNCTIONS
IN CONSOLIDATED COUNTY

Item of Expenditure	Present Settlement	Restricted Settlement
Town roads..........................	$16,300	$ 9,700
Elections	3,200	1,200
Assessment	4,000	2,900
Total	$23,500	$13,800
Estimated savings based on 1932 costs	$25,100	$34,800

THE SCHOOLS

Data for Cook and Lake counties on school indebtedness, receipts of graded and ungraded schools, net operating costs, and the percentage distribution of expenditures are given in Tables 80 to 83. The school indebtedness of Cook County is considerably greater than that of Lake, although substantial progress has been made toward its reduction.

Local taxes contribute a much larger proportion of the total receipts in Cook than in Lake County, partly because the small enrollments in Cook County are associated with comparatively high school-district valuations due to the size of the school districts. The result is that Cook County schools have a smaller claim upon state aid than any of the northeastern counties. Lake County receives a portion of the state gross earnings taxes in addition to other state aids for schools.

Although educational standards have been improved in Lake County during the period under consideration, operating costs have declined. In Cook County the decline in cost was achieved chiefly by reducing expenditures rather than by a change in organization.

Because Lake County has already established a county school system, no further changes are suggested. The results of adding the Cook County schools to the Lake County district will be consid-

TABLE 80. — SCHOOL INDEBTEDNESS IN COOK AND LAKE COUNTIES, 1929–32

Class of Obligations	1929 *	1930	1931	1932
COOK COUNTY				
School bonds............	$121,400.00	$95,800.00	$87,700.00	$81,200.00
School warrants	....	....	....	....
Total	$121,400.00	$95,800.00	$87,700.00	$81,200.00
LAKE COUNTY				
School bonds............	$ 14,500.00	$13,800.00	$13,548.76	$12,591.01
School warrants	732.34	1,126.27	577.00	....
Total	$ 15,232.34	$14,926.27	$14,125.76	$12,591.01

* As of December 31 of each year.

TABLE 81. — NET RECEIPTS OF SCHOOLS IN COOK AND LAKE COUNTIES, 1928–32

Source	1928–29	1929–30	1930–31	1931–32	1932–33
COOK COUNTY					
State aid	$ 16,708.01	$ 12,964.24	$ 19,684.96	$ 13,467.75	$ 14,195.23
Local taxes	70,532.23	46,496.65	59,938.15	33,193.89	25,508.56
Other sources	3,191.98	2,537.45	9,159.85	10,127.41	12,397.37
Total	$ 90,432.22	$ 61,998.34	$ 88,782.96	$ 56,789.05	$ 52,101.16
LAKE COUNTY					
State aid	$ 64,930.23	$ 73,080.85	$ 77,017.58	$ 85,047.80	$ 86,840.55
Local taxes	59,667.87	173,201.57	103,057.63	84,936.39	63,343.90
Other sources	2,148.44	3,050.72	2,663.04	851.75	2,758.21
Total	$126,746.54	$249,333.14	$182,738.25	$170,835.94	$152,942.66

TABLE 82. — NET OPERATING COSTS OF SCHOOLS IN COOK AND
LAKE COUNTIES, 1928–32

	1928–29	1929–30	1930–31	1931–32	1932–33
COOK COUNTY					
Ungraded					
Maintenance cost ..	$25,919.90	$29,219.94	$26,050.53	$23,950.53	$17,087.36
Transportation	9,979.89	10,683.71	7,909.48	7,006.40	5,947.99
Total	$35,899.79	$39,903.65	$33,960.01	$30,956.93	$23,035.35
Graded and high school					
Maintenance cost ..	$27,897.63	$36,834.13	$28,270.02	$24,627.31	$20,816.24
Transportation	6,364.32	5,733.49	6,236.16	5,037.24	3,887.71
Total	$34,261.95	$42,567.62	$34,506.18	$29,664.55	$24,703.95
Total operating cost	$70,161.74	$82,471.27	$68,466.19	$60,621.48	$47,739.30
LAKE COUNTY					
Ungraded and graded					
Maintenance cost ..	$152,055.36	$149,927.60	$142,927.77	$142,291.13	$127,715.25
Transportation	23,196.15	24,833.31	23,680.30	24,953.55	24,750.85
Total operating cost	$175,251.51	$174,760.91	$166,608.07	$167,244.68	$152,466.10

313

TABLE 83. — PERCENTAGE DISTRIBUTION OF EXPENDITURES FOR SCHOOLS IN COOK
AND LAKE COUNTIES

Item of Expenditure	Ungraded	Graded and Secondary	Ungraded, Graded, and Secondary
General control	3.5	4.7	6.4
Teachers' salaries	39.9	47.1	52.9
Other expenses of instruction	5.8	6.7	5.0
Operation	14.4	16.5	13.1
Maintenance	8.8	5.3	6.5
Transportation	25.3	16.5	14.5
Other expenses	2.3	3.2	1.6

ered because of the proposed consolidation of these counties. The
six school districts now in Cook County would be added to the
Lake County district and six ungraded schools and four teachers
would be dispensed with under the plan. This would leave twelve
teachers in the graded and secondary schools and eight in the rural
schools. The estimated costs of operation under the plan are given
in Table 84. Because of the basis on which supplemental state aid

TABLE 84. — ESTIMATED COSTS OF OPERATION OF COOK COUNTY
SCHOOLS IF COMBINED WITH LAKE COUNTY DISTRICT,
SETTLEMENT REMAINING AS AT PRESENT

Rural maintenance	$11,400
Graded and secondary maintenance	20,800
Transportation	11,000
Total	$43,200
Savings over 1932–33 costs	$41,500
State aid	20,000
Cost to taxpayers	23,200
Savings to taxpayers	10,300

and transportation aid are determined, total state aid might increase so that the savings to the taxpayer would be greater than
the reduction in costs. Settler relocation would make additional
savings possible. Four schools could be closed in Lake County with
savings of approximately $6,000 in maintenance costs and $4,000 in
transportation costs, a total of $10,000. In Cook County it is esti-
mated that additional savings of $4,000 would be possible under
both reorganization and settler relocation. A summary of the possible savings in Lake and Cook counties through consolidation and
reorganization is given in Table 85.

TABLE 85. — ESTIMATED TOTAL SAVINGS THROUGH CONSOLIDATION, REORGANI-
ZATION, AND SETTLER RELOCATION IN COOK AND LAKE COUNTIES

	With Present Settlement	With Restricted Settlement
County consolidation	$20,400	$20,400
County office reorganization................	7,800	7,800
Towns	25,100	34,800
Schools	4,500 *	18,000
Total	$57,800	$81,000
Percentage of 1932 operating costs........	10	14

* Cook County only.

Limitations of space make it impossible to present a detailed
analysis for the remaining eleven counties. Estimates for these
counties, however, are summarized in Tables 86 to 89 on the following pages.

TABLE 86. — ESTIMATED SAVINGS THROUGH COUNTY REORGANIZATION IN EACH OF EIGHT OTHER COUNTIES *

County	Elimination of Treasurer's Office	Consolidation of Judge of Probate and Clerk of Court	Reduction of County Commissioners	Return of Fees	Total
Beltrami	$3,300	$1,400	$1,900	$4,000	$10,600
Cass	2,000	1,300	1,900	4,200	9,400
Koochiching	2,300	1,000	1,400	3,000	7,700
Lake of the Woods	600	400	700	1,200	2,900
Clearwater	900	600	600	800	2,900
Hubbard	1,800	1,000	600	2,000	5,400
Carlton	3,000	800	900	4,300	9,000
Pine	2,800	1,200	1,000	800	5,800

* No reorganization of county offices is suggested for Crow Wing, Itasca, and St. Louis counties.

TABLE 87. — ESTIMATED COST OF COUNTY OPERATION OF TOWN FUNCTIONS IN EACH OF ELEVEN OTHER COUNTIES

County	Maintaining Town Roads	Elections	Assessment	Total	Estimated Savings Based on 1932 Costs
Beltrami					
Present settlement.......	$22,000	$3,000	$4,500	$29,500	$2,000
Concentrated settlement..	15,600	1,800	3,500	20,900	10,600
Cass					
Present settlement.......	15,300	3,100	4,100	22,500	16,600
Concentrated settlement..	11,400	2,000	3,400	16,800	22,300
Koochiching					
Present settlement.......	6,500	1,900	4,200	12,600	5,200
Concentrated settlement..	4,300	1,000	2,800	8,100	9,700
Lake of the Woods					
Present settlement.......	5,700	1,700	2,900	10,300	−2,400
Concentrated settlement..	2,800	900	2,100	5,800	2,100
Clearwater					
Present settlement.......	12,900	1,800	2,600	17,300	3,000
Concentrated settlement..	9,800	900	2,100	12,800	7,500
Hubbard					
Present settlement.......	14,700	1,700	2,400	18,800	−2,800
Concentrated settlement..	9,300	800	2,000	12,100	3,900
Carlton					
Present settlement.......	25,200	1,600	3,100	29,900	30,000
Concentrated settlement..	23,400	1,100	2,800	27,300	40,200
Pine					
Present settlement.......	29,800	2,800	3,700	36,300	25,800
Concentrated settlement..	27,200	1,700	3,000	31,900	30,200
Crow Wing					
Present settlement.......	25,200	1,800	3,500	30,500	28,000
Concentrated settlement..	20,200	1,000	3,000	24,200	36,200
Itasca					
Present settlement........	21,600	3,300	4,900	29,800	17,200
Concentrated settlement..	9,400	1,000	3,800	14,200	32,800
St. Louis					
Present settlement.......	26,600	6,800	6,900	40,300	36,400
Concentrated settlement..	16,800	2,600	2,200	21,600	55,100

TABLE 88. — ESTIMATED COSTS OF SCHOOL OPERATION WITH REORGANIZATION IN EACH OF EIGHT OTHER COUNTIES

County	Rural Maintenance	Graded and Secondary	Transportation	Total	Savings over 1932–33	State Aid	Net Cost to Local Taxpayer	Savings to Local Taxpayer
Beltrami	$89,600	$158,200	$35,000	$282,800	$27,400	$180,000	$102,800	$21,500
Cass	63,000	96,500	52,000	211,500	15,100	185,000	26,000	24,600
Clearwater	34,800	50,200	15,000	100,000	5,200	83,500	16,500	15,900
Hubbard	13,000	100,800	38,000	151,800	10,700	101,000	50,800	23,500
Carlton	64,200	250,000	50,000	364,200	14,000	170,000	194,000	17,000
Pine	67,000	153,000	45,000	265,000	15,000	160,000	105,000	24,500
Crow Wing	70,000	320,000	36,000	426,000	18,000	195,000	231,000	31,000
Itasca	......	832,000	120,000	952,000	34,000	310,000	642,000	34,000

TABLE 89. — ESTIMATED COSTS OF SCHOOL OPERATION WITH REORGANIZATION AND SETTLER RELOCATION IN ELEVEN OTHER COUNTIES

County	Rural Maintenance	Graded and Secondary	Transportation	Total	Savings over 1932–33	State Aid	Net Cost to Local Taxpayer	Savings to Local Taxpayer
Beltrami	$76,600	$158,200	$28,000	$262,800	$47,400	$176,000	$86,800	$37,500
Cass	57,400	96,500	30,000	183,900	42,700	175,000	8,900	42,200
Koochiching	......	212,000	45,000	257,000	21,800	150,000	107,000	22,000
Lake of the Woods	9,300	35,400	9,600	54,300	8,700	46,000	8,300	16,200
Clearwater	29,800	50,200	11,000	91,000	14,200	78,000	13,000	19,400
Hubbard	8,000	101,400	25,000	134,400	28,100	95,000	39,400	34,900
Carlton	55,100	250,000	40,000	345,100	33,000	165,000	180,000	31,300
Pine	56,900	153,000	35,000	244,900	35,000	150,000	94,900	35,600
Crow Wing	61,000	320,000	26,000	407,000	37,000	185,000	220,000	39,600
Itasca	......	825,000	100,000	925,000	61,000	300,000	625,000	50,100
St. Louis	365,000	......	155,000	520,000	155,000	310,000	210,000	161,000

CHAPTER XII

TRANSLATING PROPOSALS INTO
EFFECTIVE PROGRAMS *

Part I of this report is concerned mainly with giving a broad picture of the land use situation in the cut-over area of northern Minnesota. It reviews briefly some of the more important factors that have brought about this situation. After this there follows a description of the area, including its natural, economic, and social characteristics and a brief outline of governmental organization. The present uses of the land, important considerations in any program of improvement, are next considered. The economic and social consequences of this present utilization, which has developed without adequate plans, are briefly reviewed. Present public policies affecting land use are also touched upon.

Part II is devoted primarily to a consideration of the steps that may be taken to improve upon the situation described in Part I. Land classification is an important feature of any comprehensive program of land utilization, for it supplies a guide to the development and execution of a land use policy. It may serve to indicate what uses should be made of land in the interest of both the individual and society. For example, land classification will indicate what areas are best suited to agricultural use when economic conditions warrant further development, and consequently will be helpful in directing future settlers to the locations best adapted to successful farm use. Classification may also help farmers who are at present unfavorably located to find lands better suited to farming and more desirably situated with respect to schools, roads, and other community services.

A tentative classification of lands in northern Minnesota has been developed as a part of this study and is presented in this report. This is to be regarded as a first approach to a more refined classification. The limitations of funds, personnel, and time in the present study have precluded a high degree of refinement in the classification suggested. It is adequate, however, as a basis for initiating programs of improvement. It is to be hoped that the work

* This chapter was prepared by O. B. Jesness.

that has been started may be employed as a basis for further work in this field and that a more definite land classification will gradually emerge.

Recently the principle of zoning, which has long been applied to urban land, has been extended to rural lands. The object is the safeguarding of the public interest. Through zoning, land classification may be made effective. Settlement may be directed to areas suited to farming and restricted in those that are not. Because of its importance in the land use program considerable attention is given to zoning in this report.

While the emphasis at present is on state and national forests, there is considerable room for private forestry. For one thing, it appears improbable that public forestry will be expanded sufficiently to take care of all the timber requirements of the future. Private reforestation is making little headway at present and is not likely to increase much unless better methods are adopted. Successful operation requires consolidation of ownership or control into units of considerable size so that the best management methods can be employed and greater protection against fire and other losses established.

This country has passed out of the phase of its development in which emphasis was placed upon the transference of land from public to private ownership. It is now recognized that some lands are better suited to public than to private ownership. The question therefore arises as to what lands should be returned to public ownership and what processes should be employed to this end. It is pointed out that for the most part the federal government can add to its holdings for forestry or other purposes only by purchase. In Minnesota, where tax-delinquent land reverts to the state, most of the land acquired by the state will doubtless be acquired through that process. In fact, the immediate problem is to develop a policy and program for handling the extensive acreage that is coming back to state ownership because of unpaid taxes. While counties and other local units may acquire land for forestry or other purposes, it is not anticipated that they will do so on any large scale, because such units are not well equipped to manage such lands.

It is important that state and federal governments coordinate their respective programs of land acquisition in order that conflicts may be avoided. It is probable that the federal program will be directed mainly toward rounding out and expanding the areas in existing national forests. The state, it is expected, will give its ma-

jor attention to the development and management of the state forests established by the legislature in tax-delinquent areas, though
of course the acquisition of land through the process of tax delinquency is by no means restricted to these areas. It will also continue to purchase some lands, including lands especially valuable
for public use and lands needed to round out forest and other public areas.

Public land acquisition programs formulated to bring about improved land utilization must be considered in the light of their relationship to other land uses and adjustments. If the results of public
use are to be satisfactory, the best methods of development and
management must be employed. The objectives and the requirements for their attainment should be understood by the public
generally in order that adequate financial support may be provided.

This study has been concerned mainly with the lands not suited
to agriculture or not now in farms, for these are the lands in which
the land use problem centers rather than those that are being
farmed successfully. Efficient use of the latter is important, however. Consequently attention has been directed to possible improvements in farm organization and management that will increase the
financial returns from lands in agricultural use.

So long as all the cut-over area was regarded as ultimately des-
tined for agricultural settlement, little thought was given to settlement plans. Lands were sold to prospective farmers without regard
to their suitability for agriculture or to their location with respect
to existing settlement. In fact, some owners of tracts in remote regions saw an advantage in getting settlers on some of this land in
order to induce others to follow and to obtain public roads that
would make their lands more accessible. In some instances, the opportunity to obtain payment for transporting children to distant
schools appears to have been a factor in encouraging settlement in
remote locations. Consequently there are scattered settlers and settlements. Some of these are on inferior land. It would be to their
interest to move to areas where opportunities are greater. Even if
the land is physically productive, its use in farming may entail excessive public expenditures for schools, roads, and other services.
Isolated settlers scattered through forest areas increase fire hazards
and costs of protection.

Now that the picture of land use is clearer, it is apparent that
individual opportunities can often be improved and the burden of

maintaining essential public services be reduced by the relocation of settlers. While it was impossible to make a comprehensive survey covering isolated settlers who might benefit by such a move, the results of illustrative cases are given and the problems involved are discussed. Careful consideration has been given to the question of settler relocation.

Relocation involves more than the farm population. The depletion of timber and of other resources has left some stranded villages. To the extent that their inhabitants engage in farming it is desirable that they settle on good agricultural land in localities already supplied with roads and schools. The development of public forests may offer some opportunity for farm-forest communities, the residents of which will have part-time employment in the forests and will produce some of their living requirements on the land they occupy.

In some parts of the country there is a movement of industrial workers into suburban areas where they will be able to produce part of their food while relying upon industrial employment to furnish cash income. Such settlement will not become extensive in the cut-over area of Minnesota because of the limited urban and industrial development. The results obtained by a number of part-time farmers in the vicinity of Duluth are presented in connection with the discussion of this phase of the report.

The extensive territory included in the cut-over counties and the sparse population and limited taxable valuation in much of the area make it very difficult to provide the necessary public services without levying taxes that are excessive for a large part of the property. The public finance problem is aggravated by extensive indebtedness arising from expenditures previously incurred in anticipation of development that has often failed to materialize. The tax problem is an important consideration in a land use program. Conversely, the type of use to which land is devoted is an important factor in the tax burden. The questions of public finance and land use are therefore essentially parts of the same problem. In the light of this fact the report reviews somewhat extensively the public finance difficulties faced by the region and outlines suggestions for improving upon the situation. School reorganization, both with and without settler relocation, is discussed. Consideration is given also to the possibilities of reducing the costs of government through various reorganizations and realignments of township and county functions. In some cases services may have to be curtailed; in others the best step may be to transfer their performance to governmental units better equipped for the purpose. The dissolution of some units or their consolidation with adjacent units is also considered.

OBJECTIVES OF A LAND POLICY

The results of the study presented in this report speak clearly regarding the need for modifying public policies affecting land use in the cut-over area of northeastern Minnesota. It is generally agreed, probably, that public policy should be directed toward the best possible use of the available resources of the region. As to specific details, however, it is too much to expect that everyone will see them in exactly the same light.

There will be those who maintain that extensive agricultural development of northeastern Minnesota will take place in a relatively short time and that the policy should be directed to fostering such development. They may point out that the region includes extensive areas having a soil suited to farm use. They may call attention to favorable climatic factors. As pointed out elsewhere in this report, there are areas already well developed in agriculture and other areas with natural conditions favorable for such use when development is justified by economic conditions. But there are other facts that must be faced frankly in viewing agricultural possibilities. One is that agricultural development in the region as a whole has not been rapid. Many owners who expected to dispose of their holdings to settlers have been unable to find buyers and the prospects have been so poor that many have permitted the land to go tax delinquent.

Past developments suggest what are the limitations on agricultural expansion. The lands now in farm use are clearly adequate to supply present needs abundantly, and there is no reason to believe that the market will expand greatly. Population is no longer increasing rapidly. Competition from other agricultural regions is keen. Foreign outlets have decreased. In short, it is not merely a question of whether a region has soil and climate suited to farming but whether such economic factors as markets, transportation, competing areas, and costs of development are favorable. When land is in demand and high in price, it may be profitable to clear and improve land even though costs are high. But now that developed lands are available at relatively low prices, it is no longer justifiable to invest heavily in improving raw land. Unless the situation is favorable, agricultural use of the land generally will not provide the returns necessary to support an adequate standard for the people on the land and an adequate standard of schools, roads, and other services. It must be borne in mind that settlement calls for more extensive public services than are needed where the land is employed for forestry or similar purposes.

One object of a public land policy therefore should be to determine what lands are best suited to agriculture and to direct future expansion to such lands as conditions warrant. It should also include provision for the efficient use of the land being farmed.

For the land not suited to nor required for farming, the object should be to find the best alternative use. Forestry will naturally be the most important in northeastern Minnesota. Here again public interest will be served best if the lands best suited to forestry are devoted to this use. On the better lands, intensive forestry should be practiced, according to the resources available and estimated future requirements for timber. On the rest, fire protection and more limited operations may be the best program. Some lands are particularly well suited to recreation, others for game preservation and propagation. After lands have been assigned to appropriate uses, there will be some left over that are not well suited to any definite use. Public interest demands that these be handled in such a way that they will not be a heavier burden on society than necessary.

In short, a desirable land policy represents a careful weighing of the comparative benefits and costs to the public involved in various land uses and a direction of those uses to the end that the greatest benefits possible are realized.

PUBLIC OPINION

A public policy does not arise spontaneously. In a democracy its formulation evolves out of public opinion, either affirmatively expressed or indicated merely by the acceptance of certain programs of action and development. Opinion is naturally affected by the information the public has. If it has a distorted view of the problem, that distortion may lead to a shortsighted policy. The consequences of certain developments of land utilization may reach individuals and communities far removed from their immediate situs. For example, forestry is designed to provide for the future needs of people many of whom are located at a distance. Recreational opportunities frequently draw people from a distance. Ill-advised drainage operations may result in a public debt which the citizens generally will have to help pay off. These few illustrations suggest how important it is for the public generally to participate in the development of land policy. An intelligent public opinion will support constructive steps and discourage ill-advised ones and in that way force the adoption of a constructive program.

NEEDED LEGISLATION

At various points in this report attention has been directed to desirable legislation having a bearing on the land use problem. It is not necessary to mention all these proposed measures here nor to devote any extended discussion to them. The application of the principle of zoning to lands in areas where land use problems are important is receiving very favorable recognition. This is one of the steps that should be authorized by appropriate legislation at the earliest possible opportunity.

The tax-delinquency problem is acute in northeastern Minnesota. As has been pointed out previously, this is inextricably bound up with the land use problem. Considerable land is reverting to public ownership through the process of tax delinquency. It might as well be frankly recognized that under existing circumstances much of this land will serve the public interest better if it remains in public ownership. Some clarification of the laws governing tax reversion is necessary to this end.[1]

Bargain settlement of taxes has been resorted to extensively in northeastern Minnesota, and there are grounds for believing that tax delinquency has been aggravated by this practice; that is, some owners have failed to pay their taxes when due in the expectation that later on they would be able to settle back taxes at a reduced figure. While the original purpose of such adjustments may have been very laudable, it is apparent that, as a protection to taxpayers who meet their tax bills when they are due, this practice must be curtailed. In some cases these adjustments result in temporizing with a land use problem; land that would serve the public interest better if it were in public hands may be kept in an indefinite status under private ownership and thereby delay a real program of improved land use.

The possibilities of effecting economies through a reorganization of local units of government and a redistribution of functions

---

[1] The report of the Governor's Land Use Committee (*Land Utilization in Minnesota*) makes certain specific recommendations on this point.

have been reviewed in earlier chapters. The legislature has already authorized some steps toward this end, and there is opportunity for a broadening of such authority to make greater flexibility possible. The suggestion is not that state authority be employed to compel adjustments against local desires but rather that the way be cleared for readjustments that are desirable. While it is granted that the state should not force its views upon local units in these matters, it may be suggested that local units have no right to expect a continuation of state aid for uses that do not serve the best interests of the state as a whole. It is not suggested that this be held over local units as a threat but that the state should consider carefully its policies of state aid to make certain that they operate in the interest of a desirable land policy and that they do not penalize and thereby prevent desirable reorganization.

Safeguards have been thrown around the handling and disposal of state lands. The protection of such property is important. But authority should be provided for the exchange of lands in state ownership for other lands in federal or private ownership where such exchange would be advantageous to the state. A constitutional amendment authorizing such exchange has been before the voters but has not yet received the needed affirmative votes to carry.

Legislative authorization for the establishment of state forests has been granted in recent years. As rapidly as conditions permit, the acquisition of additional land in these areas and the establishment of the best practices in forest management should be provided for. Capital investments judiciously made during the next few years should in future years provide a return to the state not only in the form of merchantable timber but also in social benefits arising from well-managed forest areas.

Administrative Organization

The state took an important step toward developing a unified land program when it brought together various administrative units into a Department of Conservation. The handling of state lands was transferred to this department. It is, of course, very important that there be proper coordination of the units of the department and of its activities with those of other departments. A step to this end was taken when, in accordance with the recommendation of the Land Utilization Committee appointed by the Governor, a State Land Use Committee was established. This committee consists of representatives of some of the departments most directly concerned with land use. It is intended to operate primarily as a coordinating agency in developing and carrying out land policies. If it serves the purpose for which it was created, it will tend to overcome unnecessary conflict of action.

A few illustrations will make clear the importance of coordination. Highway construction problems fall within the jurisdiction of the Highway Department. However, the form of land use that is to be developed in an area is closely related to highway services. Highway construction designed to serve a community that should be relocated may be avoided if the situation is understood and steps are taken to move the settlement. Highway construction may likewise encourage agricultural settlement in areas where this is desirable. Highways in some forest areas may be objectionable because of resulting fire hazards.

Forests may require workers located in the vicinity. It may make considerable difference in school costs where families of such workers live. For that reason it is important that the Department of Education be represented in their location.

In the past the state has been a party to encouraging settlers to buy land that would have remained in public ownership had there been a better comprehension of the problems involved. It is because of situations such as these that it is important for each department to have in mind the relationship of its work to the program as a whole.

Any program of revised land use must have local support to make it effective. There probably is no need to create new governmental organizations to provide local participation in the program developed. Here again, however, an understanding of the objectives and a coordination of operation are of paramount importance to the success of the program.

As suggested in the body of this report, there are opportunities for cooperation in realignments of local governmental functions. School districts may combine or cooperate to effect savings. Townships may find it advantageous to have the county take care of their roads and perform other services. Counties may likewise find it advantageous to join in the performance of some of their services, and even to consolidate where this is feasible. In short, land policy must be regarded as a comprehensive cooperative undertaking based on the principle of the greatest good for the greatest number.

PROGRAM SUMMARIZED

To summarize very briefly, twelve important lines of action have been suggested in this report:

1. The general aim of a land program in northeastern Minnesota should be to make the best use of the available land resources. The attainment of this objective requires that the program be based both on the suitability of land for different uses, economic as well as physical factors considered, and on the need for land in such uses.

2. Classification of land is important as a guide in determining upon a program of land use. The information presented in Chapter VI, including the county maps showing suggested conservation zones (Figures 25–39), represents a first approach to a general land classification. It supplies a basis for further study and refinement looking to a more detailed land classification.

3. The legislature should pass a zoning law providing authority for making land classification effective and for directing land use in accordance with public interest.

4. Existing settlement on lands unsuited to agriculture or involving unnecessarily high public costs should be assisted in relocating on lands better adapted to agriculture or more advantageously situated with respect to schools, roads, and other public services.

5. State forests have been established by legislative acts. Attention now needs to be given to placing more of the land within the boundaries of these forests under definite state ownership or control and providing funds for developing, managing, and operating these forests to the end that they may provide future timber supplies and public income.

6. The uncertainty that exists under present laws regarding title to, and control of, land reverting to public ownership through tax delinquency calls for clarifying legislation. Such legislation should recognize that there are considerable areas not suited to private development under existing circumstances and that attempts to return them to private ownership will continue an uncertain status with little or no development. Such lands should be retained in public ownership, and programs should be worked out for the best methods of handling them. Some will be well suited to forestry, game preservation, recreation, or water storage or control. Others will be suitable for no specific economic use under present conditions and should be maintained at the lowest possible outlay.

7. So-called "bargain" settlement of delinquent taxes often represents temporizing with a problem rather than its solution, and should be discontinued in favor of a better land use program.

8. While it is important that there be safeguards against unwise disposal of public lands, the state should not be prohibited from making desirable exchanges of land with the federal government or with private individuals. A constitutional amendment to provide authority to do so has been submitted to the voters, but thus far has failed to obtain the necessary affirmative votes. When it is approved, the way will be cleared for legislative authorization for exchanges involving any state-owned land.

9. Coordination of and cooperation between agencies concerned with land use are important. State and federal agencies responsible for public forests, game refuges, and similar areas should be in constant contact and should have an understanding of each other's plans and programs. Highway construction, educational development, and other public services should be developed in conformity with desirable land programs.

10. Legislative provision should be made for administration of state aid to schools, roads, and other purposes in such a way that better land use programs are fostered rather than hindered by these aids.

11. Careful consideration should be given to improvements in governmental organization and in the allocation of functions. School organization on a county basis may make possible savings that are not obtainable with local districts. Some towns may be dissolved. Others may find it desirable to transfer certain functions, such as road maintenance, to the county. Legislative authorization to make these adjustments should be granted.

12. The development and adoption of constructive land policies and programs are necessarily dependent upon public understanding of the problem involved. A wider dissemination of information and more consideration of land use problems by the people are therefore important. The study on which this report is based should be followed by others that will supply additional light on land use questions.

INDEX

INDEX

Agricultural Adjustment Act, 120
Agricultural Adjustment Administration, program, 120–22
Agricultural products, markets for, 6, 49, 53, 67, 72, 85, 89, 227; transportation of, 28, 29
Agricultural zones, suggested area in, 149; acreage in, in proposed national forests, 212; suggested management of tax-reverted lands in, 218
Agriculture, lands unsuitable for, 12, 13, 14, 44, 53, 63, 66, 67, 74, 82, 200; lands suitable for, 13, 44, 50, 61, 64, 74; present development, 29–34, 45–83 *passim;* limitations on future development, 322. *See also* Agricultural products; Agricultural zones; Crops; Dairying; Development areas; Farm incomes; Farm organization and management; Farms; Livestock; Relocation areas
Aitkin, 22
Aitkin County, 71, 72, 75; iron deposits, 14; population, 23, 24; medical services, 102; business development, 25; farm development and farm incomes, 31, 34, 85, 86, 88, 94, 104, 105; governmental structure, 36; school system, 36, 280, 299; public finances, 100, 113, 114, 117, 284–99, and effects of suggested reorganization, 266, 284–301, 308; taxation and tax delinquency, 71, 72, 115, 116, 277, 288, 290, 294, 298; suggested land use zones, 149, 159; roads, 308; assessed valuations, 277, 308
Austin, subsistence homesteads project, 122

Barnum, 78
Baudette, agricultural market, 49
Beltrami County, natural characteristics, 14, 35, 61; population, 24; public relief, 42; medical services, 102; business development, 25; farm development and farm incomes, 31, 34, 53, 59, 85–89, 94, 104, 105; governmental structure, 36; public finances, 100, 101, 113, 114, 117, 127, and effects of suggested reorganization and settler relocation, 266, 275, 316, 317; taxation and tax delinquency, 115, 116; suggested land use zones, 149, 160; forest hazards, 180; ownership of forest lands, 191; assessed valuations, 275

Beltrami Island State Forest, 55, 209, 267
Bemidji, 22, 59, 61
Black River, 53
Boarders, farm income from, 34, 85, 86, 88
Blackduck, 59
Brainerd, 72; population, 25
Brimson, 58
Brimson area, soils, 58; costs of clearing land, 245; salvage value of farm buildings, 246; governmental costs, 262
Burntside Lake, 58
Burntside State Forest, 56, 209
Business development, 25

Canadians, in population, 24, 25
Carlton County, 78; population, 24; business development, 25; farm development and farm incomes, 28, 31, 34, 85–89, 104, 105; governmental structure, 36; public relief, 42; medical services, 102; public finances, 100, 113, 114, and effect of suggested governmental reorganization and settler relocation, 266, 316, 317; taxation and tax delinquency, 115, 116; suggested land use zones, 149, 161
Cass County, natural characteristics, 35, 72; population, 23, 24; business development, 25; farm development and farm incomes, 31, 34, 85–89, 104, 105; governmental structure, 36; taxation and tax delinquency, 71, 72, 115, 116; sources of farm data, 90; public finances, 100, 113, 114, and effect of suggested reorganization and settler relocation, 266, 317; suggested land use zones, 149, 162; forest ownership, 191
Cass Lake, soils in vicinity of, 64; sawmills, 188
Cedar Valley Township, 74
Chippewa National Forest, 64, 176, 210; ownership of lake shore, 35; timber types, 208; location, 209; proposed acreage, 212; management, 214
Chisholm, 67
Churches, 103
Cities, number, 36; governmental functions, 40, 42. *See also* Urban sites
Civilian Conservation Corps, 214
Classification of land, *see* Land classification
Clearwater County, population, 23, 24,